To Larry,
    prized member of "Campaigning
with Len".

        All the best,
        Bud Robertson

2/19/89

SOLDIERS
BLUE AND GRAY

AMERICAN MILITARY HISTORY
Thomas L. Connelly, Editor

Travels to Hallowed Ground
by Emory M. Thomas

*Forged by Fire: General Robert L. Eichelberger
and the Pacific War*
by John F. Shortal

Soldiers Blue and Gray
by James I. Robertson

SOLDIERS
BLUE AND GRAY

by James I. Robertson, Jr.

University of South Carolina Press

Published in Columbia, South Carolina, by the
University of South Carolina Press
First Edition

Manufactured in the United States of America

LIBRARY OF CONGRESS
Library of Congress Cataloging-in-Publication Data

Robertson, James I.
    Soldiers Blue and Gray / James I. Robertson, Jr.
        p. cm.—(American military history)
    Bibliography: p.
    Includes index.
    ISBN 0-87249-572-8
    1. United States. Army—History—Civil War, 1861–1865.
2. Confederate States of America. Army—History. 3. United States—
History—Civil War, 1861–1865. I. Title. II. Series: American
military history (Columbia, S.C.)
E492.3.R63 1988
973.7—dc19   88–17408
                                                          CIP

Contents

Preface

This is a work that could be written a dozen different times without repetition.

Of the 70,000 or more books and pamphlets treating of Civil War history, the largest single bloc consists of the letters, diaries, and reminiscences of the common soldiers. The conflict of the 1860s was the most exciting event in the lives of the highly impressionable young men of that age; and with 3,000,000 Americans in the armies of North and South, it is natural that a flood of personal recollections gushed forth both during and after the war. That great reservoir of soldiers' writings has been but lightly tapped.

Two classic studies—*The Life of Johnny Reb* and *The Life of Billy Yank*—by my mentor, Bell I. Wiley, appeared over thirty years ago. Wiley's first love in research was manuscripts. In producing his two books, he literally combed America in search of unpublished writings by Confederate and Union soldiers. So bountiful was the yield from these previously overlooked sources that Wiley bypassed a multitude of printed works such as most of the vast category of regimental histories and collections of primary material issued by the Southern Historical Society and the Military Order of the Loyal Legion of the United States (MOLLUS). Even by the late 1930s, the reservoir of available material was so full that Wiley had to be selective. For example, he extracted several picturesque nuggets from Charles E. Davis's *Three Years in the Army: The Story of the Thirteenth Massachusetts Volunteers* (Boston, 1894), but he understandably skimmed over many equally revealing unit studies.

In addition, an immense amount of primary material has come to light over the past three decades. The Civil War Centennial, which stretched some distance on either side of the 1961–1965 period, brought forth an incalculable number of soldiers' letters, journals, and unprinted recollections that had heretofore been locked in family coffers. The Centennial also inspired unprecedented interest and research in the Civil War, which in turn uncovered forgotten collections in public and private archives. New works are continuing to appear in print at the rate of two per week. Researchers could labor for years without exhausting the source material.

This situation exists despite the fact that so many Americans are guilty of historical negligence. Each year, at spring cleaning or fall cleanup, pounds of Civil War writings are thrown away as that old family trunk in the basement, or that pile of dust-covered boxes in the attic, are consigned to the garbage dump. What a loss to posterity! Every letter or fragment of a diary provides some insight into a traumatic time when our nation was a battlefield.

The major purpose of this book is to provide a new and fresh appraisal of Johnny Rebs and Billy Yanks. In no wise does this work presume to be a replacement for the two Wiley compilations. Its intent is to supplement those works, not only with material which Wiley did not use, but also with reliance on a sampling of the post-1955 tidal wave of publications. Quotations dominate the text because of the overriding desire to let the soldiers express their own feelings—and relate their own experiences—whenever possible.

Reading such material makes one conclusion inescapable: despite limitations in education and social background, an amazing number of those citizen-soldiers were extremely observant and descriptive in what they wrote. Many of them retained a delightful sense of humor from first to last. After compiling his regimental history of the 83rd Pennsylvania, Amos Judson stated in his prologue that he had some concern about two classes of readers. First were those comrades who would feel that they deserved more attention and praise in the book. To them Judson offered the explanation: "I prefer not to give my opinion of a man until he is dead; for then I can abuse him without fear of a licking, or praise him without incurring the charge of toadyism."

The second group consisted of shirkers who slipped away from battle's dangers and later told great tales of their steadfastness in the action. "I can only ask these individuals, if there be any," Judson stated, "to deal as leniently with me as possible, and not open their thunders until the first edition shall have been exhausted; otherwise they might so damage the sale of the book as to involve myself and others in a heavy pecuniary loss."[1]

Like soldiers of all ages, Civil War troops were human: they rarely spoke in praise of things. They were quick to criticize; and because they were, their writings tend to be more negative and sarcastic than one might expect. However, they had much to criticize. That war engendered an almost endless array of hardships. For starters, there was disorganization, boredom, filth, bad food (when food existed at all), primitive conditions, disease, little opportunity to go home, and sporadic delivery of mail (a soldier's only contact with loved ones).

The men naturally denounced their officers. They fidgeted at long delays on a march, when everyone stood still while knapsacks and equipment bore down with increasing weightiness. They complained about the woolen uniforms they wore year-round—uniforms that, in the dryness of summer, were veritable ovens and that, in rainy weather, became colder, heavier, and wetter until most soldiers would have preferred nakedness. Troops of the 1860s also suffered from typhoid fever, malaria, measles, smallpox and the debilitating effects of diarrhea. Unbelievable numbers of them died of such sicknesses. The revolting smell of army camps, exasperating military red tape, the exigencies of discipline, the horror of battle, the even greater horror of battle wounds—these were but some of the aspects of Civil War army life that provoked thoughts and statements which in the main comprise this book.

No attention is given here to the thousands of young men who avoided service by dubious means, or to the hundreds of guerrillas and bushwhackers who, individually or collectively, roamed the countryside and preyed unmercifully on civilians. Those soldiers who lacked the stuff of patriotism and deserted receive some discussion as a class because of the contrast they were to the vast majority of their fellow soldiers. Largely overlooked here are comments by those troops who continually bemoaned their plight, grumbled about everything, and in general were unworthy of the soldier status they possessed. Every age and every war has those elements.

The 18th Mississippi's George A. Gibbs, who lost a leg in battle, wrote in the twilight of a long life: "I look back now, after so many years, on those turbulent times, and wonder where I found the fortitude, patience and endurance to pass through so many trying experiences suffered during the four years of the war. In most cases I believe we gather strength, courage and fortitude when circumstances are such as to require them."[2]

This study concentrates on that bulk of nineteenth-century manhood: the Johnny Rebs and Billy Yanks who, through service and sacrifice, bequeathed to all Americans an unforgettable legacy.

Over the years many students and friends have kindly made available to me the Civil War writings of their forebears. My indebtedness to all is genuine and profound. I wish I could have incorporated a piece of every collection in this book. Those persons whose holdings are cited in the notes and bibliography have my deepest thanks.

I am particularly grateful to Harriet Phillips Bone, compiler of *Civil War Diary & Letters of James Martin Phillips, Company G, 92nd Illinois Volunteers*, to Joseph T. Glatthaar, author of *The March to the Sea and Beyond*, and to Bob Womack, author of *Call Forth the Mighty Men*, for permission to quote extensively from their rich studies.

Richard J. Sommers and Michael Winey introduced me to the incredible collection of Civil War photographs in the U.S. Army Military History Institute at Carlisle Barracks, Pennsylvania. My sincere appreciation goes to them for their hospitality as well as for their assistance in selecting most of the previously unpublished photographs that appear in this book. The photograph of Confederate soldier Thomas Sheppard was an unsolicited and generous donation by Tim Landis of New York City.

To good friends Guy Di Carlo and Lowell Reidenbaugh, I express thanks again for historical help given many times in many ways.

For a quarter-century, my wife Libba has lived with Johnny Rebs and Billy Yanks. She has laughed and cried, rejoiced and suffered, with them. If the men of blue and gray had a voice now, I think they would want this book dedicated to her. I fully concur, for personal reasons.

James I. Robertson, Jr.
Virginia Tech, 1987

SOLDIERS
BLUE AND GRAY

• 1 •

Rallying 'round the Flag

From farms and factories, schools and shops—from every byway and highway in the land, they came by tens of thousands to answer the call to arms. Long years of sectional debate had created an atmosphere of deepening hostility between North and South. During the stormy decade of the 1850s, Americans faced each other with accelerated feelings of self-righteousness, hurt pride, and distrust. Southerners accused the North of disobeying both the Constitution and established statutes. Northerners branded the South an un-American and immoral oligarchy whereby a few large landowners prospered through the labor of black slaves. Each side came to believe that the federal government had become the tool of the other side. The democratic process had slowly eroded away; and as it did, shouting led inexorably to shooting.

In April, 1861, the distortions of passion and the hatreds of many years burst into gunfire. A North and a South, each conscious of its superior ways, and each certain of the total evil of the other, thereupon prepared for combat in order to defend home as well as God's interests. An unparalleled war ensued, and the greatest tragedy of all was that both sides were fighting for the same thing: America, as each side envisioned what the young nation should be.

Patriotism, localized in most cases, was nevertheless deep-rooted. Over 600,000 men would die in pursuit of two opposing dreams. These sacrifices collectively form the most severe trauma in our annals. That is one explanation (but by no means the only one) why the Civil War is widely regarded as the watershed in the history of the Republic.

Nobody was ready for the conflict of the 1860s, least of all the 3,000,000 citizen-soldiers who would be its participants. By-products of an unsophisticated age, possessed of an individualism spawned in the land they inhabited, Northerners and Southerners went off to war with dreamy enthusiasm and youthful innocence. A nationwide belief existed in the spring of 1861 that one or two battles fought somewhere in the border states of Virginia and Kentucky would settle the whole issue. That is why the initial enlistment period was only three months in the North and one year in the South. Thus, the patriot's overriding fear was that peace would come before he got his first taste of battle.

William Howard Russell of the London *Times* was passing through North Carolina when news of civil war arrived. He wrote of "flushed faces, wild eyes, screaming mouths," with men and women shouting so boisterously that nearby bands playing "Dixie" could not be heard. And North Carolina had not yet left the Union! Southerners rushed to enlist in larger numbers than the brand-new Confederate States of America could accommodate. The Bureau of War informed a Mississippian: "We have more volunteers for the war and for three years than we are able to arm and equip, and hence it would be absurd to arm and equip those who wish to serve only twelve months. They cannot be accepted unless they come fully armed and equipped."[1]

Similarly, Northern recruits stepped forward in droves. Governor Oliver P. Morton of Indiana responded to President Abraham Lincoln's request for six regiments by boasting that his state alone could forward 300,000 men immediately. Morton's nextdoor neighbor, Ohio Gov. William Dennison, wired the president: "Without seriously repressing the ardor of the people, I can hardly stop short of [sending] twenty regiments." A Massachusetts volunteer arrived in New York; when asked how many Bay Staters were on the way, he exclaimed: "How many? We're all a-coming!"[2]

Military historians have long recognized that in any age an army reflects the society which it was created to defend. Civil War armies were such a reflection of the exuberance that was mid nineteenth-century America. As units on both sides rapidly took shape, war just as quickly became a reality. However, the nation as a whole at that moment was totally unprepared for armed conflict.

A 16,000-man U.S. Army was scattered across the continent and considered insufficient even to meet Indian threats. The War Department had been snoozing in peacetime lethargy. A general staff did not exist, nor did any collection of maps for battle-planning. General-in-

Chief Winfield Scott was seventy-four and fighting a losing battle with both dropsy and senility. State militia were supposed to be a reliable reserve. Yet those units had become an occasion for socializing rather than soldiering. A common weakness existed on both sides. While recruitment at the local level was energetic and widespread, efficiency decreased at each step up the chain of command to the respective war departments. Mobilization initially and in the main was a do-it-yourself process.

Concern existed rather than panic, for a peculiarly American reason. The American Revolution, War of 1812, and Mexican War had all seemed to demonstrate that patriotic amateurs were better fighters than professional soldiers; there was no reason to think otherwise when civil war swept over the land. So the call for volunteers sounded far and wide, and a new generation of Americans enthusiastically followed in the paths of their forefathers.

Men and boys who flocked to enlist did so with an excitement of the unknown. A Southern recruit stated that his company, "young, ardent, and full of enthusiasm," marched off to war "with as little thought of coming trouble, as if on the way to some festive entertainment." Tennessean James Cooper agreed. "I was a mere boy and carried away by boyish enthusiasm. I was ambitious and felt that I should be disgraced if I remained at home while other boys no older than myself were out fighting . . . I was tormented by feverish anxiety before I joined my regiment for fear the fighting would be over before I got into it." Years later an Iowa officer unknowingly replied to these sentiments. "And thus they went to war. Only a short time was needed to teach them what war was. It took a longer time to make them soldiers."[3]

Recruits in 1861 were ready to fight, of course, but very few of them had any idea about discipline, drill, life in the open, following orders unhesitatingly, mastering weapons, digging earthworks, and eating unfamiliar food. They would face the novelty of living in company with thousands of others. They would try to combat diseases they had never known, and wounds they had never imagined, with medical treatments that were both painful and pathetic.

At the same time, the men of blue and gray would experience homesickness by being out of touch with loved ones for long periods of time. Hence, they recorded their experiences and their emotions in the largest outpouring of letter-writing in American history. Many also kept journals while in the army, and some of the fortunates who returned home at war's end wrote memoirs and unit histories to perpetuate the days when hardship and suffering led to heroic death and eternal glory.

What they remembered first of all was why they enlisted.

Political persuasion was a major reason, for it quickly divided North and South into rival sections. At the news of Fort Sumter's fall, the Boston *Herald* thundered: "In order to preserve this glorious heritage, vouchsafed to us by the fathers of the Republic, it is essential that every man perform his whole duty in a crisis like the present." From Washington, abolitionist Henry B. Stanton exhorted: "I hear Old John Brown knocking on the lid of his coffin and shouting, 'Let me out! Let me out!' The doom of slavery is at hand. It is to be wiped out in blood. Amen!"

Clarion calls such as this explain why a Southern journal raised the question: "Who can calculate on getting any sense of justice out of two millions of fanatics like 'Old Brown,' who believe they will swing right off to Heaven as soon as the hangman's cart drives out from under them?" Southerners likewise shouted with religious overtones. Just before South Carolina's exodus from the Union, Congressman David Clopton of Alabama asserted: "The argument is exhausted, further remonstrance is dishonorable, hesitation is dangerous, delay is submission, 'To your tents, O Israel!' and let the God of battle decide the issue."

The first war circular to appear in Hickman County, Tennessee, proclaimed: "To Arms! Our Southern soil must be defended. We must not stop to ask who brought about war, who is at fault, but let us go and do battle . . . and then settle the question who is to blame." In Richmond, newspaper editor John M. Daniel could not have known the deep truth contained in his pronouncement: "The great event in all our lives has at last come to pass. A war of gigantic proportions, infinite consequences, and indefinite duration is on us, and will affect the interests and happiness of every man, woman, or child, lofty or humble, in this country . . . We cannot shun it, we cannot alleviate it, we cannot stop it. We have nothing left now but to fight our way through these troubles . . ."[4]

Patriotism, especially state pride, was a common inducement on both sides.

"Every one seems to be actuated by the purest and most patriotic motives and those who are going seem to be moved by a sense of duty," an Iowan wrote in his diary. After Henry E. Schafer enlisted in an

Illinois regiment, he wrote his wife: "The cause for which the majority of men now in the Army have enlisted to defend I think is sacred and should be near and dear to every true American's heart and I consider that the Union cause ought to be defended even if it costs thousands of lives and millions of treasure. . . . I consider that we should do what we can for the cause for which we enlisted and strive on until it is accomplished. If we do not succeed we will have the pleasure of saying that we done what we could." A German immigrant who took the name Peter Smith and joined the 8th Missouri wrote that he had "grasped the weapon of death for the purpose of doing my part in defending and upholding the integrity, laws, and the preservation of my adopted country from a band of contemptible traitors who would if they can accomplish their hellish designs, destroy the best and noblest government on earth."[5]

Confederate recruits, of course, did not see treason involved at all. As a North Carolinian understood the situation: "The Southern States passed ordinances of secession for the purpose of withdrawing from a partnership in which the majority were oppressing the minority, and we simply asked 'to be let alone.' " A thirty-five-year-old Louisianian explained more dramatically why he had joined the service: "If we are conquered we will be driven penniless and dishonored from the land of our birth . . . As I have often said I had rather fall in this cause than to live to see my country dismantled of its glory and independence—for of its honor it cannot be deprived."[6]

Occasionally, patriotism had its limits. A Midwestern unit was being formed, and the enlisting officer proudly announced to a prospective member that the regimental flag would bear the words: "Victory or Death."

"I object to the motto," the man said.

"Why so?" the officer asked. "How shall it be changed?"

The potential recruit answered: "Make it victory or pretty damned badly wounded, and I'm your huckleberry."[7]

Mottos might not always be inspiring, but patriotic verses were all but guaranteed to sound a rallying call. Typical of such poetry were these lines uttered by a Massachusetts orator:

> As victor exult, or in death be laid low,
> With his back to the field and his feet to the foe,

And leaving in battle no blot on his name,
Look proudly to heaven from the death-bed of fame.[8]

With war fever running high in those first days of war, many young men enlisted because it just seemed the proper thing to do. Friends and neighbors were volunteering; community pride had surged forth and could not easily be ignored. Speaking for his compatriots, one artillery-man stated that they were "bound for the front, soon to show their country and the loved ones at home, that they were 'True blue,' and that 'Johnny Reb' would have a chance to see the kind of metal that 'Yanks' were made of." An Illinois soldier (who did not survive the war) told his wife after enlistment: "I studied the cost and measured the way before I enlisted and I intend to stick it throug manfully. You must try and bear your lot Heroically . . ." Michigan's Ira Gillaspie was unable to convince his spouse that he was doing the right thing by going into the army. "I come to the conclusion that I would volunteer my cirveses to my country," he remembered. "I talked with my wife on the subject and she did not want me to enlist." Yet Gillaspie did so. "When I got home I found that the news had got thare before me. My wife was acrying. I told her to console herself that the war would soon be over and our country at peace, but she thought I had aught not to have enlisted."[9]

Other reasons why men of North and South flocked to the colors had their roots in more basic human appeals. To provincial and impression-able young men of that day, the army offered a different way of life from struggling behind a plow or hunching over a clerk's desk. Going to war would satisfy a natural desire for adventure. To others it could be a search for heroics unavailable in normal walks of life. Military service was also an opportunity to see new scenes, to take part in an exciting new life-style. Since most men of that era had never been away from their farms or home communities, the army was an enticement with pay that few of them had ever known.

Quick valor by friends and neighbors already in the field was an additional motivation. When news of the gallantry of the 1st Iowa at the battle of Wilson's Creek, Missouri, reached one Hawkeye locale, ninety-seven youths—whose average age was nineteen—promptly enlisted together and became part of a new regiment, the 11th Iowa.[10]

After conscription went into effect in 1862–1863, many eligible boys volunteered for the army to avoid the stigma of being labeled as conscripts, as well as to receive enlistment bonuses, choice of units, and the comparative pride that came with entering service on one's own free will.

The volunteers who came forth to defend the newly established Confederate States of America had additional incentives. Certainly "the flower of Southern manhood" went to war in order to protect home and everything dear from Northern hordes overrunning their lands to bring them forcibly back into the Union. As William C. Corson, a Virginia cavalryman, told his sweetheart: "Every patriot must keep his armor girded so long as the dastard foe invades the sacred soil of the South and desecrates the holy temple of Liberty."[11]

Many Southerners were fighting to preserve the political, social and economic ways inherited from their fathers and under attack by abolitionists for the past thirty years. They wanted to maintain what had been, and to be left alone with their beloved status quo. While very few Confederate soldiers could comment on the constitutional issues involved, they did understand the philosophical attacks on slavery, and the possibility of physical invasion by Northern armies.

Their usual view of Northerners was an unreasonable, tyrannical, and anarchistic people who refused to obey either the laws of Congress or the decisions of the U.S. Supreme Court. Northern leaders gave repeated indications of being hypocrites in that they damned slavery in the South but were content to overlook Northern laborers who toiled in conditions akin to, if not worse than, slave status. Contrary to popular Northern belief, the average Southerner was not fighting for slavery. Owning slaves, and profiting from their labor, were attributes only of the upper classes who constituted a very small percentage of the South's population. Most Confederate soldiers were farmers or laborers who took musket in hand to defend their homeland.

By 1861, Southerners had worked themselves into a proper frame of mind where "the enemy" was concerned. Future Confederates were thoroughly convinced of the righteousness of their cause of preserving that Union which the forefathers created. Georgia soldier John W. Hagan expressed that sentiment to his wife: "we will have to fight like Washington did, but I hope our people will never be reduced to destress & poverty as the people of that day was, but if nothing elce will give us our liberties I am willing for the time to come."[12]

Hagan and his compatriots, however, were confident of success when they went to war. Southern men, they boasted, were more accustomed to outdoor life, were more robust than Yankees locked in stuffy factories and dark shops. Men of the South further believed—or at least convinced themselves—that Northerners did not want to fight, could not fight, and would not fight if forced into a major confrontation.

It took the North longer to gear up for war. The Midwestern states, at the edge of America proper, responded to Lincoln's call for troops with more alacrity and unanimity than did the East because of the newness of country and national ideals. Yet the North had a number of inducements in its favor. Love for the Union was the most effective motivation for Northern soldiers. As Indiana private Benjamin Mabrey wrote his homefolk: "i Came out pure to do my Duty and to fight the rebes and poot Down rebelyon."[13]

The United States, Northerners were convinced, was the world's greatest experiment in freedom and democracy. Union boys could remember hearing their grandfathers tell thrilling stories of the fight for American independence in the 1770s. Preserving the union was also the overriding ideal of foreign-born soldiers who comprised a large percentage of Federal armies. Nowhere were opportunities more abundant than in America. Many immigrants had traveled halfway around the globe to reach the welcome of this country's shores, and they were not about to relinquish their premier dream without a fight. Again and again in the letters of Union troops, one encounters the phrase "fighting to maintain the best government on earth."

Economics played some part in men becoming Union soldiers. The pay of Federal privates was small by modern-day standards; yet depression was widespread when civil war began, and unemployment remained prevalent in the North until the midway point of the struggle. Army pay, in contrast, was good for that day, and it was steady. A Union private received $13 a month. With the bounties—i.e., bonuses—often given to men who enlisted or reenlisted, a volunteer could obtain several hundred dollars at one time. (Confederate soldiers generally did not have such inducements. The Southern private received $11 monthly—when he got paid. Many Confederates went a year or more without seeing a paymaster. When the money did arrive, it was so inadequate in the face of galloping inflation as to be all but worthless.)

Starting in 1863, the Civil War became in the North a crusade to end slavery in America. Soldiers either from abolitionist backgrounds or stirred by the conviction that all humans deserved all liberties, went to fight for the cause of Union and freedom. "Slavery must die," a Vermont corporal proclaimed, "and if the South insists on being buried in the same grave I shall see in it nothing but the retributive hand of

God."[14] Comparatively few Northern soldiers displayed enthusiasm for fighting on behalf of black people. For every Federal who voiced sympathy for the plight of the slaves, a dozen disclaimers could be heard. The majority saw emancipation at best as a war measure, and their acceptance of blacks was lukewarm.

Whatever the motivation, enlistments on both sides followed a general pattern. Public response to the call to arms was spontaneous if not inflammatory. It was the most exciting moment most Americans had ever known, and they reacted with unbelievable zeal. Jacob D. Cox, soon to become a distinguished Ohio general, wrote of those first exuberant weeks: "The shame, the folly, the outrage, seemed too great to believe, and we half hoped to wake from it as from a dream."[15] Yet negative thoughts such as these were drowned by the public clamor to do battle.

The appeal to arms in a community began with advertisements, posters, and word-of-mouth announcements. One interesting broadside appeared in Boston after the attack on the 6th Massachusetts: "War! War! War! Our Massachusetts citizens have been murdered in the streets of Baltimore . . . All citizens are requested to meet at the town hall this evening to see what can be done." A mass meeting or rally was the usual vehicle for actual recruitment. Such gatherings would be held on the courthouse lawn or in a meeting hall. In Boston, John Greenleaf Whittier issued his own poetic call:

> Men!—if manhood still ye claim,
>   If the Northern pulse can thrill,
> Roused by wrong or stung by shame,
>   Freely, strongly still!—
> Let the sounds of traffic die;
>   Shut the mill-gate—leave the stall—
> Fling the ax and hammer by—
>   Throng to Faneuil Hill.[16]

Bands would set the mood at these assemblies by playing "The Battle Cry of Freedom," "Dixie," "Red, White, and Blue," "The Bonnie Blue Flag," and similar patriotic airs. Leading citizens gave florid oratory and made impassioned pleas for men to come to the aid of their threatened country.[17] Aged veterans of the wars of 1812 and 1846 called on the younger generations to maintain that section's traditions and pride. Often an audience contained at least one aroused female, excitedly waving a handkerchief or small flag, and declaring loudly that she would go in a minute if she were a man; and on numerous occasions, when the call was made for volunteers, young ladies would walk out and fall in line. Sometimes a male in the crowd would offer to enlist if another person went with him. Thus, when the climactic call for volunteers finally came, there usually was a rush from the audience characteristic of sinners repenting at a backwoods revival.

Most of the volunteers North and South were farm boys who brought with them the language, ideas, and customs of rural America. Friends usually enlisted together, with companies originating in locales. Hence, neighborhood associations and attitudes were merely transferred to an army framework.

Hundreds of future Johnny Rebs and Billy Yanks (titles they adopted proudly) were already mobilized when civil war came. They were military-minded citizens who had banded together in militia companies. Raised at private expense by one or more prominent citizens, these units of 65 to 100 men had too often become social orders rather than military organizations. A member of the "Detroit Light Guard" confessed that the men in the unit were "all gentlemen of wealth and prominence, who had joined the company just for the pleasure they would derive by being a soldier."[18] Their hierarchy was heavy at the top. A Confederate official contemptuously described a typical militia company as consisting of "3 field officers, 4 staff officers, 10 captains, 30 lieutenants, and 1 private with misery in his bowels."[19]

That may have been true, but most of these militia units had a degree of organization, were usually well drilled, and were familiar with the basic rudiments of army service. John Brown's 1859 raid into Virginia had sparked the creation of scores of such local defense companies throughout the South; and when hostilities began in earnest, the "Richmond Howitzers," "Washington Artillery of New Orleans," "Danville Blues," "Oglethorpe Light Infantry," "Chatham Artillery," "Old Dominion Rifles," "Newton Light Dragoons," and many others volunteered en masse for national service.

Unique among these elitist companies was the "Liberty Hall Volunteers." It initially consisted of seventy-three students from Washington College in Virginia. Their average age was twenty; a fourth of the youths were studying for the ministry. The company commander, James J. White, was a classics professor whom the soldier-boys nicknamed "Old Zeus." He was thirty-two.

At first the volunteer companies were under state jurisdiction. Once mustered into state service, companies were then organized by regiments. Ten companies of approximately 100 men each and from the same general area were banded together to form the 1,000-man regiment. It was designated by number and state name. Thus, the "Mount Airy Rough and Readys" became Company B of the 45th Virginia Infantry Regiment, C.S.A. By long-standing military tradition, men elected the captain and lieutenants who led the company. Those officers in turn selected the regimental leaders. Although the state governor officially issued the commissions to colonels, lieutenant colonels, and majors, he usually endorsed the recommendations of company officers.

Most elections of company officers passed without incident. The occasional exceptions could have humorous overtones. A member of the 3rd North Carolina recalled how a dominating lieutenant in his company honored the election procedure. "Sergeant," he directed, "make the men fall in with arms." As the company stood in ranks at attention, the officer shouted: "Men, there are two candidates for office, and there is but one of them worth a damn, and I nominate him. All who are in favor of electing Sergeant ———— come to shoulder arms. Company, shoulder arms!"

Then turning to his orderly, the officer said: "Sergeant, take charge of the company and dismiss them."[20]

Each army recruit was normally required to sign a "volunteer enlistment" form that contained the signee's intention to serve in the army for the time specified. A surgeon then certified on the form that he had examined the recruit and that, in his opinion, the applicant was "free from all bodily defects and mental infirmity which might disqualify him from performing the duties of a soldier." Finally, the recruiting officer attested on his honor that he had "minutely examined" the volunteer and found him to be "entirely sober when enlisted," of lawful age, and qualified to perform the obligations of a soldier.[21]

Individual recruits and militia companies alike were given a few days to get their affairs in order before departing by boat, train, horse or foot for the camp of instruction. This moment of farewell was a mixture of emotions. Several enlistees in what became the 27th Alabama thoroughly enjoyed their departure. "Every young fellow who went to war got a kiss from his 'best girl,' and as it was the first that many of us had ever enjoyed, it is not surprising that a last farewell was repeated over and over again before we actually took our departure."[22]

David Johnston wrote how joy changed to sadness when his company said goodbye at its mountain village. "We seemed to be going on a holiday journey, to return in a few days. But alas! when the time of departure arrived, what a change of scene! The town was filled with people—the fathers, mothers, brothers, sisters, wives, relatives, friends and lovers of the men and boys who were starting on the errand of war. Here was a fond and loving mother clinging to her baby boy, weeping, sobbing, praying the Father of all mercies to protect and preserve the life of her darling child, amidst the fury and storm of battle. There stood the patriotic, gray haired father, the tears trickling down his cheeks, giving to his beloved son words of comfort, begging that he act the man, be brave, do his duty . . . A loving sister might be seen with her arms around a brother's neck, reminding him of her love and attachment . . . scarcely could be found an eye that was not bathed in tears on this occasion. It was weeping, shaking of hands, 'good-bye,' and 'God bless you;' and thus the scene continued until the long train of wagons drove us away."[23]

Mississippi teenager George Gibbs confessed that as the train carrying his company moved from the station, "I hid away from the other soldiers and took a big cry. It seemed to help, and after it, I felt better about leaving home." In contrast, another recruit from the same state wrote of a messmate: "Tom's sweet-heart cried [at the departure] but he would not & I had to pinch him before he would cry."[24]

Distractions shattered the drama of many of these farewell gatherings. One newly formed company was preparing to march from its New Hampshire hometown when two dogs got into a fight and disrupted the whole proceedings. A Jersey City, New Jersey, contingent stood at attention in preparation for departure when the entire audience was treated to an unusual interruption. A recruit described it: "One of our men who seemed to be very anxious to be off for a soldier, had his ardor suddenly dampened by the appearance of his wife, who told the captain that her husband was nothing but a drunkard, did not support his family as he ought, and she wanted the captain to send him home, and in order to enforce the argument she pitched into him right and left to the great amusement of the boys, who soon saw that she was the better man of the two . . . Uncle Sam lost one would be recruit."[25]

Many hastily raised companies bore no resemblance to trained warriors. Sixty-five men in Westmoreland County, Virginia, banded together into a mounted troop they called "Lee's Light Horse." As they embarked for the camp of instruction, one of their number confessed, "there was nothing very martial in the appearance of the company. The officers and men were clad in their citizens' dress, and their horses comparisoned with saddles and bridles of every description used in the country. Their only arms were sabres and double-barreled shotguns collected from the homes of the people."[26]

Many units from affluent communities left for war loaded down with every imaginable item. The "volunteer of '61," one of their numbers admitted, eagerly went off to war and "carried more baggage then than a major-general did afterwards. The knapsack was a terror, loaded with thirty to fifty pounds of surplus baggage . . . His haversack, too, hung on his shoulder, and always had a good stock of provisions, as though a march across the Sahara might at any time be imminent."[27]

Rhode Island troops, for example, became known as "pack mules." Private Ansel Dickerson recalled boarding the train at Providence for departure southward. When the new soldiers "unslung those corpulent knapsacks, the sense of relief which we experienced was, I fancy, somewhat akin to that felt by Bunyan's pilgrim when he drooped his burden. Indeed, it seemed like getting out from under a haystack or a mountain."[28]

A member of the 4th Rhode Island agreed. He gave this inventory of his gear: "There was a full supply of underclothing, woolen blanket, rubber [blanket], three or four pairs of socks, half a dozen nice handkerchiefs, dress coat, fatigue cap, supply of ink, letter paper and envelopes, portfolio, photograph album, Bible, the journal in which these notes are kept, tobacco, drinking tube, comb and brush, shaving tools, two or three pipes, pins and needles, thread, buttons, etc., and other things that went to make up a soldier's kit in those days. Add to these the regulation equipments, haversack with rations, mostly obtained from home, and consisting of cold meats, bread and butter, cheese, pie and cake, and other food. Then there was the canteen, filled with— well, say coffee; and then there were the patent water filters, knife and fork, spoon, cup and plate, shoe brush and blacking, various kinds of medicine, and flannels for sudden change of climate or weather, a pair of warm mittens for the coming winter, and other things carried in our pockets. Everything stated here was thought to be necessary to our new life as a soldier . . ."

(The same soldier then added: "What a difference one year in service made. . . . A woolen blanket and a piece of shelter tent twisted together, and thrown over our shoulders; haversack loaded with a dozen hard tack and a small piece of 'salt horse;' little bag of coffee and sugar, mixed together; all sorts of hats or caps; little to eat, but plenty of ammunition; dirty, ragged, and with a full assortment of 'gray backs.' But we were veteran soldiers then.")[29]

Military garb was of the widest variety in the war's first stages—when it was available. Units slow in receiving them became resentful to the point of rebellion. In August 1861, the 10th New York was ordered to fall in for a parade. Because it was not yet fully uniformed, Company A resolved to show its plight. Members formed ranks clad only in white shirts and drawers. The first sergeant was distinguishable by the fact that he wore a sash, belt and sword "rather too clearly defined against the ground of white." An incensed brigadier refused to let the men march in review and ordered them back to their camp under arrest.[30]

Volunteer militia generally wore fancy and ornate garb. "We were a motley looking set," wrote a Texan. "In my company were about four different shades of gray, but the trimmings were all black braid. As far as pride went, we were all generals."[31] Several Northern units adopted the Zouave uniform worn by French troops. It consisted of a red turban with white band and orange tinsel, short blue jacket with gold trimming, loose red trousers and yellow buckskin leggings. In the first weeks of mobilization General John W. Phelps, an Old Army regular, was riding through a camp when a young officer in fantastic uniform saluted him. Phelps reined to a halt in surprise.

"Who are you?" he asked.

"I'm a Zouave," the man replied.

"What is that?"

"An officer of a Zouave regiment, sir."

"An officer!" Phelps roared. "I thought you were a circus clown!"[32]

The outlandish Zouave uniform was so conspicuous in battle that high casualties resulted. Such units quickly changed to standard issue of clothing. Yet much confusion initially prevailed in official uniforms. A large number of Northern units wore gray in 1861 because that had been a favorite color of militia for years and there was abundant cloth available. Since blue had been the traditional American uniform color for many years, several Southern regiments went off to war in blue. Small wonder that several fatalities in the opening battles occurred when soldiers fired into their own ranks.

Another problem existed with government-issue uniforms. "There were four sizes of most of the clothing," a Massachusetts volunteer explained, "and he whom none of these fitted was obliged to fit himself to the size." Another New Englander observed: "Here were short men with trousers so long they had to be turned up well-nigh to the knee in order to prevent the wearer from tripping. There were tall men with nether garments so short as to clearly reveal a pair of attentuated calves and to render inevitable one of two things, the adoption of a mincing gait or a posterior disruption. Occasionally, you might find a fellow so tightly buttoned, it seemed doubtful if he could draw another breath, but more frequently those whose coats were two or three sizes too large. When their wearers came to attention their collars well-nigh forced their caps off their heads."[33]

In the 10th Rhode Island was a soldier who stood only four feet, eleven inches tall. A messmate wrote: "His first pair of army drawers reached to his chin. This he considers very economical, as it saves the necessity of shirts . . ."[34]

When young Nelson Stauffer enlisted in the 63rd Illinois, he received a uniform that he estimated at twelve sizes too long and nine sizes too big around. He donned it in order to alter it into a reasonable fit. All he succeeded in doing was generating jibes from compatriots, such as: "I say, soldier, come outen them pants. You don't fool me. I know you're there, for I can see your ears a worken."[35]

Washing the woolen uniforms, a New York private asserted, had the result of "making them too small for future use." Officers and veteran soldiers informed recruits with hats nowhere near their size that Mother Nature would come to the rescue. "One, to whose lot fell a forage cap that covered his ears, was assured it would shrink to proper proportions in the first rain-storm, while another, whose cap sat nattily upon the very tip of his crown, after the manner of the British soldier, was consoled with the assurance that the August sun would soon expand it to suit his comfort and convenience."[36]

Every shape and form of hat was in evidence, from the snappy French-inspired kepi to huge broad-brimmed coverings that resembled inverted coat scuttles. An Indiana recruit wrote home: "We have been drawing our uniforms and like them pretty well, all except the hats. They are rediculous things and make me think of the pictures of the Pilgrim Fathers."[37]

Thus, in the spring of 1861 armed mobs began congregating for a war. "Here was the broad shouldered six footer from the backwoods swearing he was a ring tailors roarer and ready to chaw up any amount of rebels," an Indiana volunteer stated. "Here we found the lawyer, the doctor, the mechanic from his shop, the ploughman from his field, the clerk from the dry goods store who, tired of measuring tape, was anxious to measure his strength with the foeman of his country. All these scattered fragments had to be consolidated by the commandant and brought to act as one man."[38]

No one really knew what the future held. Few Americans in the spring of 1861 agreed with Virginia statesman George Wythe Randolph's warning: "We are in the beginning of the greatest war that has ever been waged on this continent."[39] The youths and middle-aged men who became Johnny Rebs and Billy Yanks did so because they had been caught up in the heated atmosphere and angry words of the day, or else they had been emotionally moved (and youth is so susceptible to emotion) by swaying oratory, inspiring music, the sight of a flag waving defiantly at some moment. They were going off to war in enthusiastic expectation—in quest of excitement and accomplishment—never slowed down by any thoughts that war contains hardships and sufferings, and that soldiers often die.

Among the comparatively few serious-minded recruits in the spring of 1861 was North Carolinian William Wagner. He wrote home shortly after his enlistment: "Dear Wife if we do git in a fite all we can do is to trust God above us and try an fite thrue the best way we can but I hope to God we may be sucsesful whar Ever we go."[40]

• 2 •

Mixing the Ingredients

It is natural to think of a Civil War army as a single cohesive unit that conforms to neat arrows depicting its movements on a map. Quite the reverse was true. The fighting force of the 1860s was a conglomerate of diverse units, each with its own degree of importance, pride, proficiency, and jealousy. Whether of North or South, an army began as little more than a loosely organized mob actuated more by enthusiasm than by experience. Its composition ran the full gauntlet of humankind.

America has never seen armies as large as those put together for the sectional conflict. When the Union Army of the Potomac embarked anew on a southward movement through Virginia in the spring of 1864, its appearance was awesome. That force consisted of some 120,000 soldiers, 274 artillery pieces, 835 ambulance wagons, 4,300 supply wagons, 56,000 horses and mules, several thousand head of cattle to be slaughtered as fresh meat when needed, plus tons of food, medicine, ammunition, and other materiel. A newspaper correspondent with the army asserted that if the wagons alone could have been arranged in single file, the line would have easily stretched from the Rapidan River to Petersburg—a distance of seventy-five miles.[1]

In spite of such size, the Civil War from first to last was an infantryman's contest. Some 80% of Union fighting men were foot soldiers, with 14% serving as cavalry and the remaining 6% in the artillery. Southern infantry formed 75% of a Confederate army, 20% were cavalry, with the remaining 5% in the artillery. Rivalries were keen between armies even on the same side. In September, 1863, a member of the 7th Indiana berated the homefolk who thought the Federal force in the Western theater was of better quality than the Army of the Potomac. The Eastern army, he asserted, "can take them to a half dozen fields and count more killed & wounded on *each* side than they can in *all* their boasted engagements. . . . They fight a cowardly enemy with a superior force. We fight with an inferior force the bravest of the brave. There's the difference."[2]

The same sentiment existed on the other side. A Louisiana Confederate in the Army of Tennessee complained after the war: "The Western army got only what was left in the way of supplies after the requisitions of the Army of [Northern] Virginia had been honored. Instances occurred when six-foot men were issued clothing designed for boys, and No. 6 shoes were gravely provided for No. 10 feet."[3]

Little love was lost either between the three arms of service. Infantry held cavalry in open contempt. "These cavalry men are a positive nuisance," an officer in the 123rd Illinois wrote. "They won't fight, and whenever they are around they are always in the way of those who will fight." Confederate General D. Harvey Hill reportedly offered a "reward of Five Dollars to anybody who could find a dead man with spurs on;" and General Jubal A. Early, impatient on one occasion with the conduct of certain units, threatened that "if the cavalry did not do better, he would put them *in the army!*"[4]

Artillery likewise had little use for mounted troops. By late in the war, Quartermaster Sergeant William Brown of an Illinois battery was particularly incensed. "Written orders will not keep the cavalry in order, and I believe of all the cusses to plunder, they cap the climax. They will steal everything but a red hot stove, and I believe some would even steal that if they could pick up a mule to carry it along."[5] Yet the criticism was not all one-sided.

Gunners were reminded that they were always behind the lines away from the real action, and questions were constant about their markmanship. A group of mounted Union troops once rode out to watch artillery practice. "Well," one of them stated, "the artillerists fired their big guns and didn't hit anything but the side of the mountain; our horses curveted, capered and pranced at the sound of the big guns, scattered lots of mud, and we all returned" to camp.[6]

Gibes, good-natured and otherwise, prevailed among units from different states. North Carolinians, for example, liked to boast that they lived "in a valley of humility between two mountains of conceit [Virginia and South Carolina]." Virginians dubbed their southern neighbors "Tarheels." A regiment passing a North Carolina unit one day provoked a brief but lively exchange of taunts.

"Any more tar down in the Old North State, boys?" came a shout.

"No, not a bit," came a quick reply. "Old Jeff's bought it all up."

"Is that so? What is he going to do with it?"

A Carolinian chortled: "He's going to put it in you'ns heels to make you stick better in the next fight."[7]

The hard core of either army was the infantry company. Its 65–100 privates formed a small workable unit. Because it was raised in a single locale, the company had all the atmosphere and appearance of a large family. The captain was the father of the group; the lieutenants and sergeants acted as older brothers. Sometimes that was literally true. Following one engagement in General William T. Sherman's March to the Sea, a member of the 100th Indiana wrote of walking past a line of Confederate bodies. "It was a terrible sight. Some one was groaning. We moved a few bodies, and there was a boy with a broken arm and leg . . . and beside him, cold in death, lay his Father, two Brothers, and an Uncle. It was a harvest of death."[8]

A regiment consisted of ten companies, designated A-K with the exception of *J*. The letter *J* so resembled the letter *I* in handwriting that when the designation system was established in 1816, *J* was omitted. Generally, Companies A and B were the flank units in battle, with C-K forming the interior companies. While the men took pride in their company, however, their greatest allegiance was to their regiment.

"Every true soldier believes in his own regiment," wrote a Connecticut artillerist. "He holds himself in perpetual readiness to demonstrate that no other battalion, brigade, division, or corps ever passed in review so handsomely, marched so far, fought so bravely, or suffered so much, as his own."[9] On the Union side, a regiment's maximum strength was fixed at 39 officers and 986 enlisted men. A Confederate regiment was larger: 49 officers and 1,340 men maximum. However, and on both sides, the regiment was rarely at full strength after its muster into service. Statistics on the Federal side show that, by April 1862, an average regiment had 560 men; by July 1863, it would number only 375 soldiers.[10]

Captain John William De Forest of Connecticut explained why a regiment reached its duty station 1,000 strong but in six months could only muster 600–700 men. "Some have died . . .; as many more have been discharged for physical disability; others are absent sick, or have got furloughs by shamming sicknesses; others are on special duty as bakers, hospital nurses, wagoners, quartermaster's drudges, etc."[11]

In the North, as the war continued, governors preferred to organize new regiments rather than replenish old ones whittled down by battle and sickness. Fresh units swelled a state's contributions, and they provided the governors an opportunity to win more political favors by appointing more regimental officers. Filling gaps was left to the regiments with gaps. An officer or recruiting team was occasionally sent home to entice new men into service. Nevertheless, replacements never equaled losses.

The most glaring result of such a policy was the disbandment of the Union I Corps after two years of severe losses. At the battle of Chancellorsville, a Federal general galloped up to a small pocket of men and shouted at the lieutenant in charge: "What regiment, and where's the rest of it?"

Proudly the young officer replied: "Twelfth New Hampshire, sir, and *here's* what's left of it!"[12]

Battle indiscriminately consumed Civil War regiments. Following three days of slaughter at Gettysburg, a private in the battered 13th Massachusetts wrote: "The Thirty-ninth Massachusetts was added to our brigade to-day. Having full ranks, it looked to us more like a brigade than a regiment."[13]

While they existed, many regiments enjoyed colorful names and/or compositions.

Gaudy uniforms brought the 3rd New Jersey Cavalry the nickname "The Flying Butterflies." The 73rd Illinois, organized and commanded by the Reverend James Jaquess, a Methodist minister, contained so many officers who were clergymen that from the outset the unit was called the "Preacher Regiment." The 83rd New York was actually the "9th New York National Guard," composed of New York City's finest. It retained its original designation throughout the war because of traditions and pride. In the "Temperance Regiment" (24th Iowa) were men who had solemnly pledged to "touch not, taste not, handle not spirituous or malt liquor, wine or cider." Later in the war some of the members violated that vow, but they were excused on the grounds that "It has only been at such times as they were under the overruling power of military necessity."[14]

One of the first units to respond to Lincoln's call for troops was the 7th New York, composed of "the fashionable elite of Gramercy

Square." It left for war with 1,000 velvet-carpeted footstools—which somehow never caught up with the unit. The 23rd Pennsylvania ("Birney's Zouaves") averaged nineteen years of age. In sharp contrast was the 37th Iowa, known as the "Graybeard Regiment" because it was organized only for home guard duty and, by War Department authority, was restricted to men over forty-five years of age.

When noted prohibitionist Neal Dow announced that he was accepting recruits for a regiment, "Maine's mothers immediately opened their hearts and surrendered their sons." Some 2,600 men tried to enlist in the 1,000-man unit. The resultant 13th Marine was singular: no card-playing, swearing, drinking, or boisterous conduct was permitted. Of course, many of the men cheated along the way, but they never informed Dow. A Boston newspaper termed the unit "the quietest regiment that has ever been seen in this city!"[15]

Colonel William Chadwick called his 26th Alabama into action during the winter months; and when the men came out of the north Alabama hills without adequate clothing but with blankets of every color draped over their shoulders, the unit instantly became known as the "Bed Quilt Regiment." The 21st Indiana Heavy Artillery had to endure the designation "Jackass Regiment" because its guns were drawn by mules. A great source of pride in the 24th Michigan was the fact that 135 sets of brothers were in its ranks.

Other units acquired negative reputations. The 39th New York, nicknamed the "Garibaldi Guard," was a melting pot of a half-dozen nationalities. Members of the regiment wore the uniform of Italian infantry. Its notorious misbehavior began with the colonel, who, in 1863, went to Sing Sing Prison for a variety of offenses. The 149th New York became infamous for looting. The brigade commander expressed the opinion that this regiment "would yet steal the Southern Confederacy poor and take the shoes from off Gen. Lee's charger." At Camp Rolla, Missouri, in August 1861, a sergeant-major from Illinois wrote: "Col. Stevenson with his command, the 7th Mo., or as it is called, the 'Missouri Irish Brigade,' arrived here yesterday from Boonville. It is said that there are 800 men, and the first day they came here there were 900 fights."[16]

Battle losses brought fame to more than one regiment during the war. The 12th Massachusetts disbanded in 1864, having suffered 792 casualties in battle and having taught the nation to sing "Glory, Glory, Hallalujah!" The largest of the Bay State regiments was the 22nd Massachusetts. It departed for war with 1,177 men—the equivalent of about twelve companies. Exactly a year later, through combat losses and sickness, the regiment had no more than 200 members left.[17]

There could be humor even in valor. It was customary to inscribe battle names on the regimental flag. In the autumn of 1862, the 14th New York received a new standard to replace its tattered emblem. The new flag bore several battle names in which the regiment had taken part. After the ceremony a private stepped up, carefully surveyed the flag, and then indignantly snorted: "E Pluribus Unum! Colonel, that's a damned lie! We never had a fight there!"[18]

In the army chain of command, 3 to 5 regiments comprised a brigade. This was the fighting component of an army. Commanded by a brigadier general who led by example rather than from the rear, the brigade usually had its own quartermaster, commissary, and ammunition trains. Medical teams, and sometimes artillery, were assigned by brigades. Hence, this unit was in effect a mini-army and able to act independently.

Prior to the Civil War, the brigade was the largest unit within an army. No need existed for a higher level of command. However, the massive armies that emerged in the 1860s quickly changed that. The division, led by a major general, came into being. Composed of 2 to 5 brigades working together, it came to be the army's primary maneuvering unit. Most marching orders called for advances, time schedules, and the like to be performed by divisions.

Two or more divisions formed the army corps, led by a major general in the North and a lieutenant general in the South. Federal corps were numbered consecutively and in Roman numerals (i.e., II Corps), while Confederate were numbered by armies and spelled out (i.e., Second Corps of the Army of Northern Virginia). General Joseph Hooker in the winter of 1862–1863 took a major step in unit morale by initiating corps badges within his Federal army. The insignia were, by corps: I— a disk; II—trefoil; III—diamond; V—Maltese cross; VI—Greek cross; XI—crescent; XII—star. The badges were colored, red denoting the first division; white, second division; blue, third division. The badges were worn on the cap.

Combining two or more corps produced an army. With rare exceptions the North named armies after rivers (Potomac, Cumberland) while the South designated its armies by areas (Northern Virginia, Tennessee). A major general commanded a Union army; a full general led a Confederate army.

Mixing the Ingredients

The Johnny Rebs and Billy Yanks who formed the ranks of those forces came in every shape and size, and from every background.

More than 100 different occupations existed among southern troops. A typical unit was the 19th Virginia. Of its 749 original members, 302 were farmers, 80 were laborers, and 56 were machinists. Among the remainder were 10 lawyers, 14 teachers, 24 students, 3 blacksmiths, 2 artists, a distiller, a well-digger, a dentist, and 4 men who classified themselves as "Gentlemen."

The average Northern regiment was even more diverse in composition. Over 300 occupations can be found on Federal muster rolls. This versatility was a very positive advantage in the field. When a piece of armament of equipment malfunctioned, almost invariably a Billy Yank with experience in handling the problem could be found. Their ingenuity and self-reliance at times seemed unlimited. A Federal officer in the West wrote admiringly: "Sherman's appears to be an army of independent commands, each individual being a 'command.' "[19]

A typical Civil War soldier was a white, native-born farmer, Protestant, single, and in the 18 to 20 age bracket. Yet the ages of the men covered a broad range. A Massachusetts soldier wrote in 1864 of Confederates taken prisoner at Petersburg: "Some were grey-haired and some were not more than 15 years old."[20] Indeed, boys often marched alongside men old enough to be their fathers. While much has been written of youngsters serving as drummer boys, older soldiers performed the same duty. David Scantlon of the 4th Virginia proudly beat the drum he carried into battle, despite his fifty-two years of age. However, youthfulness was the basic characteristic of the men of blue and gray. Because eighteen was the minimum age for enlistment, many underaged boys were known to write "18" on a slip of paper, insert it into a shoe and, when asked by a recruiting officer how old they were, respond truthfully: "I'm over eighteen."

Charles C. Hay was probably the youngest Confederate soldier. He joined an Alabama regiment at the age of eleven. The champion "blue baby" was unquestionably Edward Black of Indianapolis. He joined the 21st Indiana in the first months of the war, and the nine-year-old Black served as a musician until mustered from service the following year. Hay and Black were not unique. Battle reports often mentioned the heroism of young teenagers. Fifteen-year-old John Roberts was illustrative. At Shiloh, the colonel of the 5th Tennessee stated, Roberts went down twice after being hit by spent balls, and had his musket blown to pieces, but Roberts continued throughout the fighting to display "the coolness and courage of a veteran."[21]

It was somewhat crowded on the other end of the age spectrum. William Dame of the Richmond Howitzers recalled: "I personally know of six men over sixty years who volunteered, and served in the ranks, throughout the war." In July 1862, E. Pollard joined the 5th North Carolina as a substitute. Although listed as sixty-two, some indications exist that Pollard may have been over seventy years of age. Two months after enlistment, Pollard was discharged because of chronic rheumatism.[22]

No debate exists over the identity of the oldest of all Civil War soldiers. That honor goes to Curtis King, a transplanted Virginian who enlisted in the 37th Iowa at the age of eighty. King served but a few months before being discharged for disability.[23]

Statistics on height are so fragmentary that only skeletal conclusions can be reached. Just as commanders varied in stature from Confederate General James Longstreet (6 feet, 2 inches tall) to Federal General Philip H. Sheridan (described as "scarce five feet high"), the same fluctuation prevailed in the ranks.[24] Most men of blue and gray were in the 5 feet, 5 inches to 5 feet, 9 inches range. Sixty of ninety-four members in Company F of the 18th North Carolina were six feet or more tall. In contrast, the shortest Federal on record was an Ohioan who stood 3 feet, 4 inches in his stocking feet.

Two such men standing atop one another still would not have matched the tallest known Union soldier. Captain David Van Buskirk of the 27th Indian stood 6 feet, 11 inches, and his 100-man company contained 80 men over 6 feet in height. Van Buskirk was captured in 1862 and taken to a Richmond prison. The 380-pound captain agreed to be displayed publicly as "the biggest Yankee in the world." Yet Van Buskirk had a good line for the curious who came to gawk. When he left home for war, he would say, each of his six sisters "leaned down and kissed me on top of my head."[25]

Balanced diets, enriched foods, and other basics of good nutrition were unknown at that time. As a result, the soldiers of the 1860s tended to be slight of build. This seemed to create no concern. "I am well, and I think this kind of life agrees with me," a Virginia cavalryman informed his family in the autumn of 1861. "I weigh the same as I did when I left home—one hundred and twenty-five pounds—but all there is of me is bone and muscle, very tough and very active."[26]

Mixing the Ingredients

The Civil War was never a contest strictly between white Anglo-Saxons. This became readily evident when one visited any Union camp and listened to the babel of foreign tongues. At the outbreak of the war, foreign-born elements were unusually large in America. The Second Industrial Revolution was beginning to accelerate, which added to the attractions of a nation long known for vastness, opportunity, and democracy. In addition, potato famines had driven many Irishmen to America's shores, while the revolutions of the 1848 had sent droves of Europeans westward in search of peace and prosperity. The overwhelming number of immigrants settled in the North because the land was cheaper and work-for-wages more abundant. By 1860 almost a third of the North's male population was foreign-born. One of every four Union soldiers was a first- or second-generation immigrant.

The Federal armies that those men helped to fill also reflected the national sentiment of that time. Civil war came when the country was most suspicious of immigrants. The fantastic growth and development taking place in midcentury shattered many time-honored traditions and customs. Since the flood of foreigners was part of that growth, they were widely blamed for the unwelcome changes. Prejudices therefore ran strong with native-born Johnny Rebs and Billy Yanks.

Germans were the most numerous foreign nationality in the Union armies. Some 200,000 of them wore the blue. The 9th Wisconsin was an all-German regiment. The 46th New York was one of ten Empire State units almost totally German in makeup. Many soldiers regarded such troops as "dumb Dutchmen" who were thickheaded and slow. When a German regiment marched past a native American unit, men in the latter would often sniff the air and hoot: "The air around here is rather Dutchy!"[27]

The Union XI Corps, whose twenty-six regiments included fifteen that were predominantly German, became the "unwanted orphan child" of the Army of the Potomac. That corps was always used as an illustration of the inefficiency and potential danger prevalent in relying on German troops. They even appeared to some soldiers as being of a lower order. A purebred Massachusetts infantryman once wrote contemptuously of the Germans: "Fresh meat was issued. After we had removed every particle of meat from the bones, General Blenker's corps, who were in camp near us, took the leavings, such as bones, entrails, etc., and had a regular Thanksgiving dinner on what our luxurious natures discarded as useless."[28]

It should be pointed out, however, that Germans possessed above-average technical skills, tended to adapt instantly to army discipline, and displayed a devotion to the Union cause that was unimpeachable.

Second in number to the Germans were the Irish. Some 150,000 of their number became Billy Yanks. At least twenty regiments—including the 9th and 28th Massachusetts, 69th New York, 11th Wisconsin, 9th Connecticut, and General Thomas Francis Meagher's Irish Brigade (consisting of the 9th, 63rd, and 88th New York)—were composed almost entirely of men from the Emerald Isle. Irishmen personified sparkling wit and dry humor. A Union chaplain overheard a sergeant in Meagher's Irish Brigade shout angrily during one drill: "Kape your heels together, Tim Mullaney in the rear rank, and don't be standing wid wan fut in Bull Run and the other in the Sixth Ward!"[29]

A member of the predominantly Irish 28th Massachusetts confessed at the outset of his military career: "i se there is one thing certain that irishmen as a general rule are good soldiers but they must have oficers who are strict military men." Yet the "Sons or Erin" quickly gained a reputation for their overfondness for whiskey and brawls. Hoosier soldier Theodore Upson was stationed near Vicksburg late in July 1863 when reinforcements arrived. Upson noted: "The 90th Ill., the Irish Regiment, came into camp just back of us this morning. And such a time as those fellows did have. They had got into a row about putting up their tents and had a free for all fight and were knocking each other over the head with pick handles, tent poles, or any thing they got hold of. Pretty soon their Colonel, O Marah [O'Meara], came out of his tent with a great wide bladed broadsword that is said to have belonged to some of his ancestors. And the way he did bast those Irish fellows with the flat of it was a caution. He stopped the row, and they settled down. His Regiment adore him."[30]

About 45,000 Englishmen and 15,000 Canadians also volunteered as Union soldiers. French residents of New York City manned and equipped the 55th New York and christened it "La Garde Lafayette." The 15th Wisconsin was Scandinavian, with Norwegians predominating. In one company were five men named Ole Olsen. Both the 12th and 65th Illinois were all-Scotch regiments. So was the 79th New York, known as the "Highlanders." While its members initially wore kilts, inconvenience and sarcastic barbs soon led them to adopt Cameron tartan trousers.[31] And then there was the 27th Pennsylvania, composed (wrote a New England soldier) "of Germans, French, Italians and everything else."[32] Still another Union regiment contained fifteen different nationalities. Its patient colonel grew accustomed to issuing orders in seven languages.

Although the foreign-born troops as a whole behaved no better or worse than their American compatriots, they labored under an almost automatically bad reputation. In the summer of 1864, one of General George G. Meade's staff officers sneered: "By the Lord! I wish these gentlemen who would overwhelm us with Germans, negroes, and the offscourings of great cities, could only see—only see—a Rebel regiment, in all their rags and squalor. If they had eyes they would know that these men are wolf-hounds, and not to be beaten by turnspits."[33]

Those Rebel "wolf-hounds" nevertheless contained a fair sprinkling of immigrants. Only 9 percent of the Confederate armies were foreign-born, but they made their presence known. Irishman Patrick R. Cleburne rose to the rank of major general before his death in battle. Irish, Scotch-Irish, and German companies came from every Confederate state. Louisiana sent a mixed European battalion under the command of a flamboyant Frenchman, Count Camille Armand Jules Marie, Prince de Polignac. A Texas unit that de Polignac subsequently led gave up on his name and called him "Polecat." The Frenchman was more amused than insulted.

By the time the Civil War began, most of the Indians in the so-called Five Civilized Tribes had been driven from their eastern ancestral lands to the territory that is now Oklahoma. Union and Confederate authorities promptly negotiated treaties of alliance with several of the chiefs, who then furnished troops to fight in the white man's war. Three brigades of Cherokees, Choctaws, Chickasaws, and Seminoles went into the Confederate army, while a single brigade consisting mostly of Creeks fought for the Union. The Indians participated in a number of skirmishes as well as the battles of Wilson's Creek, Missouri, Pea Ridge, Arkansas, and Honey Springs, Indian Territory.

Muster rolls of Indian units contain a fascinating array of names: George Hogtoter, Crying Bear, Spring Water, Flying Bird, and Big Mush Dirt Eater, to name a few. The most famous of all Indians in the Civil War was the Cherokee leader Stand Watie. He became a Confederate brigadier general, and he did not surrender his troops until a full month after all other Southern forces had laid down their arms.

The red men performed well in most battles. There were occasional reports of Indians scalping their captured opponents. However, given the shabby treatment they received on both sides, Indians were better soldiers than either North or South had a right to expect.

Of all the minorities in America, blacks were the largest in number—and they stood to gain the most from the Civil War. Two days after the Union setback at Manassas in July 1861, a young Massachusetts officer named Oliver Wendell Holmes, Jr., wrote his father that "this defeat tends more and more to throw the war into the hands of the radicals, and if it lasts a year, it will be a war of abolition."[34] The war did last a year, and it did become a war of abolition. That was almost natural. Slaves were a principal cause of the struggle, and thousands of them would be instrumental in determining the outcome of the contest.

Some 3,500,000 slaves and 135,000 free blacks lived in the South when civil war began. Enslaved blacks who had personal attachments to their owners, or who were holding positions of trust on a plantation, tended to remain loyal in spite of the war aims. Many affluent Confederates in the first year of the war took "body servants" with them into the army. These slaves cooked food, washed clothes, cleaned quarters, and sometimes performed picket duty while their masters lounged nearby. Most of these servants enjoyed the novelty, excitement, and importance of soldier life. In the autumn of 1861, James H. Langhorne of the 4th Virginia informed his sister: "Peter . . . is charmed with being with me & 'being a soldier.' I gave him my old uniform overcoat & he says he is going to have his picture taken in '*Regimentals*' to send to the servants. He sends a *great deal of love* to you all, white & black."[35]

Instances exist where blacks were unofficially enrolled as Confederate soldiers. Jacob Jones, a slave, was listed as a musician in the 9th Virginia. Another black shown on the rolls only as "Joe" served in the 13th Virginia Cavalry as a soldier-teamster.

Almost from the beginning of the war, Confederate authorities wrestled with the problem of whether or not to use slaves as soldiers. Blacks had served with George Washington in the American Revolution and alongside Andrew Jackson in the War of 1812. Yet Southern fears were strong that arming slaves invited insurrection. Moreover, the feeling was acute that blacks should not be given such an opportunity to know equality. As the eminent Georgia statesman Howell Cobb asserted: "The day you make soldiers of them is the beginning of the end of the revolution. If slaves will make good soldiers, our whole theory of slavery is wrong."[36]

The North at war's outset gave little attention to putting blacks in uniform. The eloquent former slave Frederick Douglass pleaded impassionately: "Give them a chance. I don't say that they will fight better than other men. All I say is, Give them a chance!"[37] Yet arming blacks for what was supposed to be a short war was a politically explosive issue, especially in Missouri, Kentucky, and other slave states still loyal to the Union. The Lincoln administration had to move cautiously because, in addition to political expediency, strong social factors were also at issue.

Some spokesmen argued that enrolling blacks in the army was unnecessary and would be degrading to America. Northerners also raised the likelihood of insurrection. Others charged that making soldiers of blacks would be a threat to white supremacy, and hundreds of Billy Yanks wrote home that they would not serve alongside blacks. A goodly number of Northerners agreed with Southerners that the black was a biologically inferior being and could not be trusted with important military responsibilities. "As to being made soldiers, they are more harm than good," Lieutenant Colonel Charles Adams of the 5th Massachusetts Cavalry wrote his brother in the summer of 1862. "Under our system . . . we might make a soldiery equal to the native Hindoo regiments in about five years. It won't pay and the idea of arming the blacks as soldiers must be abandoned." They might be useful of throwing up breastworks and digging canals, a member of the 55th Illinois commented, "but I cannot think they are a class that should be armed."[38]

As the war entered its second year, groups of abolitionists and humanitarians stepped up demands that the Lincoln government utilize blacks in the military. They would obviously strengthen every army; they would impart new meaning to the concept of American democracy; they would learn the rudiments of responsibility and self-reliance which would prepare them for admission into postwar society. By September 1862, with the Civil War going badly for the Union, Lincoln decided to act. Incorporating blacks into the armies thus came as a result partly to satisfy the demands of the abolitionists and partly to meet the demands of war.

In conjunction with the issuance of Lincoln's Emancipation Proclamation, Secretary of War Edwin Stanton authorized General Rufus Saxton "to arm, uniform, equip, and receive into the service of the United States such number of volunteers of African descent as you may deem expedient, not exceeding 5,000, and [you] may detail officers to instruct them in military drill, discipline, and duty, and to command them."[39] At the same time, the U.S. Congress passed the Confiscation

Act, which authorized the president to use escaped slaves in the Union armies. Then, in March 1863, the Enrollment Act became law, and it made free blacks eligible for conscription.

The North had not gone to war to free the slaves, yet it had resolved to free the slaves so as to win the war.

From the beginning, black troops suffered almost every discrimination. Not only were few of them entitled to enlistment bounties (bonuses), but all of them were paid less than white soldiers. In addition, they were assigned the worst tasks in the army, such as fatigue duty and digging latrines. They were segregated in all-black units and commanded—with very few exceptions—by white officers who too often treated them more as servants than as soldiers. The most constant and biting discrimination of the black, however, was the open hostility of white Northern soldiers.

Blacks wearing Federal uniforms brought forth the deep-rooted prejudices of countless Billy Yanks. Many enlisted men looked on the blacks as the reason for the whole stinking and bloody war, with the men in blue standing little to gain from it. Writing of the early stages in the struggle, an Illinois soldier expressed a common feeling: "If the Negro was thought of at all, it was only as the firebrand that had caused the conflagration—the accursed that had created enmity and bitterness between the two sections . . ." A member of the 90th Pennsylvania wrote a friend shortly after the recruitment of blacks into the Union army: "Jack what do you think about them dam niger Regiments they had better not send any of them out hear fore if they do our own Soldiers will kill more of them than the Rebs would fore a Soldier hates a niger more than they do a Reb."[40]

Complaints were loud that black soldiers were lazy, irresolute, and impudent. They would be poor soldiers, particularly in battle, several officers warned. One brigadier general, after his first look at black troops, dismissed them as "dressed up like soldiers and euphemistically styled 'Colored Troops' . . . an interesting popular and Government pet and plaything . . . not good to tie to in battle." A colonel of one of the black units had a similar opinion when he first took command. The men, he wrote, "lack the pride, spirit and intellectual energy of the whites." A former slave, he added, "cannot stand up against adversity. A sick nigger, for instance, at once gives up and lies down to die, the personification of humanity reduced to a wet rag."[41]

Most Union soldiers who openly endorsed the use of blacks as soldiers did so out of a sense of self-preservation. "Private Miles O'Reilly," the pseudonym for New York's Charles G. Halpine, combined simple logic and Gaelic wit in a poem written to the music of an old Irish tune:

> Some tell us 'tis a burnin shame
>   To make the naygers fight;
> An' that the thrade of bein' kilt
>   Belongs but to the white;
> But as for me, upon my soul!
>   So liberal are we here,
> I'll let Sambo be murthered instead of myself
>   On every day of the year.
>   On every day of the years, boys,
>   And in every hour of the day;
>   The right to be kilt I'll divide with him,
>   An' divil a word I'll say.

Only a month after emancipation went into effect, Iowa soldier Cyrus Boyd observed that "the prejudices against the [black] race seems stronger than ever." Whenever black and white troops met in a town or on other neutral grounds, fights were inevitable and fatalities were commonplace. Even worse, in combat blacks sometimes had to weather danger from friend as well as foe. Such was the case at Ship Island, Mississippi, after Federal naval gunners were ordered to give support fire for three black regiments staging an assault. The gunners, who had had recent encounters with the blacks, shortened their range and fired into the attacking troops. A Virginia soldier, describing the February 1864 battle of Olustee, Florida, wrote matter-of-factly: "The negroes saw a hard time; those who stood were shot by our men, those who ran by the Yankees. Such was the fight at Alustee."[42]

The real issue where blacks were concerned was not the propriety of uniforming them but the unknown of whether they would fight well once uniformed. It was the performance of blacks in battle that at last brought them acceptance as American soldiers.

On June 7, 1863, at Milliken's Bend, Louisiana, two untested Louisiana black regiments came under attack from a Confederate force estimated at 1,500 to 3,000 men. The blacks were shoved back; they soon held their ground and then counterattacked. A Union general stated that "it is impossible for men to show greater gallantry than the negro troops in this fight." A southern officer acknowledged that the Confederate charge "was resisted by the negro portion of the enemy's force with considerable obstinacy, while the white or true Yankee portion ran like whipped curs almost as soon as the charge was ordered."[43]

The following month, the all-black 54th Massachusetts, led by militant abolitionist Thomas Wentworth Higginson, massed for an assault across the open beach at Battery Wagner, South Carolina. The blacks had been two nights without rest, two days without food, and they had marched the better part of the day through sand and swamps to get into position. They dashed against the fort and gained a momentary toehold before lack of support forced them back. Nearly half the black troops were killed, wounded, or captured.

A Union officer who earlier had refused a commission in a black regiment watched them attack a portion of the Richmond defenses in September 1864. "The darkies rushed across the open space fronting the work, under a fire which caused them loss, into the abatis . . . down into the ditch with ladders, up and over the parapet with flying flags, and down among, and on top of, the astonished enemy, who left in utmost haste. . . . Then and there I decided that 'the black man could fight' for his freedom, and that I had made a mistake in not commanding them."

Following that same engagement, Major General Benjamin F. Butler informed his wife: "The man who says the negro will not fight is a coward. . . . His soul is blacker than the dead faces of these dead negroes, upturned to heaven in solemn protest against him and his prejudices."[44]

The Confederate government never recognized blacks as legitimate soldiers. President Jefferson Davis considered their use a "servile insurrection" on the part of the North. In May 1863, the Confederate Congress passed a resolution stating that any officer commanding, arming, training, organizing, or preparing Negroes for military service should "if captured be put to death or be otherwise punished at the discretion" of a military court. Black soldiers seized in action were "to be delivered to the authorities of the State or States in which they shall be captured to be dealt with according to the present or future law of such State or States."[45]

Lincoln publicly denounced the enslavement of "any captured person on account of his color" as a "relapse into barbarism and a crime against the civilization of the age." He then directed that "for every soldier of the United States killed in violation of the laws of war a rebel soldier shall be executed, and for every one enslaved by the enemy or sold into slavery a rebel soldier shall be placed at hard labor on the public works, and continued at such labor until the other shall be released and receive the treatment due to a prisoner of war."[46] The Confederate government would not retreat from its position; neither would the Lincoln administration. The first and immediate result was a breakdown in the cartel for prisoner-of-war exchange.

Southern troops often reacted with cold fury when they encountered former slaves fighting against them. In the last two years of the war, Northern authorities reported a number of "massacres" that became some of the darker legacies of the Civil War. Many of those so-called atrocities were exaggerated if, in fact, authentic. However, there can be no doubt that captured, unarmed, and sometimes wounded black soldiers at Fort Pillow, Tennessee, Poison Spring, Arkansas, Petersburg, Virginia, and Saltville, Virginia, were murdered by wrathful Confederates.

Debate within the wartime South was long and bitter on the subject of enlisting blacks from the huge slave populace inside the Confederacy. Finally, in March 1865 (and by the narrowest of votes), the Confederate Congress passed legislation calling for the recruitment and enrollment of 300,000 black soldiers. An all-black contingent quickly materialized in Richmond. As the blacks proudly marched down the street for the first time in their Southern uniforms, whites lining the sidewalks threw mud at them. It is fitting that this unit saw no action in defense of the Confederacy.

Many Union soldiers befriended blacks as the war continued. Writing from Tennessee in August 1862, a Wisconsin private told his parents: "One of those who are in our cook house says that he was sold 4 years ago by his own Father for $1,400. He is nearly as white as I am and he has none of the negro peculiarities about him either. Now if that aint nearly as hard a story as you read in books so often, I would like to know what is."[47]

Acts of kindness and assistance became increasingly frequent. Some soldiers taught black compatriots to read and write; others introduced former slaves to Christianity. Some social intermingling, considered out of the question in 1862, occurred in the closing months of the struggle.

Approximately 180,000 blacks served as Federal soldiers. This figure represents 9 percent of the North's fighting force. One-third of the blacks (68,178) died in service, with sickness causing thirty times more deaths than battle. As an example: the 56th U.S. Colored Troops was in service two years. It took part in three skirmishes which cost 4 officers and 21 enlisted men killed or wounded. Yet this regiment lost 6 officers and 647 men from disease.[48]

Of those blacks who saw combat, deep pride was their compensation. Two black patients in an army hospital began a conversation. One of them looked at the stump of an arm he had once had and remarked: "Oh I should like to have it, but I don't begrudge it." His ward-mate, minus a leg, replied: "Well, 'twas [lost] in a glorious cause, and if I'd lost my life I should have been satisfied. I knew what I was fighting for."[49]

After the war Colonel Norwood P. Hallowell of the 55th Massachusetts wrote proudly of the blacks he had commanded: "We called upon them in the day of our trial, when volunteering had ceased, when the draft was a partial failure, and the bounty system a senseless extravagance. They were ineligible for promotion, they were not to be treated as prisoners of war. nothing was definite except they could be shot and hanged as soldiers. Fortunate, indeed, it is for us, as well as for them, that they were equal to the crisis; that the grand historic moment which comes to a race only once in many centuries came to them, and they recognized it. They saw that the day of their redemption had arrived."[50]

That explains why marching black regiments often sang, with far more gusto than usual, a popular Union war song with the chorus:

> Yes, we'll rally round the flag, boys, we'll rally once again.
> Shouting the battle cry of freedom!

Blacks were a positive addition to the Union armies, but the same cannot be said of tens of thousands of whites who entered service in the second half of the war. As battle casualties mounted alarmingly in 1862, Lincoln issued a call for 100,000 new volunteers. Among the patriotic rallies that followed was one attended by several thousand people in Pittsburgh. A local speaker of some repute arose and began a speech that came straight out of Cato, the great Roman orator. The speaker was building momentum when he thundered: "Notwithstanding the dark and gloomy tidings of disaster to the Union army, 'my voice is still for the war!' "

A momentary pause ensued; then from the rear of the hall came a shout from a wounded soldier home on furlough: "Damn your great big voice! It's your wee small body we want!"[51]

The war by then had lost its glamor and luster; the stream of volunteers had trickled away as increasing number of youths refused patriotic entreaties to join the army. Private Henry Bear of the 116th Illinois left no doubt as to how he felt about those who remained at home. From Memphis, in mid-December 1862, Bear wrote his wife: "You must tell evry man of Doubtful Loyalty for me, up ther in the north, that he is meaner than any son of a bitch in hell. I would rather shoot one of them a great deal than one [Southerner] living here."[52]

Paying bounties to men who would enlist became less and less an enticement, except to accomplished criminals who became professional bounty jumpers. Their custom was to enlist, collect a bounty, desert at the first opportunity, enlist somewhere else for a bounty, desert again, and continue the routine as long as they could. Authorities on both sides never solved the problem of army desertions. Bounty jumpers could therefore pursue their ends almost indefinitely. Occasionally, one would be caught, and in a number of instances such culprits were executed. Yet the dangers were far less than the dividend among that unscrupulous class.

Moreover, bounties did not usually attract men who became top-quality soldiers. An officer in the 70th Indiana wrote in January 1863 that "nine-tenths of them enlisted just because somebody else was going, and the other tenth were ashamed to stay at home."[53]

Both North and South were soon forced to resort to conscription. The Confederate draft law went into effect in April 1862; Union conscription began eleven months later. Men thus forced into the army were a distinct cut below those previously stimulated by patriotism. Quality in the ranks of blue and gray declined steadily thereafter. Private David Garrett of Texas tried to belittle the crisis that followed. The new draft law, he wrote in late spring of 1862, "kicked up a fuss for a while, but since they shot about twenty-five men for mutiny whipped & shaved the heads of as many more for the same offense everything has got quiet & goes on as usual."

South Carolinian Joseph Reid did not view conscription as a temporary problem. To his wife he wrote: "The conscript Act will do away with all the patriotism we have. Whenever men are forced to fight they take no personal interest in it, knowing that, let them do as well as they can, it will be said they were forced, and their bravery was not from patriotism. . . . A more oppressive law was never enacted in the most uncivilized country or by the worst of despots."[54]

Exemption clauses subsequently added to the conscription bills made their impact more severe and their acceptance even less. When the Confederate government, for example, excused any owner or overseer of twenty or more slaves from military service, a howl of protest went up from the South's common folk. They had no such grounds for escaping duty in the army. Large numbers of them promptly turned against what had originally been a crusade for independence. Now it was "a rich man's war but a poor man's fight," the inference being that the wealthy classes had provoked the struggle but the poor people were the ones who had to fight, bleed, and die.

Even worse, North and South alike then implemented a substitute system whereby a man could avoid military service by hiring a substitute to go in his place. This seemed like still another measure aimed at benefitting the haves at the expense of the have-nots; and it brought into the armies some of the lowest classes of society. They came in large numbers: 118,000 substitutes in the Union force, more than 50,000 into Confederate service.

The first wave of conscripts and substitutes for the Federal armies was utterly worthless. Of 186 such men assigned to a Massachusetts regiment, 115 deserted, 6 were discharged for disability, 26 were transferred to the navy, and 1 was killed in action. The loyalty and behavior of these classes was so suspect that officers entrusted with getting them to an army camp generally transported them as if they were prisoners of war. An unhappy substitute in the 39th Ohio attempted to desert four times in his first three months of service. To insure that he would not escape before his scheduled court-martial, guards kept him tied to a tree. Once in camp, a New Hampshire sergeant wrote of these new soldiers, "they get drunk, fight, disturb the camp, break heads, steal, lie, fall asleep at their posts, desert the guard, and serve the evil one generally."[55]

Veteran soldiers on both sides voiced disgust over conscripts and substitutes. A New England infantryman snorted that "such another depraved, vice-hardened and desperate set of human beings never before disgraced an army." A Pennsylvania captain termed them "the grandest scoundrels that ever went unhung. These were the cream and flower, the very head and front of the New York rioters, gamblers, thieves, pickpockets and blacklegs." When a large contingent of these replacements joined the 13th Massachusetts, the veterans were appalled. A sergeant wrote: "There were two hundred of them when they started from Boston to join us, but about a dozen had been shot or drowned on the voyage out in trying to escape. After breakfast we went up to hear the roll call . . . Many had forgotten the name they gave when they enlisted, and others would try to make them believe that was their name when one was called and there was no answer. . . . Their conversation was foul, with almost every other word an oath."[56]

The situation was the same on the Confederate side. In 1864, after the 1st Virginia received a company of draftees and substitutes, Sergeant Charles Loehr sneered: "Some of them looked like they had been resurrected from the grave, after laying therein for twenty years or more." Private J. W. Eggleston of the 24th Virginia was more emphatic on the subject, even to his mother: "ther is no nues in camp Worth yo attention moer than Congress has past A bil to fetch the dam substitute men back an aint I glad dam the Sobs I want them to fite an die an buley for them."[57]

Medical examiners in the Union army were horrified at the condition of the 1863–1864 waves of men sent to the armies. Cripples, the incapacitated, and persons in the final stages of incurable diseases were in large evidence. Of fifty-seven recruits for the 6th New York Heavy Artillery, seventeen could not muster. In March 1864, one-third of the replacements sent to a cavalry division were already on the sick list when they reached camp. There was even a case where recruitment brokers persuaded an idiot to leave a New York asylum and join the army.[58]

In December 1863, a field officer in the 34th Massachusetts told of a contingent of substitutes assigned to his regiment. "Six recruits joined us to-day, making twenty whom we have received. Three of them are given to fits; are entirely worthless, not having done a day's duty since joining; and the worst one of the lot cost the most, being what is termed a 'Veteran Recruit' at $700." Yet these new and "purchased" recruits often had to fight a war against their experienced comrades before they fought the enemy. One veteran stated: "Our boys don't play fair with [the substitutes] they steal their knapsacks and guns and everything else. They will find out how to watch their things closer after they soldier a year or two."[59]

Of course, many of the soldiers who enlisted or who were drafted into the army after 1862 were sincerely motivated, conscientious, and demonstrably good fighting men; but they appeared to be a distinct minority. Conscripts and substitutes as a rule had to be guarded in camp to prevent them from plundering their compatriots or deserting the army. In battle, they were an almost total liability. They would not fight under any inducement; and if somehow forced to the front lines, they would go over to the enemy at the first chance. They were so unreliable that any regiment that had them in large numbers was decidedly weaker than it would have been without them.

The one positive aspect of the class of bounty jumpers and substitutes was to make the good soldiers look even better. Henry Orendorff of the 103rd Illinois was one such soldier. From Mississippi in July 1863, he informed his sister: "It is hard for a person to imagine how much a man sacrifices in the way pleasure and enjoyment by going into the 'Army,' but I think I shall never regret being in the 'Army' if I get out alive & well." He did.[60]

• 3 •

Novelties of Camp Life

The army camp was the place where the recruit ceased to be a civilian and learned how to become a soldier. He would spend more time in camp than on marches and in battle combined. It was in camp that he was introduced to the mysteries of the army: bugle calls and drum beats, the military chain of command, discipline, the necessity of taking care of equipment, and obedience to orders. He drilled as best he could; he learned something about pitching a tent and using a weapon.

Youngsters, as well as volunteers from isolated rural areas, especially liked the novelty of army life. The men of blue and gray tended to be volatile, fun-loving, and sociably engaging. In their new surroundings, they at first reacted with pleasure.

"Everything goes on very agreeable," Iowa soldier Peter Wilson wrote home. Charles Wills of an Illinois regiment was more exuberant. "I never enjoyed anything in the world as I do this life." Virginia recruit William Morgan informed his sister: "we are the livliest set of men you ever saw together without they had Liquor to drink, singing, Whooping, talking & laughing. . . . All we have to do when not on drill is to cook and eat and do a little washing and the balance of the time we lay flat on our backs . . . I have got so lazy that if I was discharged and returned home it would be some time before I could take hold of work wright." At almost the same time, New Yorker Edwin Weller was writing his wife: "There is Something about Soldiering that is romantic and a great many get So much accustomed to the life that they like no other. I sometimes think that if I was to go home now to remain I should not be contented . . . "[1]

All of these men, however, were describing their first days in camp. Recruits entering the field quickly found themselves confronting a number of adversities.

Excess and ill-fitting equipment became apparent first. New Hampshire recruit Millet Thompson declared at his regiment's arrival in Washington that "we are warriors now in full feathers and trappings: ten pounds of gun: eighty rounds per man of ball cartridge, one pound of powder, five pounds of lead, heavy equipments; knapsack, haversack, three-pint canteen, all full; three days' rations; rubber blanket, woolen blanket, shelter tent, full winter clothing; tin cup, tin plate, knife, fork, spoon, spider, et cetera too numerous to mention, and too many to carry, and a pound of mud on each shoe. We are a baggage train, freight train, ammunition train, commissary train, gravel train, and a train-band, all in one."[2]

The fancy-looking havelock did not long remain popular. Made of white linen, it was "to be worn on the head as a protection from the rays of the sun. As it was made sufficiently large to cover the neck and shoulders, the effect, when properly adjusted, was to deprive the wearer of any air he might otherwise enjoy."[3] Overnight havelocks came to be used as dishcloths and coffee strainers. Other superfluous items met similar fates. Almost without fail, the large items were discarded first. Lining the route of any new army could be seen overcoats, extra blankets, homemade quilts, knapsacks, and the like.

Some gear had to be tolerated. While the knapsack remained indispensable as a carryall, to more than one soldier it was "a miserable thing of painted cloth which daubs everything it touches." A haversack was a black canvas bag with a strap attached to the opposite side and worn around the neck or shoulders. One Rhode Islander exclaimed: "Your haversack's to carry your grub in! It'll be the best friend you'll find in the army!" A messmate did not see it that way. "When we left Providence our haversacks had neat white cotton linings, but after they had been in use a few weeks as receptacles for chunks of fat meat, damp sugar tied up in a rag, broken crackers and bread, with a lump of cheese or two, they took the color of a printing-office towel. . . . Very likely you would have gone hungry a good while before eating anything out of them."[4]

Some units raised in 1861 were issued "bulletproof vests," which soldiers generally regarded with contempt. A sergeant in the 15th Iowa observed that when some of these items were brought into camp and submitted to trial, "about one half were bored through by musket balls. If the bullet did not go through it it would knock a man into the middle of next week so that he might as well be killed first as last."[5] Few of these vests ever saw battle.

A Confederate soldier noted that "wisdom is born of experience." Before many weeks had passed, "the private soldier, reduced to the minimum, consisted of one man, one hat, one jacket, one pair pants, one pair drawers, one pair socks, one pair shoes, and his baggage was one blanket, one gum-cloth, and one haversack . . ."[6]

Rare indeed was the soldier who did not have a problem with government-issue boots. The shoes, a Marine private asserted, "were made for feet of all shapes and sizes, but when a soldier had selected a pair which he thought came nearest to his size, there was always plenty of room to spare in all directions, except one or two places where they pinched." Billy Yanks gave their new shoes a variety of nicknames, including "Ferry-boats," "Tanyards," and "Pontoons." A Rhode Islander with a sense of humor characterized his shoes as "easy to march in, easy to drill in, and large enough to sleep in. They are so broad-soled, that I have taken one off, and, putting a piece of brown paper on it, have improvised a satisfactory writing-desk."[7]

Field camps were the places where, a Louisianian understated, "we were fairly initiated into the mysteries and miseries of a soldier's life."[8] The first army camps of the war gave every appearance of orderliness. Army regulations prescribed how an encampment was to follow a systematic grid pattern. Officers' quarters were at the front of each street, with enlisted men's quarters precisely aligned to the rear. Streets were to be of specific width; the locations of kitchens and latrines were responsibly pinpointed; picket lines formed a symetrical perimeter around the whole plat. A nearby creek or river was essential for water supply.

Everything was that way initially. Adherence to regulations worked in inverse proportion to the length of the war. When war became drudgery, latrines and horse pens often were located upstream—which at the least affected the taste of the coffee.

A tent was the soldier's home away from home during the spring, summer, and autumn months. Three types were used in the first part of the war. The wall tent was a large, box-shaped canvas structure with upright sides and sloping roofs. The walls were high enough to permit a man to move around while standing erect. However, the wall tent was expensive to manufacture and heavy to transport; as a result, its use was confined to hospitals and officers.

Easily recognizable was the Sibley tent, named for Henry H. Sibley, who designed it and who later became a Confederate brigadier. A conical structure 18 feet in diameter and 12 feet tall, it resembled an oversized Indian tepee. A New England soldier remembered the Sibley tent with anything but fondness. "It was quite a spacious pavilion, large enough almost for a good size circus side show. . . . The foot of the centre pole was held in position by an iron frame, called a tri-pod, the three legs of which straddled out like those of a daddy-long-legs. This straddling attachment seems to have been invented expressly for the soldiers to stumble over when moving about at night. It served its purpose admirably. . . . The men were packed like sardines in a box, from fifteen to twenty in each tent. At night they lay with their feet mixed up around the centre-pole, their heads fringing the outer line. Each man's knapsack marked the particular section of ground that belonged to him. . . . The men slept like a great circular row of spoons, and if one wanted to turn over to give the bones on the other side a chance, he would yell out the order to 'flop' and all would go together . . . "[9]

Abner Dunham of the 12th Iowa adjudged the Sibleys "a great deal healthier than barracks and just as comfortable and there is not so many men put together so there is not much confusion." Not many soldiers would have agreed with that assessment. A Confederate who lived in a Sibley only a short time called the tents "those abominations, those breeders of disease." Inclement weather had an adverse effect on the atmosphere of the shelter. Massachusetts artilleryman John Billings avowed that to enter a Sibley on a rainy morning "and encounter the night's accumulation of nauseating exhalations from the bodies of twelve men (differing widely in their habits of personal cleanliness) was an experience which no old soldier has ever been known to recall with great enthusiasm."[10] Sibley tents went out of use in 1862 because they proved too cumbersome for transportation and field operations.

Wedge tents were popular on the union side. Known also as "A" tents because they resembled the letter without the crossbar when viewed from the end, they consisted of six-foot-long canvas stretched over a horizontal ridgepole which was staked on both sides. The tent had flaps for closing the front and rear ends. A wedge tent normally contained seven square feet of space and accommodated four men. It was not uncommon for six soldiers to crowd inside when the weather was bad or tents were in short supply. With the ridgepole less than five feet off the ground, everyone had to stoop before entering—and endure cramped quarters thereafter.

Near Fredericksburg, Virginia, late in December 1862, a New York soldier wrote: "Our one tent is a pig-sty. Four of us sleep and six of us eat and write in it. We have nothing either in our own stove inside or on the little space outside that can be called a fire. The wood is all green pine. The smoke hangs to the ground and there is no wind to blow off what comes from a whole division crowded into an acre or two of land. Everybody is crying. Everybody is cross."[11]

Beginning in the war's second year, the standard abode for soldiers was the shelter tent. It rapidly became known as the dog tent or dog shanty since "it would only comfortably accommodate a dog, and a small one at that." Such statements were not exactly true. Laforest Dunham of the 129th Illinois once interrupted a letter home because "we have got to draw purp tents as we call them. They are little tents big enough a for too."[12]

The always cynical Charles Davis of the 13th Massachusetts complained loudly when he had to abandon his Sibley for a shelter tent. "In place thereof [of the Sibley] we received a piece of thin sheeting about four feet by six feet, in the binding of which were buttons and buttonholes. Each man was given one piece, with instructions to find two other men supplied with a similar piece, and combine the three into a tent. In order to pitch your tent you must first go into the woods and cut crotches with a stick to rest across the top, forming a ridgepole, on which two of the pieces, buttoned together, were to rest, then to be stretched out in the shape of the letter A and fastened to the ground. The third piece was to cover one end. . . . To enter one of these 'dog-kennels,' as they were called, you had to get down on your knees, with your head near the earth, as though you were approaching the throne of an Arabian monarch, and crawl in."[13]

If only two canvas pieces were available, soldiers used coats and blankets to enclose the tent. The men learned in sultry weather to elevate the tent so that air could circulate around the bottom. Small, airy, and offering little head room, the dog tents were a far cry from homely comforts—especially in extremes of weather. A soldier in the 17th Virginia remembered that "during the early part of the [summer day] and until the late noon, the heat inside was worse than that of the blazing sun without; the canvas seemed only to draw the rays to a focus and keep them there in one white blaze. And to add to the discomfort, swarms of flies infested the tents and could never be induced on any account to leave them; they seemed to think exposure to the outer air not at all conducive to their health, while anything like a walk abroad would be positively fatal."

James M. Phillips of the 92nd Illinois was of the same mind where shelter tents were concerned. They "are the worst things that was ever invented for soldiers, I think," he wrote his wife. "when the weather is cool and rainy, as it was last night and this morning, a person almost suffers. the wind and rain blows through both ends. being open gives a good chance for circulation of the wind, but they shed rain a great deal better than I expected they would. but still I am talking about suffering."[14]

Ill-supplied Confederates, always in want of tents, utilized every piece of canvas seized from the enemy. Southerners came to rely on homemade shelters known as "shebangs." Built with whatever material was available, a shebang could be erected in one day by four men and a single axe. Two wooden forks were imbedded in the ground; a ridge-pole was placed on the forks; barns and fences provided most of the siding, with heavy wooden posts used for the frame and thinner boards for the siding. If wood was not available to cover the frame, Johnny Rebs resorted to bushes, "blankets, oil cloths, or anything else which could be made available to protect from the weather." Naturally, the quality of these huts depended on the skill of the builders. The finished structures housed three to four men and, in spite of their appearance, were generally pronounced "very comfortable in warm weather."[15]

Over the entrance of many tents and shebangs, soldiers placed boards crudely labeled with the name of their homestead. Titles included "Uncle Tom's Cabin," "Hawkins's Happy Family," "Fifth Avenue Hotel," "Social Circle," "Mess of Cabbage, Company F," "Old Abe's Parlor," and "Chateau de Salt Junk." Another differentiation in the quarters resulted from the way residents treated them. An Iowa soldier noted that "some tents will be made in a few days as snug and cosy as parlors, while others will have become like stables." Wet weather put them all on an equal level, he added. "At such a time as this, it is next to impossible to make any tent comfortable. The rain soaks through the canvas and drips, drips, drips inside, while outside is deep mud, and, of course, this is carried by boots and shoes inside."[16]

Beds varied more than the canvas homes. Massachusetts soldier William Lincoln listed some of the types he had seen. "A. spreads his blanket upon his tent floor, of dirt or wood, as the case may be, and uses his boots for a pillow; B. nails up a long narrow box, strongly suggestive of that unpleasant, black looking shell, in which we all sleep our last slumber; another makes his couch of small cedar or arbor vitae twigs, carefully laid one upon the other; while he who is more fastidious, drives into the ground four forked sticks, rests upon them two slender poles, to which a proper number of barrel staves are fastened cross ways, and, spreading his blankets, enjoys a spring bed as luxurious as any which crowd the warehouses at home."[17]

Whatever the accommodation, a New Englander stated, "one cannot describe his feelings during the first night under a tent—the beginning of his real soldier life. There was so much to look forward to, so much to look back upon! Thoughts of separation from home and loved ones, never, perhaps, to be seen again, occupied the mind. All the hopes and ambitions of the young soldier were crowding through the brain, and ending in the one dearest wish to go speedily to the front."[18]

First, however, came the training process. The normal camp day began with reveille near 5 A.M. and usually with "a combination of all the unhuman sounds possible to be made on an army bugle." Ted Barclay of the 4th Virginia did not mind. "I have gotten so used to it that I jump up before the drum beats." Few others shared Barclay's exuberance. Most soldiers, wrote New Yorker George Collins, "slept in the major part of their clothes, yet it was not an unusual thing to see officers and men present [for roll-call] in partial *dishabille*, shivering in the cold morning wind . . . the men standing in line rubbing their eyes with the backs of their hands to get the 'sticks' out of them while the hairs of their heads stood on end like the quills of a porcupine." Troops responded to roll call, another Billy Yank commented, "in every tone and compass of which the human voice is capable, a perfect Babel."[19]

The assembled troops might have a short drill before receiving a summary of their duties for the day, "if the First Sergeants can possibly find out beforehand what their duties are to be." Then the men were dismissed to prepare breakfast. This they did either individually or in groups known as "messes." Around 8 A.M. would come a drum or bugle call summoning guard details to their posts and alerting the sick to report to the regimental surgeon. The morning was devoted to a number of activities. Building roads, policing the camp, making pathways of pine logs, extending latrine pits, gathering firewood and water wherever they could be found, repairing equipment, were but a few of the daily chores. Most recruits who had rushed to enlist were unprepared for such menial tasks as these. "Men who at home were accustomed to nothing more strenuous than the handling of a yard stick and dry goods from over the counter, or light clerical work, lawyers, book keepers, school teachers, and among them were men of wealth, now [found] themselves as privates in the ranks subject to the orders of superior officers, doing the work of porters and laborers in all kinds of necessary drudgery."[20]

A noon call announced the time for lunch. Regimental drill then occupied two or three hours. Following that, the men returned to their quarters, cleaned weapons, and got uniforms into inspectable condition. Dress parade, if held, occurred around 6 P.M. After retreat, the men had supper. Free time prevailed until 9 P.M., when the call for lights-out sounded. Loud snores and coughs soon marked the end of the day.

One Billy Yank left no doubt about his feelings in regard to the principal activity that filled most of the soldier's first weeks in camp. "The first thing in the morning is drill, then drill, then drill again. Then drill, drill, a little more drill. Then drill, and lastly drill. Between drills, we drill and sometimes stop to eat a little and have roll-call."[21]

Several reasons existed for the concentration on drill. Cultivating discipline was a principal factor. Then there were the "how-to-fight-a-war" manuals of that day. Although termed "books on tactics," the volumes were actually drill regulations. Not only had they been written in peacetime (when parade appearance counts more than battle activity); a couple of the more popular works were so ancient that explanatory plates depicted flintlock muskets—which had been out of use twenty years before the Civil War began!

Officers on both side relied heavily on Winfield Scott's *Infantry Tactics* (3 volumes) and William J. Hardee's *Rifle and Infantry Tactics*. The former, published in 1835, was simply reprinted in 1861 without changes. A year later, General Silas Casey produced what was to be a modern, 3-volume manual for the army: *Infantry Tactics, for the Instruction, Exercise, and Manouevres of the Soldier* Yet by the author's own admission, the finished work wɔ somewhat disorganized and in need of revisions. Such improvements in the text came slowly and through the experience of war.

Army drill in the 1860s was far simpler and less rigorous than that now prescribed for recruits because the citizen-soldiers were less prepared mentally for army service. Drill officers regularly discovered that they were dealing with untutored farmboys who often and literally did not know their left foot from the right foot. One unique audiovisual aid was devised. A wisp of hay would be attached to the left shoe, a piece of straw to the right. Then, when the squad began marching, the men would look down at their feet and follow the drill instructor's chant: "Hayfoot, Strawfoot, Hayfoot, Strawfoot!"

Simply executing a left-face or right-face while standing in ranks created problems to the uninitiated. As a Pennsylvania soldier recalled: "The drill in the 'facings' disclosed the fact that many, otherwise intelligent men were not certain as to which was their right hand or their left. Consequently, when the order 'Right face!' was given, face met face in inquiring astonishment, and frantic attempts to obey the order properly made still greater confusion."[22]

Only occasionally did practice drills extend beyond the regimental level of an army, and for a basic reason. Most officers and men in the Civil War started out together as complete novices. Hence, drill was often akin to the ignorant leading the uneducated. As a Virginia artillerist concluded: "Maneuvers of the most utterly impossible sort were taught to the men. Every amateur officer had his own pet system of tactics, and the effect of the incongruous teachings, when brought out in battalion drill, closely resembled that of the music at Mr. Bob Sawyer's party, where each guest sang the chorus to the tune he knew best." A New Hampshire infantryman stated that "the appearance of the line can be better imagined than described. Drill is aching funny. We are all green. Mistakes are corrected by making still worse mistakes. The men in the ranks grin, giggle and snicker, and now and then break out into a coarse, country hee-haw."[23]

Officers generally took unkindly to such reactions, and the stalwarts among them sometimes got the last laugh. A favorite Civil War anecdote of unknown origin concerned a young and inexperienced lieutenant who was assigned to a new company of rough-hewn men. The lieutenant was small, inept, and weak in appearance. When he rode in front of the men for the first time, out of the rear ranks came a shout: "And a little child shall lead them!" That drew a roar of laughter from the entire company.

Seemingly undisturbed by this reception, the lieutenant calmly went about the day's business. The next morning the men awakened to discover a surprise notice that the company in full gear would be going on a twenty-mile march that day. "And a little child shall lead them," continued the proclamation, "on a damned big horse!"

The men drilled and marched four-abreast in column. They had to learn to shift promptly from column of fours to two closely aligned ranks, which was the usual line of battle. Green officers giving such commands while scores of men attempted to maintain lines and proper cadence could be a nerve-wracking ordeal for all concerned. A member of the 14th New Hampshire noted: "The men were serene in their ignorance of tactics; but ambitious officers of the line, who had been cramming Casey for a fortnight, were in a vetrebral cold-shiver temperature. . . . That the men got into a snarl, a tangle, a double and twisted, inextricable tactical knot, is tame delineation. The drill caused a great deal of serious reflection . . . "[24]

Marching drills certainly had their humorous moments. A newly commissioned captain was putting his men through close-order drill. He wanted them to spread out in skirmish formation, but he did not know the proper command. Finally the captain thundered: "Get out there as skirmishers, every one of you, or I'll put you all in the guardhouse!" Similarly, an inexperienced lieutenant assigned to drill a company one morning was doing fairly well until his troops rapidly approached a huge mudhole in the drillfield. The officer could not think of the proper commands to give. Desperately he called out: "Boys! Break up, scoot the hole, and git together on t'other side!"[25]

First efforts at drilling were strenuous and exhausting. "We made so much nois coughing that no one could hear the commands," Ira Gillaspie of the 11th Michigan stated. A Connecticut soldier wrote after a two-hour drill that his company "looked and felt as though they had been through a forced march of thirty miles." The men would customarily return from full-gear drill, he added, "with eyes, noses, mouths, ears, teeth and hair full of dust, and their rations, as well as themselves, were gritty for a week thereafter . . . "[26]

Infantry drill, a Virginian solemnly concluded, was "an infliction to be endured while it lasted." Should a company go awry while trying to execute some regimental maneuver, the results were disastrous to the whole command. When such occurred, a soldier in the 17th Virginia wrote, "our colonel, genial and sociable off the field, and a martinet on, would fume and fret, until the luckless captain, losing what little self-possession he had, blundered more and more and generally ended up tying his company in a hard knot."[27]

Artillery drill was no more proficient. Batteries practiced over and over galloping up to a line, halting and unlimbering, disassembling their cannon until every piece lay on the ground in order, then reassembling the weapon, packing up, and galloping away. Of course, mistakes and errors occurred at every step. Improvement was noticeably slow.

All of this routine, a young gunner growled, "was of as much practical use to us as if we had been assiduously drilled to walk on stilts."[28]

Men on drill-practice welcomed any distraction. "Very often in manoeuvering in the field," a Virginian reminisced, "an old hare would jump up, shake his white tail by way of challenge and bound off. In that case good-by to all discipline. Regardless of officers' commands, the soldiers with one shout would start after him. . . . A strange characteristic of this Southern army was their insane desire to run a hare."[29]

The inexperience of officers was readily apparent in the first months of service. Thomas Head of Tennessee was correct when he noted: "The first officers were good men, although they were selected more through their standing and influence in private life than through efficiency." A Mississippi captain wrote his wife during his first days as a company commander: "My post is no sinecure, be assured of it. My hands are full—perfectly full. I have no hope of being a popular Capt. I am only trying to make a good one. . . . No one can imagine the amt. of work required of an officer as green as I am in Tactics."[30]

When Walter Lenoir received word that he had been elected a lieutenant in his North Carolina company, he was horrified at the thought of having to drill men who knew more than he did. "Oh! that I could but once have gone to school for two or three months as a diligent student of the company and battalion drills, learning to give and superintend the execution of the commands belonging to my new office!" Val Giles of the 4th Texas added that "the volunteers of the early sixties were hard to manage at best, and when they were commanded by former playmates it was a trying ordeal for the officers." These factors led a recruit in the 92nd Illinois to state in a letter home: "There is a great deal of disatisfaction with the Capt. he [is] so bigoted that he will not learn any thing and he cannot drill half as good as the men and the other commissioned officers are not much better."[31]

One Tennessee colonel acknowledged that he knew only three commands: "Form line," "Forward march," and "Fix bayonets." Several officers devised their own unique commands. The 28th Virginia's Robert T. Preston would shout: "Fall in, Twenty-eighth, fall in! If you don't fall in, I will march the regiment off and leave every one of you behind!" Whenever an alarm sounded in the camp of the 19th Virginia, Colonel John Bowie Strange would bellow: "Attention, my people, fall in! Them fellers are a-coming!"[32]

Some officers sought to conceal inexperience with bluster. A Confederate became quite bemused at his green captain. "If you could see him strutting along as proud as a peacock," he wrote to the homefolk, "you would think he was Jeff Davis, Gen. Johnston, or some other big bug. Today whilst out drilling, he was walking so big and his head so high that when he came across a ledge of rocks, he could not see them and fell head over heels and great was the fall thereof. . . . I reckon he wont walk so big hereafter."[33]

Even the simplest order could sometimes be misunderstood. A Confederate major was taking a group of men single file up a mountainside. Straggling increased, despite the major's command: "Tell them that the order is to 'double quick'!" When the order reached the rear elements by word-of-mouth, it came out: "The order is to 'double quick back there'!" Whereupon the rear portion of the regiment bolted back down the mountain. The major "was upset," his chaplain noted, "and flat on his back and with heels in the air he poured forth benedictions of an unusual kind for a Presbyterian elder."[34]

Other officers were content to rely totally on what they regarded as the high quality of their men. When a commander once asked Captain John Trice of the 4th Kentucky how he would deploy his troops in battle, the untutored Confederate replied: "Well, Major, I can't answer that according to the books, but I would risk myself with the Trigg County boys, and go in on main strength and awkwardness."[35]

Parades and reviews offered units a formal opportunity to display their abilities, and they usually engendered patriotism and pride. A sergeant in the 105th Illinois wrote his sister of a recent parade. "It was a fine sight to see them all dressed in clean uniforms and bright arms and polished accoutrements and nice packed knapsacks on their backs marching to the music of four splendid brass bands . . . Oh! who would not be a soldier. I would sell a small farm to become a soldier if I could not be one any other way."[36] However, distractions or a lack of respect for the occasion could shatter a parade's aura.

A Massachusetts officer sadly noted: "At parades, if a head itches, off comes the cap, that a good scratching may be had; noses get many a brush and buffet, as intrusive flies light upon and tickle such members; and many a time, a good natured fellow turns upon his heel to exchange a friendly word with his rear rank neighbor."[37]

The 118th Pennsylvania never forgot its first grand review. The men were immaculately dressed, with bayonets gleaming in the summer sun. The regiment marched snappily onto the parade ground—and promptly stepped into several nests of yellowjackets. Startled insects attacked in force; the Pennsylvanians wavered, then "fled in confusion, covered with stings instead of glory." The first review of the 36th New York was even more hilarious. That unit was composed in the main of Irishmen under twenty-one years of age. They knew fighting and little else, a member of a sister regiment asserted. "On their first dress parade, or attempt at it, when the officers marched in front to receive the colonel's instructions, the loafers around camp and the sentinels on duty, doubtless thinking that so many could not get together in one crowd without a fight, all ran and gathered around the officers, and staid there till the colonel dismissed them!"[38]

Many new soldiers saw no glamor in the pageantry of a review. A private in the 10th Illinois wrote of one parade: "To us poor tired soldiers, after having marched ten miles, loaded down as we were with all the paraphernalia of war, and then to be obliged to go through all the evolutions described in Hardee for half a day for the gratification of every military upstart who might happen to come along, we just thought it too much of a good thing, and in our hearts voted the thing a gigantic fraud."[39]

A Maine soldier was witness to another parade that lost its seriousness. "Gen. Slocum reviewed us, or tried to, but his horse and Gen. Williams's became frightened at 'Present arms,' and went jumping all around the field, scattering the staffs and orderlies to the four winds. This made the review interesting to us, but we enjoyed it more when a small dog came running down to bite the heels of Gen. Slocum's horse. Lieut. Pittman drew his sabre and slashed at the cur . . . but the dog flanked him and ran back to Slocum, leaving the lieutenant to charge on."[40]

Obviously, being an officer in the Civil War was far from an easy task. For the most part, officers were inexperienced and poorly trained for the responsibilities they bore. An officer had to get maximum effort from the men while maintaining maximum morale. He had to walk a fine line between providing for the needs of subordinates and meeting the demands of superiors. Some officers could not meet the test. A Texas major gave up in despair and resigned from the army. According to one of the men, "he said when he left them that if he had to associate with devils he would wait till he went to hell, where he could select his own company."[41]

Learning to use weapons was an even more traumatic ordeal for new soldiers.

In the first weeks of any unit's training, accidents with weapons just distributed were commonplace. Cavalrymen drilling with sabers regularly pricked their mounts and caused stampedes. Recruits trying to master the basics of artillery fared little better. Members of a Massachusetts battery one quiet day decided to test their markmanship at a large tree on a hilltop 1,000 yards away. The gunners clumsily set the sights at 1,600 yards and almost killed the inhabitants of a village on the other side of the hill.[42]

For infantrymen, trying to learn how to handle their arms was an exercise in patience and luck. The Civil War was a foot soldier's contest from the first to last; thus, shoulder arms were of paramount importance. Both sides in 1861 were woefully delinquent in supplying quality weapons for their troops. The governor of Iowa sought to belittle the shortage of arms by declaring that "double-barreled shotguns and hunting rifles, although not the best, are good arms in the hands of brave men."[43] Such a viewpoint was unrealistic for the struggle which the Civil War came to be.

Those who volunteered in 1861 took into service whatever weapons they had. The 27th Alabama left for war allegedly armed with 1,000 double-barreled shotguns and 1,000 crudely made bowie knives. One huge Pennsylvanian who entered service without any arms purchased "a great butcher knife" and pranced through camp for weeks thereafter "bellowing to be let loose on the rebels." In contrast, when young John McDonald arrived to join the newly formed 6th Tennessee, he could be heard long before he came into view. He was literally sagging from a veritable arsenal of weapons. "His idea," a compatriot stated, "was to use the Minie [musket] at long range, then his shotgun, then his [two] pistols; then, as the hostile lines came closer, to throw his tomahawk, and then, with sword in one hand and a big knife in another, to wade in and dispatch the ten traditional Yankees" any respectable Southerner was expected to defeat.[44]

Arms issued by the government to many units were hardly an improvement. A North Carolinian described the weapons his company received as "old flint-and-steel, smooth-bore muskets, a species of ordnance . . . supposed to have descended from 1776, and to have been wrestled by order of the Governor from the worms and rust of the arsenal at Fayetteville." A New Hampshire colonel dismissed the arms given his regiment as "about as efficient as pitchforks."[45]

Some of the first Northern units organized were equipped with huge .69 caliber smoothbore muskets, which had been popular for a generation or more. Newspaper reporter Franc B. Wilkie once examined a shipment of these weapons and concluded: "I think it would be a master stroke of policy to allow the secessionists to steal them. They are the old-fashioned-brass-mounted-and-of-such-is-the-kingdom-of-Heaven kind that are infinitely more dangerous to friend than enemy—will kick further than they will shoot . . . "[46]

These muskets were so short-ranged and inaccurate that enemy soldiers, aware of the weapons their adversaries were using, often "took advantage of the situation and would expose themselves on their works and tantalize our boys." At one early musket-practice with this particular gun, members of the 14th Illinois set a barrel 180 yards away as a target. Of 160 shots fired, 157 missed. A disgusted Gen. U.S. Grant observed that a soldier using such a musket at any appreciable range "might fire at you all day without you finding it out."[47]

North and South alike looked initially to Europe for arms purchases. The results were generally disappointing, for too often foreign nations foisted off their armament refuse to America. One shipment of 3,000 Austrian muskets contained only 500 that were usable. A Massachusetts private was confident that the Austrian musket "would hardly carry a ball clear of its muzzle and [would] send it anywhere but in the desired direction."[48]

Belgian muskets were blunderbuss-like .70 caliber weapons and cursed as well by crooked barrels. American soldiers called them "pumpkin slingers" and "European stovepipes." One Federal officer stated that many Prussian-manufactured muskets "burst at the first firing, and were more dangerous at their butts than at their muzzles."[49] In contrast to such imports was the musket produced at the Enfield arsenal in England. It was a direct copy of the rifle-musket whose name is synonymous with the Civil War.

That weapon was the .577 Springfield, named for a Massachusetts armory. More than 1,600,000 of this gun were manufactured in the United States (at a cost of $14.93 each).[50] The rifle-musket was the most important military development of the Civil War. It was a muzzle-loading weapon with a long, relatively thin barrel and a spinning, grooved track inside the barrel. This enabled the bullet to spin as it started down the barrel, and the tube's extra length helped to increase range fivefold and accuracy even more. Confederates never missed an opportunity to exchange their weapons for the Northern-made Springfields.

Loading a musket was a multistage process. The soldier reached into his cartridge box and got a cartridge, which consisted of a ball and a charge of powder wrapped together in paper. He tore open the cartridge with his teeth, emptied the powder down the barrel of the musket, and inserted the bullet with the pointed end up. The soldier then drew the ramrod from beneath the barrel and tamped down ball and powder, then returned the ramrod to its place (unless, of course, he was in battle). Next he half-cocked the hammer and placed a firing cap atop the little protrusion at the back end of the barrel. He then took position, cocked the hammer fully, aimed the musket, and pulled the trigger.

It was a complicated procedure, even in quiet surroundings. Recruits in a Rhode Island company remembered the first day they nervously began the step-by-step procedure of loading their muskets. The captain gave the familiar order "Load in nine times—load!" Then he added: "If you can do it, go ahead. I can't!"[51]

Muskets, wrote an Ohio soldier, "weighed seemingly a ton before the drill was ended." Then came time to fire; and once all weapons were up to shoulder-height and in aiming position, the drill sergeant—"that wretch in charge of us would deliberately walk up and down the line, raising the muzzle of one gun, depressing another, correcting the position of this or that, until our arms and shoulders would ache as though a team of horses had been tugging at them. This drill . . . was a great outrage. . . . It took a great deal of muscle to get the thing out straight even long enough to pull the trigger. There is no denying it—the boys did say bad words sometimes, when this performance was being enacted."[52]

Most recruits "cringed at every shot. Quite a number of men had never fired a gun in their lives; and several of them, when commanded to fire, would shut their eyes, turn their heads in the opposite direction, and blaze away." A Wisconsin enlistee "feared the result of the service to be performed with one of these 'howitzers.' " Those fears were realized the first time he pulled the trigger. "The next moment I was on my back, kicking for all that was out."[53]

In spite of the advancement in firepower made by the advent of the rifle-musket (or perhaps because of it), commanders were reluctant to issue live ammunition in camp or for skirmish drill because eagerness and inexperience led to numerous mishaps. A large number of soldiers were killed by shots accidentally fired by a compatriot. Men lost fingers, eyesight, even their lives, by having weapons discharge when they were handling them carelessly.

Marksmanship did not improve noticeably in the Civil War. A quartermaster in the 34th New York swore that one of his companies "had one hundred men, more or less, that could, at a hundred yards, knock an apple off a man's head without touching a hair." A Pennsylvania veteran boasted to everyone within hearing that "he hit an enemy every time he pulled the trigger."[54] Such claims are patently false. Statistics kept of target-practices were consistent in showing that at a distance of 150 yards, one shot out of three hitting the target was indeed a good score. After one June 1861 target-practice, a South Carolina soldier predicted: "If our men shoot at the enemy like they did at that barrel, they will not kill very many of the enemy unless they climb like squirrels or get in the ground like moles; for those that did not hit the tree top hit the ground about half way to the target."[55]

Reluctance by commanders to have soldiers practice with live ammunition was but one reason for the inaccuracy of Johnny Rebs and Billy Yanks. Although troops were instructed repeatedly to "shoot low so as to hit them in the stomach," in battle they tended to aim too high. Moreover, the thick heavy smoke from the gunpowder of that day usually reduced visibility in an engagement to zero. One authority on logistics asserted that the average Civil War soldier expended 900 pounds of lead and 240 pounds of powder in taking out one of the enemy.[56]

No weapon in that war was more awesome in appearance or more disliked by the men than the bayonet. It was a triangular-type blade, eighteen inches long, with deep grooves to permit easy drainage of blood. Most soldiers acquired an instantaneous revulsion at the thought of ramming that instrument into an enemy. A Connecticut regiment never forgot the nausea that swept through its ranks when, in an early engagement, General Emory Upton pointed to attacking Confederates and shouted: "If they come there, catch them on your bayonets and pitch them over your heads!"[57]

Bayonets in the Civil War were used almost exclusively as candlestick holders and as spits on which to cook rations. A postwar medical report revealed that only four-tenths of one percent of all battle wounds treated on the Union side were attributable to bayonets and sabers. Nevertheless, bayonet-drill was a regular routine in camps of instruction. Some of them apparently were wondrous to behold. A New Hampshire soldier watched his regiment go through the various steps and lunges. To him the men looked "like a line of beings made up about equally of the frog, the sand-hill crane, the sentinel crab, and the grasshopper; all of them rapidly jumping, thrusting, swinging, striking, jerking every which way, and all gone stark mad."[58] Severe cuts, and an occasional fatality, sometimes marked these exercises.

Guard duty was a necessary facet of camp life. Early in the war inexperienced sentries were armed only with fence-posts; and if a recruit seeking a good time ran past the guard station, the sentry could only give chase and hope to catch the culprit.[59]

Later, to the green soldier armed with a weapon he tended to regard as more his master than vice versa, walking a beat in the lonely darkness of night could be harrowing. A company of the 4th Georgia arrived at Norfolk, Virginia, and was assigned guard duty its first night. Private Louis Merz later wrote of the task: "Jasper got mighty scared. [He] had in one hand his revolver in the other his musket. The boys teased him right much. He is the only scared man we got."[60]

False alarms were understandably frequent. On the first night the 13th Massachusetts was encamped in the field, the "long roll" beat and the entire regiment massed for battle. "When it was discovered . . . that all this excitement was caused by a pig who strolled into camp and was mistaken by the officer of the guard for the rebel army, many of us were imbued with a courage we hardly felt before."[61]

On more than one occasion, night guards sounded the alarm and roused the entire camp because of claps of thunder or drunken soldiers firing their weapons. A Mississippi recruit confided in his diary: "Came very near shooting a loose horse while on guard to-night because he would not halt & give the countersign." Sentinels were often victimized by other soldiers who had wandered out of camp and who learned to return through the picket line in a large group. A new and frightened sentry would call out: "Halt! Who goes there?" or "Stop! What's yer name?" The returning men would walk rapidly by the bewildered picket and shout: "Pete," "Jim," "Dick," "Bill," "Tiger," "Reb," "The Devil," "Spoons," "Beans," or any other name that came to mind.[62]

Many sentinels were more apathetic than apprehensive. In some instances they were "so absorbed in their duties as seemingly to have lost the sense both of sight and hearing." General Nathan A. M. Dudley decided to make an example of one such laggard. He ordered the picket to mount the general's horse, ride up the road, turn and gallop back toward the picket post. The man did as ordered. Just as the horse was almost upon the post, Dudley hollered "Halt!" The horse, following his master's command, braked immediately and totally, while the sentinel continued several feet farther in the air. Thereafter, at least one soldier patrolled his beat alertly.[63]

Corporal Peter Welsh of the 28th Massachusetts assured his wife after three months in the field: "i am heartier and stronger then i ever remember to be before i will be quite handy when i get home."[64] In truth, however, the wartime process of making obedient soldiers out of carefree citizens was painful for all concerned, and the adaptation became more difficult as the war continued and intensified.

· 4 ·

The Novelties Wear Off

A new Illinois regiment proudly marched onto a Mississippi paddle-wheeler. The troops were heading south for their first duty in the field. It proved to be a disillusioning trip, wrote one of the recruits. "We was aboard the steamer *Memphis* 8 or 9 days. We was in dirt, lice, shit, grease & hard crackers."[1]

Homesickness, foul weather, filth, lack of privacy, stern discipline, and general discomfort all combined in time to produce negative views of soldier life. Happy enlistees who gaily tramped away to be part of a neat little war full of glory soon found themselves part of an environment none of them had ever imagined. Captain Oliver Wendell Holmes, Jr., surmounted the problem confronting all Civil War soldiers. "I started in this thing a boy," he wrote his mother late in the war. "I'm now a man."[2] Achieving that transition involved enduring a host of hardships.

The first rude awakening was weather and how quickly it caused army life to lose its glamor.

Oppressive heat and stifling humidity prevailed during most of the months in the field. Flies and mosquitoes swarmed at every movement. Army camps acquired an overbearing stench because of the lack of attention given to garbage pits and latrine procedures. The drinking water was usually muddy and warm. A surgeon in the 5th New Hampshire arrived at a Virginia camp in 1862 and recoiled at "the barefooted boys, the sallow men, the threadbare officers and seedy generals, the diarrhea and dysentery, the yellow eyes and malarious faces, the beds upon the bare earth on the mud, mist and the rain."

Such sights, he concluded, totally shattered his "pre-conceived ideas of knight-errantry."[3]

When mud was not reducing a camp to the status of a swamp, dust was stifling. A Connecticut soldier observed in the summer of 1864 that taking a stroll around the regimental area was akin to walking in an ash heap, that within minutes "one's mouth will be so full of dust that you do not want your teeth to touch one another." During one severely dry period, a Federal artillerist swore that whenever a grasshopper jumped up, it raised so much dust as to cause the Confederates to report the Union army on the move.[4]

The second shock to most soldiers came with the marches the units had to make. A Civil War army moved by foot. It often journeyed great distances to maneuver into position. Men were walking more at one time than they had ever done previously. The ordeal quickly lost all vacation-like aspects. A soldier in the 83rd Pennsylvania wrote of his first military hike: "After we had gone three or four miles, the men began to throw off blankets, coats and knapsacks, and towards night the road was strewn with them. I saw men fall down who could not rise without help. The rain soaked everything woolen full of water and made our loads almost mule loads. . . . I never was so tired before." A Massachusetts soldier was even more opinionated by late 1863. "Here we are marching from one end of Virginia to the other, wearing our-selves out and yet nothing seems to be accomplished by it. . . . this everlasting advancing and retreating I am sick of. My God! Hasten the end of this accursed war."[5]

Men usually marched four abreast, sometimes in the road and some-times alongside it. The average speed was about two and a half miles per hour. The manner of march was "route step," which meant "go as you please." However, a Massachusetts soldier pointed out, "the men were generally in step, because it was easier." Wagon trains and artil-lery traveled the same roads as infantry, and their faster pace forced the marching columns repeatedly to take to the ditches. Moreover, as vet-erans rapidly learned, marching outside the road raised less choking dust and thereby reduced "trouble and annoyance."[6]

A typical day's march began somewhat awkwardly, a private in the 19th Massachusetts recalled. "The men threw their muskets over their shoulders like men starting out to hunt, regardless of the manual of arms; others were at the right or left shoulder shift, while occasionally a man would carry his musket with the hammer resting on the shoul-der. Another who had been slow at preparing came stumbling along, trying to fasten his roundabout with his musket under his arm and the barrel punching his file leader in the back. So the day's work began."[7]

Being at the head of the column was very much preferred. Front-liners got skirmish and picket-duty first and thus could get a night of uninterrupted sleep. Men in the van also used the road when it was in its best shape. In addition, being the first elements to halt, they got the jump on foraging and gathering firewood for the bivouac. Troops at the end of the line fared miserably. For one thing, as the 22nd Massachusetts once discovered, they had to eat the dust of the whole procession. "The perspiration flowed in streams," the regimental historian wrote, "the dust almost suffocated, and soon . . . one could hardly distinguish an object a dozen yards away. Fine and penetrating, the dust sifted into the eyes, nose and mouth, and soon changed the appearance of the marching column. The expressions of the countenances were certainly very ludicrous and one could scarcely refrain from laughing as the dust-and-sweat-streaked face of some individual would look up with rueful glance, with such a pleading, beseeching expression, seemingly asking for sympathies which under the circumstances could not be given, so nearly alike was the condition of all."[8]

When there was no dust, there was mud. "We took one step forward and two backward," Private Bissell of Connecticut wrote of one struggling march. A member of the 10th Illinois wrote of a similar trek: "At times it seemed almost as if pandemonium had let loose. Everybody and everything seemed to be out of sorts. The horses and mules were mad, and some of them balky, the drivers were mad, and the soldiers were not in the best of humor . . . I mean by this that bad words were issued."[9]

For at least nine months of the year, heat was another impediment.

Massachusetts soldier Ernest Waitt captured the misery of marching under the summer's fireball: "The sun was now well up and the air intensely hot, causing the perspiration to run out and, running down the face, drip from the nose and chin. The salty liquid got into the eyes, causing them to burn and smart and it ran down from under the cap, through the dust and down the sides of the face which was soon covered with muddy streaks, the result of repeated wipings upon the sleeves of the blouse."[10]

Scarcity of water characterized most marches. After one all-day tramp, a New England soldier confessed: "I never was so thirsty in my life and I hope I never shall be again." Soldiers learned to grab a handful of water from any nearby pond they passed on a march. "How many wiggletails and tadpoles I have drunk will never be known," wrote a Confederate. Gullies where rainwater had collected became veritable oases. When a soldier took a drink from one, a member of the 5th New Jersey swore, "the sand could be felt and almost heard as it rattled down your throat."[11]

Troops marched accordion-style all day as terrain changed elevations or wagons broke down in the road. "We plodded along at various rates of speed," an artilleryman noted, "now a walk, now a trot, then a halt, then a slow, hardly perceptible movement, then a rapid motion, as if we were struck with compunction for having tarried at all, and felt bound to make amends." If the march was strenuous, and a mounted officer was setting the pace in front, shouts would soon arise from the ranks: "Halt! Give us a rest!" or "Give the horse a rest, never mind the men!"[12] The column would wind through woods, across fields, and up and down hills; soon there was the inevitable dribbling to the rear as ne'er-do-wells, skulkers, and men genuinely ill began to drop back. By the time the rear elements finally reached camp, the men in the front lines were already cooking rations or had fallen asleep.

Night marches were especially fatiguing, a New York soldier emphasized. The most difficult part "is usually the frequent halts. The column often goes by jerks, making sometimes only a few yards at a time, halting from five minutes to an hour, and then moving a few yards further to halt in the same manner. This tries the patience more than anything else. The poor men sit down or lay down by the road, and just as they are wandering off into dreams, their ears are rudely stunned by the gruff 'Forward!' and up they scramble, half asleep and half awake." An Arkansas officer noted: "I have seen numbers of men go to sleep marching along the Roads at night and stager off just like a Drunk man."[13]

If the troops were marching through a battle zone, or were on an especially severe jaunt, another negative element appeared. The 129th Illinois' Laforest Dunham wrote home in March 1864: "Let people talk about thare balm of a thousand flower, but we can beat that heare, we have the balm of a thousand mules. The roads ar strewd with dead mules. It beats any thing I ever hurd tell of."[14]

Any long trek sorely taxed the physical condition of most soldiers. Ill-fitting shoes triggered widespread lameness. The feet of a New Jersey sergeant became swollen, blistered, and infected during the several marches attendant to the Fredericksburg campaign. Every time the regiment halted and the sergeant removed his shoes, he found blood and pus acting as glue between sock and skin. When the march resumed, fresh scabs "cut into the raw flesh like a knife."

Justus Silliman of the 17th Connecticut likewise developed foot blisters. On the second day's hike, he stated, "my gait was somewhat like that of a lame duck, but I waddled along at first as fast as the remainder of our crew, but towards noon I brought up the rear." One of the classic quotations by a Civil War soldier was the Rhode Island private who unthinkingly wrote his wife after a painful march: "I'm all right except [for] the doggorned blisters on my feet, and I hope these few lines will find you enjoying the same blessings."[15]

Corporal Cort of the 92nd Illinois observed after one gruelling advance: "Some of the largest and stoutest men were the first to give out while the small ones stuck to it but I find that it is not the phisical strength but the determination that carrys one through a long march." Ted Barclay of the 4th Virginia said the same thing but in a lighter vein. "Well, here I am at the old camp near Winchester, broken down, halt, lame, blind, crippled, and whatever else you can think of—but I am still kicking."[16]

The fortitude these citizen-soldiers displayed was extraordinary on a regular basis. In January 1863, a Texas officer wrote proudly of his troops: "It appears almost incredible that men could exhibit such reckless indifference, such strength of will and determination . . . The war, however, developed and decided some strange theories as to the amount of physical powers which the human frame contained—powers of enduring fatigue, hunger, thirst, heat and cold—which would scarcely have been believed before, if asserted."[17]

Two or three times a day, Johnny Rebs and Billy Yanks confronted food supplies. What they had to eat prompted the loudest and most widespread complaints by Civil War soldiers. Army rations of that day offered little sustenance, for what the troops received was poor in quality and monotonous; and so often it was in small quantities. Richmond artillerist George Eggleston offered one explanation for scanty issues. "Red tape was supreme, and no sword was permitted to cut it. From the beginning to the end of the war the commissariat was just sufficiently well managed to keep the troops in a state of semi-starvation. On one occasion the company of artillery to which I was attached lived for thirteen days, *in winter quarters*, on a daily dole of half a pound of corn meal per man, while food in abundance was stored within five miles of its camp." Such "was the omnipotence of routine." D. P. Chamberlain of the 9th Tennessee Cavalry stated more succinctly:

"Sometimes we had a good meal, but generally we . . . had to buckle up our belts to find whether we possessed stomachs."[18]

The thinking on both sides during he war was that if the government supplied the basic foodstuffs to the men in large enough proportions, the troops would make out satisfactorily. Such thinking worked out fairly well during long encampments, when rations were regular and unencumbered by government bureaucracy. Yet when the armies were on the move, or in battle, food was both scarce and of suspect quality. As an Indiana soldier wrote after the Seven Days' campaign: "Rotten meat, mouldy bread & parched beans for coffee are common occurrences now."[19]

Rations issued to the soldier by commissary departments ranged from mediocre to downright awful. Considering the combination of irregular and unbalanced diet, the ignorance of cooking methods, and a preference of the men for frying everything in a sea of grease, one might wonder how the troops kept their health. The answer, of course, is that many of them did not. That is why rations were the worst problem in keeping an army fully supplied. One Union surgeon reported that he was having difficulty saving men from "death from the frying pan." A member of the 1st North Carolina concluded a description of skimpy rations by stating to his father: "A soldier's life is calculated to ruin a young man for business afterwards."[20]

Preparation of meals went through a trial-and-error period at war's outset. A Pennsylvanian noted that "the company-cook system introduced was found to be a total failure, principally because of the selection for the trying position of the most uncouth and disqualified men in the companies. As a result of dissatisfaction, company cooks were discontinued, and each mess of three or four comrades accepted the raw rations distributed to the companies and did their own cooking in messes."[21] Different tastes, among other factors, eventually led most soldiers to prepare their meals individually. This required no great talent; the average soldier did little more than fry a slab of bacon or salt pork, and boil coffee to accompany the hard bread which completed the normal meal.

"Coffee was the main stay," a private in the 10th Massachusetts stated. "Without it was misery indeed." This "subtle poison," a Maine soldier added, was "considered as indispensable to him as the air he breathes." Army officials worked hard to insure that if only one commodity of nourishment was issued, it would be coffee. Union surgeon A. C. Swartwelder provided a long discourse on army coffee.

The bean "is furnished to the soldier in the crude state—that is, just from the sack. The first thing, therefore, he has to do is to 'toast' it." Such was done in a camp kettle for 10–15 minutes or longer. The result was often that "instead of 'toasted' coffee, the soldier had charcoal." To reduce the beans to powder, men used rifle butts and flat boulders, or else left it in the kettle and tamped it down with a bayonet or other instrument. "More properly it should be called cracked coffee. If there were such a thing, I would call it black hominy." The surgeon concluded: "I am thoroughly convinced that a pint of good coffee is a better beverage for the soldier than all the rye, bourbon, brandy . . . or any alcoholic nostrum that ever flowed from a worm. . . . It has no equal as a preparation for a hard day's march, nor any rival as a restorative after one."[22]

Give soldiers five minutes' idle time and most of them would start boiling water for coffee. "Coffee and sugar we kept in a bag mixed together," Alfred Bellard of the 5th New Jersey wrote, "and when we wanted a cup of coffee we put two tablespoons full of the mixture in a pint cup of water and placing the cup on two sticks with some hot coals beneath it let it boil." A normal day's coffee ration was sufficient to make three to four pints.[23]

Confederates rarely had coffee in adequate quantities. The blockade of Southern ports cut off much of this luxury and forced soldiers (as well as civilians) to resort to substitutes brewed from peanuts, potatoes, peas, corn, and rye.

The meat rations of the Civil War literally defy belief. Meat was always in short supply—and that may have been good fortune. Beef rations were distributed either fresh or pickled. When chewable, the fresh meat was sometimes eaten raw because it tasted just as good that way as cooked. William Lincoln of the 34th Massachusetts recalled an occasion when beeves were driven into camp, slaughtered, and the meat distributed immediately to hungry soldiers. The ration, he wrote, was "eaten, in many cases, raw and quivering." A North Carolina Confederate stated: "I learned to eat fat bacon raw, and to like it. The beef roasted on sticks and the hard and dry army crackers which I generally used for bread were so delicious to my taste after the fierce appetite gained by hard marching that I never enjoyed eating so much." Yet this rapid consumption of raw meat had its dangers. Private Bellard noted after one issue of meat: "Every man who had eaton any of the stuf was laid up, and what with the heaving up and the back door trot, we had a sorry time of it."[24]

A soldier from Woburn, Massachusetts, unknowingly gave one reason for such illnesses. "As to the meat, I have seen as good meat as ever was in Woburn fly blown in twenty minutes after it was killed before it was cut up to be delivered out. We do not pay any more attention to that than if it was the wind blowing. We scrape them off and lay the meat in the sun which stops the flies work."[25]

One Virginia company serving under "Stonewall" Jackson raised such protests over a meat ration that the general appointed an investigating board. That body declared the beef "worthless, being infested with maggots and fit only to be burned." William Stephens of the 46th Alabama informed his wife in February 1863 that his meat ration was "the Porest Beaf you ever saw men eat and nearlest the Porest you ever saw Walk you would not beleave me if I worst to tel you how pore tha are." The following winter, while the Army of Tennessee was in winter camp at Dalton, Georgia, a soldier in the 4th Louisiana judged the issues of meat "worse than any we had had yet. It was thrown down in the butcher pen and was covered with mud and dung and a decent dog would have turned up his nose at it, but a hungry man will eat almost anything."[26]

Pickled beef was usually so foul-smelling as to stunt the appetite. If properly preserved, it was too salty to eat. If not properly preserved, it was too tainted to swallow. "The boys call it salt horse," the 13th New Hampshire's Millett Thompson declared, "because they say that iron horse shoes and mule shoes have been found in the barrels, with the meat, but never an ox shoe." A New Jersey private swore that "the maggots had to be scraped off before it was put into the pot . . . The salt junk as we called our pork was sometimes alive with worms . . . "[27]

Much of the "old bull" issued to the troops, another soldier commented, "was musty and rancid . . . and much more was flabby, stringy, 'sow-belly.' " On the outside it "was black as a shoe; on the inside, often yellow with putrefaction." Rhode Island's William Spicer sought to make light of it all by stating: "We have eaten so much salt pork of late that we are inclined to speak in grunts, prick up our ears, and perform other animal demonstrations."[28]

Cornbread was the staple of every Confederate's diet. The meal was coarse, unsifted, and sometimes of amazing consistency when cooked. Private Ted Barclay of Virginia was astonished at the first bread ration he received. It would "have thrown our black mammies into spasms." It was panfried, "in consistency resembling india rubber. It could be stretched into ropes and pressed into balls. One bite of it would have raised enough nightmares [to cause one] to ride a regiment of horses for a week."[29]

The meal got worse as the war continued, John Casler of the famed Stonewall Brigade remembered. "The corn bread would get so hard and moldy that when we broke it, it looked like it had cobwebs in it." By 1863 the pint of cornmeal issued daily to Confederate soldiers had no appeal. "Nothing more or less than a mixture of corn cobs, husks and saw dust," another Virginian said of it. "This was often every morsel [the men] would have for their rations, and they dared not sift it, for there would not have been enough of pure meal to fill a cup. Full rations consisted of a pound of this acidulated dry bran and a quarter of a pound of fat pork, which served to grease the skillet." In the autumn of 1864, a sergeant in the 9th Kentucky asserted: "The only way we had to cook it was to mix it with a little water & salt & then fry it . . . My share gave me such a pain in my stomach that I could hardly walk."[30]

Known as "slapjacks," these corn cakes were cooked over an open fire. The result was a bread consisting of alternate layers of paste and soot. "It would kill a horse to digest them," a Texan believed.[31]

Confederate soldiers became fond of "cush" or "slosh." It came into being on the premise that cooking much meat together was better than preparing small portions at a time. Chunks of beef or pork donated by several soldiers were fried in grease, with some water added, to form the base of the stew. Cornbread was crumbled and added. The mixture cooked until it reached a desired thickness. Cush was not the most digestible of dishes, but it was easy to prepare and hence a favorite on a march.[32]

On the Union side, the bread ration was—in the testimony of Billy Yanks—even worse. The standard bread issued to the Federal armies was hardtack, a cracker three inches square, a half-inch thick, generally so stale as to be well-nigh unbreakable, and, as often as not, densely populated with worms. In November 1861, a Pennsylvanian confided in his diary: "Camp gossip says that the crackers have been in storage since the Mexican War. They are . . . almost as hard as a brick, and undoubtedly would keep for years and be as palatable as they now are."

A Massachusetts soldier agreed on the texture and age of hardtack. "To break it was impossible; water made but very little impression on it. I saw some that had been soaked for twenty-four hours; when scraped with a knife, just a little could be started from the outside. . . .

The boys say that [Admiral] Perry carried it with him to Japan for balls for his cannon; as he had no occasion to use them, they were issued by mistake to the infantry for food." An Illinois private added: "We live on crackers so hard that if we had of loaded our guns with them we could of killed seceshs in a hurry." Writing of tough meat and hard crackers, a New York soldier resumed a letter to his sweetheart with the statement: "Well, I have been to dinner and my teeth have become easier and I will make another trial at writing."[33]

Some men referred to hardtack as "sheet-iron crackers," and one group of artillerists used the crackers as pavingstones in front of their tents. Other soldiers labeled them "teeth-dullers." A Midwesterner proclaimed: "This hard bread is a great institution. You might soak a biscuit in a cup of coffee six weeks, and then you would have to have a good set of teeth to eat it. This kind of bread I suppose was made to keep." The crackers were shipped south in large crates on the sides of which were stamped the letters "B. C.," signifying that the hardtack was consigned to the brigade commissary. Not so, said the troops; the letters referred to the date of their manufacture.[34]

The favorite designation for hardtack was "worm castles." After soaking biscuits in coffee, a New Englander suggested, "lay them on your tin plate, being careful not to shake the worms out; they eat better than they look, and are so much clear gain in the way of fresh meat." Another Billy Yank downplayed the worms by stating of hardtack that "eaten in the dark no one could tell the difference between it and hardtack that was untenanted." John Tallman of the 76th Illinois was philosophical about the matter, but in a belligerent way. "Some say the crackers have magets in them, but I don't look for them. All I have to say is if they get between my teeth they will get hurt."[35]

Soaked in water and then fried in pork grease, hardtack became a dish the men called "skillygalee." If the biscuits could be crushed before soaking, the resultant concoction was "hellfire stew." A soup made of salt pork, hardtack, and whatever else was available bore the general label "lobcourse."[36]

The men in blue were always seeking an alternative to hardtack. Some of them found it on the rare occasions when they obtained corn. A Massachusetts recalled in a letter home: "when the corn was standing in the fields we used to pull the ears and grind them to meal by punching holds in a piece of tin and rubing the ear of corn on the rough side of it thus by a goodeal of labour one could get a good mess of meal and it is quite a treat when one has been a long time on hard bread."[37]

Troops on both sides eagerly accepted the first issuance of flour. As a rule, however, it proved less palatable than the hard crackers. At Murfreesboro, Tennessee, men in the 101st Ohio received flour rations. Lewis Day of that regiment stated: "We knew not what to do with the flour. We poured [it] upon our rubber blankets and then doused it with water until it was wet—if too wet we borrowed and tried to thicken it, or went partnership with some one whose flour was not wet enough. When mixed we tried to bake it. Some wrapped it around ramrods and set it up to roast; some fastened it in a wad at the end of the ramrod and held it over the blazing fire; some rolled it in paper and put it in the hot ashes; some pegged the stuff to trees near the fire and swore at it. . . . We had lots of fun if we did go hungry."[38]

A soldier in the 21st Iowa told of being issued ten days' rations of flour "without a particle of soda, saleratus, or any other rising material." The men nevertheless tried to make bread. "The biscuits have uniformly turned out when warm to be like leather, and when cold, like lead."[39]

Lack of fresh vegetables was the worst deficiency in Civil War rations. Scurvy lurked in every camp. Federal quartermasters tried to remedy the situation by issuing what officially was called "desicated compressed mixed vegetables." The soldiers termed it "desecrated vegetables," "son-of-a-sea-dog," or simply "baled hay." The mixture supposedly contained string beans, turnips, carrots, beets, onions—and, soldiers charged, roots, leaves, vegetable tops and stalks—all compressed into hard, dry cakes. When soaked in water, the cakes expanded to an awesome degree. Charles Davis of the 13th Massachusetts observed that a cooked cake "tastes like herb tea. From the flow of language which followed, we suspected it contained powerful stimulating properties." Sergeant Cyrus Boyd of the 15th Iowa declared in his diary: "I ate a lot of desicated vegetables yesterday and they made me the sickest of my life. I shall never want any more such fodder."[40]

Experiments with other foods were equally disappointing. "We had a few beans that the devil would not eat," a member of the 9th Massachusetts Battery wrote from camp. Robert Moore of the 17th Mississippi related how two of his comrades "thought they would be smart to-day and make a peach pie. They baked the peaches without any water or anything else in them & cooked them only about half. Such a pie no one ever ate." In contrast, soldiers North and South coveted blackberries, not merely because of their tasty quality but also because they were regarded as medicine. A New Englander was certain that "many who were suffering from stomach and bowel affections were greatly helped or entirely cured" by the berries.[41]

Much of the sickness so prevalent in army camps was a direct result of poor army rations. Diarrhea, dysentery, and malnutrition were attributable to the steady diet of fried meat, hard bread, and strong coffee—supplemented on occasion with green peaches and unripe apples. Moreover, a New Jersey soldier admitted, "these mess pans were used to fry our pork in and also as a wash bason. Our soup, coffee and meat were boiled in camp kettles . . . which were also used for boiling our dirty clothes."[42]

That government-issued food was often in short supply heightened the problem still further. "Hunger is one thing that is dreaded more than balls from the enemy guns," stated an Illinois private. Lack of food, a Confederate asserted, was "the one thing that we suffered from most. We were always hungry."[43] Both men were correct.

It seems unbelievable that in a country long praised as "the land of plenty," hunger was prevalent in the armies. Yet countless soldiers wrote of it. "I never knew what it was to be hungry [until] I came into the service," Illinois soldier Charles Cort wrote in 1864. A private in the 36th Virginia once stated dejectedly: "I have had nothing to eat for four days & I don't feel very hungry now but I know damned well I'm starving to death."[44]

Soldiers were known to go to extreme degrees to quell the pangs of hunger. When the Union army was at Chattanooga in 1863, rations were so scarce that guards had to be posted when the livestock were fed to keep soldiers from stealing the forage. A member of the 6th Indiana once described his compatriots as "starved into walking skeletons— pale, thin-faced, sickly looking men, so weak they would stagger as they walked." A couple of the men found some meat skins "hard as raw-hide leather;" yet they washed and eagerly chewed the pieces as if they were "a sweet morsel."[45]

Pennsylvania soldiers once came upon some rations "mouldy and almost rotten from exposure in transit [and] which had been condemned as unsafe for us." The food "was seized by the famishing men and greedily devoured." Sergeant Thomas Ford of the 24th Wisconsin told of hunting desperately around camp for something to eat. He chanced upon an old tin that had earlier been filled with grease and rags for use as a candle. Finding that the can still had "considerable grease in it, mixed with some flies and the old rag wick," Ford stated, "I ate them all and relished them very much of the time." A Virginia soldier once boiled his greasy haversack in an effort to make soup.[46]

In the autumn of 1863, hunger was widespread in the Confederate Army of Tennessee. "When the army was most dissatisfied and unhappy," Private Sam Watkins wrote, "we were ordered into line of battle to be reviewed by Honorable Jefferson Davis. When he passed by us, with his great retinue of staff officers . . . cheers greeted them, with the words, 'Send us something to eat, Massa Jeff! Give us something to eat, Massa Jeff! I'm hungry! I'm hungry!'"

Even the officers suffered. A South Carolinian wrote in 1864 of his "bold and aggressive" appetite. He then confessed: "I devoured the hindquarters of a muskrat with vindictive relish, and looked with longing eyes upon our adjutant general's young pointer."[48]

Three avenues existed for supplementing army rations. One was to have food sent from home, but the long delays and rough handling of food packages rendered the contents all but useless most of the time. One Massachusetts soldier asserted that it was easy to tell when a box of food had finally arrived. Throughout the camp could be heard a series of cries such as "Run to the sutler's, Jim, and get a hammer!" "Oh, use a bayonet!" "Damn the thing! We can get another!"[49]

A second source for food were army sutlers. These civilian vendors appeared in camps from the beginning of the war. Military panels were supposed to regulate their prices but seldom gave them much heed. Largely unsupervised as a result, and with no competition because peddlers were not allowed in camp areas, sutlers jacked their prices upward until they made several hundred percent on each ware. Further, "that throng of vultures" always seemed to "follow in the trail of the paymaster" and hence were present to take soldiers' money as fast as it was distributed.

Condemnation of sutlers was universal. "He would skin a louse for its hide and tallow," an Illinois soldier wrote of one sutler. In the spring of 1863, a member of the 38th North Carolina informed his father that thanks to a sutler, "a common size chicken sold in camp the other day for $6.00. At such outrageous prices, what good does a soldiers wages do him! . . . In the course of 12 months longer, if this unhappy and cruel war should continue, I dont believe the soldiers wages will be sufficient to keep him in chewing tobacco."[50]

To the soldiers, therefore, the sutler became both a natural enemy and a natural prey. "Occasionally," a Massachusetts veteran admitted, "when they were located near the road leading through our camp, and the boys' indignation had been aroused to the proper pitch, the cry 'Rally! Rally!' was raised, and in a moment a perfect cloud of men issuing like magic from the ground, charged in from sides and rear, overturned the cart, took every thing from it, and quickly retiring, in five minutes not a soldier was visible."[51]

Johnny Rebs and Billy Yanks alike eventually learned that the best source for extra food was through a means known euphemistically as "foraging." Translated, it meant stealing from farms in the neighborhood of an army's march or camp. Union soldiers appear to have developed the practice into a fine art. Many declared that it "was their bounden duty to forage upon all inhabitants of the enemy's country." Others made light of confiscation by defining it as a process whereby a soldier "bought chickens, turkeys, porkers and sheep while the owners were absent." Quite often the men would help themselves to a country store or filled barn, then cheerily tell the proprietor: "Charge it to Uncle Sam."[52]

Hungry soldiers could easily rationalize the procurement of fresh food, by whatever means. Henry Schafer of the 103rd Illinois wrote from Mississippi: "Last night was a jolly time in camp with some of the boys as hogs, calves, sugar, honey, mollases &c. came into camp plentifully. The excuse offered as a reason for bringing them into camp was that they would not take the oath."

The same situation existed in the Eastern theater. A Maine soldier once confessed: "Despite most stringent orders against foraging, every morning, the ground between the different encampments of the regiments was covered with sheep skins and feathers from turkeys, geese and hens that had given their lives, during the preceding night, for the relief of the hungry soldiers." John Casler of the 33rd Virginia devised a unique excuse for his foraging: "We would not allow any man's chickens to run out in the road and bite us as we marched along."[53]

By far the worst incidence of foraging occurred on General William T. Sherman's march through Georgia and the Carolinas. Writing shortly after Sherman headed east from Atlanta, Major James Connolly of the 123rd Illinois stated: "Our men are foraging on the country with the greatest liberality. Foraging parties start out in the morning; they go where they please, seize wagons, mules, horses, and harness; make the negroes of the plantation hitch up, load the wagons with sweet potatoes, flour, meal, hogs, sheep, chickens, turkeys, barrels of molasses and in fact everything good to eat, and sometimes considerable that's good to drink. Our men are living well as they could at home and are in excellent health."[54]

Not all soldiers approved of the practice. A member of the 24th New Jersey stated that his conscience bothered him when he saw Union troops in Virginia "robbing the poor families of all the little they possessed." Around the campfire, he added, it was disgusting to hear his comrades tell how "helpless women cried to see their small stock of poultry carried away."[55]

Foraging continued throughout the war, however, and some soldiers became proficient at it. A Georgia soldier parlayed his natural forlorn-look into successful and peaceful foraging. He would knock on a farm door and, when the door opened, ask almost tearfully: "Please, m'am, give me a drink of water. I hain't had a single bite for the last three days, and hain't slept on a bed for a week."[56]

Another of "Stonewall" Jackson's soldiers composed a parody of a well-known passage of Scripture: "Man that is born of a woman, and enlisteth in Jackson's army, is of few days and short rations. He cometh forth at reveille, is present also at retreat, and retireth apparently at taps. When lo! he striketh a bee-line for the nearest hen-roost, from which he taketh sundry chickens, and stealthily returneth to his camp. He then maketh a savory dish, wherewith he feasteth himself and a chosen friend. But the Captain sleepeth, and knoweth not that his men are feasting."[57]

In spite of hunger, indigestion, occasional food poisoning, and regular bouts with diarrhea as a result of tainted food, most soldiers of the 1860s followed the human trait of adapting to that which they could not change. With respect to food, the men tolerated it, swallowed it— and hoped for the best.

The youths and men who rushed to arms at war's outset discovered as the months passed that active campaigning was but a small part of this civil war. Long static intervals followed battles and were devoted to recuperation, reorganization, and waiting to see what next the opposing side would do. As year's end approached and the weather grew colder, soldiers generally became "muddy, wet, ugly, sour, and insubordinate." A youngster in the 1st Michigan Engineers wrote one late autumn: "The boys will hudel round the cooks fire after the roll call in the morning like a lot of half grown chickens under an old hen."[58]

Orders finally would come down the line for the army to go into winter quarters. The men responded with speed and zest because frigid temperatures were usually at hand by the time the commanding generals suspended army movements until springtime. Axes at once became the most sought-after weapons; and so armed, men fanned out in every direction and felled trees for logs until the land for miles around the campsite stood naked in the winter sunlight. When trees were in abundance, troops constructed log cabins reminiscent of frontier life. Tents with dirt walls, as well as materials confiscated from buildings in the neighborhood, also came into use.

Those troops without any shelter material were left to fend for themselves. During the frigid winter of 1862–1863, Louisianians unable to procure tents dug furrows and, like animals, burrowed below ground while using blankets and anything else available to cover the holes. These Confederates labeled their area "Camp Hole in the Ground."[59]

Winter camp for an army quickly assumed the appearance of a rustic city. The huts were arranged in orderly fashion along company and regimental streets. Open fields were maintained for drill and parade. Private homes nearby served—voluntarily or otherwise where the owners were concerned—as quarters for ranking officers.

The log huts that became soldiers' homes through the winter followed a general pattern. As a rule, four men worked together to erect the shelter. Using bayonets for picks and tin plates for shovels, they first would dig out the flooring into a rectangular area about twelve feet long, six feet wide, and at least a foot deep. Pine or hardwood logs would then be arranged horizontally to a height of four feet, with mud and wood chips used to chink the cracks. Boards or thatch comprised the roofs, depending upon availability of materials.

If lumber was not plentiful, soldiers took their half-shelter tents (each half being four by six feet), buttoned them together, and secured them over a ridgepole and down to the top of the log sidings. Some men claimed they made their tents warmer by sprinkling them with water at sundown. The water froze, with the ice "windproofing" the shelter through the night.

To complete the hut, soldiers built a chimney of short logs split in half and covered well inside with mud. Barrels obtained from the commissary were placed at the top of the chimney to enhance the fireplace's draw. There was always danger of the barrels catching fire from sparks shooting up the chimney. Conversely, it was difficult during the rainy periods to make fires out of wet wood; and when one succeeded, the smoke settled in the cabin so thickly that visibility was reduced to near zero. Over the door, customarily located on the leeward side to minimize drafts, was hung "an old blanket or other cloth that we could beg, borrow or steal."[60]

Furnishings inside the cabins varied with the needs, artistry, and materials at hand of the occupants. At the far end from the door were double bunks extending the length of the wall. These beds were made of boards and logs, with barrel staves or thin poles stretching across the bed as springs. Mattresses were of pine needles, straw, or leaves. On the cold nights a few men donned all the clothing they had—including overcoat—before going to bed. The veterans insisted, however, that it was warmer to undress, then pile everything on top as covering.

To impede the intrusion of mud, the men would spread straw, leaves, and planks on the floor. Pine slabs, boxes, or upended logs served as stools. In the absence of such items, the lower bunks served as seats. (However, most soldiers sought to avoid that practice because visitors who were infested with fleas or lice might leave "calling cards" on the beds.) Rough wood or shipping crates became crude tables. Bayonets driven into the ground served as candlestick holders. When candles were unavailable, troops made "slush lamps" by filling containers with grease and placing a rag in one corner as a wick.[61]

For a finishing touch, imaginative soldiers bestowed names on their homes. Members of a Louisiana battery used wooden signs to christen two of their huts "Sans Souci" and "Buzzard's Roost." Other favorite nicknames were "Swine Hotel," "Yahoos," "Rest for the Pilgrims," "Hole in the Wall," "Pot-pourri," "Uncle Tom's Cabin," "Devil's Inn," "The House That Jack Built," and "We're Out." While camp streets initially bore such titles as "Lincoln Avenue" and "Lee Boulevard," they soon became "Mud Lane" and "Starvation Alley." A quagmire near a chaplain's tent was promptly dubbed "Holy Park."[62]

Naturally, the men took pride in their residential creations. A member of the 7th Indiana wrote lightheartedly that "instead of appearing like a camp of rusty soldiers," the scores of winter huts resembled "a city of magnificent splendor." New Yorker Robert Tilney commented: "The coziness of the loghouse after dark, with its blazing and cheerful fire, compensated in a measure for the toils of the day." Resinor Etter of the 16th Tennessee was likewise pleased with his log cabin. "every thig is complet every thing looks nice Our bed is composed of some chestnut lathing . . . covered with sage grass We have got a big fire took our seat befour it and feel with great obligation to our Heavenly father for giving us the comfortable dwelling that I now sit in."[63] Yet in reality the encampment and the log and canvas shelters were potential sickness traps.

Weather played havoc with the winter encampments. Of one unattractive site, a Massachusetts soldier sneered: "In our childhood we were taught that 'God is everywhere,' but after seeing this place, we concluded that there were exceptions to this statement." The historian of the 22nd Massachusetts recalled a winter near Fredericksburg, Virginia: "This plain became a wallow-hole; the clay surface freezing at night and thawing by day, trampled by thousands of men, made a vast sea of mud. . . . It had to be scraped and washed off to prevent our tents from becoming hog pens."

A Virginia soldier wrote—with some imagination—of his first winter home: "Manassas and its vicinity is literally a lake of mud. Wherever you go the ground is so soft that you have to hold your breath to keep from sinking. Men and horses are often completely buried in driving over the roads, and you see their heads protruding above the mire, they pulling and laboring to extricate themselves, and finally you would be perplexed whether to laugh or sympathize."[64]

Few men laughed. A Minnesota private recalled one evening in which rain poured and the water "persisted in running under our beds all night. . . . Our blankets, tents and overcoats were saturated with mud and water which made our loads exceedingly heavy. I estimated mine as follows, wool blanket twenty-five hundred pounds. Overcoat one ton, shelter tents fifteen hundred pounds. other traps a trifle." A Connecticut private described his winter misery more succinctly: "the snot runs and I am shivering like a dog you know what over a briar."[65]

Certainly by the time of the first winter encampment, uniforms were a far cry from their original pristine appearance. Duties in the field, in all kinds of weather and without anything akin to a full change of clothing, reduced most soldiers North and South to some stages of raggedness. In late summer 1862, a Billy Yank complained: "Our uniforms at this time would have disgraced a beggar. Our pants had worn away so much that they hardly reached the knee, and the bottoms were in tatters. Our overcoats were not much better being burnt here and there in the skirts, by laying too near the fire. The whole uniform being pretty well stained up with mud and ashes. The shirt that I had on had seen active service for some 3 or 4 weeks and needed washing."

A year later, a private in the 57th North Carolina informed his brother that he had "onely one shirt & one pair of draws & when I wash them I hafta put on my coat." The major of the 123rd Illinois confessed to his wife: "If you could see me in my rags and dirt as I am now, you would laugh first and then cry . . . " A South Carolina veteran gave his wife a report on the state of his trousers. "They will soon be gone forever, but I am perfectly satisfied that they will go in peace, for there is no doubt of their hol(e)iness . . . if you were to see me in [them] you might mistake me for a zebra, leopard, or something else equally outrageous." Tennessee's James Anthony declared: "Our uniforms were uniform in one respect only. We were uniformly ragged! We had rags of all sizes . . . Rags of all colors textures and makes; Rags of bright colors and gloomy ones."[66]

In lieu of shoes in 1864, soldiers in one Union regiment were given rawhide strips to bind around their feet. A Bay State volunteer, after seeing his "squares of green hide," exclaimed that they "put one in mind of the foot of an elephant. The boys called these moccasins 'thanks-of-Congress-shoes.' " A Texas soldier who also had to endure rawhide strips for shoes claimed that his feet "looked as big as two 20-pound canvas hams." To anyone who asked about his foot coverings, the Texas replied that he "had a slight attack of gout, caused by rich food and riotous living."[67]

That the men could make fun of themselves, in the face of such adversity, remains one of the most sterling qualities of Civil War soldiers. The ability to accept what they could not change was one of their most notable characteristics. When Sherman's army pulled to a halt at Goldsboro, North Carolina, after a two-month ordeal of marching and fighting, a Wisconsin corporal made a self-evaluation of his condition. "Arrived in camp out of rations & out of clothing. The soles of my shoes were gone . . . Had no socks, only one shirt which Had not been washed in 5 weeks . . . Trousers were all in rags . . . coat was the same . . . But Thank God I was far ahead of the general run in my general appearance."[68]

One irregular event—even in the most squalid of camps—would send spirits momentarily upward. An Illinois soldier described it in a September 1862 letter: "About 12 o'clock of Thursday the camp was set afire with the announcement that the paymaster had come . . . a thousand pairs of eyes anxiously watched the road for the approach of the man who carried the panacea for all ills." A compatriot from Massachusetts was even more emphatic: "A paymaster's arrival will produce more joy in camp than is said to have been produced in heaven over the one sinner that repenth."[69]

Another soldier likened pay-time to Christmas. Men quickly gathered to collect accumulated wages. Each company, with the men in alphabetical order, marched to the paymaster's table. "Some men stepped forward with countenance wreathed in smiles," a Rhode Islander noticed. Others bore "solemn visage and an air of 'I wish there was more of it.' "[70] Individuals watched the bills counted out, then collected their little bundle and walked away with varying degrees of uncertainty over what to do with their newly acquired treasure.

In comparison to modern-day standards, Civil War troops were grossly underpaid. A private in the 10th Illinois once looked at the meager two months' pay he had received and snorted: "I trust our children's children will never have it in their hearts to say of us, we were governed entirely by mercenary motives."[71] Privates on both sides at first received $11 monthly. In 1864, the stipend for Union soldiers increased to $16 per month and that of Confederates to $18 monthly. Yet with inflation running out of control in the beleaguered South, the additional stipend for Johnny Rebs was meaningless. For example, a pair of shoes bought inside the Confederacy in 1864 cost $125—the equivalent of seven months' pay for a private!

Nevertheless, a Maine soldier spoke for men on both sides when he observed: "It is wonderful how having money in the pocket improves the appearance of a soldier. He stands straighter, walks prouder, looks happier, acts more independent and enjoys better health."[72] Equally as bad on both sides, however, was the fact that monthly payments to soldiers were notoriously tardy.

In January 1862, Confederate General John B. Floyd stated of a Virginia regiment: "One half of the fifty-first have never received one dollar since they entered the service [six months earlier]. They are generally poor men entirely without support for their wives and little children, except their wages . . . They have not a single dollar to purchase the least little comfort, even for the sick." A year later, the U.S. government owed troops in the 1st Massachusetts Cavalry more than $200,000 in back pay; and many of the troopers, having not been paid in nine months, were receiving frantic appeals from families back home.[73]

Although the North had a system whereby a portion of a soldier's pay could be automatically sent home, the South failed to adopt such a relief measure. The repercussions from this were suffering at home and desertions from the army. Adding to the incidence of desertion was the fact that a soldier in the 1860s had little opportunity for a short vacation from army duties. Both sides opposed granting leaves of absence during the months of campaigning. At other times, furloughs were exceptions rather than the rule. In the case of Billy Yanks, they generally were too far from home—and transportational facilities were too limited and slow—for a leave of two or three weeks to be feasible. The Confederacy was too hard-pressed for manpower to permit any widespread granting of furloughs. This prohibition led the ever caustic General D. Harvey Hill to speculate: "If our brave soldiers are not permitted to visit their homes, the next generation in the South will be composed of the descendants of skulkers and cowards."[74]

The unlikelihood of securing a furlough did not prevent hundreds of applications being submitted at appropriate times. In December 1863, a Maine sergeant resolved to use a distinctive approach with his request to go home for Christmas. He justified his petition on the basis of Holy Scripture, specifically Deuteronomy 20:7: "And what man is there, that have betrothed a wife, and hath not taken her? Let him go and return unto his house, lest he die in battle and another man take her." The strategy worked: the sergeant spent Christmas at home.[75]

Confederates and Federals alike, subjected to tribulations for which they had never been prepared, displayed amazing stamina and fortitude. This is not to imply that they were emotionless or void of resentment. A Pennsylvania soldier spoke for thousands when he mused: "If Congressmen at Washington, or the Rebel Congress at Richmond, were required to endure the hardships of a soldier's life during one campaign, the war would then end."[76] Yet it was the soldiers to which the two countries looked for a solution to the war; and it was their devotion and determination that kept the war going.

· 5 ·

Fun, Frolics, and Firewater

The Civil War was barely a year old when Adam S. Rader of the 28th Virginia wrote from camp: "there is some of the most onerest men here that I ever saw and the most swearing and card playing and fitin and drunkenness that I ever saw at any place." Musician Henry E. Schafer of the 103rd Illinois voiced the same feeling more eloquently. "In our camps wickedness prevails to almost unlimited extent. It looks to me as though some men try to see how depraved they can be. Gambling, Card Playing, Profanity, Sabbath Breaking &c are among the many vices practiced by many of the men. . . . It is indeed wonderful what a demoralizing influence the vices of army life have upon the minds of a great many. It sometimes seems to me that the Almighty would never bless the efforts of our army to put down this rebellion while it is so depraved."[1]

Infrequently, soldiers confessed pleasure with the camp environment. The 4th Georgia's Louis Merz, who died at Antietam Creek, wrote in the war's first spring: "I'm just enjoying myself because the days of men are few and I want to be as merry as long as I can, and when we get home again I [will] make it all up."[2] Yet the overwhelming number of those who wrote letters or kept diaries were repelled by camp behavior. "the more wee see the more wee are convinced that this war is the most damnable curse that ever was brung upon the human family," a young recruit stated. Writing of "the vitiating influences of war," an Alabama private told the homefolk: "Few there are who have escaped the contagious effects of being mixed up with the vile and low. The bad are not reformed while the good are made bad." An Iowa sergeant was just as shocked. "I see enough every day to almost make one curse the race to which he belongs."[3]

An Ohioan correctly analyzed the population of an army camp. "Many of the men had not been much from home, and to say that they were homesick is to state the fact very mildly. Others, throwing off the restraints of home, acted more like wild colts than anything else. A very large majority were, however, steady, earnest men, as reliable in camp as out of it." Private Schafer commented that in service "almost every one thinks more about the best way to kill time than anything else."[4] Hence, the homesick, the "wild colts," and the earnest men spent the long inactive months in a multitude of camp activities. Most of them were peaceful in intent; some of them were not.

Letter-writing, discussed in detail in another chapter, occupied many idle hours. So did reading—among those who could read. Printed matter was more in evidence in Northern army camps because reading materials were more available and the literacy rate was much higher. *Harper's Weekly* and *Frank Leslie's Illustrated Newspaper* were by far the most popular pictorial newspapers in the Union ranks, while the *American Review* and *Atlantic* were the more widely read magazines. Confederates enjoyed such serials as the *Southern Illustrated News, Southern Literary Messenger,* and *Field and Fireside. Waverly Magazine* was always in demand for its personal ads placed by young women seeking "a soldier correspondent."

The book in a revered class by itself in any Civil War army was the Bible. Chaplains and colporteurs alike scoured every outlet to keep soldiers supplied with testaments. Yet there were never enough to meet the demand. A few soldiers displayed a fondness for the classics, and they read Shakespeare or works in Latin and Greek. The ones who appreciated good literature, however, were so small in number as to appear out of place. Of the morale-building books that appeared in print during the war, the most memorable was Edward Everett Hale's 1863 story, *The Man without a Country.*

Those reading materials that generally flooded an army were twenty-five-cent thrillers, Beadle's famous "Dime Novels," and picture books offering "spirited and spicy scenes." An Indiana soldier thought such paperbacks, "miserable" and "worthless," but he added that they "were sold by the thousands." While some field missionaries reported disgustingly that "licentious books," and "obcene pictures" were to be found in encampments, more men North and South simply read what was available. A Baptist missionary observed early in the war that "the soldiers here are *starving* for reading matter. They will read anything." Charles Ross of the 11th Vermont gave credence to that statement. He once noted in his diary: "Have been reading all day in a bok I got of the Chaplin. It is a history of Missiens on the Haley island in the north sea."[5]

More than American servicemen of any other age, Civil War troops were singing soldiers. This is not to imply that all of them were accomplished at the art. A soldier stationed in Baton Rouge once commented: "I wish you could hear a greaser of the 1st Texas Cavalry sing. His song is a cross between the bray of a jackass and the note of a turkey buzzard, and far excels either in melody." A Federal officer felt the same way. "The pleasure of music predominated, but it was more noted for diversity of tune and noise in execution than artistic skill."[6]

Next to letter-writing, music was the most popular diversion found in the armies of the 1860s. Men left for war with a song on their lips; they sang while marching or waiting behind earthworks; they hummed melodies on the battlefield and in the guardhouse; music swelled from every nighttime bivouac. Singing was such a natural release of emotion that occasionally men hidden on outpost duty endangered themselves by raising their voices in song. It is hardly surprising, therefore, that no other event in the nation's history produced more enduring melodies than the Civil War. Never since has music been so integral a part of American military affairs.

Brass bands accompanied many units into service at the war's first year, and most of them were a joy to hear. A Midwesterner termed the musicians of the 8th New York "the gayest band I have ever seen. Their music fairly made me take the double shuffle right on the parade ground, before I thought where I was."[7] Often, however, the quality of the musicians was less than commendable. The scarcity of instruments, limited talent among band members, and weariness from campaigning led to inferior renditions on occasion. At the same time, many men possessed of good musical ability preferred instead to shoulder a musket alongside comrades rather than to defend home and country with a cornet.

As a result, an English officer visiting in Texas wrote of hearing one Confederate band "braying discordantly," while another Britisher observed that the performance of most bands was "wretched" and their "dismal noises an intolerable nuisance." Robert Moore of the 17th Mississippi once wrote that his regiment's band "has been practicing for more than a week but are not learning very fast. I think I am getting very tired of hearing the noise they make."[8]

The band of the 6th Wisconsin apparently had a perverse pride. Satisfaction within its ranks existed not because the group was so good but because it was so bad, and the reason for this was because the regimental colonel regularly punished soldiers for misdemeanors by assigning them to the band. The musicians could play only one selection, an obscure tune known as "The Village Quickstep." Their only asset seems to have been the drum major, William Whaley. He became widely esteemed for his high and fancy twirling of the baton. Everything came to a climax one day during a grand review for General George B. McClellan. The band was parading past the general, giving off sounds as if each musician were playing a different tune to a different tempo. McClellan raised his hat in bemused salute. Whaley was so overcome by the gesture that he stumbled and dropped his baton in the mud. The 6th Wisconsin's band faded into history shortly thereafter.[9]

A similar misfortune befell the band of the 19th Virginia. Although it was an accomplished ensemble, its activities were severely curtailed the night the bandmaster got drunk. The leader felt that the regimental commander did not fully appreciate his services. He thereupon staggered to the colonel's tent, pulled aside the flap and, poking his head inside, shouted: "Strange, you are a damned old louse!" The bandmaster awakened the next morning in the guardhouse.[10]

Regimental and brigade bands were nevertheless always welcomed by encamped soldiers in search of any entertainment. Yet for the most part, music in Civil War camps came from individual musicians. Any sizable body of men contained at least one fiddler of ability. Consequently, such foot-stomping tunes as "Arkansas Traveler," "The Goose Hangs High," "Billy in the Low Grounds," "Oh Lord, Gals, One Friday," and "Hell Broke Loose in Georgia" could be heard regularly. Many other soldiers were proficient with the harmonica, Jew's harp, or banjo. These performers would make music at the least invitation, while any two men could and usually did form an impromptu chorus.

Dancing was similarly popular with the generations of that day. In the autumn of 1862, a recruit in the 107th New York wrote his sweetheart: "I hope you will be favored with a few Hops this Winter So as to Keep in practice for I want to have one good old Dance when I get out of this War." Men in camp oftentimes staged company or regimental dances. They especially liked the cotillion and the Virginia reel. A Tar-heel soldier described one of the all-male dances: "A handkerchief, if you had one, or a rag, of which there was no lack, tied around the left arm denoted the lady. We would trip the light fantastic toe on the greensward with as much zest as at home in the dance hall with the girls, but not with the same pleasure, affection and love, defined by one of our boys as 'an inward impressibility and an outward all-over-ishness.' "[11]

Civil War armies were deeply sentimental. This was so in great part because the overriding emotion of Johnny Rebs and Billy Yanks alike was loneliness. On a long march, regiments often broke out in song. The singing would eventually stop. Then, all along the ranks would come the cry: "I want to go home!"[12]

The truly popular songs in camp were not stirring airs that the folks back home (and generations of Americans thereafter) sang inspirationally. Rather, they were melodies with tones of sadness and homesickness. The all-time favorite of Civil War troops was "Home, Sweet Home." Early in December 1862, two mighty armies gathered at Fredericksburg to do battle. Only the Rappahannock River separated the opposing hosts. One evening a Confederate band came to the front and played "Dixie." Immediately, across the way, a Union band responded with "John Brown's Body." The Confederates "retaliated" with "The Bonnie Blue Flag" and received "The Star-Spangled Banner" in return. The music ceased; silence descended over the battle arena. Then a lone Union bugler played the notes of "Home, Sweet Home." A New Hampshire soldier commented: "As the sweet sounds rose and fell on the evening air, . . . all listened intently, and I don't believe there was a dry eye in all those assembled thousands."[13]

Another song popular on both sides was "When This Cruel War is Over." It sold 1,000,000 copies during the war—roughly equivalent to sales of perhaps 10,000,000 copies today. The sentiments of its chorus touched the soul:

Weeping sad and lonely,

Hopes and fears in vain!

Yet praying, when this cruel war is over,

Praying that we meet again.

High also in popularity were "Auld Lang Syne," "Just before the Battle, Mother," "My Old Kentucky Home," "Drink to Me Only with Thine Eyes," "Maryland, My Maryland," "When Johnny Comes

Marching Home Again," and "All Quiet along the Potomac Tonight." Morale in the main Union army dropped so low in the winter of 1862–1863 that orders went forth forbidding Federal bands from playing "Home, Sweet Home" and "Auld Lang Syne."[14]

A particular favorite of Union soldiers was "Tenting Tonight on the Old Camp Ground," composed by a young New England songwriter. Its chorus began:

Many are the hearts that are weary tonight,

Waiting for the war to cease;

Many are the hearts that are looking for the right,

To see the dawn of peace.

Then came the final lines:

Dying tonight; dying tonight,

Dying on the old camp ground.

Interestingly, some Federal soldiers despised "Tenting Tonight." As a New Hampshire soldier explained: "That song is especially dedicated to the brave and stalwart home-stayers: while they do furious battle with the ferocious minnow, the deadly trout, the blood-thirsty angle-worm and the awe-inspiring bull-frog, along the bold and dangerous shores of New England summer mill-ponds and meadow brooks. For real soldiers all the color such songs ever had is just now washed out with an ocean of mud and water."[15]

Each side had its own group of patriotic and happy melodies.

For the embattled South, and despite the fact that the song was written by Northerner Daniel Decatur Emmett for use in minstrel shows, "Dixie" became an unofficial national anthem. "It is marvelous with what wild-fire rapidity this tune of 'Dixie' has spread over the whole South," an Alabama recruit stated in May 1861. "Considered as an intolerable nuisance when first the streets re-echoed it from the repertoire of wandering minstrels, it now bids fair to become the musical symbol of a new nationality, and we shall be fortunate if it does not impose its very name on our country."[16]

"The Bonnie Blue Flag" ran a strong second in Confederate popularity. Western troops were fond of "The Yellow Rose of Texas." To belittle both the Southern diet and the soldiers from one particular state, Confederates teasingly sang:

Just before the battle, the General hears a row.
He says the Yanks are coming, I hear their rifles now.
He turns around in wonder, and what do you think he sees,
The Georgia militia, eating goober peas.

Union soldiers' letters and diaries make it clear that "John Brown's Body" (which gained stanzas on a seemingly monthly basis as the war progressed) was a beloved marching song.[17] In November 1861, Julia Ward Howe wrote new lyrics so as to give the majestic melody more dignity and power. Soldiers were slow in accepting the new words, but the resultant "Battle Hymn of the Republic" is the war's greatest musical legacy.

"The Girl I Left Behind Me" enjoyed constant popularity among Federal soldiers. Other favorites were "Yankee Doodle Dandy," "Tramp, Tramp, Tramp," and, for those with a good voice range, "The Star-Spangled Banner." High also on the list of patriotic songs was "The Battle Cry of Freedom." On May 6, 1864, a Union brigade struggled to reform its lines after taking a fearsome beating in the Virginia Wilderness. As survivors caught their breath amid an air of deepening gloom, one began singing:

Yes, we'll rally round the flag, boys, we'll rally once again,
Shouting the battle cry of freedom!

Soon scores of comrades were singing lustily:

The Union forever, Hurrah! boys, Hurrah!
Down with the traitor, up with the star!
While we rally 'round the flag, boys, rally once again,
Shouting the battle cry of freedom![18]

One new and unforgettable bugle call emerged from the Civil War. Federal General Daniel Butterfield enjoyed music. Shortly after the war commenced, he invented a bugle call for assembling his troops. The following spring, while campaigning on the Virginia peninsula, Butterfield summoned his bugler and whistled for him a little tune he had been muddling over of late. The general and the musician played with the tune, changed a little here and there, and then the bugler wrote the music on the back of an envelope. Thereafter, Butterfield directed, the tune was to signal lights-out at day's end, for he thought its melody denoted tired men settling down for sleep.

The bugler played the new song. Other buglers throughout the Union army picked up the tune. In time, it went west with troops. It soon became regulation. It has remained so since, for "Taps" does indeed signify the weary settling down to peaceful rest.[19]

A number of regiments gave their attention and love to mascots. "Old Abe," the bald eagle of the 8th Wisconsin, was the most famous of all. The 10th Maine had a dog, "Major," who "behaved well under fire, barking fiercely, and keeping up a steady growl from the time it went in [to battle] till we came out." The 104th Pennsylvania adopted a Newfoundland dog, a cat, and a tamed raccoon. Few of these animals survived the battles of which their regiment were a part.[20]

Physical activities were much in evidence at every encampment. Boxing, broad jumping, wrestling, footracing, hurdling, wheelbarrow racing, and occasional free-for-all scuffles were all popular pastimes. Of competitive sports, none was more visible in warm months than baseball. It was new and easy to play. High scores were the general rule; for even though the ball was soft, the base runner had to be hit by a thrown or batted ball before he was out. In one game between teams from the 13th Massachusetts and 104th New York, the Bay Staters won by a 66–20 score.

Another summertime diversion was animal chasing. A rabbit scurrying through a camp would create a riot of excitement. Any small mammal attracted attention. On November 4, 1861, Private Moore of the 17th Mississippi recorded in his diary: "This is Sunday in camp & a number of the boys are amusing theselves after squirrels. They have caught 3 or 4. I never heard such a noise in my life. Cpt. Duff was up a tree with a stick after a squirrel."[21]

Any loose animal in camp seemed to produce some degree of pandemonium. James Warnell of the 5th Georgia Cavalry recalled one evening in camp: "between nine & 10 oclock Jake Fasterlings mare broke off the tree to which she was tied and run through the camp racking Deans buggy and running the sentinels off there posts as she came to them and playing hell generaly."[22]

In wintertime, snowball fights became familiar sights. They generally were contests between individuals or small groups, but several "snow wars" of regimental and even brigade proportions took place. Snowball battles, a Virginia private observed, "were sometimes fought with such vigor as to disable the combatants. The result of such a battle was the capture of the defeated party's cooking utensils, and any food that might be contained in them." A particularly severe engagement erupted between the 2nd and 12th New Hampshire. In the action (according to a participant), "tents were wrecked, bones broken, eyes blacked, and teeth knocked out—all in *fun*."[23]

A good fistfight always attracted a large crowd, with betting on the outcome oftentimes spirited. Officers were inclined to ignore minor alterations between men and to let them settle their differences. Authorities usually intervened only if insubordination, striking an officer, or some other military violation was involved. Given such laxity, soldiers of a belligerent bent were quick to throw a punch when provoked.

Less athletically inclined soldiers sometimes concentrated on handiwork. This became a common diversion in hospitals and prisons as well as in camps. The men carved pipes from brierroot. Bones, sea shells, and soft wood were also raw materials for rings and other ornaments. A number of men became quite proficient at the art. An Indiana soldier sent two rings home in the space of a month, with one of the rings having an elaborately etched American eagle on its face.[24]

Checkers and chess were the most popular two-man games. Any large encampment had at least one Masonic lodge. Literary societies and debating clubs originated among the more educated men, with formal discussions ranging far afield in subject matter. A private debate was once held on the question, "Which Has the Most Influence on Man, to-wit Money or Women?" The latter argument was proclaimed the winner. One group in the Richmond Howitzers specialized in reversing the normal patterns of life. Known as the "Independent Battalion of Fusiliers," it met weekly and enjoyed such pursuits as: "In an advance, always [be] in the rear—in a retreat, always in front. Never do anything that you can help. The chief aim of life is to rest."[25]

Theatrical productions were sources of pleasure for large numbers of soldiers. Professional casts made an occasional visit into the field, but camp productions were the usual and more enjoyed of the presentations. The 48th New York and 45th Massachusetts acquired wide reputations for excellent stage plays on the Northern side. A troup from the Washington Artillery of New Orleans staged several productions during long wintry months. Its satires were so popular as to attract overflow audiences that included "some ladies from the adjacent country."[26]

Sometimes the presentations amounted to a community theater. At Plymouth, North Carolina, in 1862, a New York artillery regiment built a theater, the 5th Rhode Island constructed the stage scenery, and the 23rd Massachusetts supplied the cast. The audience consisted of all Union troops in the area. "Imagine Juliet," a Pennsylvanian commented, "with a sun-browned face, fierce mustache, and close-cropped hair, in a blue dress-coat, baggy blue pantaloons, and heavy brogans, wailing out her grief at the death of Romeo! Or Claud Melnotte saying to a fellow dressed in the same fashion, except a pair of cavalry boots in the place of brogans: 'We read no books that are not tales of love; we'll have no friends that are not lovers.' "[27]

"Bombasties Furioso," a farce staged by the Confederate 9th Kentucky, was the hit of the 1862–1863 season in the West. Minstrels and comedy performances were highly coveted, as were burlesques satirizing officers, surgeons, and other figures of authority. A production that poked fun at any aspect of army life was a guaranteed success, regardless of how unpolished it might be.

One of the most prevalent diversions in camp were bull sessions. Topics ranged from politics and the progress of the war to gossip about individual soldiers, reminiscences of childhood, boasts of the beauty of a wife or sweetheart, tales of pleasure from a visit to a "center of sin," and speculations about the future. The men of blue and gray utilized a variety of slang expressions that were a product of the ruralism from which most of the soldiers came. A brave soldier, for example, was "cool as a man hoeing corn" or "so cool water froze in his canteen." The panicky soldier was one who "jumped up and down like a bob-tailed dog in high oats." If only frightened, the man "mumbled like a treed coon." Asking a compatriot to have a drink was an offer to "change his breath." Occasionally, unknown words came forth—such as one soldier admitting: "I was squashmolished;" and another confessing: "I flumixed right in front of him."[28]

Many soldiers, related a private in the 10th Illinois, "would reel off yarns by the yard of their adventures both here and elsewhere, and build air castles, without number, as to what great things they would do when this cruel war was over." Stretching the truth became a source of pride. A Georgia private once noted: "Frank Reed wrote a letter home to Ben Cooper and if Frank cannot beat any man lying then I give it up. He wrote a right smart about me and made it a heap worse then it really is."[29]

Spreading rumors was a natural outgrowth of such conversation. "Every one tries to see what kind of rumor he can start," a member of the 21st Virginia stated, "so when our bodys are still we have our minds puzzled and harrassed by things from the reliable man." It was the same on the Northern side. "In camp," an Iowan stated, " 'Rumor' furnishes the morning and the evening news—some of it well founded, much of it baseless and imaginary."[30]

A Massachusetts soldier summarized the general course of a rumor. "After supper the men gathered around the fires for a smoke and to listen to the gossip of the regiment. It frequently happens that someone will invent a story, requesting the strictest secrecy, in order that it may travel the faster. In the course of twenty-four hours or so it will return, not exactly as it went forth, but so enlarged and exaggerated that you could scarcely recognize the original. Frequent repetition of this amusement very soon created such disbelief in camp stories, that it was difficult to get one well started except by the exercise of considerable ingenuity."[31]

Rumor-spreading in a regiment was therefore a short-lived enterprise. The frequency and unreliability of such reports caused them to lose their effect, and soldiers came to regard "confidential information" as nothing more than "chin music." However, if the rumor was personal, it could provoke anger. Daniel B. Holmes of the 1st Kansas Cavalry wrote home early in the war: "I don't know how the report of my being killed could of started. *I believe that I am alive.*"[32]

Some camp humor in the 1860s might appear adolescent by modern standards, yet in view of the limited recreational outlets for Civil War troops, anything that offered a laugh was eagerly sought. Suddenly, on a dull day, a soldier would loudly mimic a cow, donkey, or chicken—and, like echoes, hundreds of voices all over the camp would respond in similar sounds. These vocal exercises became very popular occurrences at nighttime. After all the men had bedded down and supposedly were reaching for sleep, one man would begin making loud noises. The chain reaction in the dark would then begin. A regiment quickly "represented the entire animal creation," a New Hampshire private wrote, and sometimes for hours "men together howled, crowed, bleated, barked, roared, squealed, yelled, screamed, sung, and laughed to the limit of vocal powers."[33]

Soldiers on both sides were chronic teasers. "The army laughs far more than it weeps," New Englander Millett Thompson asserted. "Camp jokes are common property." Visitors to army camp were popular prey. A civilian wearing one of the stovepipe hats fashionable in that era was likely to be greeted with: "Come down out of that hat and join the soldier-boys, and help whip the Yankees!" Other men would pick up the shout and add another, such as: "Come down! Come down! I know you are up there! I see your legs!" Should a gullible visitor enter camp and innocently ask the location, for example, of Company B, somewhere down the line would come the reply: "Here's Company B!" followed by dozens of the same shout from all over the encampment.³⁴

On rare occasions, the visitor would enjoy the last laugh. Men in the 7th Virginia once saw an elderly minister, long white beard flowing in the wind, riding into their camp. One of the soldiers immediately called out: "Boys, here is Father Abraham!"

"Young men, you are mistaken," the cleric immediately replied. "I am Saul, the son of Kish, searching for his father's asses, and I have found them!"³⁵

Practical jokes on compatriots were as frequent as drill. Hiding a musket, or stripping a man's tent while he was absent, were mild pranks. In wintertime, covering a chimney with boards was a sure bet to send the occupants of the hut choking and cursing into the cold air— and to a chorus of laughs and catcalls. Similarly, some jokesters would take several rounds of ammunition, place them inside a paper bag which, tied to a string, was lowered down the chimney of a log hut. In short time, several explosions would follow, and chaos inside momentarily prevailed.

Sleeping soldiers were easy prey. A common trick was to pour a bucket of water on the man; everyone would then hide or feign sleep while the sputtering, wet, and angry soldier pranced around the area in search of revenge. In warm weather, if molasses or honey was available, pranksters would sneak up on a sleeping comrade and gently pour the sweet liquid into the ragged holes of his uniform. The men would then sit nearby and watch flies, mosquitoes, and the like drive the rudely awakened man to cover.³⁶

One recorded prank almost had fatal consequences. Members of the 103rd Illinois decided to take advantage of Mike Augustine, who thoroughly enjoyed smoking his pipe. They found the pipe half-full of tobacco and promptly laced the tobacco with gunpowder. Augustine returned to his tent and commenced smoking. A messmate told what happened next. "he said it was pleasant to have the privelige of taking a good old smoke. pretty soon it (the powder) ignited and blowed the fire & tobacco up in his face set his hair on fire. he jumped up leaped out of the tent. he flew around . . . I never laughfed so much in my life. the blamed fool thought some buddy had throwed a cartridge from the chimney."[37]

Recruits assigned for the first time to night guard duty often received dire warnings and ominous forebodings about the responsibilities they were assuming. Then older soldiers would hide in the woods and emit loud screams; or a prankster might dress in some outlandish costume, steal to within a few yards of the sentry and, when challenged for identity by the frightened recruit, would moan eerily in the darkness: "The devil!" Of course, such practical jokes were running a deadly risk, for stray cows and pigs, stumps, clothes hanging out to dry, even leaves rustling in the wind, were often shot for failing to identify themselves.

Too often ignored in the literature is the seamier side of camp life. It beclouded every encampment. Peter Wilson of the 14th Iowa stated to his father after two years in service: "There is no mistake but the majority of soldiers are a hard set. It would be hard for you to imagine anything worse than they are. They have every temptation to do wrong and if a man has not firmness enough to keep from the excesses common to soldiers he will soon be as bad as the worst."[38]

The men of blue and gray were, in the main, a robust, plain-speaking and earthy folk. Much of army life in the 1860s aroused displeasure and frustrations. As a result, "profanity of the worst form from morning to night" characterized any gathering of troops. In June, 1862, Mississippi soldier T. J. Koger told his wife: "One of my greatest annoyances is my proximity to one tent of the Co. next [to] me, Co. F, in which are 9 or 10 [of] the most vile, obcene blackguards that could be raked up this side [of] the bad place, outside of a jail or penitentiary. From early morn to dewey eve there is one uninterrupted flow of the dirtiest talk I ever heard in my life. . . . those fellows have 'had no raising.' " A Union recruit confided in his journal: "Around me is the gibber of reckless men & I am compelled to Listen day and night to their profanity, filthy talk and vulgar songs. I have some conception how Lot felt in Sodom when he had to listen to and be cursed by the filthy conversation of the wicked."[39]

Some generals issued orders of admonition against profanity, and Union army regulations expressly forbade it under fine of one dollar per offense. Such directives went against the tide of army behavior and were futile gestures. Only occasionally did a soldier express remorse over his language. When a member of an Ohio company illegally shot a buzzard, the lieutenant in the company called the men together and verbally fired "sulphurous expletives, the use of which is strictly forbidden by the Bible." A short while later, the officer again formed the company and "made a full apology for his lapse from self-control." The men cheered this free confession.[40]

Most of the profanity heard in camp was idle, uninspired, and meant for no offense other than to enliven normal conversation. To some men, cursing became wearisome. "Virginia weather, and mud, is responsible for nine tenths of the profanity in the army," a New Hampshire soldier believed. "One man in the Thirteenth has suddenly given up the use of profane language, declaring that 'no hard words can possibly do the weather and mud here any degree of justice,' and he is tired of trying."[41]

Gambling was almost as common among Johnny Rebs and Billy Yanks as profanity. It certainly was a universal time-killer in every camp. Betting was always in evidence at horse races, cockfights, boxing and wrestling matches, athletic contests, raffles, and any other competition that lent itself to waging money. Dice games were always popular, with "craps" heading the list. Close behind was "sweet-cloth" (or "bird-cage"), in which players bet on the various numbers that might appear when three dice were rolled from a cup. The man who had guessed the correct total beforehand won the pot.

Card games—"throwing the papers," they were sometimes called—were the overwhelmingly prevalent forms of gambling. It would not be too much of an exaggeration to paraphrase a biblical passage and state that "when two or three soldiers were gathered together, there did a deck of cards make its appearance among them and they did proceed to exchange their meager earnings." Virginian Alexander Hunter was convinced that five of every six soldiers played cards, "and some gambled day and night; draw poker of course being the game. When out of money, a man stayed in the game by resorting to the use of 'O. P.'s (order on the paymaster)."[42]

Another Southerner noted: "I have seen men gamble all night, and do a great deal of nodding on duty the next day." Texas soldier Val Giles philosophized: "There is a strange, unaccountable fascination about gambling. I have known men who never threw a card before the war began, or have bet a cent since it closed, to lose the last Confederate dollar they had, betting at a game they really knew nothing about."[43]

A private in the 14th Wisconsin wrote home from near Vicksburg in June 1863: "Since we were paid off a person cannot go five rods in any part of our camp without seeing someone gambling. The day after we were paid there were a good many of the boys to be found who had not a cent left of their two months pay." A Massachusetts artilleryman reported "many ugly fights indulged in, caused by their cheating each other at cards."[44]

So prevalent was gambling by 1864 that the Army of the James was known among Federals as the "Army of the Games." Officers as well as privates could be seen in camp "taking a twist at the tiger." Draw poker was the chief card game, but there were others: twenty-one, faro, euchre, keno, and a contest dubbed "chuck-a-luck." In February 1863, John T. Smith of the 13th Alabama solemnly informed his family: "You ought to hear your pious preacher curse. And you ought to see him bet on chuck-luck and farrer. Poor boy, I fear he is "forever fallen' from his high estate."[45]

Strict rules against gambling existed in the armies, and from time to time authorities sought to control the practice. General James H. Lane warned his North Carolinians that "gambling in this Brigade is prohibited and those caught at it will be severely punished."[46] The usual punishment was extra duty and forfeiture of a month's pay. So rarely was the prohibition enforced, however, that soldiers placed bets on the outcome of the cases involving men who were arraigned. No one seems to have regarded gambling as a serious offense. In February 1864, Federal General John C. Cleveland issued a directive: "Gambling within the limits of this division is prohibited. The attention of brigade and regimental commanders is called to the suppression of this evil."

Massachusetts soldiers read the order and "immediately concluded that the 'old man' had been 'roasted' the night before by some of his brigade and regimental commanders."[47]

The one development that could bring an abrupt halt to gambling was the call to battle. Men would promptly throw away cards, dice, and other gambling instruments so that, if wounded or killed, no "passports to sin" would be found on their persons. Avid gamblers could then be seen intently reading their Bibles as they awaited the command to form ranks.[48] Such repentance was generally short-lived. The more ardent gamblers who survived the battle would rush frantically into woods and fields in search of the discarded items.

A "minor sin" among an ever growing number of Civil War soldiers was the use of tobacco. Sutlers normally had a plentiful supply, both for chewing and for smoking, and it was moderately priced. If a youth had never been addicted to the use of tobacco at home, it required but a short period after enlistment for him to acquire a taste for the weed. Moreover, a Pennsylvania chewer observed, "the appetite always increases with the scarcity."[49]

In December 1862, Lieutenant James P. Douglas of a Texas battery wrote his fiancée: "Sallie, I have not learned to drink and swear like nearly everybody else in the army but have become a constant companion of the pipe, what do you think of that? I have not resorted to this disagreeable practice for the purpose of drowning my sorrows so much as from a love of the weed . . . " The average soldier, wrote a Wisconsin private, "can bear cold, heat, hunger, thirst, forced marches and lost sleep with comparative cheerfulness, but when he is out of tobacco he is as 'cross as a bear.' "[50]

A member of the 5th New York recalled how the men customarily shared the contents of packages from home. Yet "if there were any exception to this generosity, it would be in the case of tobacco; that was jealously guarded. It is said that many a man who was the fortunate recipient of a package or a plug of tobacco would carefully secrete it, and walk half a mile or more to a friendly patch of woods, that he might take a 'chew' unobserved. If known to be the possessor of such a luxury, his stock would be exhausted before he was an hour older."[51]

When tobacco was not available, soldiers resorted to a number of unsatisfactory substitutes. White-oak bark or dried tea leaves came into use regularly. Billy Yanks also learned to smoke coffee. "The fragrance is rather agreeable than otherwise," one man stated. "How the Yankees did enjoy smoking the Rebel tobacco!" Virginia Alexander Hunter exclaimed. "At the North they sold the soldiers a vile compound made of chickory, cabbage and sumac leaves ground together and christened tobacco. It burned the tongue, parched the throat, and almost salivated the consumer."[52]

The craving for tobacco caused some soldiers to go to extraordinary lengths in quest of it. On one occasion, a Confederate regiment was marching past General Lee and his staff. The commander was peering intently through field glasses. A private left the ranks, walked up to the general, saluted obediently, and then inquired if General Lee had an extra chew of tobacco. The amused commander turned to a member of his staff and that man quickly supplied a much-coveted quid.[53]

What triggered genuinely unpredictable behavior in army camps was consumption of alcohol.

Overimbibing in civilian life drove an untold number of men into the armies. Peter Welsh was a case in point. In his first letter to his wife after enlisting in the 28th Massachusetts, Welsh confessed: "you know i never would have left you only i was crazy from that acursed misfortune i fell intoo however, you need not be afraid of my drinking now for there is no licker alowed in the army nor no person is alowed to sell to soldiers and that is much the best."[54]

Welsh either was reassuring his wife with falsehoods, or else he was incredibly ignorant of in-ranks behavior. "Whiskey was the most troublesome enemy the army had to fight" in camp, a Pennsylvania officer asserted. "Through the instrumentality of 'red eye' and 'tribulated tanglefoot,' many a good fellow was brought to grief." No one evil so much obstructed an army "as the degrading vice of drunkenness," General George McClellan stated in 1862. "It is impossible to estimate the benefits that would accrue to the service from . . . total abstinence from intoxicating liquors. It would be worth 50,000 men to the armies of the United States."[55]

Thousands of soldiers had a far different perspective of the influence of whiskey. Removal of home restraints, the desire to be "one of the boys," the rationale that drinking in the army was first excusable and then necessary, loneliness, uncertainty about the future—these were some of the major factors that explain the high incidence of drinking in Civil War armies. "I can't get Liquor of any sort to drink," the 24th Virginia's John H. Morgan told his sister. "If I had some I think it would be an advantage to me sometimes." A member of the 13th Massachusetts was more philosophical. "The life of the common soldier is such an irksome guard that it is not to be wondered that he welcomes anything that will put a polish on the hard surface of his daily duties. There was nothing that so effectually removed the wrinkles from 'grim-visaged war' as a noggin of old rye."[56]

What created a problem, however, was overimbibing. A soldier in the 4th Louisiana wrote of a messmate: "I never knew before that Clarence was so much addicted to drinking. If he had been as fond of his mother's milk, as he is of whiskey, he would have been awful hard to wean." Ira Gillaspie of the 11th Michigan wrote from Kentucky in 1862: "One Tomey Crow was put in the guard house to keep until he gits sober. He is as tite as you pleas. I felt sorey for the oald fellow for shure. His oald wife died back in Mich. and he was acrying."[57]

Excessive drinking occurred more often in the Federal ranks because Billy Yank received periodic rations of whiskey, they were more frequently encamped near large cities, and they had more money with which to purchase beverages. In the early stages of the war, however, liquor was readily available in any locale. A recruit in the 4th South Carolina told how the trip from home to camp inspired much drinking. "It seems that every man in the regiment mistook himself for Commander-in-Chief of the regiment. Whiskey was plentiful and cheap; every man had as much as he wanted, and a great many had a great deal more than they needed."[58]

Special occasions were "good reasons" to have a drink or two. A Maine soldier wrote of July 4, 1861: "The sutler of the 5th New York Militia must have coined money in dealing out liquor to our boys. Almost everyone who ever got drunk felt it to be his duty to do so now, and this, with running guard, made the day attractive." One Rhode Island private always got drunk on payday, his company commander stated, "in order, as he said, that he would see double, and thus in imagination, get double pay."[59]

Adding to the evil was the fact that being intoxicated was not a punishable military offense. However, just as in the case of profanity, any misconduct resulting from liquor could result in a military trial. Captain Joseph Newell of the 10th Massachusetts remembered one comical incident. "General [Don Carlos] Buell, upon riding up, left his horse in charge of a Company A man, while he went inside. The man, thinking the opportunity a good one to secure a hasty drink, jumped upon the horse's back and started for Graves' store, a mile away, the general's staff in hot pursuit. As the general's horse naturally made the best time, the man had secured his drink, and was on his way back, when he was overhauled by the provost guard. . . . For this little freak, the soldier had to perform a week's penance, mounted on the head of a barrel, carrying on his back a knapsack of sand."[60]

Most of the whiskey that made its way into camps was considered "mean" in those days and would be adjudged vile by modern standards. What was inside a bottle varied between raw, rough, and unknown. It contained a taste, and packed a wallop, that few men ever forgot. A soldier in the 14th Indiana analyzed one issue of whiskey as a combination of "bark juice, tar-water, turpentine, brown sugar, lamp-oil, and alcohol." Massachusetts cavalryman Ben Crowninshield recalled that the commissary whiskey "was new and fiery, rough and nasty to take."[61]

Some soldiers, on acquiring a supply of whiskey, would simmer it over a campfire in an effort to reduce the harshness. Others would set it afire in the belief that this would destroy the fusel oil and similarly harmful ingredients it possessed. Charles Davis of the 13th Massachusetts termed a sizable quantity of "apple-jack" he and several friends secured as "a decoction which many of us became acquainted with for the first time, and which discretion suggested ought to be the last."[62]

The potency of the whiskey is evident from some of the nicknames given to it: "Rot Gut," "Old Red Eye," "Spider Juice," "Bust Skull," "Rifle Knock-Knee," "How Come You So," and "Help Me to Sleep, Mother." One fact was irrefutable: the whiskey of the Civil War times produced some startling and unpredictable reactions because, wrote one man, "it takes but little to make me feel funny."[63]

A soldier in the 14th New Hampshire obtained a bottle whose lineage was untraceable. He drank steadily for a few minutes; afterwards, wrote a comrade, he "had a bad case of delirium tremens that night, and saw snakes and devils and howled in terror, until the captain got forty drops of laudunum chasing the liquor down his gullet and he became quiet."[64]

One night Colonel Edward Cross of the 5th New Hampshire personally broke up a drunken party by storming into the tent with a saber in one hand and manacles in the other. Yet when large numbers of troops were imbibing heavily, officers sent to quiet the rowdiness were "received with jeers, groans, hisses, sticks of wood, stones, old shoes." Calling out the guard was only marginally successful.[65]

A principal reason why drunkenness among the troops could not be effectively controlled was the prevalence of the same sin at officer level. "The company is going down the hill," a private in the 2nd Michigan wrote his wife in the war's first winter. "The Capt. is *dead drunk* more than half his time. He doesn't get out of his tent to take command of the company more than two days in the week." Writing of an 1862 skirmish in Kentucky, an Illinois soldier made the simple statement: "Major Mellinger was so drunk that he fell off his horse." On one occasion an intoxicated Union corps commander walked straight into a tree in front of his tent, and then had to be restrained from arresting the officer of the guard on charges of felonious assault.[66]

Men in the 95th Illinois celebrated a Christmas season that had a painful aftermath. Wrote one fortunate survivor: "Col. Tom turned out 15 gall of Rotgut & several of the boys got Happy, and some got pugilistic, and as a consequence some had Eyes Red & some Black and all felt as though they had been poorly staid with at best."[67] In February 1864, the officers of the 126th Ohio had a farewell party for their colonel. A bucket each of egg nog and whiskey were the centers of attention. The result, according to a disgusted bystander, "was a big drunk, and such a weaving, spewing, sick set of men I have not seen for many a day. . . . Col. Harlan was dead drunk. One Capt. who is a Presbyterian elder at home was not much better."[68]

Liquor, a Virginia soldier concluded, "has different effects on different men. It induces a Frenchman to talk, and he shines out, the very embodiment of the graces. A German becomes gloomy and morose; an Englishman grows affectionate; four fingers of stone-fence whiskey will set an Irishman fighting as surely as St. Patrick was a gentleman."[69]

After soldiers had overimbibed sufficiently to dull common sense, fights inevitably followed. In December 1861, several members of the 5th New Jersey rejoined their regiment at a dramatic moment. "By the time we arrived the whiskey had begun to operate and a fight had commenced between two officers who were jealous of each other. Swords were drawn and sheathed again without any whiskey being spilt. This started the ball rolling between two companies and a regular old fashioned free fight was the consequence for about half an hour, during which bloody noses and black eyes were freely given and received."[70]

Fatalities from drunkenness were not uncommon. A member of the 129th Illinois informed the homefolk in November, 1863: "One of the boys in the company died day before yesterday. He got into a row and got stabd so that he died in two days after. He was a tip top solder only he could get on a spree once in a while." Also in the Western theater, Sergeant Boyd of the 15th Iowa once wrote solemnly in his diary: "Col. Dewey of the 23d Iowa is *dead*. Old Whiskey at last laid him *out* as it is laying out many a thousand other men in this Army. It is killing more than the Confederates are killing."[71]

An unusual death from the effects of alcohol occurred in July 1862 at Tybee's Island, Georgia. The 48th New York, commanded by the Reverend James H. Perry, was such a model of good behavior that his regiment had become known as "Perry's Saints." However, while performing coastal duty in Georgia, the unit was beneficiary of a large cargo of beer and wine that washed ashore after a storm. The New Yorkers proceeded to get collectively and wildly drunk. This spree is generally believed to have been a major factor in Colonel Perry collapsing fatally the next day at his desk.[72]

Several regiments organized temperance societies in an effort to abolish the widespread consumption of whiskey. "The cause needs to be agitated in the army," Alburtus Dunham of the 129th Illinois declared, "for there is a great many that never drank a drop at home [who will] return tipplers, if they stay long."[73] Yet temperance movements almost without exception were short-lived undertakings that ended in failure.

Drinking, cursing, gambling, and similar vices were always present in camps North and South. They were escape vehicles from both horror and loneliness. All too quickly, a Billy Yank from Massachusetts explained, soldiering "was no longer an enthusiasm, nor a consciously difficult endurance; it had become ordinary every-day life . . . "[74]

An Illinois officer correctly observed: "There is a warmth of feeling which irresistibly springs up which unites us all as brothers. One common danger and one common impulse brings us very close together in friendship, and truer and more steadfast friends outside of one's own family would indeed be very hard to find." On the other hand, camp life for the majority of the soldiers was a struggle with boredom. "Give me campaigning, where there is something new and exciting all the time," one man wrote in his diary. "Fighting, marching, and building breastworks is preferable to this." Unless some diversion occurred soon, a South Carolina soldier once wrote, "I will turn to a high land terrapin or an oyster." One Billy Yank took a more long-range view of life in the field. "Staying in camp will never bring us home again so the quicker we are on the move again the better."[75]

Most Civil War soldiers who indulged freely in raucous camp activities just as freely relinquished them on returning home at war's end. Every army has its quota of rogues and weaklings, to be sure; but the evidence is overwhelming that the majority of Confederates and Federals were conscientious, devoted men possessed of simple but indelible virtues. They sought to do the best they could in an atmosphere over which they had no control. How well they met hardships and temptations during long months in camp varied with the individual. Nevertheless, an Iowa private spoke for all of them—indeed, for soldiers of all ages—when he declared: "There is one thing certain, the Army will either make a man better or worse morally speaking."[76]

·6·

Heartstrings vs. Playthings

Homesickness broke the moral fiber of countless numbers of Civil War participants. Nostalgia is always the great enemy of soldier morale. Most Johnny Rebs and Billy Yanks were away from home for the first time. Life then was far less encumbered. Therefore, absence from loved ones quickly created a pain that was at first acute and ultimately chronic.

A Texas lieutenant was flagrantly in error when he observed that "the boys don't think a great deal about home as they must stay for the war, hence are much better satisfied when [they] enlisted . . . " Much closer to reality was the statement in August 1862 by a member of Hilliard's Alabama Legion: "I never new what pleasure home afforded to a man before. If it were not for the love of my country and family and the patriotism that bury in my bosom for them I would bee glad to come home and stay there but I no I have as much to fite for as any body else but if I were there I no I could not stay so I have to take it as easy as possible."[1]

Even more akin to the universal feeling was a Pennsylvania soldier's confession to his family: "If I had been suddenly thrown from the comforts of home, and the scenes of prosperity around me into such a place as this I should have thought it horrible, very horrible, but we have become used to it, we are as cheerful and happy as you are; only when we think of home, then oh then how our hearts sicken." Samuel Sawyer of the 32nd North Carolina expressed the same yearning more succinctly: "Mother, I hope to live to See you all face to face and to take you all by the hand once mour before long." An Illinois private displayed more anguish in his feeling. "O would that I was at home. I used to talk about being away from home when I was thare but little did I know what it was till now. . . . I have often drempt that I was at home and how nice it was, but lo and behold when I wake up I am in this blame old tent."[2]

Virginia's Royal Figg borrowed a popular poem to convey his sentiments to the homefolk.

> Oh, there's a power to make each hour
> As sweet as Heaven designed it;
> Nor need we roam to bring it home,
> Though few there be that find it!
> We seek too high for things close by,
> And lose what nature found us;
> For life here has no charm so dear
> As home and friends around us.[3]

The yearning for home became painful for most soldiers. In the closing days of 1861, Lieutenant Warren Magee of the 6th Mississippi confided to his wife: "I had thought I would not write to [you] for afew days as I have just written to you, but some how or other I studdy about Home to day i feel like I must write you afew lines. I have been studdying about you and the children all day. oh how I wish I was at home with you this day. it seems as if there is nothing else in this world would please me better than to be with my family."

Confederate John C. Tillery of Barnard's Battalion wrote in a similar vein to his wife in October 1864: "I got a letter from you last week and am looking for another today. I hope I will get one for it would cure the Bluse if there was good noose in it for if I was where I could not hear from you all it dont seem to me like I could Stand it for you are my dailey Study."[4]

A wife's letter filled with loneliness would accelerate the pangs of emptiness the soldier already felt. Joel Angle of the 36th Virginia had to have been moved when he read these lines from his wife Mary Ann: "I sit and study ten thousand things to make me miserable and unhappy and when I sleep I see you in my sleep sometimes sick and sometimes wounded. Sometimes I see you comeing home and wake myself jumping up to meet you but when I wake you are gone and I lay down to cry myself to sleep again."[5]

The death of a child could be especially traumatic to a soldier far from home. In the autumn of 1862, Alabamian John Cotton received word that an infant daughter had succumbed to measles. Weeks later, Cotton was still benumbed by grief. "I could not help shead tears when I red your letter the other day," he stated to his wife. "you said you got worse about the loss of little cricket. I shall dread to come home for I no I shall miss her so much she will not bee there to fondle on my nees with the rest of the little fellows but I try to study about it as little as possible for I no she is a great deal better off than I am we should not grieve that she is gone to a better world than this and gone where she never can come to us but we can go to her I can't help sheading tears ever time I get to studdying about you all."[6]

Many soldiers, probably in an effort to conceal their own feelings, made light of homesickness to comrades and chided those afflicted by the ailment. Yet, a member of the 4th Texas asserted after the war, "I honestly believe that genuine homesickness killed more soldiers in the army than died from measles." Cyrus Boyd of the 15th Iowa agreed emphatically. "More men die of homesickness than all other diseases," he exclaimed, "and when a man gives up and lies down he is a *goner*. Keep the mind occupied with something new and keep *going all the time* except when asleep."[7]

Such loneliness and longing explain why letter-writing was by far the most popular occupation of Civil War troops, on the march as well as in camp. A New Jersey soldier voiced a common sentiment when he wrote: "You can have no idea what a blessing letters from home are to the men in camp. They make us better men, better soldiers." On the other side, a member of the 10th Virginia gave one reason why letters were so valued. "We lead the *dullest imaginable* life here," he wrote his fiancée. "Shut out from the world, hid away in a pine thicket, we have nothing to think of but the loved ones at home."[8]

Soldiers gravitated naturally from thinking to writing. The volume of soldier mail in the Civil War was literally staggering. A U.S. Christian Commission representative who visited several Federal camps estimated that in some 1,000-man regiments, an average of 600 letters were being mailed daily. Members of an Iowa regiment dispatched 7,136 letters home during one autumn month. At the height of the war, some 45,000 letters passed daily through Washington to the Union armies, while an equal number went the opposite direction. Twice that number reportedly went through Louisville, Kentucky, for the Union forces in the West.[9]

With the struggle of the 1860s being the first time in American history that so large a percentage of the common folk were pulled from home, and with letter-writing the sole contact available with loved ones, men wrote home at any and every opportunity. A member of the 3rd Virginia Cavalry informed his sweetheart in the war's first summer: "Your letters and those of my Mother are the only consolations I have in my solemn hours. Write my dear as often as you can." Letters, an Illinois captain was convinced, "are the only link a soldier has to bind him to civilization." An Indiana corporal added: "Nothing will make the heart of a soldier glader than to receive some little token from home no difference how small."[10]

The majority of soldiers seem genuinely to have enjoyed writing letters. They were seeing new things as well as living an exciting life. They were in a flashing, strange world that they wanted eagerly to share with the folks back home; and despite the fact that military campaigns, lack of writing material, weariness from marches and battles, plus other and similar causes brought a slowdown in letter-writing as the war progressed, most servicemen sent hastily scribbled lines home whenever an opportunity existed.

Stationery varied from quality paper to rough parchment. Generally, the sheets were five-by-eight inches in size. Sometimes they were lined. While the men preferred to write with pen and ink, they were usually forced to rely on pencils. "A lead pencil is a poor thing to write with," a private in the 116th Illinois once commented, "but you must try and figer it out."[11]

Most Civil War letters were remarkably similar in format and content. The soldier began with a salutation such as: "My Dear and effectionat wife, I seit myself this cold morning to drop you a few lines to inform you that I am well at present & trust when this reach you it find you all well." Sometimes the man would begin in picturesque fashion. After Lee's army crossed the Potomac River into Maryland in September 1862, a member of the 6th North Carolina started a letter to his mother with the words: "I seat myself once in the United States of America flat down on the ground bare-footed and lousy to write you a few lines to inform [you] where and how I am."[12]

The soldier-writer would next give a report on his health, for sickness in the army was more feared than the enemy. Following that would be inquiries or comments on affairs at home. The bulk of the letter, however, treated of his military situation: battles, camp life, rations, clothing, religious expressions, marches, opinions on officers and comrades, the weather, and other things he had witnessed.

A few soldiers expressed difficulty in putting thoughts on paper. "I could rite a heap," an Alabama private told his wife, "but when I go to rite I cant think of half I want to rite   if I could see you all I could tell you a heap."[13] That statement, in the middle of a letter which runs in small script to almost three printed pages, is ample evidence that soldiers always had something to say in a letter.

Indeed, Johnny Rebs and Billy Yanks were prone to mention anything, especially the conditions under which they were writing. "I seat myself on the ground (or rather in a mudhole) with a knapsack for a desk," began a letter from one Iowan. Leo Faller of the 36th Pennsylvania explained the difficulty he was experiencing at the outset of one letter: "I am siting on my knapsac in front of my tent with a Segar box on my knees to write on." The 2nd Michigan's Perry Mayo encountered more discomfort when writing his wife. "The only desk I have to write on is on my knee and my pen is more like a crowbar than an instrument to write with."[14]

On the day after Christmas 1863, a Massachusetts soldier in Virginia sought sympathy from his sweetheart with the opening lines: "You can imagine me sitting on a log close by the fire writing to you. The trouble with a outdoor fire, the smoke will take a turn and blow into my face. I have to shut my eyes and wait until it takes another turn." During a freezing night at Fredericksburg, Virginia, a private in the 22nd North Carolina closed a letter with the forlorn thought: "I will have to stop this time for it is now night and Soldiers has no candels." John D. Shank of the 125th Illinois was an unusually observant soldier. He once broke his train of thought in a letter with the statement: "they is a fly on my pen. i just rights What ever Comes in my head."[15]

Soldiers and loved ones in letters often posed questions that ranged from the pertinent to the absurd. Characteristic of the latter was a query from the wife of Emory Sweetland, a bluecoat in Sherman's army. Following the Atlanta campaign, Mrs. Sweetland asked if she should purchase a cemetery plot back home. Sweetland replied disjointedly that he would have to rely on her judgement in the matter.[16]

A small percentage of Civil War letters were models of literary excellence. The majority, however, were examples of phonetic spelling and crude handwriting reflective of the limited educational standards of that era. Civil War troops employed a number of slang expressions still in vogue today: "snug as a bug in a rug," "let 'er rip," "scarce as hen's teeth," and the like. Others conceived homespun, blunt, and sometimes near obscene expressions in messages to loved ones. Writing about the sparseness of his camp, a Billy Yank stated solemnly: "To tell the truth we are between sh-t and a sweat out here."[17]

Large numbers of soldiers took pride in improving their letter-composition through practice. Yet it was a difficult process because of their environment. "I am sitting by a camp fire writing on my knee and am unable to see the lines by the dim light," Virginian Green Samuels wrote, "and consequently write very crooked and I suppose scarcely intelligibly to you." Henry Orendorff of the 103rd Illinois once apologized to his sister: "Sarah please excuse my poorly composed & badly written letter. I would like to know how any body could write good or compose where there is so much confusion and fun going on." A similar but somewhat boastful apology came in a letter from a private in the 4th Virginia. "Excuse this scratch," he stated. "I believe I am getting more careless about my writing every day but I console myself by saying that all great men wrote badly."[18]

Drummerboy John Tallman of the 76th Illinois sought to help his sister with her correspondence. On February 12, 1863, he replied by mail while on duty in Florida: "I rote you a letter the other day in answer to one that Ulysses coppyed for you, but last Sunday evening I received an other from you in your own hand wrighting whitch was the best of all I could read every word except one. If you will keep trying you will soon get so as to wright first rate. You must learn to spell, to."[19]

Soldiers closed their letters generally with sentimental thoughts; or occasionally the writer would ask forgiveness for the messy sheets. "Pleas excuse this dirty looking letter," James Phillips wrote to his wife back in Illinois. "It was raining yesterday when I wrote and my ink was poor and upon the whole I made rather a poor looking job of it."[20] A surprising number of soldiers employed poetry to express farewells—and their true feelings. A popular verse with soldiers on both sides ran: "my pen is poor, my ink is pail, my love to you shall never fail." Another favorite couplet (which appeared in many derivatives) was: "if me no mor on earth you see, when you here of war remember me."[21]

That same writer once tried his hand at original verse. It was more revealing than artistic.

> Now in a fare land I rome
> fare from my friend at home
> but I hope the time is near

when we shall all meet again
I have not heard from home since
I left there.[22]

Because letters were the only link between soldiers and those close in heart, writers regarded their communiques as highly private. A soldier in the 137th New York wrote home in October 1862: "You must not show this to enny boddy for it is very poorly wrote and badly composed but I have not got no chance to do enny thing tonight but I was bound to write enny how."[23] Confederate soldier George White felt even stronger about the confidentiality of letters. In the summer of 1862 he told his wife Annie: "Any as I could not get no letters from you I taken all my oald leters and red them which gave me grate consolation and I distroid them   I hated to distroy them but I thaut it bes for I did not no hoos hands tha mite get in too."[24]

Letters being the only direct contact from home, mail call was an event that took precedence over everything in camp. The arrival of letters, a soldier in the 15th Massachusetts asserted, "was looked upon as a most important event, and it always found a crowd eagerly waiting for its delivery." The shout that a packet of mail had reached camp sent men scampering to the postman with unmatched fervor. William Wagner of the 57th North Carolina displayed the eagerness the men felt when he told his wife: "Dear I have bin loocking for a letter this hole week and I haint got none yet but I hope I may git one to day."[25]

John Worsham summed up the reactions of men in the 21st Virginia at mail call. "Those who received letters went off with radiant countenances. If it was night, each built a fire for light and, sitting on the ground, read his letter over and over. Those unfortunates who got none went off looking as if they had not a friend on earth."[26]

The lucky ones at mail call gave full attention to their gifts. A Federal sentinel on the outskirts of the camp was seen walking his beat, a musket in one hand and a hometown newspaper in the other. Whit Johnson of the 2nd Virginia Cavalry told his cousin after a profitable mail call: "It had been so long since I had gotten a letter I had nearly forgotten what a letter was." Receiving letters brought a marked rise in morale, a Wisconsin captain observed. "The boys all feel as well if not better than if they had got there Hard Tack." The 92nd Illinois' James Phillips informed his wife in May 1863: "I look with wishful eyes nearly every mail that comes for a letter from you. So you can judge how harde it is to wait ten days or two weeks as I have to sometimes. however I am happy to say it happens but seldom." A Minnesota private once exclaimed: "I can live a month now without eating, I have got five letters from my dear wife."[27]

Reactions were markedly different with men who walked away empty-handed from mail call. "I stood by the post master when he called out the mail," a forlorn soldier in the 10th Virginia related to his fiancée. "My heart at times was in my throat at the sight of some of the letters with small white envelopes *so much like yours* which some loving sweetheart had written to *her devoted swain.* I could scarcely hide my disappointment when the last letter was called out, and none from you."[28]

Alabama's John Cotton, after being in the army two months, sent a single but cogent plea home: "rite I hanent got nary letter from you yet." In February 1863, a Wisconsin soldier became disheartened at the lack of mail from home. "I cant afford to write many more letters unless I get an answer to some of them pretty soon," he announced. A month later, he moaned: "I expected to get a letter from you today when the mail came in but I was disappointed *as usual.*"[29]

Soldiers on more than one occasion blamed the mail service rather than the homefolk when mail call left them empty handed. John H. Morgan of the 24th Virginia vented his anger early in the war over what he thought was poor mail delivery. "There is something wrong in the Post Office affairs somewhere and the villainous perpetrator of the deed ought to be found out, and no punishment too bad to be administered to him, not even the burning pit of H-ll."[30]

The long periods without mail caused the most even-tempered of men to deliver emotional outbursts at the folks back home. Private Phillips of the 92nd Illinois wrote his wife an apology in the last month of 1862: "you must not think hard of me for writing as I did. I didn't mean what I said. I had not received a letter from you for some time and was getting a little out of patience." A Texas cannoneer likewise grew angry at no mail. To his fiancée he wrote belligerently: "If you have discontinued writing to me, please inform me of the fact at once, for however much I might regret such a determination on your part, I am not so weak but that I can endure it." On one occasion—either with sarcasm or with desperation, a Michigan officer wrote home: "tell me which or when all my correspondents died."[31]

A New England private spoke for tens of thousands of Civil War soldiers when he observed late in 1862: "If the people at home could realize how valuable letters are to the soldiers, and especially to the sick, they would be more generous with their pen and ink and spare time." Virginia soldier William Sutherland felt precisely the same way. "I have often thought it strange why our friends at home, who have so much time and opertunity, do not write more frequently to their soldier boys in the army. There is nothing more encouraging to the soldiers . . . than to know that they are held in remembrance by the loved ones at home. It seems to lighten their many arduous duties, gives them an elastic step upon the weary, dusty march, and nerves the soul for the dreadful shock of battle."[32]

In 1863 the semiliterate James Parrott of the 28th Tennessee opened his heart in a letter to his wife. "I all waz love to read as kind letters as you send mee   that lets mee now that you are living a christian . . . I love you and my children Better than every thing in the world   you must kiss the boys for mee and hug the Baby Bless his hart   I want to kiss him   I now he is sweat By his Being so fat." Parrott added in a subsequent letter: "if I could get one kiss from you it would be more pleasure to mee than every thing here."[33]

Johnny Rebs and Billy Yanks, far from home, displayed the rude strength of youth, but large numbers of them had youth's terrible capacity for loneliness. "Oh! that I was a boy once more at home in peace and knew nothing of the horrors of war," young William Rogers of the 13th Tennessee scrawled in his journal. "When I think of my native home, in a moment I seem to be there. But, alas! recollection soon hurries me back to dispair. Oh! Tell me I yet have a home; a home I am never to see."[34]

Accentuating that loneliness was a sentimentality characteristic of midnineteenth century America. The Civil War brought those two emotions together and gave them added strength. Combining loneliness and sentimentality had the result of increasing interest in romance, as well as some loosening of relations between the sexes. A Virginia cavalryman remembered: "The girls—bright, beautiful, charming girls— were abundant, and acted their part nobly, and if a susceptible soldier now and then had a couple or more sweethearts, the fault was pardonable, as the temptation was irresistible. The girls understood the situation as well as the boys, and patriotism frequently impelled them to court more than one champion."[35]

Many young ladies, filled with martial spirit, became unofficial recruiting agents by bestowing attention only on those willing to join the army. Roscoe Carper of the 5th North Carolina informed a friend that a woman's kindness more than anything else made a soldier willing to face the hardships of war. "Nothing goes harder with us than to be treated with indifference by the ladies. I can face the enemy's bullets but not the frowns of the ladies."[36]

Theodore Upson found himself showered with affection when he enlisted in the 100th Indiana. "If a fellow wants to go with a girl now," he stated, "he had better enlist. The girls sing 'I am Bound to be a Soldier's Wife or Die an Old Maid.' " One Alabama lass made her feelings on the matter painfully clear. To a suitor who was displaying reluctance to enter the army, she sent a skirt and petticoat with the message: "Wear these or enlist."[37]

Once single men got into the army, it did not take long before absence from females engendered acute pain. A boastful Virginia soldier told his sister in the war's first summer: "I begin to want to see the pretty Girls of my acquaintance very bad. If you see any of them tell them I say God bless their sweet souls for it wouldn't be a world at all without them. Give my love to all and [say] that they must keep a sharp look as I am going to speak before I return [home] as I am a candidate for a higher office than I could get in the army (that is, Matrimony) . . . I think it best to put in my claims in due time."[38]

Acquiring a sweetheart became a triumph just short of victory in battle. In May 1862, Virginia cavalryman Andy Crockett wrote to a friend: "I must tell you a secret, down on the Jeems River the other day I saw a—a—gal, that is a lady.   right thar, I lost my heart, as well as the little bit of sense I had   Ef I could get that gal, I'd give anything that I've got. Yes! I'd even part with my new red cotton Handkerchief."[39]

Many were the boasts and promises made after romance had taken root, and each successful suitor was convinced that he had found—and secured—the perfect mate. Illinois soldier John Shank confidently informed his homefolk: "I wrote a letter to my sweet Hart—one that i intend to Have for my Wedded Wief if i ever get Home Safe again. she is Bout 16 years old. She has Black Eyes and dark Hair and fair skin and plenty of land and that hant all." Another Billy Yank was more specific about the new love in his life. "My girl is none of your one-horse girls. She is a regular stub and twister. She is well-educated and refined, all wildcat and fur, and union from the muzzle to the crupper."[40]

What most soldiers sought in a sweetheart were women of modesty and femininity rather than girls who were outgoing, robust, hardy, or athletic. Beauty did not seem to be a paramount consideration, although Civil War troops usually commented at length on the lack of beauty among women on the other side. An Indiana soldier, after visiting a community in northern Mississippi (and obviously writing with exaggeration) asserted that the females there were "sharp-nosed, tobacco-chewing, snuff-rubbing, flax-headed, hatchet-faced, yellow-eyed, sallow-skinned, cotton-dressed, flat-breasted, bare-headed, long-waisted, hump-shouldered, stoop-necked, big-footed, straddle-toed, sharp-shinned, thin-lipped, pale-faced, lantern-jawed, silly-looking damsels."[41]

Northern soldiers went to lengths to criticize Southern women, probably as a display of fidelity to wives and sweethearts hundreds of miles away. "The girls down here," Union Private Shank informed the family, "hant half as good looking as the girls up in Illinois, and not half as deasent neather." Of the grammar used by Southern ladies, a Union infantryman remarked: "if one were to talk the english Language they would no more comprehend wat you were saying then is you were talking Latin." A Rhode Islander was struck at how "babies at every farmhouse were almost as abundant as chickens." The regimental surgeon, he added, "relates that he saw five persons riding one horse: the mother, one before, one behind, one at her breast, and one in embryo."[42]

Even the drummer boy of the 76th Illinois made fun of Confederate belles. From Mississippi in April 1864, he stated in a letter to his sister: "Thare are some nice looking girls, but they will chew tobacco, sweet little things. Don't you think that I, for instance, would *look*, or rather *make* a nice show, rideing along in a carriage with a young lady, me spitting tobacco juice out of one side of the carriage, and she out the other. Then we would each of us take a cigar and have a real old fashioned smook together. Wall, ain't that nice, Oh Cow!"[43]

With so many men in the armies, statements of love and campaigns of courtship all had to be done by mail. A soldier who overlooked telling his wife how much he missed her was likely to hear about it in her next letter. An Indiana artilleryman, after proclaiming enjoyment of army life, received the following response from home: "You say that you have lots of fun in camp. I am glad that you enjoy yourselves well and hope that you will think of poor lonely me sometimes."[44]

Actually, soldiers thought of loved ones at all times. "Lige" Cavins of the 14th Indiana penned a note one night while on picket duty: "I think more of home if possible when the moon is bright than at any other time. So when you see a beautiful bright moon, you may know that while you are looking upon it, I am thinking of you." After one bloody engagement, a Texas gunner wrote his fiancée: "Sallie, I remembered you on the battlefield and do not flatter when I say that I fought for you as well as for my country."[45]

Absence from home, another Confederate artilleryman felt, "can never conquer true love and the longer away the more ardent grows the flame." Romantic expressions abound in letters from husbands to wives. Ruffin Barnes of the 43rd North Carolina, for example, poured out his heart to his wife in an August 1864 letter. "Last night about sunset while I was going to my Picket Post all alone & it being Sunday Evening I began to think about you & Home & thinking I did wish I knew where you were at the time. It appeared to me I could almost see you sitting on the Porch & see the children Playing around you. It seemed so Plain to me I thought maybe it was a sign I would see you Before long. Oh, I do want to see you so Bad! I cannot Express by affections for you by letter as I wish to. You must guess at the Balance."[46]

From camp in November 1861, Albion Martin of the 33rd Virginia expressed similar sentiments to his wife Nannie. "By my honor, I never realized fully till since I left you how much I love you—I have thought of a good many harsh words I have given you in moments of ill humor though not one of them with intent or forethought from the heart for that has always been true and warm for you and must ever be while life lasts. I have been punished for every unkind word given you . . . I have no words to express my desire to see my Dear Nannie . . . "[47]

That soldiers ever had love and its attendant physical expressions on their minds is substantiated by what they did to the standard manual of arms in the Civil War. Known as "Hardee's *Tactics*," the book contained highly stilted, purely military language. Soldiers delighted in composing parodies of nonmilitary subjects in the vernacular of Hardee's *Tactics*. The most popular of these treatises was:

"Tactics of Kissing—Recruit is placed in front of the piece. First motion—Bend the right knee; straighten the left; bring the head on a level with the face of the piece; at the same time, extend the arms and clasp the cheeks of the piece firmly in both hands. Second motion—Bend the body slightly forward; pucker the mouth, and apply the lips smartly to the muzzle mouldings. Third motion—Break off promptly on both legs, to escape the jarring or injury should the piece recoil."[48]

While there was general hesitation in being too open in a letter, many Civil War soldiers resorted to poignant and moving lines to court sweethearts back home. In June 1861, a member of the 3rd Virginia

Cavalry wrote his betrothed: "If I ever return in safety from the campaign I shall lose no times in having our nuptials celebrated and I hope we will be permitted to enjoy a long and happy life. When I think of embracing you as my wife the thought is perfectly blissful . . . I have nearly worn out the little curl you gave me. I take it out every day to gaze upon and kiss."[49]

Private Charles Cook of Indiana utilized dramatic prose to court his girlfriend. His romance with "Maggie" began when he added a postscript to a messmate's letter home in November 1862. Six months later, even though he still had not laid eyes on the young lady, Cook wrote: "Maggie you are mine and I am yours and may the attachment that has sprung up in each of our hearts . . . be the germ that shall bud and bloom in heaven." By the latter months of 1864, Cooke had advanced in literary efforts to this point: "In the springtime we will plant flowers & they will spring up in the pathway and shed their fragrance around our happy home. the tiny humming bird will visit us and feast on the bouquet that Jupiter sips.   our paths will be pleasantness & the end thereof will be peace."[50]

Husbands and wives—as much so as sweethearts—tended to be reserved in what they wrote about sexual matters. Some wives were so timid about giving expressions to their affections that they initially addressed a husband as "my dear friend." Yet time, continuing absence, and the volume of correspondence usually lessened inhibitions. Peter Dekle of the 29th Georgia grew uneasy after hearing about the infidelity of the women back home. Whether unsure of his mate or of his neighbors, he wrote his wife: "I want you to be on your guard and not let no one get a holt on you."[51]

"Lige" Cavins also fell victim to the rumors that the menfolk back home were exploiting the soldiers' absence. The Indianian sermonized to his wife in a January 1863 letter: "A great many soldiers will find strangers added to their household upon their return to their homes— and some may find strangers of less number of years or months than will be pleasing to the soldier husband. I have heard of such instances, but have no fears for any of us who came out first."[52]

Soldiers and loved ones often carried on a delightful repartee in their letters for the obvious purpose of bolstering morale and easing the pain of separation. A Hoosier infantryman, in telling his wife how much he missed her, came to the edge of propriety by stating: "For some cause I can never get used to sleeping with a man. I always hitch off and my fellow sleeper hitches up, so by morning I generally find myself hitched out of bed."[53]

On the other hand, the correspondence between a couple in love was often touching as they sought devotion amid destruction. Especially tender were the sentiments of a Lexington, Virginia, soldier and a Caroline County lass who fell in love at the war's midway point. Alexander "Sandie" Pendleton was a Virginia staff officer when he became engaged to vivacious Catherine Corbin. Both were in their early twenties. In the summer of 1863, Sandie wrote Kate: "My whole being is welling out in joy and thankfulness for the great blessing and happiness which has come into my life." The couple picked a wedding date, but a new Federal threat on Virginia caused a postponement. Sandie expressed his disappointment by observing that "if 'hope deferred maketh the heart sick,' then my poor organ is well nigh unto death."

They set a new wedding date; and as the Confederate officer counted the days, he told Kate: "I am, I know, now a much better man than before I loved you. And oh! I do love you so much & deem it a privilege to be able to minister to your happiness, to bear your sorrows & lighten your burdens, to share your joys, and heighten your enjoyments. I have been very happy since I first loved you and you ought to be thankful that you have been able to brighten one life amid the sorrows of the times."

On December 29, 1863, the couple were married in a home ceremony. Three months later, writing from camp, Sandie proudly informed his bride: "How I do love to think about providing for you . . . How I do cherish the hope that soon we shall be together for good, & all the pleasures of home & peace will be ours to enjoy together."

Such was not to be. On September 22, 1864, Sandie Pendleton was killed in the battle of Fisher's Hill. His widow gave birth to a son six weeks later. The child lived ten months before dying of diptheria. It was then that Kate Corbin Pendleton gave way to total grief. To her father she wrote: "I wonder people's hearts don't break when they have ached and ached as mine has done till feeling seems to be almost worn out of them. My poor empty arms, with their sweet burden torn away forever." She then reached out for strength by adding: "If God loves all he chastens, surely I have good reason to believe he loves me."[54]

Other soldiers struck by homesickness eventually acknowledged their helplessness in changing the situation. In 1864, a member of the 10th Confederate Cavalry wrote home: "I dont no that I will ever live to see it but I still live in hopes that I will live til this war will end so we can live in peace and harmony once more   I think if this war was ended I would bee the happiest man living." At the same time a Louisianian stated in despair: "I am almost wild. I do not think that I will ever be fit again to associate with respectable people. I have not spoken to a lady for two years [because] I have been in the woods since I left home."[55]

W. A. Stephens of the 46th Alabama likewise sought to make the most of his state of affairs. He wrote his wife: "I cold in joy my self in serves as good as a most any one if I new that you was faring as well as you wold if I was with you and cold hear from you oftener. I no I am a way and canot get back and I no thare is no use in bein down in the mouth a bout it   we just as well laugh as cry."[56]

Younger soldiers tended to retain buoyant spirits and to accommodate better to the sternness of army life. Similarly, unmarried men displayed higher morale more consistently. Yet the desire for female companionship was so universal among all troops as to transcend most sentiment. In January 1862, while stationed in the mountains of western Virginia, the 14th Indiana's Elijah Cavins flirted with a number of local females—and he freely admitted it to his wife. He spent several evenings in the company of "good looking and intelligent" ladies. "You must not get jealous at what is coming now," he stated in a letter home, "you know I always tell the truth and the whole truth. The truth is that I stayed at Philippi so long that when I did leave, I had quite a big job of kissing to do up. It may be some consolation to you to know that I done it up right as I usually do."[57]

Later that year, a Richmond infantryman moaned: "I should go perfectly wild with delight to spend a day with a party of young ladies in camp to day, but [we] have just received marching orders, so all that is knocked in the head."[58]

Longings such as these, plus the vicissitudes of military life, taxed the morality of many soldiers. The army did not breed evil, nor did it condone moral laxity. In the military, sin competed with salvation on an equal footing for quite human reasons. Impressionable country boys away from home for the first (and probably the last) time found excitement in the unusual attractions and novel experiences that soldiering offered.

Every camp and nearby community had its temptations. Being a soldier provided a man with a degree of anonymity. The removal of restraints that the men had known at home gave an opportunity to "experiment with the forbidden" before returning home to the straight and narrow of former ways. Moreover, soldiers quickly learned the truism that individuals have less inhibitions when involved in group activity. Hence, immorality developed naturally in the armies of blue and gray.

This immorality was recreational and rarely criminal. Sexual assaults were not commonplace during the Civil War. Both sides looked sternly on such offenses and enacted justice accordingly. In June 1864, a Wisconsin private stationed at Memphis told his parents of "three men shot that day for committing an outrage upon the person of a defenseless female who lived a short distance from this place." A month later in Virginia, two wagoners in the 72nd New York were put to death for raping a married woman who lived alone near the Union lines. Some 10,000 Federals were in attendance at the execution. The two culprits were hanged together on a double gallows, a Union officer stated, "in full view of the enemy's lines, to show the rebels how justice was done amongst us."[59]

Sexual references are difficult to find in the writings of Civil War soldiers. Johnny Rebs and Billy Yanks were explicit in their boasts only to a brother or friend. Letters commenting on the subject of sex were usually destroyed at war's end, and "gentlemen-soldiers" writing in the postwar years almost never alluded to the subject. Nevertheless, immorality was present whenever an army bivouacked near any sizable community.

James Greenalch of the 1st Michigan Engineers was stunned at the conduct he beheld after the Union army occupied Savannah, Georgia. On the day after Christmas 1864, he wrote his wife: "I am satisfide from what I have seen that some of the women . . . have been convinced that the Yankees have hornes but not horns on the top of the head. I should have hesitated to of believed that men or those that pretend to be men would become so demoralized and void of all decency or respect. I would expect if I had ben guilty of what I have seen, to have some plague or sin come upon me for it."[60]

Practically every large city in the path of war had dozens of bawdy houses catering to soldiers. An Iowa soldier arrived in Mississippi and noted in mid-July 1862: "Corinth is full of 'fast womin' who have come in within a few days and are demoralizing many of the men and with the help of bad whiskey will lay many of them out."[61] On the Northern side, Chicago, Cincinnati, New York, and Boston became especially notorious as "sex centers." Yet Washington, the focal point of military and political activity, rapidly developed into a capital of prostitution as well.

A Massachusetts soldier delighted in telling a friend of the "gay old time" he had in Washington, drinking lager beer all day and "riding a Dutch gal" all night. By 1863, Washington had 450 known houses of ill repute, and the Washington *Star* reported no less than 7,000 prostitutes at work. Several blocks on the south side of Pennsylvania Avenue contained nothing but bordellos. All had names, and some did little to conceal the business conducted inside: "The Haystack," "Hooker's Headquarters," "The Ironclad," and "Mother Russell's Bake Oven."[62]

David Beem accompanied some of his 14th Indiana comrades to Washington one evening. "They wanted me to go to a performance called the 'Varieties,'" he later told his wife, "but I very respectfully declined, as I knew the performances consisted mostly of dancing by ladies who, although they may be good loooking, yet exhibit too many charms to suit modest eyes, and you know how *very modest* I am."[63]

Even the ever romantic Lige Cavins of the same regiment drew back from the wild life he encountered in occupied Alexandria, Virginia. "I would rather be farther off from town," he declared. "It is said that one house of every ten in the city is a bawdy house—it is a perfect Sodom. The result will be that in a week or two, there will be an increase of sickness in camp. . . . Women pass along the bank of the Potomac and look at men while they are bathing. I believe I have seen more loathsome and disgusting sights here than I ever saw before, notwithstanding I have been in the streets but few times."[64]

Richmond became the true mecca of prostitution in the Confederacy. Available women promenaded on every major street, shouted invitations from scores of boardinghouse doorways and windows, and brazenly used the Capitol grounds as a major soliciting site. In May 1862, one madam opened a bawdy house immediately across the street from a soldier hospital. Shortly thereafter, the hospital superintendent complained angrily that the prognoses of many of his patients had taken sharp turns for the worse. Prostitutes were appearing at their windows in various stages of nudity, and they were making highly provocative gestures. As a result, the superintendent declared, patients were sneaking and hobbling out of the hospital with little thought to the seriousness of their condition.[65]

The superintendent of a Northern soldier hospital took matters into his own hands. In August 1864, the Davenport (Iowa) *Gazette* reported: "On last week several women of easy virtue, who were trifling with the soldiers about Camp McClellan Hospital, were treated to a cold bath in the Mississippi by order of the officer in charge. They will probably not stroll about camp again for some time to come."[66]

Illicit sexual behavior ("horizontal refreshments," it was popularly termed) occurred more often than might be supposed. Behind every major army camp was a second force: so-called laundresses and camp followers who displayed total impartiality as to whose army they were serving. A Norwegian lad in a Minnesota unit wrote home in late November 1861: "We have about forty women in the regiment, some of them make lots of money natures' way. One of them had a bill today against a soldier for forty dollars."[67]

James Phillips of the 92nd Illinois gave his wife a vivid description of Lexington, Kentucky, women who congregated around the Union camps. "I have seen wenches here that would weigh one to four hundred. they are great fat greecy looking things. . . . they Strut around here to day with there hoops and shakers on and plaid dresses. our boys have plenty of fun with them. . . . The Boys are having great times with the wenches here to day ketching them and squeesing them. They are all dressed to fits. that new dress of yours that you was bragging about I want you to throw away because I saw a wench with one just like it here to day."[68]

Prostitutes generally conducted business in their own huts or occasionally in the tents of the soldiers. A South Carolina soldier, writing in June 1861, dutifully told his wife about the number of women visiting his camp. "If you could be here on those occasions you would think that there was not a married man in the regiment but me. A great many of them are married men, but they are not obliged to say so."[69]

Instances existed when women of easy virtue literally joined a unit. In the 116th Illinois, a lieutenant tried to keep a woman disguised as a soldier. A private in the regiment voiced satisfaction at what transpired. "The Colonel give our first Lieut. fits to day after drill about Kate. She goes in mens clothes. She has been with the Regt ever since we left Memphis. . . . There is a few in our Company that would like to have such rips as her in camp, and on account of them our lieutenant was talked to as was some of the rest. You could hardly tell her from a man."[70]

Late in October 1864, the Richmond *Enquirer* reported that two females named Mary and Mollie Bell, "alias Tom Parker and Bob Morgan," were brought to the capital under guard. "They were dressed in Confederate uniforms, and were sent to this city from Southwestern

Virginia, where they have been in the service during the past two years." The two women were subsequently convicted and imprisoned for "aiding in the demoralization of General Early's veterans."[71]

Venereal disease became prevalent in all Civil War armies. A medical report revealed that in the first year of the war one of every twelve Federal soldiers had syphilis, gonorrhea, or other sexually transmitted maladies. By 1863, it was not uncommon to read in soldiers' letters such statements as this by a member of the 14th Indiana: "The health of the regiment is tolerably good, except there are quite a number diseased from their conduct at Alexandria and New York."[72] The incidence among Northern troops for the whole war period was 82 cases per 1,000 men. If figures were known for the number of infections not reported, the statistics would be double or possibly triple.

Confederate records are too fragmentary to provide an accurate gauge of the incidence of venereal disease in the southern forces. Johnny Rebs were not so well or so frequently paid, and not so often stationed near the heavily populated cities in the Border and Northern states. Hence, they had less opportunity for contacts with prostitutes. Given the same circumstances as Billy Yanks, Southern soldiers undoubtedly would have compiled equally disastrous statistics.

Medical treatment for venereal infections did nothing to stem the spread of the diseases. The treatments of that day were a combination of guesswork and hope. Medications included poke roots, elder berries, mercury, sarsaparilla, sassafras, zinc sulfate, silver nitrate, and—in some cases—cauterization. A surgeon in the Confederacy's western army boasted that "silk weed root put in whiskey and drank, giving at the same time pills of resin from the pine tree with very small pieces of blue vitrol, would cure severe cases of gonorrhea."[73]

Perry Mayo of the 2nd Michigan once wrote his wife from Washington: "There is a good many sick now mostly caused by imprudence. That fellow (Hollman) that you told to see after me . . . has been caught in bad company and is so bad off he has not been on duty since we have been here and stands a good chance to be discharged and sent home."[74] Mayo was writing in June 1861, when the war was barely two months old.

On rare occasions, soldiers and their wives would openly discuss sexual matters. Their comments are more humorous than stimulating. In July 1864, Michigan soldier James Greenalch begged in a letter home: "O Fidelia I herd sometime ago that Gilberts wife that lived on the hill by McKerchers had run away with another man. You never wrote me about it, if it is so. I have herd men when they were talking about old men being guilty of such [a] thing that the older the Back the Stifer the horn and the women, some of them, apear to have the same disease. I hope you won't ketch it." When Private Phillips of Illinois told his spouse of the boys "having great times with the wenches here to day," she promptly wrote back and warned Phillips to leave those women alone because they "might have some mixed bread."[75]

One of the most explicit preserved collections of letters is between Elnathan Keeler of the 16th New York and his wife Jane. While stationed at Petersburg, Virginia, in 1864, Keeler received a box of food from home. His wife's accompanying note stated: "don't let that horseradish make you horney for I am not there you know and I don't believe them blacks taste good unless it is in the dark."

Later, when her husband advised her to get another man if he were killed, Jane Keeler replied that she preferred in such a case to have his hide stuffed with straw.[76]

Like all wars, the conflict of the 1860s tested the moral as well as physical fiber of soldiers. Vice offered to some a pleasurable albeit momentary escape from war's realities. However, thoughts of loved ones occupied the mind and warmed the heart; and the longer the absence from home, the deeper the yearning for wives or sweethearts became. The Civil War had its seamy side, to be sure, but the evidence is overwhelming that a majority of soldiers North and South displayed fidelity through words in a letter, longing in the heart, and hopes for the future.

Thomas Cliburn of the 6th Mississippi was representative of that class. He went to war to defend his native state, but his real love was the wife he left behind. On May 5, 1863, Cliburn wrote her: "I am so tired I cant hardly right honey. O may God bless you honey is my prair & O how bad I want To see you all no man cant tell."

A week later, Cliburn was killed in action.[77]

·7·

Problems of Discipline

Civil War troops were the worst soldiers and the best fighters that America has ever produced.

Most of the men who went off to war in 1861–1865 were citizen-soldiers: volunteers who tended to remain more citizen than soldier. Once in service, they operated under a common belief that constructive thinking was the domain of officers only. A company commander in the 125th New York once observed: "A captain has as much to do as—in fact, he is practically—the father of ninety children. Men in camp, sensible men, lose all their good judgment and almost their good sense; they become puerile, and come to the captain on a multitude of silly, childish matters. A captain does not only his own, but all the thinking of the company."[1]

One private from Pennsylvania expressed a somewhat similar view. The average soldier, he commented, "was not required to do much, if any thinking for himself, as his officers were expected to do that for him. He was simply expected to act a good deal as an automaton; so that his brain was never burdened about 'manoeuvres,' 'advances,' 're-treats,' and 'strategy;' but he was simply expected to act when required, and to obey orders."[2]

It did not work out that way for the vast majority of soldiers North and South. They entered service with an ignorance of army life and an indifference to discipline. The former disappeared out of necessity; the latter remained a constant problem throughout the war. Confederate General Joseph E. Johnston snarled in the first weeks of hostilities that the volunteers were so lacking in "discipline and instruction" as to make it "difficult to use them in the field." Johnston added: "I would not give one company of regulars for a whole regiment!"[3]

The general was a professional soldier with strong and slanted opinions, to be sure. Yet the situation he described did not disappear as the war seemingly became more organized and sophisticated. A Southern inspector-general wrote near the end of the conflict that "the source of almost every evil existing in the army is due to the difficulty of having orders properly and promptly executed. There is not that spirit of respect for and obedience to general orders which should pervade a military organization."[4]

Writing after the war, Iowa General William W. Belknap noted: "Discipline is the basis of armies. Without it, they are but organized mobs. Men drawn suddenly from home, where liberty was the rule and licence was its companion, and placed instantly under the stern control of martial authority, could not be expected to yield to restraint, without showing that change was irksome."[5]

Adjutant James R. Binford of the 15th Mississippi unknowingly agreed with Belknap. "The officers and men all being raw recruits, discipline was very galling to them, and as they would be brought under rigid military discipline a large amount of first-class swearing could be heard every day; but soon the boys began to learn the 'Old Soldier' tricks and learned to yield gracefully to the inevitable when they could not dodge the officers."[6]

Binford's last statement was more wishful thinking than reality. Much of formal military life appeared to Johnny Rebs and Billy Yanks alike as a useless waste of time. An Indiana private complained: "We had enlisted to put down the rebellion and had no patience with the red-tape tomfoolery of the regular service. Furthermore, the boys recognized no superiors, except in the line of legitimate duty."[7]

This was no exaggeration. Discipline was never tight enough to keep soldiers from doing something which they believed was justified at a particular time. Hence, maintaining firm control over the rank and file was a critical problem on both sides, especially in the first years of the war.

Most of the men had been longtime acquaintances with their company captains, and in some instances even with their regimental commanders, before civil war erupted. They had addressed one another then as Tom, Dick, or Harry. Once in the army, usage and friendship were often stronger than military necessity—particularly since the men expected to return to being neighbors when that unnatural war ended.

As an example, Missouri soldiers in one company could never bring themselves to show proper respect for Brigadier General Thomas Harris. To them, he was always "the sole and modest-salaried operator in our telegraph office" back in Hannibal. A North Carolinian wrote of his company at the outset of the war: "The rank and file of the Anson Guards were the equals, and superiors to some of their officers; socially, in wealth, in position and in education, and it was a hard lesson to learn respectful obedience."[8] The citizen-soldiers, in other words, were willing to obey all orders that were sensible, so long as the man giving them did not get too stuffy about it.

Troops on both sides demonstrated that they could be led but they could not be driven; and any officer who attempted the latter was going to encounter at least resistance and at most rebellion. After all, historically minded soldiers would say, American government rested on the consent of the governed. A member of Hood's Texas Brigade summed it up neatly: "Tell a soldier that he must not do a certain thing or go to a certain place and he will immediately want to know the reason why and begin to investigate."[9]

Soldiers balked almost naturally at blind obedience. In the war's first months, one young recruit informed a friend: "we are not lowd to go to the Shops without a permit and we are not lowd to miss a drill without a furlo sickness or permit, we are under tite rules you dont know how tite they are   I wish I could see you and then I could tell you what I thought of campt life   it is very tite rules and confinen." A Georgia soldier, writing at the same time, was more pointed in his opinions. "I love my country as well as any one but I don't believe in the plan of making myself a slave. . . . A private soldier is nothing more than a slave and is often treated worse. I have during the past six months gone through more hardships then anyone of ours or Grandma's negroes; their life is a luxury to what mine is sometimes."[10]

Disrespect for authority was the first and most prevalent offense committed by the men of blue and gray. Prewar acquaintance with one or more of their officers initially led men to take discipline lightly. Much of the insubordination also resulted from factors common in any war: recruits adjusting badly to army regimentation, the natural tendency of subalterns to find fault with those placed in command, plus the disillusionment that came when the harsh reality of war erased the rosy dreams of glory. Intensifying these denominators was the strong individualism characteristic of midnineteenth century America. Confederates and Federals who answered the call to arms were products of a new nation dedicated to the ideal that one man was as good as another. At the same time, many of the recruits of the 1860s were independent small farmers to whom teamwork was alien.

When a North Carolina brigadier early in the war displayed too authoritarian an air, a soldier with a sense of humor "proposed to auction off General Hoke, and mounting a box proceeded to cry him off to the highest bidder." The general was sold for six cents, the auctioneer declaring solemnly that "the purchaser was cheated in his property."[11]

One other encumbrance hampered discipline in Civil War armies. A large number of the first wave of officers were either appointed because of their political influence or elected because of their popularity. "We like our Captain verry well," a New York soldier wrote early in his army career. "he Is full of fun and makes a good deal of noise but if we was a going into battle I should rather he would stay behind for he is no milatary man at all." Some men were chosen on the basis of prior service in the Black Hawk or Mexican wars, which appeared to give them an aura of experience and prestige that in fact did not always exist. One of the first captains in the 61st Illinois was such a "veteran;" yet at drill his commands to the men were such shouts as "Swing around, boys, just like a gate!"[12]

Pomposity was guaranteed to produce negative repercussions. A member of the 13th Massachusetts wrote of his colonel: "He was one of a class of men who labor under the astronomical error of thinking the earth cannot move in its orbit nor revolve on its axis without their consent, and who, having a feeling of responsibility for all matters that take place on the land or in the sea, become very wroth when anything happens to mar their beautiful conceit."[13]

The colonel of the 19th Iowa must have belonged to the same class. According to one of his men. "Col. Crabb made the remark to day that the regiment was getting sick laying around camp and eating too much and it would require a tramp to bring them out   Hurrah for Crabb   laying by dont seem to hurt him much & he is very particular about the time we leave to be such so as not to be able to go   The same medicine operates differently on soldiers & officers." Another soldier dismissed one of his superiors with the observation: "Of Captain Blackmer, I have but a word to say. He entered at the big end of the horn, with a loud flourish, declaring he would 'wade in blood to his ears,' and then in three months came out the little end, from a hole too small to be seen with the naked eye."[14]

Drunkenness among officers also limited their effectiveness as leaders and disciplinarians. John Cotton of the 10th Confederate Cavalry wrote home in 1863: "there is a great deal of dissatisfaction about our colonel they dont like him atall I hant got no use for him he is always drunk when he can get whiskey." The 61st Illinois' James Lawrence became even more articulate about one of his officers. "Lieut. Dawes is here and seems to be like a sheep steeler. His money is run out, and now he keeps sober he is very submissive, but he has repented so often that I have no confadence in him. He will be discharged in a few days, and then I shall be clear of the mean, pucelanamous, low bread, nigerdly, unprincupled drinking sot."[15]

Even in battle, soldiers were quick to recognize a tipsy officer. Writing of the two days of fighting at Shiloh, Sergeant Cyrus Boyd of the 15th Iowa made no attempt to hide his disgust. "We were in great confusion as Col. Reid and [Lt. Col.] Dewey did a considerable amount of hard *swearing* and I had time to notice him wheel his horse around and take some *consolation* through the neck of a pint bottle. This seemed to give him a stronger flow of swear language than before."[16]

Two measures early in the war went far in stabilizing the Union officer corps.

A July 1861 regulation authorized screening boards to eliminate obviously incapable officers. Included among this group were those popular men of limited education who simply could not read orders and dispatches. Screening boards had the additional advantage of causing many officers of marginal ability to resign rather than face the board. The second measure, enacted a month later, allowed any officer with forty years' army experience to retire with appropriate pay and privileges. This cleared the way for many aged officers to leave the army with dignity.

In one three-month period thereafter, a Midwestern regiment rid itself of seventeen officers through resignation or dismissal. An Iowa soldier wrote of one such departee from his regiment: "He is one of those noiseless *vipers* that lie in the sunshine and when no warning can be given his victim he will strike at him when defenseless."[17] However, and in spite of flagrant incompetence, far too many officers managed to retain their position long after their worthlessness was an accomplished fact.

One such martinet was Captain Walter G. Dunn of the 109th Pennsylvania. After he died in a freak boat accident near the end of the war, a soldier under him wrote that Dunn "has been a tyrant to the men since he has been in command of the Regt, and had he lived and shewed himself after our boys got home, in all probability he would have been killed, for he was brutal almost beyond Endurance. at the least provocation he would catch a man by the throat and nearly choke him, the men not daring to Interfere."[18]

In defense of some of the officers, it should be noted that many who were thrust by circumstances into command status were no older, wiser, or more learned than the men they led. Hence, they themselves had to learn while teaching others. In 1862 an Iowa soldier informed his brother: "I never saw so many green officers as are in some of the new Regs. There is fun for us to see them go through their maneuvers. It is rather a funny operation for one man to teach another what he don't know himself . . . " Iowa's Sergeant Boyd saw no humor in the situation. "The Col.," he wrote, "does not know the difference between file right and file left and is as ignorant of Military Maneuvers as a child."[19]

What the soldiers did not understand was that most officers were painfully aware of their shortcomings. Youthful Lieutenant Samuel A. Craig several times during his first weeks in the army would sneak off alone in the woods. There he would shout commands in the manual of arms, marches, and the like so that he would appear more experienced when he was in front of his company.[20]

There were embarrassing moments, nevertheless. One was the first day the colonel of the 5th Wisconsin proudly led his regiment in daily drill. A band suddenly began playing, the colonel's horse shied, and a shower of paper slips floated in the wind. The colonel halted the men, called the company commanders together, and had them march their individual units back to camp. Without his notes, he was helpless.[21]

Colonel William C. Scott of the 44th Virginia underwent even greater humiliation. New to regimental leadership—and war—the colonel learned one afternoon that Federal cavalry were advancing down a road his troops held. Scott immediately dispersed his men along both sides of the road so as to ambush the column. One of the Virginians described in his diary what happened next. Colonel Scott "placed the men on each side of the road facing each other and commanded them to fix bayonets and insert their bayonets through the fence, at the same time cautioning them not to fire until the enemy has passed. . . . The folly of the thing was so apparent that such a peal of laughter went up that he had to command silence lest the enemy should discover our whereabouts." What ensued thereafter is not recorded.[22]

Officers in the Civil War were expected to lead by example. The overwhelming majority of Johnny Rebs and Billy Yanks acknowledged that death was an integral part of war. Yet an officer who endangered his men unnecessarily, or who squandered troops haphazardly, appalled and angered the men. When one did not measure up to expectations where courage, fairness, and inspiration were concerned, soldiers in the ranks were unsparing in their criticisms.

The longer the troops remained idle in camp, the more argumentative they became. As a New Yorker wrote: "The men talked about the officers, and the officers talked about each other, in a manner that led strangers to believe that like Ishmael of old, 'Every man's hand turned against his neighbor, and his neighbor's hand against him.' "[23]

Cowardice by an officer in the face of the enemy was simply not tolerated. After the battle of Perryville, Kentucky, the colonel of the 50th Ohio resigned in the face of widespread derision and a threatened court-martial. The colonel "was of no service" to his troops in the fighting, an adjutant general stated. "The first position that I saw him in was lying on his face, crouching behind a stump, and twice subsequently I saw him far to the rear of his regiment, while his men were in line of battle, apparently trying to rally some half a dozen stragglers."[24]

The most common form of disrespect to authority was contemptuous language. Nicknames were given to officers and used freely. "Falstaff," "Hudibras," "Satan," "Ironsides," "Colonel Martinet," and "Old Bowels" were but a few titles employed. Verbal attacks were more profane. In letters and diaries can be found such officer-references as "a vain, stuck-up, illiterate ass," "whore-house pimp," and "horse's ass." A Louisiana soldier dismissed his lieutenant as "a whining methodist class leader." George N. Bliss of the 1st Rhode Island Cavalry had no affection for his colonel, whom he once termed an "old puke." Later, when that officer made Bliss angrier, the cavalryman branded the colonel a "God damned fussy old pisspot."[25] Yet the overheard phrase that got most men hauled before a military court was the time honored "son of a bitch."

Derisions of officers came in a wide variety of expressions. A Federal prisoner being led southward through Virginia stated to one of his captors that his captain "never told him the truth but once in his life & that was when he told him he would be in Richmond in a few days." In mid-August 1864, a member of the 123rd Illinois wrote his wife: "I feel certain that if our Generals hadn't fallen to quarreling among themselves, Atlanta would have been ours now. I'm glad I'm not a General to be quarreling with my companions about questions of rank, like a bunch of children quarreling about their painted toys."[26]

Blanket denunciations were commonplace with the men in the ranks. An Iowan asserted that "nine tenths of the officers in the army do not care any more for the principle at stake than a savage cares about the Bible." After the battle of Fredericksburg, a member of the 33rd Massachusetts expressed the opinion that "our poppycorn generals kill men as Herod killed the innocents."

Another Illinois soldier once wrote in exasperation: "I wish to God one half of our officers was knocked in the head by slinging them Against A part of those still left." An even more sweeping condemnation came during the siege of Vicksburg, when a section of the opposing lines struck an informal truce and discussed the war at length. Confederates "agreed with us perfectly on one thing," a Wisconsin soldier asserted. "If the settlement of this war was left to the Enlisted men on both sides we would soon go home."[27]

Such an atmosphere was bound to produce insubordinate behavior on a regular basis. Much of that misconduct stemmed not from an order but from the brusque manner in which the order was delivered. A natural opposition to discipline, plus personal dislike of some superior, often combined to produce reactions that went beyond verbal disputes. Incidences were many when soldiers physically attacked officers.

One evening early in the war, an intoxicated captain rode along his picket line; and when guards dutifully challenged him, the captain became belligerent and insulting. Whereupon the pickets pulled him from his horse, gave him a good beating, and sent him walking back to camp. Later in the war, an inspector general of the Union XX Corps interrupted a group of men at breakfast, berated them for some supposed breach of duty, and threatened to beat each of them with the blunt end of his sword. At that point, the soldiers dragged the officer from his saddle, blackened his eyes and bloodied his nose, then made a hasty flight into the middle of the camp. They were never punished because the inspector general could not identify them.[28]

More often, soldiers would "settle a score" with a disliked officer through subtle means. Any unpopular captain or colonel who prided his appearance on a horse could be prepared one morning to find his mount with a shaved mane and tail.[29]

"The hole regiment I think would be glad if he was dead," a Confederate cavalryman once wrote of his regimental commander. One known instance exists when a group of soldiers repeatedly tried to take matters into their own hands. Writing of duty on Roanoke Island, North Carolina, the historian of the 6th New Hampshire stated openly that General Thomas Williams "was a tyrant in every sense of the word, and all the troops on the island hated him. They would shoot at him as he rode through the bushes, and when he was in his tent, they put the balls into his bedpost."[30]

On occasion, some soldiers vowed "to get even" with an officer in the confusion of the next battle. One such case involved General Charles S. Winder, who in 1862 succeeded a highly popular brigadier in command of the South's proud Stonewall Brigade. Winder, stated a member of that unit, "was very severe, and very tyrannical, so much so that he was 'spotted' by some of the brigade; and we could hear it remarked by some one near every day that the next fight we got in would be the last for Winder." It was. The general was killed by a Federal shell at the battle of Cedar Mountain.[31]

Those officers who led with gentle persuasiveness and possessed genuine concern for their men almost without exception received obedience and respect. An Alabama soldier wrote of his company leaders: "A more impartial set of officers, so far as my observation extends, cannot be found in any company in the Army, nor is there a set of officers more urbane, dignified and gentlemanly in their bearing. Capt. Clarke is noted throughout the whole regiment for [such] kindness, care, attention, and watchfulness . . . that hundreds of [soldiers] would defend him to the last, and follow him into the most imminent danger."[32]

One of the most beloved of Civil War regimental commanders was Colonel Edward E. Cross of the 5th New Hampshire. He was a stern disciplinarian, but he tempered his severity with levity and true concern for the welfare of his men. Brave to the point of reckless, Cross was wounded an incredible eleven times in his first two years of service. He was struck in the groin during the battle of Seven Pines; yet as he lay on the ground, Cross told his aides: "Never mind me, men, whip the enemy first, and take care of me afterwards."

Then came Gettysburg. Cross went down from a mortal shell wound. His last words, conveyed to his weeping troops, were: "I did hope I should live to see peace restored to our distressed country. I think the boys will miss me. Say goodbye to all."[33]

In the early days of the war, discipline occasionally and literally had to be hammered into some units. The skillful organizer, General

George B. McClellan, dealt with balky troops in a straightforward and peremptory manner. When the 2nd Maine mutinied for a variety of reasons, McClellan sent sixty-three of its members to Dry Tortugas Prison for the remainder of the war. Likewise, the 4th Connecticut almost rebelled—but with due cause. Stationed in Maryland, it was subjected to bad officers, poor rations, and such skimpy clothing that many of the soldiers appeared for dress parade in their underclothing. McClellan also arrested a sizable number of the 79th New York and threatened to have them shot for insubordination.[34]

Next to insubordination, drunkenness got the most men in trouble. A Michigan recruit in September 1862 was assigned to duty at a guard-house. What he beheld was a shock. "Our first tower [tour] was the worst, it was in the first part of the evening, some fifteen or twenty drunk and some not, and fetching them in all the time holering and swaring, some of them the officers, two or three of them, would pitch on one man and knock him down and pound him all up, some of them handcofed and some tied down to the benches groaning and yeling. They made so much disturbance and noise that one of the officers went out and got a revolver and pointed it at two or three of them and told them if they did not sit down and be still he would give them the contence."[35]

The guardhouse was a frequent form of punishment for minor offenses. What was termed "guardhouse" varied from a tent or stockade to an open pen or—sometimes—merely a marked-off area patrolled by sentries. Guardhouse confinement usually ranged in time from a few hours to a month. It was hardly a terrible sentence, since it provided a welcome relief from regular camp duties; and unless a bread-and-water diet was included in the penalty, men sentenced there did not seem to mind it too much.

Another common offense in the armies was theft. It varied in content and intensity from single soldiers committing petty larceny in camp to small bands carrying on a sort of roving robbery to entire regiments pilfering a community. An Iowa soldier once recorded somewhat humorously in his diary: "A member of the Company by the name of Locker was arrested for letting things stick to his fingers. Capt found a revolver upon him which he lost some time ago." From camp in Virginia late in August 1861, the following order emanated from a regimental headquarters: "Commanding officers of Companies A and B will cause to be returned to headquarters one chair each belonging to the Field and Staff."[36]

Certain units gained quick and unsavory reputations for "sticky fingers." A member of the 29th Georgia once stated indignantly to his wife: "some of the brigades behaves badly, vis the north Carolina troops.   they have bin caught in squads of 30 stealing hogs & chickens & plundering houses &c. but the troops from Georgia have did thare State honer by behaving honerable on every march cince we left Georgia. I am truly Sorry thoughs troops are with us. it is calculated to corrupt the Whole Brigade."[37]

Similarly, it was often said that no farmer's henhouse was safe when the 21st Illinois was in the vicinity. Over in the Army of the Potomac, the 6th New York appears to have been in a class by itself. The regiment contained a large segment of men from the rough Bowery section of New York City. One officer described the regiment as "the very flower of the Dead Rabbits, creme de la creme of Bowery society." Rumor circulated that before a man was accepted into the 6th New York, he had to prove that he had a jail record. In any event, just before the regiment left for war, its colonel gave the men a pep talk. He held up his gold watch and proclaimed that Southern plantation owners all had such luxuries that awaited confiscation by Union soldiers. Five minutes later, the colonel reached in his pocket to check the time and found his watch gone.[38]

Punishments were necessary, if discipline was to survive. Yet the leading characteristics of Civil War punishments were inequity and capriciousness. Too often, soldiers convicted of the worst crimes were given such light or reduced sentences as to make a mockery of justice, while others found guilty of trifling offenses sometimes received punishments that ranged from severe to inhuman. The frequency and degree of army punishments also depended in great part on the whims of the commanding officer, and such leaders ran the gauntlet from strict and harsh to condescending and lenient. Some officers were too benevolent; others, wrote John Billings, "felt that every violation of camp rules should be visited with the infliction of bodily pain." For example, six Confederates who deserted the army in late 1862 were returned to duty after "a little fatherly advice." At about the same time, a dull-witted Union soldier who took five days' unauthorized leave was sentenced to a prison term of three years at hard labor.

The most frequently employed punishments in the Civil War were exhibitionistic, and little doubt existed as to what the man had done. A Federal cavalryman paraded for several hours with a saddle on his back—a saddle he had stolen. When a trigger-happy Confederate shot a stray dog, he was forced to double-time around camp with the dead animal in his arms. Six soldiers caught in the act of stealing a rowboat received a picturesque penalty. Four of them had to carry the boat through camp all day while the other two sat in the boat and rowed vigorously in the empty air. During an 1863 skirmish in Virginia, five New England soldiers lost their resolve and broke to the rear. For their misbehavior, the men were forced to stand atop barrels in camp and turn periodically so that everyone could see the wooden signs draped on their backs: "I shirked," "I skedaddled," "So did I," "I did too," and "Ditto."[39]

"Riding the horse" was a similar indignity. Two uprights extended eight to ten feet in the air and had a pole between them. One or more culprits were placed astride the crossbar and their ankles then bound. Wearing placards reading "Deserter," "I am a coward," "Thief," and the like, the guilty men sat there for several hours and endured the hoots and jeers of passersby.[40]

Ball-and-chain sentences were popular if the materials were available. In such a punishment, one end of a heavy chain two to six feet in length was attached to a man's leg, the other end to a cannon ball weighing up to thirty pounds. The convicted soldier was then required to march through camp, dragging his shackles behind him. Another punishment for medium-serious offenses was to tie a man by his thumbs to a tree branch, pulling him just high enough so that he could keep his thumbs from being torn from the joints only by standing on tiptoe.

Bucking and gagging was a frequent punishment for some cases of mild insubordination, unauthorized leave ("French furloughs," soldiers called them), and cowardice. A New Jersey soldier described the procedure: "A bayonette or piece of wood was placed in his mouth and a string tied behind his ears kept it in position;" after that, the man was "seated on the ground with his knees drawn up to his body. A piece of wood is run through his legs, and placing his arms under the stick on each side of his knees, his hands are then tied in front, and he is as secure as a traped rat."[41]

Such a punishment extended over several hours and was excruciatingly painful. It produced cramps and thirst while subjecting the culprit to a chorus of derisive remarks from passing soldiers. A Pennsylvania soldier who fled the field at Spotsylvania received this penalty. In addition, he was placed in front of regimental headquarters; the man's company passed in single file and, under orders from the colonel, each man spat in the face of the coward. This was considered ample justice.[42]

Courts-martial were in session throughout the war. Usually the court consisted of eight officers appointed by a division commander. The officers were generally company commanders (captains and sometimes lieutenants). Another officer, the judge advocate, served as prosecutor. The defendant was entitled to have legal counsel, but as often as not the accused defended himself. All of this was well and good, but the Civil War created a situation that quickly made a log jam of the court-martial system.

The overnight mobilization of tens of thousands of civilians totally unfamiliar with—and resentful of—army behavior led to an epidemic of pending court cases. Once military campaigning began, however, officers were so needed at the front that finding enough capable ones to serve as judges was a constant problem. So was scheduling a court time convenient to all parties. As delays mounted, likewise did the risks that witnesses would be killed or lost in the shuffle of war. Finally, the failure to bring culprits promptly to trial and to mete out sure and rapid punishment weakened the court-martial structure on both sides.

Many officers therefore took the matter of justice into their own hands; and when such occurred, punishments tended to be harsh for two reasons: the officer passed judgment while his anger was high, and he generally inflicted a penalty that he thought would deter similar offenses in the future.

Being dishonorably discharged and drummed out of service were humiliations usually inflicted on some cowards, deserters, as well as men convicted of gross insubordination. When this punishment was employed, the guilty man was brought before his brigade, which was drawn up in a two-column formation. The sentence was formally read, after which the man's head was shaved and the buttons and insignia ripped from his uniform. He was then marched between the rows of his comrades, each man standing silently with lowered musket. One or more soldiers behind the convicted man would prod him along with bayonets, while a band played the "Rogue's March:"

Poor old soldier—poor old soldier
Tarred and feathered
And then drummed out
Because he wouldn't soldier.[43]

Very rarely were prisoners sentenced to perform extra guard duty. As one Confederate general explained, "Standing guard is the most honorable duty of a soldier, except fighting, and must not be degraded."[44]

Capital punishment occurred more times in the Civil War than in all other American wars combined. Of some five hundred men shot or hanged by order of court-martial in the 1861–1865 period, almost two-thirds of them were executed for the crime of desertion. Lack of adequate discipline, prevailing individualism, and proximity to home were basic reasons why one of every ten Federals and one of every seven Confederates deserted the armies. Presidents Lincoln and Davis, as well as commanding generals, utilized proclamations of pardon, general amnesties, and impassioned pleas to try and persuade absentees to return to the armies.

The efforts were futile. At the beginning of 1865, over 420,000 soldiers North and South were absent from their commands. A sizable percentage of those absences was justified for one reason or another, but the majority of them were not. Since the chances were about three to one that a deserter could make a successful escape from the army, disgruntled soldiers took advantage of both the opportunities and the odds.

Desertion followed a natural and chronological pattern in the Civil War. On both sides the desertion rate was lowest at the outset of the struggle, then increased steadily as the war progressed until it reached highest levels in the last year of hostilities. The high proportion of desertion on the Union side in 1864–1865 was attributable in large part to the huge influx of conscripts, reluctant recruits, and men whose patriotism was bought with bounties. Concern over tightening affairs at home, and pleas from loved ones, became major factors that spurred desertions.

A New England officer asserted that desertion was "encouraged and aided by letters and citizens' clothing from relatives or acquaintances at home." Indeed, a favorite system by a Northern soldier was to inform the family that he wished to come home. Loved ones then mailed him a box of civilian clothing. The soldier donned that garb at an opportune moment, slipped away from camp, and usually was not seen again. More poignantly was a Virginia artilleryman's diary entry for January 8, 1864: "Saw a man shot today for desertion. Poor fellow! His crime was only going home to see after his wife and children. It was his third or fourth offense."[45]

Punishments for desertion became more severe as the war continued. Commanders initially treated desertion cases more as delinquencies than as felons. When the crime remained unabated, the penalties increased. A convicted deserter in 1862 might be branded on the hip with the letter "D" and then dismissed from service. Sometimes a prison term was added to the branding and dismissal.

These punishments had little effect in stemming the steady leakages from the army. In March 1865, Private Luther Mills of North Carolina wrote from the trenches at Petersburg: "It is useless to conceal the truth any longer. Most of our people at home have become so demoralized that they write to their husbands, sons and brothers that desertion *now* is not *dishonorable*."[46]

Chaplain Thomas H. Davenport of the 3rd Tennessee wrote after watching fourteen deserters shot to death at one time: "I think they were objects of pity, they were ignorant, poor, and had families dependent upon them. War is a cruel thing, it heeds not the widow's tear, the orphan's moan, or the lover's anguish."[47]

Southerners felt the ravages of civil war far more severely than Northerners. Shortages of basic needs ranging from food and medicine to clothing and money, out-of-control inflation, lack of adequate menfolk to maintain the home front, and depravations by invading Federal armies were but some of the factors that combined to bring painful hardships on the Confederate population in general and its rural classes in particular. That entreaties from home had a major impact on soldiers was emotionally evident at the court-martial of North Carolina Private Edward Cooper. Introduced at his trial for desertion was this letter he had received from his wife: "My dear Edward—I have always been proud of you, and since your connection with the Confederate army, I have been prouder of you than ever before. I would not have you do anything wrong for the world, but before God, Edward, unless you come home we must die. Last night I was aroused by little Eddie's crying. I called and said, 'What is the matter, Eddie?' and he said 'O Mamma, I am so hungry.' And Lucy, Edward, your darling Lucy, she never complains, but she is getting thinner and thinner every day. And before God, Edward, unless you come home, we must die."[48]

The letter saved Cooper from a firing squad. Others were not so fortunate. Courts-martial for capital offenses were a regular part of army routine starting at the midway point of the war. Some commanders, unwilling or impatient with the lengthy procedure involved in legally condemning a soldier to death, took matters into their own hands. A Massachusetts colonel, acting alone as a drumhead court, once pronounced a captured deserter from his regiment guilty as charged and ordered his immediate execution. The man was shot two days later, without his case passing through channels. Desertion in the regiment decreased noticeably thereafter.[49]

The case of Frank McElhenny is illustrative of a capital crime in the Civil War and the execution that followed.

McElhenny was a product of the Boston slums. He endured a bitter, hard youth and entered the Union army in November 1861, after reportedly killing a neighbor. Records listed him as an eighteen-year-old teamster when he became a member of Company F, 24th Massachusetts. McElhenny, one of his officers testified, was "from the start a troublesome, insubordinate soldier." In the spring of 1862, he "got into trouble with his officers" and was jailed at New Berne, North Carolina. Shortly thereafter, McElhenny escaped from the guardhouse and disappeared.

One afternoon two years later, a Confederate soldier dashed to safety into the Federal lines at Deep Bottom, Virginia. The Southern deserter was McElhenny, and with incredibly bad luck he came into the Union lines at exactly the point where Company F of the 24th Massachusetts was on picket. Instantly recognized, McElhenny was subsequently court-martialled for desertion to the enemy and sentenced to death by firing squad.

Monday, August 8, 1864, was hot and cloudless. In midafternoon, McElhenny's brigade formed three sides of a square two columns deep. At the open end was a freshly dug grave. Two firing parties of twelve men each had been chosen by lot from Company F. The first squad would carry out the sentence; the second would act as a backup squad, if needed. In each of the two groups was a musket loaded only with powder; no one in either party knew who had the harmless weapons.

Suddenly that afternoon, stated a chaplain in attendance, the oppressive silence of the clearing "was broken by a low, soft, plaintive strain of music, which came floating on the sultry air across the plain, from beyond the rise of ground in the direction of the camp we had left. It was the sound of a funeral dirge from muffled drums, with the subdued notes of an accompanying band. A funeral dirge, for a living man! Hearts quickened, and hearts stood still, at the sound.

"A cart drawn by a pair of white horses bore the condemned soldier, seated on his coffin, accompanied by a kindly priest, while a military escort marched on each side with arms reversed, as though the man were already dead. The firing party, the guard, and the music, completed the gloomy procession. It was nearly half a mile away, and it seemed a long, long while in coming.

"Low and soft as the breathings of an aeolian harp, mournful and oppressive as a midnight funeral knell, the approaching music rose and fell in swelling and dying cadences, while listening ears ached in sympathy and waiting hearts throbbed in responsive tenderness. It was hard to bear. Faces paled and hands shook which were not accustomed to show fear; and officers and men alike would have welcomed a call to battle in exchange for that terrible inaction in the sight of coming death."

McElhenny had been jocular and defiant up to that point; but as he descended from the wagon and was led to the coffin now lying beside the grave, he displayed a mixture of fear and repentance. Prisoner and priest knelt beside the grave in prayer. An officer advanced and read the proceedings of the court-martial. Provost guards then bound McElhenny's arms, placed him in a kneeling position on the rough pine coffin, and wrapped a white handkerchief around his eyes.

Quickly the firing party moved to within several paces of the condemned prisoner, and with equal speed the officer in charge gave the commands "Ready! Aim! Fire!" A sharp explosion of musketry shattered the silence. McElhenny tottered for a moment, then pitched forward to the ground. Two surgeons examined the victim. Five bullets had pierced the chest; but a pulse still beat, and there was a low respiration. The second firing party rushed forward as McElhenny was propped against the casket. A second volley sent eight bullets tearing through the deserter and snuffed out the remaining life.

So that every aspect of the execution might serve as an unforgettable deterrent, the entire brigade was thereupon formed in column and marched slowly past what one soldier termed "a gory, ghastly sight, lying where it fell." A member of the burial detail summarized the execution's final events: "The body was placed face downward in the box and lowered into the grave. The grave was then filled and the earth levelled. No mound or headboard marked the spot where the deserter was lying. Such was the ignominious ending."[50]

In a distressing number of instances, executions were horribly botched. Most Civil War soldiers were mediocre marksmen at best; and when forced by orders to shoot an unarmed comrade, their accuracy could be terribly erratic.

Problems of Discipline

A case in point occurred December 21, 1864, when five convicted deserters from the 1st Connecticut Heavy Artillery were to be shot at the same time near Laurel Hill, Virginia. The condemned men, under guard and wearing balls and chains, shuffled onto the field where three Union brigades were formed in a U-shaped "hollow square." Each man was placed in a standing position beside freshly dug, parallel graves. The charges and sentences of the court-martial were read, after which a chaplain prayed briefly with each prisoner. The five men were blindfolded. Firing squads of twelve men each silently took position about twenty-five yards from the culprits. Reserve squads of the same number took their places in the rear. The provost marshal dropped a white handkerchief, and sixty muskets fired in unison. A New Hampshire officer in attendance described what happened thereafter.

"We looked towards the graves, but to our astonishment each man yet remained standing, showing conclusively that the detail had fired high. The second or reserve detail was at once marched into position while the first detail retired to the place occupied by the reserve, and at the same signal the smoke puffed from their carbines, and their fire proved more accurate, but not entirely effective. The prisoners all fell. Three were dead, while two were trying hard to rise again, and one of them even got upon his knees, when a bullet from the revolver of the provost marshall sent him down. Again he attempted to rise, getting upon his elbow and raising his body nearly to a sitting posture, when a second bullet in the head from the marshal's revolver suddenly extinguished what little life was left and a third shot put out the life of the second prisoner, thus ending the execution."[51]

It is easy but erroneous to conclude from the preceding that crime and punishment were widespread in Civil War armies. Discipline was not always as bad as it seemed. Units on both sides were supposed to give prompt obedience to orders; their failure to do so attracted more attention than regiments exhibiting good conduct. The misbehavior that appears so often in soldiers' letters and reminiscences is there in large part because it was the exception to normal soldier behavior. Yet it was a prevalent enough exception to be regarded as an integral part of army life in the 1860s.

While troops of that era could punish their own numbers cruelly, they were equally capable of displaying friendship—and even compassion—toward the enemy. America has never known a war where fraternization ran so rampant. "It was curious to observe the sort of *entente cordiale* which the soldiers on both sides established during the siege," a Vermonter wrote of the Port Hudson, Louisiana, campaign. "When they were tired of trying to pick each other off through the loop-holes, one of them would tie a white handkerchief to his bayonet and wave it above the parapet. Pretty soon a handkerchief, or its equivalent . . . would be seen on the other side. This meant truce. In a moment the men would swarm out on both sides, sitting with their legs dangling over the parapet, chaffing each other . . . "[52]

Antipathy between Federals and Confederates varied considerably with individuals and circumstances. Some soldiers regarded their enemy with deep hatred from beginning to end, while others acquired bitterness toward the foe through military experiences. During the siege of Petersburg, Northern and Southern earthworks were within voice-call of one another. One day a Federal put his hat and shirt on a ramrod and raised them above the trench. From across the way came a shout: "It won't do, Yank, your neck is too skinny! Place your head under the hat and we'll accomodate you!"[53]

The majority of men on both sides never felt any strong animosity toward those "across the way." The reasons for this are not difficult to ascertain. Opposing forces spoke the same language; they had the same likes and dislikes, the same backgrounds and cultures, the same roots in America's soil. A private in the 85th Illinois wrote that opposing pickets in the Atlanta campaign agreed not to shoot at one another. They left their guns, "shuck" hands and swapped "canteens and caterages." The same soldier informed his homefolk: "Now you might think that strange but I cant help but be just friendly to one of them as I would to one of my own country."[54]

Kinfolk fighting on opposite sides promoted fraternization. So did a general unawareness in the ranks of the deep issues that had sparked the conflict, camp boredom, and war weariness as the struggle dragged on interminably. Common desires among soldiers for Northern coffee and Southern tobacco contributed to friendly relations. And because the Civil War was a series of battles with much idle time between contests, not only was anger difficult to sustain during lulls but ample opportunity also existed to become acquainted with counterparts across a field or on the other side of a river.

Friendly intercourse between Johnny Rebs and Billy Yanks was in evidence as early as the summer of 1861. When the Potomac River was all that separated Union and Confederate forces, long-distance shouting opened "negotiations" between outposts. A member of the 15th

Massachusetts wrote home: "We have agreed with the pickets on the opposite shore, who are Mississippians, not to fire at each other, but be on friendly terms as long as they are posted as pickets. . . . Yesterday, one of our boys agreed to meet one of the Mississippians half-way across the river and exchange newspapers. . . . I have just learned that one of the Mississippians is coming over in a boat to take dinner with the boys today."[55]

In 1862 the fraternization increased. Federal General Darius N. Couch reportedly issued an order for his men not to fire on the Confederate picket-line because it was "nothing but murder to kill a poor picket while on duty." On one occasion in Tennessee, opposing pickets were so close as to overlap. An irate Iowa officer walked out, informed the Confederates that they were too close, and personally placed one Reb several yards farther back. At that, a Southerner shouted happily: "Here is a kettle of fish. This Yankee is posting both his own picket and ours!"[56]

Military campaigns occupied the spring, summer, and autumn months of that year, and the bloodshed that ensued would seem to have put a permanent end to fraternization. It did not. During the long winter of 1862–1863, as two mighty hosts faced each other along the Rappahannock River, "trade was opened up. Sugar, coffee, tobacco, newspapers, and lies were the chief commodities freely swapped all along the river front." One particular sector became known as "Outpost Liar."[57]

Opposing soldiers regularly visited each other's lines that winter. Confederate General John B. Gordon wrote somewhat indignantly of catching a group of Yankees in a Southern camp and of ordering their arrest and transfer to a military prison. Yet the Confederates pled almost tearfully with Gordon to rescind the order. They had given their word, they exclaimed, that the Yanks would be safe. Gordon finally relented, ordered the bluecoats to return to their side of their river, and warned them not to make any other visits.[58]

After the two armies in the East returned to Virginia from Gettysburg, a Massachusetts soldier noted that the pickets on both sides "became more friendly than ever, often exchanging courtesies, and chatting freely on matters pertaining to the war."[59]

Three years of camp and battle weariness, coupled with immobile siege operations at Atlanta and Petersburg, are the major explanations why 1864 witnessed the greatest degree of fraternization. Loss of enthusiasm for the struggle certainly was in the mind of a Confederate who leaped from his breastwork at Spotsylvania one day and dashed toward the Union line. He had almost made it when a Union bullet sent him sprawling. "I'm so sorry you shot me," he moaned to Federals who came to take him into the lines. "I was coming over to take the oath of allegiance."

His captors apologized for the misunderstanding and explained that there was no oath of allegiance at hand. One Billy Yank remarked that all he had at the moment was a canteen with a little whiskey in it.

"That will do just as well," the Confederate replied eagerly. "I surrender."[60]

In late August 1864, while in front of Atlanta, Private Laforest Dunham of the 129th Illinois wrote his parents: "We maid a bargain with the rebs not to shoot at one annother heare on the scourmish line unless one side or the other went to advance, so it makes it mutch plesanter." A Pennsylvania soldier described the full extent of fraternization present during the besiegement of Petersburg. "Although intercourse with the enemy was strictly forbidden," he stated, "the men were on the most friendly terms, amicably conversing and exchanging such commodities as coffee, sugar, tobacco, corn meal and newspapers.

"It was a singular sight to see the soldiers of the two great hostile armies walking about unconcernedly within a few yards of each other, with their bayonets sticking in the ground, bantering and joking together, exchanging the compliments of the day and even saluting officers of the opposing forces with as much ceremony, decorum and respect as they did their own. The keenest sense of honor existed among the enlisted men of each side. It was no uncommon sight, when visiting the picket posts, to see an equal number of 'graybacks' and 'bluebellies,' as they facetiously termed each other, enjoying a social game of euchre or seven-up and sometimes the great national game of draw poker, with army rations and sutler's delicacies as the stakes."[61]

Soldiers often found it unbearable to fire unexpectedly on acquaintances in the other trenches. If suddenly ordered to deliver volleys at friends across the way, troops would often holler: "Look out, Johnny!" or "Hunt your holes, Billy, I'm going to shoot!" A fusillade would take place for some length of time—generally until the officers were satisfied. Then, wrote an eyewitness to such a scene, "the boys from both sides would walk around us as leisurely as if there was not an enemy in a thousand miles."[62]

The longer the armies were immobile and near one another, the more pronounced the fraternization became. One day at Petersburg,

Federal General Samuel W. Crawford climbed atop a parapet and be-gan surveying the Confederate positions through a telescope. A couple of moments later, a rock bounced into the Union rifle pit. Around the stone was a piece of paper on which were the words: "Tell the fellow with the spy glass to clear out or we shall have to shoot him."[63]

Incredibly, there was even an unwritten code of honor among Civil War soldiers "that forbade the shooting of men while attending to the imperative calls of nature."[64]

Men of blue and gray alike were capable of extreme kindnesses to the enemy. One of the most startling examples of this occurred Christmas Day, 1864. A Michigan captain and ninety of his men loaded several wagons with foodstuffs to take to Georgia civilians rendered destitute by the ravages of war. The Yankees tied tree branches to the heads of the mules to make them "resemble" reindeer as they gaily distributed food to thankful Southerners.[65]

Nor were acts of mercy by enemy soldiers unusual. The compassion displayed at Fredericksburg by Sergeant Richard Kirkland of South Carolina, thereafter known as the "Angel of Marye's Heights," are im-mortalized in prose and bronze. Patrick McNeil of Parker's Virginia Battery saw a wounded Federal lying in front of the guns at Gettys-burg. McNeil risked his life to drag the soldier into the safety of the lines; and as he was completing his deed, a cannonball ripped off both his legs. "Oh, my poor wife and children!" McNeil screamed just before he died."[66]

Of course, compassion and friendly feelings never approached the hatred that prevailed between opposing armies. Countless soldiers har-bored a real hatred, even in winter encampments when action was minimal. Writing of a minor skirmish with Federals early in March 1864, G. W. Waggoner of the 20th Tennessee stated: "I am fond of that [skirmish] duty. I fired several rounds at the sons of bitches if I should say such a word. I cant tell whether I hit one or not but I tride like the devil."[67]

Verbal exchanges could sometimes be barbed. Describing one period in the siege of Vicksburg, Illinois soldier Henry Schafer wrote his wife: "Sometimes one party would tell the other to look out they were going to shoot when bang would go the gun and then the one shot at would laugh and tell the other he shot too high or too low as the case would be. They would curse and blackguard each other almost all the time they were firing." In his diary at this same time, Schafer noted: "It is quite laughable to listen to their conversation. If our boys tell them anything which they do not believe they will say it is a damned lie. They will call us damned yankee sons of bitches and everything else of the kind."[68]

In spite of the horror and hardness produced by the war, however, fraternization persisted to such a degree as to give commanding generals on both sides deep concern throughout the Civil War. "Johnny Reb and Billy Yank had great respect for each other," a Virginian stated simply.[69] Men of blue and gray looted, they killed, they robbed corpses; and yet deep within most Civil War participants was an absence of animosity, and that lack of smoldering resentment goes far in explaining why North and South were able to come back together after a war that tore the nation asunder.

· 8 ·

The Grimmest Reaper

Corinth, Mississippi, in early May 1862, seemed like a frightening dream come true. A two-day bloodbath had occurred a month earlier at Shiloh, a dozen miles to the north. Now sinister yellow flags denoting the Confederate hospital corps hung limply over hotels, public buildings, schools, churches, and dozens of private homes. Yet the facilities were woefully inadequate for 20,000 sick and wounded soldiers. Men howling in agony or silently awaiting death were sprawled on sidewalks, front porches, and railroad platforms. Every clearing, every open space where a sick man could be laid full length, was seemingly in use.

Surgeons were so few in number as to be at times nonexistent. Medical supplies were low; lack of food was producing malnutrition at an alarming rate; the available water, a reporter noted, "smells so offensively that the men have to hold their noses while drinking it." Mud and human excrement, mixed together, extended in every direction. Erysipelas and dysentery were out of control. In addition to typhoid fever raging through the town, an outbreak of measles was fast reaching epidemic proportions. A volunteer nurse on reaching Corinth lamented: "Alas! Nothing that I had ever heard or read had given me the faintest idea of the horrors witnessed here. . . . Certainly, none of the glories of the war were presented here. But I must not say that; for if uncomplaining endurance is glory, we had plenty of it."[1]

More Confederates died of illness during the seven-week aftermath at Corinth than fell in the two days of intense fighting at Shiloh. Yet this was anything but an isolated tragedy in the Civil War. Calamities of a similar degree were an aftermath of every major battle. Barely five months after Shiloh, a youthful member of the 84th New York informed his parents following the bloodbath at Antietam Creek: "all the way from frederick and in every church, stable, hemty houses was full of wonded men with legs and arms of . . . and dount you think that is aenought to see."[2]

For three days in July 1863, Union and Confederate armies mangled each other at Gettysburg, Pa. One medical inspector wrote that the week following the battle was "the occasion of the greatest amount of human suffering known to this nation since its birth." Some 22,000 injured soldiers were jammed into a town of 2,000 inhabitants. The number awaiting treatment grew so large that surgeons grimly separated the wounded into two groups: those who were obviously going to die, and those who had a chance of being saved. The former were taken into woods and laid in rows. There, semiconscious, they moaned and twitched painfully while waiting alone for the end.

A young Quakeress who answered the frantic call for nurses was shocked on her arrival at Gettysburg. The foul stench of infection and death was overpowering. It was an atmosphere, she wrote, that "robbed the battlefield of its glory, the survivors of their victory, and the wounded of what little chance of life was left to them."[3]

Disease and disability were constant companions of the men of blue and gray from the outset of the war. In December 1861, Company A of the 44th Tennessee arrived at Bowling Green, Kentucky. Its inexperienced captain ordered the unit to bivouack in an open expanse outside town. The troops did not know it was low ground until the entire encampment went under water a day later from an icy rainstorm. A third of the men promptly fell ill with intense chills. A steady number began dying in the camp's crude infirmary. The survivors were ordered to return to Nashville. They rode in drafty freight cars, received no medical aid en route, arrived in Nashville during a sleetstorm, and were abandoned at the depot. All were "wet and chill[ed] Beyond reason," one of the Tennesseans wrote, and several of his comrades "fainted and Died Before they go to their hospital."

A month later, a Michigan soldier in the same area commented: "From two to four dies evry day from the many diseases around." A South Carolina surgeon, then stationed at Richmond, asserted that the sick were "dying by the thousands."[4]

When a Virginia private wrote home that he "had rather face the Yankees than the sickness and there is allways more men die from sickness than in battle," he was sadly correct in his analysis. Just being in the army killed more men than were slain in battle. Total Union deaths in the war were 360,222 men. Only about 110,000 of these deaths were enemy-induced; the remaining quarter of a million came largely from disease. The Confederate side did not maintain complete figures. However, some 258,000 Southern soldiers perished in the war. According to conservative estimates, three-fourths of them succumbed to sickness.[5]

Union statistics show 6,454,834 *recorded* cases of wounds and disease, and that figure only begins to highlight the suffering present in the conflict of the 1860s.[6]

Several factors explain the high incidence of sickness and disease in Civil War armies.

The ease with which a man could enter the army in the first stages of the war, and the poor condition of many volunteers taken into service, were initial factors. Physical examinations in the beginning were a sham. The basic if not sole requirement of a potential soldier seems to have been that he possess all of his limbs and most of his sensory organs. A man performing adequately in any civilian job was proof that he was fit for military duty.

Hence, near comical activities marked many so-called induction examinations. Recruits for the 5th Massachusetts received informal inspections from men who were not even physicians. Soldiers in the 27th Indiana never saw a surgeon until their first battle. One contract surgeon in Chicago "examined" a regiment by having the 1,000 men parade past him in rapid fashion in the rain. A New Jersey recruit penned a vivid picture of his unit's more thorough medical inspection. "The company was drawn up in line on one side of the room and when a man's name was called he would step up to the doctor, who put to him the following questions. Were you ever sick in your life, have you got the rhiumatism, have you got varicose veins, and other questions of like matters, instead of finding out for himself by actual examination wether you had or not. If the questions were answered in the affirmative and he had no reason to doubt it, he would give us a thump on the chest, and if we were not floored nor showed any other signs of inconvenience, we were pronounced in good condition and ordered to fall in on the other side of the room, where while waiting for the examination to end, we amused ourselves by grinning at each other."[7]

During 1861–1862 alone, some 200,000 men were accepted for service and discharged within a few months. One of every three members of the 39th New York was sent home before the regiment left its home state. A New England recruit mustered into service at the age of forty-four was discharged two years later at the age of sixty-two. "So fast do men grow old in active service!" a compatriot sneered.[8]

A Southern newspaper editor, attempting to explain the poor quality of so many volunteers, advanced the theory that the call to arms "brings to the field the most patriotic, but the most excitable and nervous portion of the population. These people, however gallant in the field, have rarely the constitution to stand the real burden of war." The medical director of the Union's Army of the Potomac disagreed in outspoken and blunt fashion. Complaining of the first waves of volunteers, he stated: "It seemed as if the Army called out to defend the life of the nation has been made use of as a grand eleemosynary institution for the reception of the aged and infirm, the blind, the lame, and the deaf, where they might be housed, fed, paid, clothed, and pensioned, and their townships relieved of the burden of their support."[9]

Once in the army, camp life did what physical examinations failed to do: namely, weed out those who could not measure up to soldier life. Johnny Rebs and Billy Yanks were in the wrong place at the wrong time. They not only went into the army just when the killing power of weapons was being brought to a new peak of efficiency, they also enlisted in the closing years of a period when the science of medicine was woefully imperfect. Thus, the Civil War soldier got the worst of it in two ways. When he fought, he was likely to be injured severely. When he was in camp, he lived under conditions that were apt to make him sick. In either case, he had no chance of getting the kind of medical treatment that a generation or so later would be routine. "The 34th is in bad shape," an Iowa soldier wrote in January 1863, "about nine tenths of the men are sick and such a discouraged and disheartened lot of men I never saw."[10]

Sickness, poor rations and insufficient medical care became the worst enemies that Civil War troops faced. These maladies played havoc on the regiment's effectiveness and strength, for a steady attrition of manpower began practically the moment they reached their first camp. Records for scores of regiments show that sickness had depleted the ranks as much as 50 percent before the unit saw action against the enemy. Taking one period as an example: in the autumn of 1862, the 22nd Massachusetts listed 915 men on its rolls—with 588 of them "absent sick." Six weeks after the 125th Ohio departed for war, it numbered only 572 men fit for duty. The 12th Connecticut headed southward with a full complement of 1,000 troops but was down to 600 men when it entered its first battle.[11]

Before soldiers heard the first hostile bullet, they encountered two onslaughts of sickness. The first were maladies normally associated with childhood. Most recruits were farm boys who left good health at home. Comparatively few of them had previously been exposed to chicken pox, measles, mumps, and whooping cough. These common communicable diseases struck immediately when the men congregated in large numbers, and they devastated units in quick fashion.

The worst of these illnesses, all soldiers agreed, was measles. A member of the 1st Maine recalled: "Though we enlisted to fight, bleed and die, nothing happened to us so serious as the measles." The disease struck with savage intensity. "It seemed that half or more of the army had the disease the first year of the war," a Virginia soldier wrote without exaggeration. Surgeons had no treatment to offer; they knew so little about measles that some of them attributed the malady to wheat straw used in the bunks.[12]

Surgeon Legrand Wilson of the 42nd Mississippi stated that the sudden onset of measles in his brigade "was something that astonished everyone, even the surgeons," in the summer of 1861. Over the three-month period that followed, 204 men in three regiments died from measles or its side effects. Wilson made his first visit to a tobacco warehouse where the afflicted had been sent. "About one hundred sick men crowded in a room sixty by one hundred feet in all stages of measles. The poor boys lying on the hard floor, with only one or two blankets under them, not even straw, and anything they could find for a pillow. Many sick and vomiting, many already showing unmistakable signs of blood poisoning."[13]

John Green of the 9th Kentucky survived the disease. Yet in the process, he stated, "I knew nothing for a few days & when my fever began to abate I could not speak above a whisper." One Confederate, recuperating from measles in late 1861, sent a slightly garbled report to his sweetheart. "The measels affected my lungs considerably and has left me with a wretched cough which I fear I shall not recover this winter." An Iowa surgeon felt that the disease left a lingering after-effect on soldiers. "These 'measly boys' were easily recognized for months by peculiar signs. They seemed of all the men to be most frequently and most easily impressed by other maladies . . . "[14]

Another equally feared disease was smallpox. In December 1861, Ira

Gillaspie of the 11th Michigan wrote in his diary: "Thare was a man died in the hospitlle. Some said he had the small pox. It raised an aufull excitement amongst the boys. Some was on the point of leaving. Well it come very near causing a general mutiny." For centuries, smallpox had been one of the most feared of diseases. It remained highly contagious and dangerous at the time of the Civil War. During one period of thirty months, 1,020 of 2,513 cases of smallpox in Virginia general hospitals proved fatal.[15]

Physicians sought to control smallpox through isolation of cases and a fifteen-day quarantine of anyone suspected of having the disease. Vaccination was used as much as possible, with human scabs the source for most vaccine. Yet this relatively new procedure was a long way from perfection. A Massachusetts soldier whose regiment had to undergo vaccination remembered: "Such a wholesale slashing and cutting of arms never was witnessed before. The commanding officer of each company would march up the men, all with bared arms. The doctor would make three or four passes with his knife, cutting through the skin, punch a little of the vaccinating matter into the wound, and the thing was done. The doctors went through the thousand men in about three hours, and the sore arms for ten days afterwards was a sight to behold." The entire 7th Rhode Island "was well-nigh disabled for service" following smallpox vaccination.[16]

While the troops struggled helplessly against these "childrens' diseases," they also had to withstand camp illnesses triggered by impure water, mosquitoes, exposure, poor food, and general filth. Such conditions bred the principal killers of the Civil War: typhoid fever, malaria, diarrhea, and dysentery.

Typhoid fever was extremely prevalent early in the war, then tapered off in the armies as the sectional conflict progressed. That impure water and typhoid fever were inexorably linked was a theory of the future. A Texas surgeon, bemoaning an outbreak of typhoid in his regiment, added in the same letter: "We have had an awful time drinking the meanest water not fit for a horse (indeed I could hardly get my horse to drink it)."

The disease caused more than 17,000 Confederate deaths during an eighteen-month period. A Kentucky soldier who came down with "break bone fever" was "delirrious for days" but managed to recover. One of the regiments hardest hit by typhoid fever was the 23rd Massachusetts. In April 1862, while the unit was on duty near the North Carolina coast, typhoid fever struck so severely that only 150 of the 800

Bay Staters escaped the disease. A number of Civil War regiments—the 18th Virginia being a prime example—had more fatalities from typhoid fever than from battle.[17]

Writing from a Potomac River bottomland in 1862, a Connecticut soldier stated: "Malaria, like a nightmare, settled on the camp, crushing all energy and hope out of the men."[18] Soldiers referred to malaria as "the ague," "the shakes," and "intermittent fever." Surgeons knew little more about the disease. The prevailing theory at that time was that malaria originated from the poisonous vapors of nearby ponds. Burning tar in hospitals was considered the best preventive measure against the disease.

Malaria accounted for twenty percent of all sickness reported by Northern and Southern surgeons. "Our soldiers, being unacclimated, rapidly succumbed to 'the shakes,' " a Billy Yank wrote from North Carolina, "and the morning [sick] call showed a rapid increase. Men were taken down sick, unfit for duty, who a few hours before felt all right; but with the shivers running down the spine, which a little later would turn to fever, they would throng to the doctor's tent." Fluctuating temperatures would continue for several days and generally until the man "had taken so much quinine that he was no longer able to master the 'hard tack' with his loosened teeth."[19]

Northern troops seemed more vulnerable to malaria. The 38th Iowa journeyed to Mississippi with 910 men. Eighteen months later, 311 had died and another 110 had been discharged as permanently incapacitated. The single cause of these staggering casualties was malaria.[20]

The most prevalent illness in all Civil War armies, however, was a combination of diarrhea and dysentery. "No matter what else a patient had," a surgeon noted of hospital admissions, "he had diarrhea." A recruit in the 57th North Carolina wrote his wife after being in service three months: "I think I look as well as Ever I wasent sick since I left home onley bad cole and caugh and the Bowel complaint that is nothing much in camp for they nearly all git it."[21]

In those days physicians made a simple differentiation between the two intestinal disorders. Loose bowels alone was diarrhea; loose bowels with blood denoted dysentery. The two diseases were labeled *alvine flux* and treated similarly. To the soldiers the ailment was diarrhea, "the bowel complaint," "Virginia Quick Steps," "Tennessee Trots," and "the runs."

An oft-repeated wartime assertion that "bowels are of more consequence than brains" was no attempt at humor. A greater number of soldiers died of diarrhea-type illnesses than fell in combat. If a man was "fortunate" to be discharged because of chronic diarrhea, a slang phrase was that "he hasn't got the guts to stand it."[22]

What to do about the disease was as uncertain as what caused it. Surgeons employed the full gauntlet of medical treatments, ranging from overdoses of drugs to cauterization of the anal opening. Such procedures too often proved fatal. A case in point was Private John Leopold of the 74th Pennsylvania. On October 12, 1863, Leopold was admitted to a Philadelphia general hospital after suffering with chronic diarrhea for three months. Physicians prescribed heavy doses of lead acetate, opium, aromatic sulfuric acid, tincture of opium, silver nitrate, belladonna, calomel, and ipecac. When Leopold showed no improvement, he received steaming mustard plasters to the chest area. Leopold died after two weeks of treatment.[23]

Another factor that bred so much illness among Civil War soldiers was normal camp conduct. Encampment sites were selected primarily for military reasons and rarely for health considerations. Locations tended to be used repeatedly, and more often than not for months at a time. Inadequate drainage, an ignorance of sanitation practices, and the natural carelessness associated with army life, abounded.

Regulations specifically called for the daily washing of hands and feet, plus a complete bath once a week. Not a soldier, North or South, who served in the field complied with that directive. Lacking soap, warm water and opportunities, the men would go for months without any semblance of a bath—either for themselves or for their clothing.

A popular joke in the 92nd Illinois late in 1862 concerned the soldier who lost his socks, searched everywhere for them in vain, and then decided to go ahead and bathe his feet anyway. He found that he was wearing his socks after washing away "one thickness of dirt." When the colonel of the 70th New York ordered his grubby troops to undergo short haircuts, he discovered that "the pile of dirt disclosed beneath the earlocks of some must have been accumulating all winter and . . . would grow a hill of corn."[24]

Every campsite had (or was supposed to have) several latrines. These "sinks" were straddle trenches 30 feet long, 2½ feet wide, and 3 feet deep. In front of each—according to orders but rarely enforced—was to be "a screen of boughs so arranged as to secure a degree of privacy and decency for the proper performance of natural functions common to all humanity."[25] Fresh dirt was to be added to the pit daily.

A number of things made the latrines not only ineffective but dangerous as well. Little attention was given to the fact that many of the "sinks" were located upstream from the camps. Most men had a shyness in being seen in an open field in an undignified position. Moreover, the odor grew increasingly repulsive with time. Soldiers therefore were inclined to answer nature's calls when and where they beckoned, which was usually in woods, behind boulders, or merely outside the tents. The resulting pollution was widespread, in every sense.

Uncollected garbage accumulated throughout camps and added to the problem. The emanations from slaughtered cattle and sheep, the rubbish from field kitchens, and the like all combined to produce what one writer termed "an olfactory sensation which has yet to be duplicated in the Western Hemisphere."[26]

This contaminated atmosphere led in turn to hordes of flies, mosquitoes, lice, and fleas, which themselves became hazards to health. Vermin swarmed wherever an army assembled. The human body was their favorite habitat. In 1863 a New York soldier wrote in his diary: "Some of our men are well Stocked with Vermin. I Saw [a] coat that was a Sight to behold. The Seems and even the lining was matted with Nats and Some of [the] largest Lice that I ever Saw. they must have been well fed."[27]

An Iowa sergeant, writing at almost the same time, noted: "I have seen men literally wear out their underclothese without a change and when they threw them off they would swarm with Vermin like a live Ant hill when disturbed." A Massachusetts infantryman asserted somewhat glibly: "Our new position would furnish an excellent study for the naturalist. Every species in the bug and insect line, that can kick, jump, bite, or sting, is here represented in astonishing numbers."[28]

Mosquitoes "seem resolved to take me dead or alive," a Confederate soldier once snorted. A compatriot in the siege of Petersburg solemnly informed his mother: "An officer who is located near me here sends the worst cases he has for punishment to the picket lines in the swamp to fight and be fought by, not Yankees but mosquitoes. They are not allowed to take their guns lest shooting at and being shot at by the Yankees might divert their minds from the agony. No wonder the inhabitants of the James River low ground look pale and sallow after having their veins depleted by these merciless blood-letters."[29]

Lice were an even worse nuisance. A member of the 10th Confederate Cavalry, in a letter home, reported of a comrade: "Mr. Brown says he is getting very home sick the body lice bothers him very bad you ort to see him rakeing and scratching and cracking them." According to an Illinois captain, General William T. Sherman became so concerned on one long march that the "graybacks" would bodily carry off his army that he ordered the ranks to halt so that every man could divest himself of the pests.[30]

A Virginia soldier wrote of the embarrassing introduction to lice in the autumn of 1861: "At first the soldier was mortified and almost felt disgraced when he discovered the van-guard of the coming crowd upon his person. Their crawling made his flesh creep; their attacks inflamed his blood and skin. He made energetic efforts to hide the secret and eliminate the cause; he would quietly and with an abstracted air most artfully withdraw from the company of his comrades, and then with considerable alacrity . . . steal out into the woods. Once hidden from the eyes of men he lost no time in pursuing and murdering with a vengeful pleasure the lively descendants of Egypt's third plague, flattering himself the while, poor soul, that he would then have peace and comfort of mind and body, and be able to hold his head up once more before his fellows. On his stealthy way back he would be sure to run in on a dozen solitary individuals, who did their best to look unconcerned, as if indeed they were in the habit of retiring into the dim recesses of the forest for meditation and self communion."[31]

"Hunting graybacks" quickly became a daily and unconcealed morning chore for most soldiers. Another popular remedy was to boil clothes in water. Still another method was to hold shirts and trousers directly over a fire (which at least guaranteed them an intense smoky odor for days thereafter). Turning one's shirt inside out, a Billy Yank observed, at least forced the vermin to make "a day's march" before locating their victim again. James Phillips of the 92nd Illinois saw futility in all such labors. "I change shirts and boil the gray backs pretty well which is death to most of them but there is jenerly enough kept for seed somewhere in the co[mpany]." Virginia infantryman Ted Barclay was appalled at the lice he discovered on himself. To his sister he confessed: "This evening I caught between 50 and 100 on my shirt and drawers. Excuse plain speaking but it is certainly not an *exaggerated* state of affairs."[32]

If possible, fleas outnumbered lice. When an Illinois battery arrived at its first duty station in Kentucky, it discovered that the fleas were everywhere and, "without rations, ready on the arrival of the battery boys to help themselves to a rich feast on the well fed and fattened men, much to their dismay and torture." A mathematically inclined Ohio soldier asserted that he had "given about 100,000 a dishonorable discharge," but to no avail. Fleas became so bad in one Union division that the general posted a placard outside his headquarters: "All persons carrying uncles or aunts about their person are requested to keep away from this tent."[33]

Lack of proper clothing caused immeasurable suffering among Bill Yanks and—especially—Johnny Rebs. Exposure to the elements brought colds, which in turn could trigger bronchitis, pneumonia, and/or death. Tents and oilcloths were never in abundance. Worn government-issue uniforms offered little protection from the icy blasts of winter. In February 1862, Cyrus Boyd of the 15th Iowa noted in his diary: "Uniforms in bad light—feet wet and cold and patriotism down to zero." Late in 1864, after the Confederate army retreated from Nashville, Resinor Etter of a Tennessee regiment stated: "It snowed very hard and the ground was hard froze my feet suffered much as I was barefooted . . . It was so cold I came nigh freezing."[34] Soldiers wrote casually in every winter of the war of rising in the morning with blankets and haversacks white from frost, and with a solid cake of ice in their canteens.

Union soldiers likened the winter of 1862–1863 around Fredericksburg, Virginia, to the agony of the Continental Army at Valley Forge. A member of the 13th New Hampshire observed: "It is fearful to wake at night, and to hear the sounds made by the men about you. All night long the sounds go up of men coughing, breathing heavy and hoarse with half-choked throats, moaning and groaning with acute pain. . . . This camp of 100,000 men is practically a vast hospital."[35] Untold numbers of men during the war froze to death while huddled around skimpy campfires.

Exacerbating all of these conditions were the critical need for army surgeons and the limited knowledge of medical care. The Union forces had 11,000 surgeons, the Confederate armies but 2,600 physicians. This broke down to the North having one surgeon per 133 men and in the South to one surgeon per 324 men. Close personal attention to a single ill soldier was all but out of the question.

Furthermore, no one in America at that time had any experience in the handling of large-scale medical problems as would develop inside the huge armies of the Civil War. Heading the U.S. Medical Department in 1861 was Colonel Thomas Lawson. A veteran of the War of 1812 and over eighty years of age, Lawson was a penny-pincher more concerned with budgets than with medical advances. He regarded the purchase of medical books to be crass extravagance. In answer to an 1862 request that a field hospital be established at Port Royal, South Carolina, the Surgeon-General denied the petition on the grounds that "the mild climate of South Carolina deletes the necessity of a hospital."[36]

The training of a majority of the physicians of that era further hampered the treatment of soldiers. Nearly all of the older surgeons had received their medical tutorage through apprenticeship with a practicing physician. The younger doctors (who comprised the bulk of Civil War army surgeons) had usually acquired a medical degree. However, that formal education was deceiving. Admission to medical school in those days required nothing more than an age stipulation and the ability to pay the tuition. Worse, medical school training was a two-year curriculum in which the second year was but a repetition of the first. Mastering what was known of medicine in the midnineteenth century could be learned in twelve months of study.

Small wonder that ignorance and assumption existed where understanding and knowledge would someday reside. As examples: little or nothing was known of germs; temperature was thought to be of so little importance to a man's condition that only twenty thermometers were used in all of the Union armies. Such things as X-rays, antibiotics, most vaccines, all vitamins, plus areas that comprise ninety percent of today's surgery, all were nonexistent in the 1860s. Most physicians were unfamiliar with the use of the scalpel and far less familiar with its life-saving potentialities.

Pneumonia was typical of an illness that perplexed the surgeons. Some physicians resorted to bleeding the patient by applying burning alcohol to the chest or slashing the man's wrists. Using external heat to "draw out" internal illness was a pet treatment of the time. When Ben Pearson, the elder member of a father-son team in the 36th Iowa, fell ill with "violent Congestion of the Stomach," he endured a painful siege. "for three hours, I suffered about all it was possible for me to suffer & live. Dr. Strong our Regtl. Surg., our Chaplain & my Son done all they could for me. they kept hot bricks to my feet & hot cloths on my stomach but the Cold clamy Sweat ran out at every poar cold as death. Oh such hours of suffering, but the Lord was with me praise his holy name."[37]

The practice of medicine for most physicians devolved into administering drugs and potions of all known types and in heavy quantities. In

The Grimmest Reaper

August 1861, Private Theodore Mandeville of the 5th Louisiana described to a friend the treatment he was receiving for a liver complaint. "I believe these damn quacks they have got for Drs. in this regt. are doing me more harm than good. They know nothing but Calomet & Quinine. . . . Yesterday they dosed me with Elixor of Vitriol and to day, intend giving me Iodine of Potash & paint me in the region of the liver with Iodine which burns like the devil."[38]

One dispenser in the 13th Massachusetts habitually plied ill men with castor oil while cheerily saying: "Down with it, my boy, the more you take the less I carry." Regulating the bowels, the kidneys, and the blood were the basic rudiments. One authority has stated: "If a dose of this or a dose of that could force a stool or provoke a healthy stream of urine, the result had to be salutary;" and so long as the dosages had a medical odor or interesting taste, they were considered beneficial.[39]

Favorite "medicines" for intestinal disorders were calomel, strychnine, castor oil, green persimmons, turpentine, blackberry juice, repeated doses of whiskey, a mercury and chalk compound known as "blue mass," and rainwater that had collected in tree stumps. A mixture of whiskey, quinine, and red pepper was thought to ward off colds. (It certainly must have performed wonders with clogged sinuses.) Mustard seed and hickory leaves were prescribed regularly after the first signs of pneumonia.

A favorite ministration for snakebite was whiskey and gunpowder. The former did not necessarily kill the venom, but the victim cared less with repeated doses. Confederate surgeons often administered a cure-all aptly named "Old Indigenous." It consisted of the bark of dogwood, poplar, and willow trees mixed with whiskey. The bitter taste was proof of its medicinal value. Among the more popular substitutes for quinine was boneset, "nature's herb remedy." One Confederate subjected to boneset was unimpressed. "Bitter, most bitter weed imaginable. It was used by soaking it in whisky. No one was ever made a drunkard by using this decoction and acquiring the taste."[40]

Calomel was the drug most given for ailments. Physicians regarded this mercury compound as a cathartic. It was administered so lavishly that mercury poisoning commonly resulted. The "wonder drug" of the Civil War was quinine. Its primary use was in the treatment and prevention of malaria. Yet surgeons also prescribed it for syphilis, rheumatism, diarrhea, or general fever—and when sufficient quantities were available, it was also used as a dentifrice and a hair tonic.

In February 1863, an ailing soldier in the 4th Louisiana summed up the medical situation in his regiment. "It is astonishing what an amount of ignorance there is amongst the Medical fraternity. The most of them will administer a large dose of calomel to the patient, it doesn't matter what his disease may be, without caring how much the constitution may be injured. Then comes dose after dose of quinine and other strong medicines until they either kill the individual or ruin his constitution for life." A newspaper correspondent wrote in similar vein: "Nine physicians out of ten scare their patients by long faces, looking at the tongue often, thumping the chest, shake their heads significantly, and dosing them with quinine and ipecac. The first makes you deaf and dumb, the other turns you inside out."

A sizable percentage of Johnny Rebs and Billy Yanks were openly contemptuous of their surgeons. On Christmas Eve, 1862, Private Henry Bear of the 116th Illinois wrote his wife: "The Damed Surgeons are not worth a Curse. They dont no any thing." Ten days later, Bear sneered that the army doctors "are perfect cuthroats. The bloody hounds would just as soon a man would die as not." Tennessee soldier Joseph Hoover never forgot delirious patients cursing "the Doctors for all they were worth;" and a half-century after the war another Tennesseean stated bitterly that "nine tenths of the Doctors ought to have been hung."[41]

On rare occasions, soldiers exacted a measure of "revenge" on a physician. A surgeon of the 20th New York proved to be so "decidedly gruff" that several of the troops seized him and repeatedly bounced him into the air with a tent fly. This come-uppance, one private observed, proved to be "a great blow to his vanity."[42]

Soldiers accused their surgeons of every form of malpractice. The most common charge leveled against them was drunkenness. Medicinal spirits in hospitals, coupled with the inept performances of surgeons on occasion, led to obvious and negative deductions.

Enough accidents caused by "the knife of a tipsy operator" occurred to give credence to some of these charges. In one example, a Union soldier bled to death on the operating table because the surgeon allegedly "was too drunk to take up the arteries." An inebriated Confederate surgeon set a broken leg and discovered a day later that he had treated the wrong limb. By the time corrections were made, it was too late. The injured soldier died of shock and complications.[43]

Surgeons understandably became the target of a host of uncomplimentary nicknames. "Sawbones," "Old Quinine," "Long John the Shoemaker," and "Loose Bowels" were some of the less offensive titles.

The Grimmest Reaper

A disgusted Pennsylvania infantryman once asserted: "Many of these fellows, if compelled to depend upon their profession in civil life, would have starved, but having, through the influence of political friends, been appointed army surgeons . . . blossomed out into miserable tyrants. Brutal as well as ignorant and careless of the poor soldiers placed in their care, they helped to fill many graves where our army marched."[44]

Such denunciations were not merely unfair; they were untrue. Mrs. Fannie Beers, a nurse in several Confederate hospitals, praised every doctor with whom she worked. "I never saw or heard of a more self-sacrificing set of men than the surgeons," she wrote. They were "devoted to their patients and as attentive as in private practice or as the immense number of sick allowed them to be." A Massachusetts soldier wounded in battle later stated of Northern surgeons: "Their sympathetic devotion, their professional skill, their unselfish, untiring energy, saved many a poor, mangled sufferer from an untimely grave."[45]

As a matter of fact, charges of incompetence and neglect made by soldiers usually vanished when the men shifted from the calmness of bivouac to the chaos of battle. In combat the soldiers beheld the handicaps under which surgeons labored. It became clear then that the great majority of army physicians were conscientious and hard-working men who sought to ease pain under the worst of circumstances.

Soldiers wounded in action generally suffered more than those who fell ill from disease. Getting prompt and proper battlefield attention was a rare thing in this war. So many crises faced the downed soldier that they can best be described by following him from the time he fell on the field.

His nightmare began with his first cries for help. If he were lucky, someone might respond to his calls within a few minutes. More often, however, he would wait unattended for hours; and in the case of major battles such as Shiloh, Second Manassas, and the Wilderness, he might lie ignored among the dead for several days. One of the most extreme examples of the latter occurred at the February 1862 battle of Fort Donelson, Tennessee. The weather was bitingly cold; and when medical personnel discovered a still-living Illinois soldier on the field a day or so after the action, they had to chop him loose from the frozen earth.[46]

Once found by friends or stretcher-bearers, the wounded man then started to a field hospital by one or two types of conveyance—either of which increased the agony.

Stretcher-bearers were supposed to provide immediate transportation, but their appearance on the field was a mixed blessing. These "angels of mercy," as the troops sarcastically termed them, were both undependable and unsympathetic. Each regiment had to furnish twenty-five to thirty men for stretcher duty. Naturally, the regimental commander was not going to detail his better men for rear-echelon service, so he usually assigned musicians, loafers, and rogues. This class, Dr. Frank Vickery of the 2nd Michigan charged, "were generally wretches," and "the less [the surgeon] calculates on aid from them, the better."[47] In many instances, stretcher-bearers hid or ran away from their duty at the first opportunity.

The other conveyance for a battle victim was by hospital wagon. There were never enough of these ambulances for the wounded. When a soldier did find room in one, the ride became verily a survival of the fittest. Ambulances were of two-wheeled or four-wheeled variety. The two-wheeled cart (which soldiers called "avalanche") was especially uncomfortable as it bounced, swayed, and jostled on even the smoothest ground. The four-wheeled ambulance was scant improvement, especially when six to ten suffering men were jammed onto the rough lumber boards of the wagon bed.

None of the wagons had springs. The broken, wooded country, and roads rutted by artillery and supply wagons, caused the hospital wagons to bounce constantly and painfully. Heavy downpours of rain—which seemed to follow every battle—caused wagons to become mired in the mud, during which wounded men were drenched by rain falling through the leaky canvas covers. The drivers were not always considerate of their passengers and often drove at breakneck speeds to get clear of the battle zone. Sometimes "blood trailed from the ambulances like water from an ice cart."[48]

Whether by stretcher, or wagon, or assisted by a comrade, the wounded soldier eventually reached the field hospital a mile or so behind the lines. This medical station was in fact a home or outbuilding that had a well or stream nearby. Straw, pine needles, or brush was scattered on the ground for patients. On a front porch, in a tent, or under the shade of a tree, the surgeons worked. Their tables were boards, the tailgate of a wagon, a door placed atop barrels or boxes—in short, anything on which the patient could be placed for surgery.

Dr. J. R. Weist of an Ohio regiment penned one of the most vivid descriptions of wounded soldiers at a field hospital. "There are a few tents and improvised tables . . . Wounded men are lying everywhere.

What a horrible sight they present! Here the bones of a leg or an arm have been shattered like glass by a minnie ball. Here a great hole has been torn into an abdomen by a grape shot. Nearby see that blood and froth covering the chest of one choking with blood from a wound of the lungs. By his side lies this beardless boy with his right leg remaining attached to his body only by a few shreds of blackened flesh. This one's lower jaw has been carried entirely away; fragments of shell have done this cruel work. Over yonder lies an old man, oblivious to all his surroundings, his grizzly hair matted with brain and blood slowly oozing from a great gaping wound in the head. Here is a bayonet wound; there a slash from a saber. Here is one bruised and mangled until the semblance of humanity is almost lost . . . This one has been crushed by the wheel of a passing cannon. Here is one dead, and over yonder another; they died while waiting for help that never came. Here are others whose quivering flesh contains balls, jagged fragments of shell, pieces of iron, and splinters of wood, from a gun blown to pieces by an exploding shell, and even pieces of bone from the head of a comrade who was torn to pieces by the explosion of a caisson. The faces of some are black with powder; others are blanched from loss of blood, or covered with the sweat of death. All are parched with thirst, and many suffer horrible pain; yet there are few groans or complaints."[49]

The relatively slow moving .57 caliber bullet of that day made a jagged and nasty wound. (A Michigan soldier once tried to downgrade the seriousness of being shot by informing a friend back home: "I hope you will pardon me for not wrighting before but a hole through my leg caused by a minney has caused me some inconvenicnce as it has kept me from doing enny verry big running around. the ball went in a little above my knee and came out just under my a-s so it made a pretty big hole.") If the wound was not in the torso or did not involve a fractured bone, one Virginia soldier asserted, treatment was simple. "Their wounds were bandaged with a handful of lint, over which was a bandage of cotton; then a canteen of water was placed in the patient's free hand, that he might keep the cloth always wet. In the other hand was a branch with which to wave the flies away."[50]

In addition to the extent of the injury, the limited knowledge of how to treat gunshot wounds reduced the surgeon's duties to three principal tasks. First, he probed for imbedded missiles—usually with his fingers in the interest of speed. The idea that damage done by the bullet might stretch beyond the bullethole was rarely considered. Second, the surgeon utilized a crude form of ligature to stop hemorrhaging. This consisted of applying a loop of threat around the ruptured artery and leaving one end of the thread dangling loosely. Some days later, the surgeon would exercise "judicious tugging" until the thread, having rotted, fell away. However, if a clot had not formed, or if infection had developed, such jerking could reopen the artery and bring speedy death to the patient.

The third option occupied the surgeon three-fourths of his time at a field hospital: he performed hasty amputations of limbs too mangled for repair.

Ether had come into use in 1846, chloroform five years later. Neither was always in ample supply. Instances were many when the only "anaethesia" used was a bullet or piece of wood thrust between the soldier's teeth to keep him from biting his tongue while the surgeon cut, sawed, and sutured. A New Jersey soldier who watched two amputations wrote of the patients: "Neither of them seemed to be under the influence of cloreform, but were held down by some four men, while nothing but a groan escaped them, as the operation proceeded."[51]

Screams of agony and pain, however, usually accompanied every case placed on the operating table. Such sounds were clearly audible to masses of prostrate men lying nearby on the ground and awaiting their turn.

More arms and legs were removed in the Civil War than at any other time in the nation's history. Confederate soldier Richard Slade considered himself lucky after a battle wound left a hand mangled. He informed the homefolk: "My fingers are getting better I did not have but one of them taken off the second one was broken & the Doctors insisted on taking it off but I would not let them & I saved my finger by this means. It looks rather hard to see them take off legs & arms & fingers & cut the men all into pieces but thank God they have not got only a small part of me."[52]

Of the disposition of severed limbs, a private in the 22nd Massachusetts being treated at one field hospital wrote: "A large hole was dug in the yard, about the size of a small cellar, and into this the legs and arms were thrown as they were lopped off by the surgeons, with a coolness that would be a terror to persons unaccustomed to the sights of military surgery after a battle. The day was hot and sultry, and the odor of the ether used in the operations and the effluvia from the receptacle of mangled limbs, was sickening in the extreme. Flies came down upon us in clouds, torturing us with their bite . . . "[53]

Surgeons of that day were convinced that suppuration was an essential part of healing. Therefore, what was known as "laudable pus" was encouraged as much as possible—even to the extent of tearing off scabs from a wound. In addition to probing injuries with ungloved fingers, the physicians went from case to case wiping their hands on dirty, often pus-laden rags. Bloodstained bandages were used over and over again; instruments went unwashed for days. More than one surgeon honed his scalpel on the sole of his shoe. Flies and other insects in the operating areas were considered a nuisance, not a danger.

Small wonder that a day or so after every engagement, a steady wave of deaths began from wound complications. Tennessee soldier W. W. Wilson wrote home from Corinth, Mississippi, a month after the battle of Shiloh: "theire is an A avredge A Bout four or five Deths Pur Day They Beary ten men Pur Day . . . I was at the graveyard yeasday and they aire still Buring ten Pur day on A avredge."[54]

Despite crude surroundings and limited knowledge, physicians in the field were anything but an indifferent lot. They labored indefatigably at their duties, often with an emotion as heavy as was their weariness. Surgeon George T. Stevens of the 77th New York is a good case in point. In May 1864, intense fighting extended over two days in the Wilderness of Virginia. For almost a week thereafter, hospital wagons crammed with disabled men snaked over the roads to Fredericksburg. Most of the wounded were dumped on any floor that had space. Many buildings half-destroyed in 1862 contained stagnant rain water that had fallen through large holes in the roof, and the water soon turned blood-red because of the wounded. In one warehouse, where leaky barrels of molasses had left a half-inch of gummy treacle all over the floor, maimed soldiers had to contend with the stickiness in addition to polluted water, oozing wounds, and lack of straw or blankets.

Fredericksburg became "a great charnel house," wrote a New York infantryman. "Thousands of maimed soldiers filled the dwelling houses, peopled the dingy tobacco warehouses and in many instances lay along the sidewalks, where they clutched at the dresses of the passing nurses, and in the delirium of fever and pain prayed for succor."[55] Worst of all, Stevens was but one of only 40 surgeons entrusted with the care of 7,000 wounded men. It was taking twenty-four hours just to get a wounded man from a wagon to a line awaiting the surgeon's examination.

In letters hastily written to his wife at that time, the thirty-one-year-old Albany physician revealed the physical and mental fatigue he was enduring. "We are almost worked to death," Stevens confessed. "My feet are terribly swollen; yet we cannot rest for there are so many poor fellows who are suffering. All day yesterday I worked at those terrible operations since the battle commenced, and I have also worked at the tables two whole nights and part of another. Oh! it is awful. It does not seem as though I could take a knife in my hand to-day, yet there are a hundred cases of amputation waiting for me. Poor fellows come and beg almost on their knees for the first chance to have an arm taken off. It is a scene of horror such as I never saw. God forbid that I should see another."

A few days later, Stevens wrote that the situation had not improved. "I see so many grand men dropping one by one. They are acquaintances and my friends. They look to me for help, and I have to turn away heartsick at my want of ability to relieve their sufferings. . . . Oh! can I ever write anything beside these mournful details? Hundreds of ambulances are coming into town now, and it is almost midnight. So they come every night."[56]

Following treatment at the field hospital, wounded soldiers then proceeded to one of the general hospitals located in cities near the war zone. The use of railroads was one of the greatest advancements in the removal of Civil War wounded to general hospitals. Over 15,400 of the 20,300 Federal soldiers wounded at Gettysburg were transferred by rail to Washington, Baltimore, and other points. Less fortunate soldier-patients leaving the war zone had to endure a second bone-wrenching wagon ride to a hospital in the rear. A few men evinced astounding endurance by making this journey on foot. One Union soldier who had an arm amputated on the Manassas battlefield walked twenty-five miles to reach a hospital in Washington. Another Billy Yank made the same trek with "a hole in both cheeks, a broken jaw and his tongue nearly off."[57]

The general hospital was where the wounded soldier began the long and dangerous road toward recovery. A hospital stay of less than six weeks for anything other than minor ailments was rare in Civil War times. For a serious wound (or protracted disease such as diarrhea), hospitalization for a year was common.

When an Alabama soldier wrote his wife in 1862: "I never want to go to a horse pital again men are dying there constant," he was not being dramatic. The odds of regaining health were not strongly in the patient's favor. Medicines were as limited as medical know-how, while food was anything but conducive to a patient's welfare. Spencer Talley of Tennessee was repelled by the food rations he received in one Confederate military hospital. "Our fare was not palatable to say the least of it, consisting of corn bread and beef soup & rice meted out to us on crochery ware plates and wooden spoons . . . when our meals were brought in, we had to 'shoo' and knock for sometime before we could tell what was on our plates other than flies."[58]

A popular and bitter joke among patients was "shadow soup." As a Rhode Island soldier described it, "a chicken was provided, and hung up in the sun where its shadow would strike into the kettle. A quantity of water was put into the kettle and the shadow boiled therein. Salt, pepper, and other spice were added to make it palatable, and it was then served out."[59]

Even worse, filth and overcrowding in hospitals produced deadly results. Single diseases assumed malignant characters. Cases were many of soldiers prostrated by mumps or measles also becoming infected by typhoid fever or pneumonia. The foul exhalations in the wards brought regular outbreaks of erysipelas, pyemia, osteomyelitis, gangrene, and other equally deadly illnesses.

If one of those diseases did not kill the soldier, there was another, equally lethal malady. Alexander Hunter of the 17th Virginia asserted after a brief hospitalization that "many, very many, of the sick died in the hospitals simply from nostalgia or homesickness. A soldier from the far South would be brought in with a wound or a long, lingering camp fever [and] as the days passed with no familiar face by his cot, one might observe . . . that his features grew paler and thinner, his looks more weary and listless . . . The simple truth of the matter was, the poor soldier had grown hopeless and despairing. He had lost all control over himself and would cry like a child; and then, not having been roused from this fatal, nervous apathy and weakness, . . . dying because he had not nervous force enough to hold on to the attenuated thread of life."[60]

The political capitals of Washington and Richmond became the chief medical centers for their respective sides. By 1864 the Washington area had twenty-five military hospitals with a bed capacity for 21,000 men. The largest of the North's 204 general hospitals was the Lincoln facility in Washington. It provided care for 56,000 men in the course of the war. Trained Catholic nuns ministered to some of the hospitalized soldiers; but most of the nurses, North as well as South, were volunteers who gained ability through experience.

Among their number was Walt Whitman. Before 1861 the poet had been engrossed with the meaning of stars and flowers and with the soul of man. War shocked Whitman's sensitivities, and for three years he mused on the meaning of it all while giving comfort in Northern hospitals and occasionally on Virginia battlefields. Whitman was always taken aback when overloaded wagons arrived in Washington to deposit fearfully injured soldiers at hospitals already crowded beyond capacity. "It is the most pitiful sight I think when first the men are brought in," he wrote his mother. "I have to bustle around to keep from crying."

Whitman often became discouraged at the tens of thousands of suffering men he encountered. At one point he asserted that "future years will never know the seething hell and black infernal background" of the war, "and it is best they should not." Just as often, on the other hand, he found satisfaction in befriending the helpless. To a friend he once confided:

"I still live here [in Washington] as a hospital missionary after my own style and on my own hook—I go every day or night without fail to some of the great government hospitals. O the sad scenes I witness—scenes of death, anguish, the fevers, amputations, friendlessness, hungering and thirsting young hearts, for some loving presence—such noble young men as some of these wounded are—such endurance, such native decorum, such candor—I will confess . . . that in some respects I find I supply often to some of these dear suffering boys in my presence and magnetism that which no doctors, nor medicines, nor skill, nor any routine assistance can give."[61]

Thirty-four military hospitals were in Richmond. Winder Hospital, with a bed capacity of 4,300 men, was the largest. The most famous of the Richmond medical facilities was Chimborazo. It was located on a high forty-acre plateau just to the east of the downtown. Its south side dropped sharply to the James River; a similarly steep slope marked the east face. Such topography offered good drainage. The site also had excellent well water.

Constructed in the late months of 1861, the "hospital on the hill" (as locals termed it) was a seemingly endless arrangement of 1-story white ward buildings divided into 5 divisions, with 15 wards in each division. A barracks or ward was 75 feet long and built of undressed 2-inch-thick pine boards. Some 30–40 men occupied each of the 120 buildings.[62]

Dr. James B. McCaw, a native of Richmond, was the chief surgeon. He was highly organized and generally well liked. Each division had a surgeon-in-charge, a physician for every 70–80 patients, hospital stewards, nurses, and support elements. This chain of command lasted throughout the war and provided usually sound efficiency. Yet Chimborazo was not as orderly as it looked from afar.

One surgeon called the wards "nothing but shanties." Another staff member wrote of living "in a whitewashed board house through the planks of which I can see the stars and the snow too." Before any repairs or improvements could be made, the 1862 Peninsular Campaign began to the east of Richmond. Soon thousands of injured Confederates were flowing into the city in a seemingly endless crimson tide. When Chimborazo quickly reached its 3,000 capacity, Dr. McCaw refused to accept any more wounded men. Ambulance drivers and stretcher-bearers thereupon dumped their cargo in the hospital streets and departed. At one time, 3,500 maimed soldiers were packed into Chimborazo.

Such overcrowding, combined with short supplies and inadequate hospital personnel, produced a medical hell. Chimborazo became infamous for its odors. The putrid smell of gangrene merged with the stench of suppurating wounds and the foul aroma of torn flesh trying to heal. Piles of dirty rags littered floors wet from blood and water. Shortages of soap left bedding and patients' clothing perpetually filthy. The limited number of mattresses and blankets were used again and again until they rotted.

A Texas chaplain visited Chimborazo and termed it "that charnal house of living sufferers." Everything inside the complex was foul, he stated. "Then take into account the privys under the hill, all along the N. & S sides so that when the wind blows from either direction, which during the summer is not very infrequent, and then imagine the chambers carried a little below the brow of the hill and emptied. Together with the stench of several thousand wounds, you can imagine how 'sweet' the atmosphere was."[63]

In all, Chimborazo was a refuge for 77,889 soldiers. Some 16,000 of those patients are buried in nearby Oakwood Cemetery. That number does not include those deceased men taken home for burial.

These general hospitals provided the first opportunity for an ill soldier regularly to feel a woman's soothing touch. The Civil War was a breakthrough in American history for women nurses on a large scale, and many of them won national fame for their efforts. Yet for every heralded Dorothea Dix, Clara Barton, Sally Tompkins, Mary A. ("Mother") Bickerdyke, and Annie Wittenmyer who gained distinction, there were scores of ladies who unpretentiously did everything they could to relieve the pain, suffering, and fear of soldiers. In spite of being hampered by lack of knowledge, and hated by many of the physicians for whom they worked, women nurses went about their duties faithfully.

Phoebe Yates Pember was illustrative of a nurse who learned from experience and persistence. In 1862 this thirty-nine-year-old Jewish widow obtained a nurse's appointment and literally forced her way into Chimborazo Hospital over solid male opposition. She became the hospital's first matron. For the remainder of the war Mrs. Pember labored unceasingly. She later explained why. "Scenes of pathos occurred daily—scenes that wrung the heart and forced the dew of pity from the eyes; but feeling that enervated the mind and relaxed the body was a sentimental luxury that was not to be indulged in. There was too much work to be done, too much active exertion required, to allow the mental or physical powers to succumb. They were severely taxed every day. Perhaps they balanced, and so kept each from thinking."

To criticisms that the horrible sights inside a soldier's hospital was something no lady's eyes should see, Mrs. Pember snapped back: "In the midst of suffering and death, hoping with those almost beyond hope in this world; praying by the bedside of the lonely and heart-stricken; closing the eyes of boys hardly old enough to realize man's sorrows, much less suffer man's fierce hate, a woman must soar beyond the conventional modesty considered correct under different circumstances."[64]

Some nurses paid dearly for their volunteer service. Noted author Louisa May Alcott worked but a month in the hospitals when she contracted typhoid fever. Surgeons plied her with calomel, which resulted in a mercury poisoning that brought loss of teeth and hair as well as a deterioration of the nervous system. Miss Alcott was never the same for her brief war experience.

The only remuneration for these nurses was the gratitude of the patients they served. One Union matron wrote shortly after her work in a makeshift Gettysburg hospital: "I have been for weeks the only lady in a camp of seven hundred men, and have never been treated with more deference, respect, and kindness." Several weeks later, with the emergency under control, one group of women nurses left the hospital camp for home. Two regimental bands in gratitude escorted them to the railroad depot. Similarly, a Virginia artilleryman wrote after leaving a Confederate hospital: "The ladies of Richmond, may God ever bless them, from the maiden of sixty to the young girl in her teens, moved like ministering angels among these sufferers, doing all in their power to relieve the soldiers' pain and sufferings."[65]

Neither North nor South could boast of any outstanding medical achievement in the Civil War. No pathbreaking new treatments emerged, no lifesaving medications appeared. Ventilation of hospitals evolved as a positive procedure. Some important lessons in hygiene became a new part of medicine. A hospital system for large armies developed on the basis of trial and error. The ambulance corps, organized in the North in 1864 to provide systematized transportation of the wounded from battlefield to hospital, may have been the most significant advance of the war.

Informing and involving the public of medical needs made its debut in this war. The work of the U.S. Sanitary Commission was precedent-setting in many respects. Two New Yorkers, the Reverend Henry W. Bellows and Dr. Elisha Harris, organized the commission in the first months of the struggle. Its purpose was to inspect military camps and advise on matters of "sanitary and hygienic interests" so as to reduce the incidence of disease. To practice what it preached, the Sanitary Commission sent representatives to assist in the field and in the hospitals. It conducted fund-raising drives throughout the North to accomplish its ends. Army surgeons at first looked on the agency as intrusive and snooping, but the good work of the commission soon brought a change of mind and close cooperation.

All of these innovations were positive advances in the field of medicine, to be sure, but the little progress made seems terribly out of balance with the immense amount of suffering and death so ever-present in Civil War armies.

·9·

Gathering at the River

"I can not see any reason why men can not be religious in the army, for there is no plase in the world whare there is the disaplin there is here," a semiliterate Illinois soldier wrote home in mid-1862. "You perceve we are in the very best mode to rise in the scales of morrels. My constant prayer is, 'Save us in this dredful war from the moral miasma.'" Yet another infantryman from the same state, and writing at the same time, lamented: "If there is any place on God's fair earth where wickedness 'stalketh abroad in daylight,' it is in the army."[1] Obviously, the presence and importance of religion among soldiers elicited varying opinions.

The years leading to civil war had sorely traumatized the foundation of faith on which the young nation had been built. Religious liberty had been the major impetus in the colonization of America; church growth and revival movements were an integral part of society well into the nineteenth century. One commentator noted that while there might often be a wide divergence between the preacher's exhortations and the laity's response, "religious sanction was demanded by the righteous, approved by the lukewarm, and tolerated by the wicked. All felt better to have had the blessing of the church."[2]

It was somewhat natural that the major religious denominations were the first large groups of any kind in American society to face the issue of slavery (with its subsequent, attendant by-product of secession); and in doing so, the larger of the sects became the first casualties of the war.

Religion in the antebellum South was more conservative and more orthodox than anywhere else in the nation. The Bible was the authoritative Word of God, and that was all there was to it. New denominations spawned in the eighteenth century by the Enlightenment movement—Congregationalists, Unitarians, and Universalists, for example—never took root below the Potomac River.

Evangelical sects prevailed in Dixieland. Their tenets called for a personal religious experience and a life consistent with the teachings of Jesus. For most of these fundamentalists, the primary purpose of existence was to prepare for eternal salvation. The individual was expected to conduct his daily affairs in harmony with the wishes of a just and stern God. Such dedication in beliefs and actions goes far in explaining why 25 percent of all Southerners, as compared to 15 percent of the Northern population, were active members of some religious group at the outbreak of the Civil War.[3]

Moreover, and by that time, slavery had shattered the national character of the larger denominations. In 1845, after a fierce debate among its bishops, the Methodist church had divided into northern and southern wings. The Baptist church did not undergo such a formal division, since each congregation was an entity unto itself. However, when Northerners in 1840 organized the American Baptist Convention in New York, Southerners responded a few years later by creating the Southern Baptist Convention. The rift became permanent.

Civil war did not split the Presbyterians only because they had already divided earlier in the century over theological issues. The northern-dominated New School Presbyterians strongly backed the Union in 1861, while the Old School Presbyterians just as ardently supported the Confederacy. Lutheran synods found too that they could not withstand the pressures of secession and war. When the Virginia Synod left the main church body in October 1861, the Carolina synods followed suit. No southern wing of the Lutheran church was ever organized, but Lutherans in that section displayed strong loyalty to the Confederate cause.

Although the Episcopal church managed to hold together through the years of the slavery crisis, secession ripped that sect asunder. In July 1861, delegates from a majority of southern states met in Montgomery, Alabama, and established the Protestant Episcopal Church of the Confederate States of America. Its existence lasted only as long as the nation it supported.

No such official cleavage occurred among American Catholics, even though some of its clergy and many of its laity staunchly defended the Southern nation. The same can be said of the Jewish people who, operating under no denominational restraints, were left individually free to determine which side they would support.

The fractured state of the major religious sects not only contributed to the breakup of the Union; such schisms helped widen the breach between North and South once war began because each section could insist fervently that God was on its side in this holy American crusade. The Confederacy became noteworthy for its reliance on God as an ally. Not merely in sermons and church publications, but in the Confederate Constitution, presidential proclamations, and generals' announcements of victory, thankfulness to the Almighty was a dominant theme.

Mrs. Fannie Beers of Louisiana captured this fervor in her reminiscences. "From the very first there was among the people of the South an earnest dependence upon God, a habit of appeal to His mercy and loving-kindness, and a marked attention to religious duties. On Sundays the churches were crowded with devout worshippers. Every service was attended by more or less Confederate soldiers, generally in squads, but sometimes even in companies, marshalled by some of their officers."[4]

Few Johnny Rebs and Billy Yanks had been directly embroiled in the denominational struggles, nor had they entered service with any feelings of participating in some sort of crusade for Christ. For most soldiers of the 1860s, religion was a personal matter; joining the army only strengthened their conviction to follow home-learned Christian principles down the uncertain road of war.

Faith in God became the single greatest institution in the maintenance of morale in the armies. To the devout soldier, religion "was the connecting link between camp life and home. As he prayed and sang hymns of praise, his thoughts could not help but wander to his home church wherein he felt a mother, a father, a wife, or a child might be united with him in asking for his speedy return." Furthermore, many soldiers North and South agreed with Louisiana Sergeant Edwin Fay, who did not "believe a bullet can go through a prayer" because faith was a "much better shield than . . . steel armor."[5]

War inevitably dented the faith of many Civil War participants. Leaving the restraints of home and loved ones, and then cast as soldiers in a novel environment that alternated between apathy and loneliness on the one hand to excitement and danger on the other, invited a wandering from the straight and narrow. A Midwesterner wrote his fiancée after several months in the army: "I must say that I doe not live faithful as I ought to . . . You can not Imagine the temptations that beset a Soldier on every hand." Large numbers of men found more important things to do than worship. In June 1861, a minister in the field complained that "it seems impossible to draw out the men at all numerously to a morning service. They want to 'wash up,' put their quarters in order, prepare their arms for inspection, write home and the like . . . "[6]

Some men scorned faith after witnessing the hell of a battle or experiencing the loss of messmates and friends. A New Yorker felt war and religion to be at odds. "There is something inconsistent in fighting the enemy and attending divine service, therefore, these services so efficiently commenced were in the course of time interrupted and in the end almost entirely discontinued."[7]

For a majority of the soldiers, however, war and its uncertainties led to an affirmation of faith similar in sentiment to Abraham Lincoln's observation: "I have often been driven to my knees by the realization that I had nowhere else to go." Carroll Clark of the 16th Tennessee confessed: "We were cut off from home Communication & had not much hope of ever meeting again the loved ones at home. . . . I thought of earthly home sweet home & cried . . . "[8]

An untold number of soldiers performed devotionals by reading the Bible alone, reciting the Rosary without assistance, or praying in the seclusion of a tent or nearby woods. One Confederate wrote his brother in May 1862: "the greatest pleasure that I have is when I am reading my Bible and praying to my Creater my Heavenly Father for in his car a lon do I feel safe. I som time tak my Bible on the Sabath and go to some grove where I have no on in my way."[9]

This personal religion also manifested itself in rather intimate and informal prayers. During one trying period, a North Carolinian made this supplication: "Oh Lord, we have a mighty big fight down here, and a sight of trouble; and we hope, Lord, that you will take the proper view of the matter, and give us the victory." A war-weary Virginian once offered this testimonial at a prayer service: "My brethren, I'se got nothin' agin nobody, and I hope nobody's got nothin' agin me."

Similarly, there were instances when an individual's deep faith was momentary. On one occasion, as Federals began attacking en masse, a Virginia artilleryman dropped to his knees and prayed: "O Lord, drive them back! O Lord, drive them back!" Gunfire roared as the battle began. A few moments later, the man arose partly and asked: "Boys, are they coming or going?"

"Coming!" was the reply.

The gunner knelt quickly and, with even more intensity, he intoned: "O Lord, drive them back! O Lord, drive them back!" He soon asked again: "Are they coming or going?"

"Coming!" his comrades exclaimed.

Both sides were firing furiously as the man dropped to his knees a third time and begged:" "O Lord, drive them back!" Desperation was in his voice as he asked once more if the enemy were coming or going.

"The Yankees are going!" his comrades now shouted.

Whereupon the devout worshipper became a "son of mars," sprang atop the earthworks, and yelled defiantly: "Come back here, you cowards! Come back here! We'll whip you!"[10]

Many soldiers followed the lead of General "Stonewall" Jackson by giving credit for survival—as well as victories—to the Almighty. "I can say thank god that I have never bin harmed," James Parrott of the 16th Tennessee once stated to his wife. "when I go into a fite I say God be my helper and when I come out I say thank God I feel like he has bin with mee." Similarly, when Confederates began retiring from the field after prolonged and bitter fighting at Murfreesboro, Tennessee, an Ohio soldier began singing the old-time doxology, "Praise God from Whom All Blessings Flow." Union comrades around him quickly picked up the words, as did the regiment in time, and soon the familiar lyrics were being sung by an entire segment of the Federal lines.[11]

Guarding and guiding the spiritual well-being of the soldiers was the primary responsibility of army chaplains. On both sides, chaplains received officer status. Their salaries—$80 monthly in Confederate armies, $100 a month in the Union forces—seemed a respectable stipend for that day. Nevertheless, and for a number of reasons, chaplains as a group had difficulty in obtaining security, requisitions, and recognition.

Galloping inflation in the South reduced the chaplain's salary to a paltry sum. He also labored under severe military restrictions. The clergyman had no standard uniform and his rank was at best a quasi-official position. A chaplain received the rations of a private rather than an officer; he could not draw government forage for his own horse but had to purchase its feed with whatever money he had; he was not even entitled to issues of paper and ink, even though he had to write out sermons.

Chaplains for the most part lived a spartan existence. In November 1861, the Reverend Charles Quintard of the 1st Tennessee described his housing facilities. He had a tent, an old box containing various items such as a handkerchief, an extra shirt, and a pair of socks. On the box rested a Bible and a volume of sermons, writing paper, and an inkstand. Candles inserted into bayonets stuck in the ground were on each side of the box. The remainder of Quintard's clothes were wrapped in a blanket. His bed was a pile of hay.[12]

Frederic Denison, an energetic minister who served as chaplain of two different Rhode Island units, was surprised on entering the army to learn that a chaplain had "no appointment or recognized place . . . on a march, in a bivouac, or in a line of battle; he was a supernumerary, a kind of fifth wheel to a coach, being in place nowhere and out of place everywhere." Moreover, some regimental commanders openly opposed their mere presence. In the eyes of many officers, religion made men more fearful of death, it preached against popular sins and vices, and it was a challenge to blind discipline, which made an army efficient. One officer had a reverse reason for his antichaplain feelings. Having a clergyman in the ranks, he stated "was a standing reproof of [our] wicked conduct; and the sooner [officers] could discourage and dishearten the chaplain, the better they were pleased."[13]

The chaplaincy service, especially in the first stages of the war, did not always attract men of ability and devotion. Most of the accomplished clergy North and South were reluctant to abandon the peaceful security of civilian positions for the hardships and perils of army life. They much preferred to serve as occasional evangelists or short-term missionaries, thereby gaining a maximum of patriotic satisfaction at a minimum of personal risk. In addition, many ministers of the gospel entered the army as soldiers or officers rather than as chaplains. Of one hundred clergy serving in the Confederate Army of Tennessee in 1863, only half of that number held chaplains' posts.

A shortage of army chaplains existed at the beginning of hostilities and became worse as the struggle continued. In a phrase, the army and the churches together demanded too much. Not enough clergymen existed to meet the demands in military service and, at the same time, maintain church organization on the homefront. The soldiers had one kind of need; the church hierarchies had another.

The U.S. War Department announced in June 1862 that of 676 regiments in the field, only 395 had chaplains on official assignment; and of that number, 29 were absent on detached service while another 13 were absent without leave.[14] Fully a third of the Federal regiments had no chaplain. It was even worse on the Confederate side. The C.S. Chaplains Association reported in 1863 that half of the Southern units were without a minister.

In April of that year, Chaplain John S. Paris of the 54th Carolina in "Stonewall" Jackson's corps begged a fellow clergyman back home to give assistance. "Can you not find a man who will volunteer as a chaplain in some of our regiments in this Corps? Here are fifteen regiments from North Carolina without chaplains. I am the only one in my Brigade . . . Such a life is rough." A Georgia officer commented the same spring that his men had not heard a sermon in five months, despite every effort to obtain some kind of chaplain. The situation worsened rather than improved. A year later, General John B. Gordon wrote a Presbyterian newspaper to ask why there were so few preachers in the army. "Was it that they did not wish to cast pearls before swine? Whole groups seldom hear a sermon. Send more ministers!"[15]

Quality was often needed as much as quantity. Lieutenant Colonel Edwin Bennett of the 5th Massachusetts was convinced that "at least seventy-five per cent of the chaplains commissioned during the first year of the war were practically unfit for their work."[16] Bennett's figure is exaggerated. Yet it is undeniably true that many of the chaplains were too old or too physically unfit for heavy responsibilities in the field; and ne'er-do-wells were numerous enough to give the chaplaincy branch on both sides a tainted reputation. These misfits were men who had chosen the wrong profession, clergy unable to find or maintain a church at home, and individuals unqualified to perform even the basic duties of chaplains. Many of them were demonstrably deficient in education; too many were lazy; others possessed little concern for the welfare of their charges; some were rogues and sots; a handful were cowards.

In the last-named class was the chaplain of the 3rd Alabama. A member of that regiment once wrote: "We got into a little row with the Yankees a few days ago and our parson, deeming, no doubt, that 'discretion was the better part of valor,' took to his heels when the shells commenced flying and I have not seem him since." A New England officer who had witnessed the same misbehavior insisted that "undue susceptibility to cannon fever" were ample grounds for the disqualification of a chaplain.[17]

Soldiers in need of spiritual guidance were quick to recognize and criticize poor sermons. On July 16, 1862, James Warnell of the 5th Georgia Cavalry wrote in his diary: "Preaching at 4 oclock by the Rev. Mr. Paine. Sermon not very consoling to the friends of those who has fell on our battle fields. after role call Mr. Paine made a speach, I suppose, on the criciss of the day in which he informed us that he would have been a capt. in the confedrate army if he would & his health would have admitted, also that he was willing to be in the confedrate servis for 20 year rather than be sub[ju]gated. How unfortunate it is so many Patriots are in such bad health."

Five weeks later, Warnell had apparently resolved the problem of how to attend church services without having to endure dull messages from the chaplains. "Preaching at 11 by the Rev. J. W. Turner. unfortunately I went to sleep and did not wake until he was singing the last Hymn."[18]

Excessive absenteeism from the ranks also brought complaints about chaplains. "I think Brother Murphy would be an entire stranger to the 19th Regiment," an Iowan asserted of the minister in his unit. Confederate John Sale sneered that the rarely seen chaplains in his brigade "are so careful of their precious bodies that they can take none for souls which is their business."[19]

Lack of scruples characterized a number of the early army ministers. A Wisconsin chaplain displayed the basest conduct by boarding in a brothel while his regiment camped in the field. One cleric was court-martialed for stealing a horse; another deserted with ninety dollars in regimental funds; a third entered a stud-poker game in the camp of the 2nd Connecticut Heavy Artillery one evening and promptly cleaned out an entire company.[20]

According to a Federal surgeon at Fort Monroe, Virginia, the chaplains there were "pharisees" and "rotten to the core, not caring half as much for their souls' welfare or anybody else's as for the dollars they received." That was not completely true. One chaplain in the group became a demoralizing element with his habit of sitting on the edge of some soldier's hospital cot, telling the man he looked close to death, and urging him to prepare to die. This was too much for one patient: he threw a plate at the cleric and told him to go to the devil.[21]

A chaplain recently assigned to the field sought to improve his condition by commandeering a horse from a Virginia farmer. He then joined his regimental commander, who promptly asked him where he got the horse.

"Down the road there," the chaplain replied.

Angrily the colonel told the chaplain to return the horse.

Protesting strongly, the chaplain sought to justify what he had done by stating: "Why Jesus Christ, when He was on earth, took an ass whereon to ride to Jerusalem."

The colonel snapped back: "You are not Jesus Christ; that is not an ass; you are not on your way to Jerusalem; and the sooner you restore that horse to its owner, the better it will be for you."[22]

"Holy Joe" and "Holy John" were common nicknames the soldiers used for chaplains, but there were other, derogatory titles as well, such as "The Great Thunderer," "Death on the Pale Horse," and "The Old Woman" (because "he ain't fit to be called a Chaplain").[23]

In a steady stream these incompetent ministers soon left the armies. The apathy or hostility of the soldiers, physical strain, homesickness, the perils of camp life and battle, oppressive routines, real or imagined illnesses, plus the elevation of standards for the chaplaincy service, all led to a healthy weeding out of the misfits.

The unpretentious men who in the main filled most chaplain posts in the Civil War were genuinely motivated, filled with both patriotism and righteousness, and able to bring a sense of caring to a war atmosphere of callousness. These chaplains performed a host of important activities. All of them held church services and prayer meetings as regularly as military operations would permit. They baptized and they buried; they exhorted during the great revivals that periodically swept through the armies. All of them visited the sick, and they were usually nearby to comfort the wounded brought back from battle. Chaplain Alexander Betts of the 30th North Carolina embodied the spirit of these field ministers when he extolled: "God help our men to fight! Have mercy on those who are to die!"[24]

Comforting the homesick and sorrowful, as well as offering counsel of other kinds to individual soldiers, occupied much of a chaplain's time. He was expected to perform individual therapy as well as group presentations. In January 1863, a New England soldier wrote in his diary: "Our chaplain made a speech to us on dress parade last night, and its subject was 'Cultivate a Cheerful Spirit;' and it is just so. If a man makes the best of everything, he will be much happier than if he looks on the dark side all the time."[25]

In addition, chaplains begged supplies from congregations back home. They secured religious literature and became roving libraries in their regiments. Some chaplains acted as correspondents for hometown newspapers. Many became one-man postal services. Not only did they read letters to, and write letters for, the illiterate in their care; they likewise took charge of all outgoing and incoming mail. Chaplain William G. Scandlin of the 15th Massachusetts handled as many as 500 letters at a typical mail call. His counterpart in the 60th New York, Richard Eddy, processed 3,063 letters in a one-month period.[26]

The respected Holy Joes willingly made sacrifices for their flock. Chaplain Scandlin was known to carry as many as three muskets on a march so that a like number of soldiers could get momentary relief. Men in the 1st Tennessee remembered Reverend Charles T. Quintard, who would fill his canteen each morning with whiskey and, throughout the regiment's advance, dispense drinks "to help the wearied and broken down to keep up in the march." The Reverent John F. Moors of the 52nd Massachusetts was of the same mold. During a long and hot advance, he agreed to carry a soldier's blanket on his horse. Others rapidly made the same request. Soon little more than Moors's head was visible above the saddle. Good-natured cheers came from the ranks: "The chaplain is well barricaded! The rebels can't hit him! Nothing short of a shell can reach him!" Moor laughed along with the men.[27]

Enduring hardships cheerfully while setting moral examples for the troops to follow was the hallmark of the accomplished chaplain. One such cleric was Thomas D. Witherspoon of the 42nd Mississippi. The regimental surgeon stated: "Chaplain Witherspoon endeared himself to every man in [the] brigade by his kindly disposition and genial manner. He was every man's friend, and the oldest and youngest soldier felt no hesitation in approaching him in time of trouble. He was, physically, a delicate man, but intellectually a giant. He was a devout, humble, hopeful Christian, and his daily walk and example was a benediction to his brigade."[28]

Although chaplains were under orders not to take part in combat, many of them nevertheless went to the front lines, reassured the men with prayers and words of encouragement, gave aid to the fallen, and often displayed incredible bravado. Colonel John Beatty of Ohio told of seeing "a fighting parson" who "had two revolvers and a hatchet in his belt and appeared more like a firebrand than a minister of peace." At Mine Run, Virginia, in 1863, Federals assaulted a Confederate camp as the Southerners were preparing breakfast. Chaplain Abner Hopkins of the 2nd Virginia leaped up from the campfire, grabbed a frying pan and, using that utensil as a weapon, rallied his brethren.[29]

More dramatic was the conduct at Shiloh of Isaac T. Tichenor. This Alabama chaplain wrote that "we were under a crossfire . . . from three directions. Under it the boys wavered. I had been wearied and was sitting down, but seeing them waver, I sprang to my feet, took off my hat, waved it over my head, walked up and down the line, and, as they say, 'preached them a sermon.' I reminded them that it was Sunday. That at that hour all their home folk were praying for them . . . I called upon them to stand there and die, if need be, for their country. The effect was evident. Every man stood to his post, every eye flashed, and ever heart beat high with desperate resolve to conquer or die."

According to one source, Tichenor then set an example in the fighting that ensued by killing a Federal colonel, a major, and four privates.[30]

After one engagement, Chaplain William P. McBryde found bullet holes in his shoe, haversack, the back of his coat, the front of the vest, his sleeve, and his Bible—yet he was not wounded. The Reverend T. L. Duke of the 19th Mississippi is the only Confederate chaplain cited for gallant conduct in the Official Records. At Chancellorsville, Duke "remained in front of his regiment with his musket during the series of engagements and mainly directed the movements of the skirmishes of that regiment."[31]

At least fifty chaplains died in battle. In the 1864 struggle for Jonesboro, Georgia, Father Emmeran Bliemel of the 4th Kentucky knelt beside a dying soldier and had just lifted his hands in prayer when he was decapitated by a cannonball. Chaplain Arthur B. Fuller of the 16th Massachusetts fell at Fredericksburg, Virginia, musket in hand, while participating in a skirmish. Fuller had been officially discharged from service two days earlier, but he delayed his departure to remain a while longer with his friends.[32]

Over fifty Confederate chaplains fell wounded or died from disease or natural causes. Chaplain A. G. Burrow of the 30th Mississippi returned to camp after a skirmish with a four-inch gash in his skull. "It was winter and bitter cold," a fellow minister stated. "The wounded chaplain had no overcoat. His other coat was thin and ragged. All his clothing was worn out." The Mississippi clergyman succumbed in the field, "his devotion to his God and his country" having "cost him his life." The Reverend George L. Winchester died from fatigue after struggling to minister daily to two different regiments.[33]

Thomas G. Sheppard of the 1st South Carolina. A year later, the nineteen-year-old private fell mortally wounded at Second Manassas. *Tim Landis*

An unidentified but fully equipped Union recruit in the early stages of the war.
U.S. Army Military History Institute

Part of a company of the 40th Massachusetts practicing bayonet drill in Virginia during the winter of 1862–1863.
U.S. Army Military History Institute

Inside the Washington defenses in the war's first winter, these Carlisle-area soldiers in the 36th Pennsylvania posed for a formal group photograph. *U.S. Army Military History Institute*

This reversed 1861 photograph shows members of the "Clinch Rifles" (Company A, 5th Georgia) relaxing in camp. Note the black servant and the Confederate flag. *U.S Army Military History Institute*

Unidentified Federals, some of whom are overacting for the benefit of the photographer. *U.S. Army Military History Institute*

A union squad demonstrates preparedness for battle in this early camp photograph. *U.S. Army Military History Institute*

Camaraderie prevailed when this group of Federal officers and enlisted men—as well as someone's pet dog—gathered together. *U.S. Army Military History Institute*

Chaplains were judged far more for what they did than for what they said; but if they turned out to be good preachers as well, that was an extra point in their favor. All of them aspired toward that goal, but comparatively few attained it. "I attend church some," Edward Botts of the 101st Pennsylvania informed his mother, "but there is but one Chaplain here & he is so poor a preacher that it is painful for me to listen to him." Chaplain J. William Jones exulted that the war "brought a truce to denominational bickerings—there are no sectarian sermons preached and no sectarian tracts circulated, but all seem to work together to make men Christians." In truth, that ecumenical approach was not always accepted with Christian joy. Charles Cort was unimpressed by the new chaplain in his Illinois regiment. He was "of the Methodist denomination. he appears to be very earnest in his work but has got the regular shouting style."[34]

On the other hand, the 17th Connecticut's James C. Beecher was extremely popular with the men. "he used no notes and preached in conversational style. his sermon was well delivered and its teaching plain so that the simplest could understand." A Maine sergeant wrote of a service he attended immediately after the battle of Cedar Mountain: "Chaplain Knox gathered us together this forenoon and spoke words of cheer, but the cheers choked him and he ended with a prayer. Those were divine services that we appreciated."[35]

Biblical texts with a martial flavor were the favorite sources for chaplains' sermons. Homilies occurred repeatedly on: "Fight the good fight of faith . . . Put on the whole armor of God . . . "I will stir up the nations and I will fill this house with glory, saith the Lord of Hosts" . . . If God be for us, who can be against us?" . . . The Lord is my helper, and I will not fear what men should do to me." A Virginia minister once lashed out at the Yankees by preaching on a passage from Deuteronomy: "For they are a nation void of counsel, neither is there any understanding in them. O that they were wise, that they understood this, that they would consider their latter end."[36]

If their side was winning, chaplains stressed that it was because the men were keeping the faith. If they were losing, it was a temporary setback caused by sinfulness. The ministers rationalized protracted reverses by comparing the current plight to the tribulations faced by the Israelites of old as they struggled toward the Promised Land.

Sometimes interspersed with the pleas for guidance were warnings for the men to keep their muskets clean and their powder dry. One Alabama chaplain, whose patriotism momentarily exceeded his piety, closed a camp meeting by praying that the Yankees' "moral sensibilities might be awakened by the roar of our cannon and the gleam of our bayonets and that the stars and bars might soon wave in triumph through these beleaguered states!"[37]

Chaplains also emphasized the basic tenets of faith, warned against the evils of army life, and sought to prepare the men for death and salvation. A number of sermons therefore sprang from such biblical texts as: "Seek ye first the kingdom of God . . . So teach us to number our days, that we may apply our hearts unto wisdom . . . Be thou faithful unto death, and I will give thee a crown of life."

Sermons occasionally provoked unexpected reactions. At one service, when a soldier suddenly let out a loud scream, a general in attendance ordered his adjutant to take the disrespectful listener to the guardhouse. Yet "when the officer went to arrest him," the cleric proudly noted, "he found him in tears, and was told that the man did not intend to interrupt but he was a Methodist and that was only *his way of enjoying the sermon*."[38]

In contrast, a company of Louisiana soldiers known as "Wilson's Zouaves" once met to hear a visiting chaplain. The troops knew little English, but the minister was unaware of it. The chaplain spoke earnestly as the congregation listened silently. When the sermon ended, Captain Wilson stood and stated: "Boys, I want you to remember what the minister has told you. It is all for your good. Take his advice and follow it, for there is no knowing but what in less than six months every damned one of you will be in hell!"

At that point, a loud voice came from the rear: "Three cheers for hell!" Hurrahs came forth lustfully.

The irate chaplain demanded an explanation for such behavior.

Wilson replied calmly: "The boys don't know much about Scripture. They think hell is somewhere between Montgomery and New Orleans, and they are damned anxious to get down in that neighborhood!"[39]

Many soldiers, especially officers, did not take kindly to hellfire sermons with their threats of eternal damnation. "There is of necessity solemnity enough here without any shadow of yielding to it," commented a lieutenant in the 13th New Hampshire. A Wisconsin colonel, after listening to a long "prophecy of doom," levied a verbal blast at the chaplain. "I don't want any more of that doctrine preached in this regiment. Every one of my boys who fall fighting in this great battle of liberty is going to Heaven, and I won't allow any other principle to be promulgated to them while I command the regiment."[40]

The leading religious service in camp took place on Sunday afternoon so as not to interfere with morning duties and inspections. Such meetings were generally outdoors in front of a tent or in the woods. Listeners either stood or sat on logs and boxes in irregular fashion. A barrel, camp stool, or caisson served as the altar.

The men would sing one or two hymns, sometimes to the accompaniment of a banjo, fiddle, or other musical instrument. Some congregations organized singing groups to perform at services. (One such choir, promptly nicknamed the "Bull-Frog Club," disbanded after a couple of performances.) Northerners and southerners enjoyed the same songs of praise and hope. Many of the hymns had verses appropriate to the war environment, such as: "O God, our help in ages past, Our hope for years to come, Our shelter from the stormy blast, And our eternal home." A similar hymn proclaimed: "My soul, be on thy guard: Ten thousand foes arise; A host of sins are pressing hard To draw thee from the skies." Other favorites were cherished hymns of childhood: "Rock of Ages," "Amazing Grace," "Nearer, My God, to Thee," "All Hail the Power of Jesus' Name," "How Firm a Foundation," "Sweet Hour of Prayer," and "Praise God from Whom All Blessings Flow."

A scripture-reading preceded the sermon, which was the highlight of the service. Closing prayers then sent the men on their way.

Prayer meetings of an informal nature took place more frequently than structured services. Held whenever the desire arose, these sessions consisted of a small gathering of soldiers who each participated by offering testimonials and supplications. John H. Kiracofe of the 18th Virginia Cavalry voiced the benefits of such meetings in a letter to his wife: "We had an experience meeting and the Lord was with us, our hearts were made to lep for joy to know that though we war far from home among strangers that the Lord would condecend to bless us."[41]

Distractions and interruptions were commonplace with religious gatherings in camp. Soldiers entered and exited throughout a service; noise from the camp marred the solemnity; a loose horse might bolt through the assemblage; marching orders could come at any time—as well as enemy fire. One service ended abruptly when "the Parson from the concussion of a shell had all discussion knocked out of him for awhile."[42]

Less heroic competition hampered the 7th Wisconsin on one occasion. The colonel of the regiment sent a hasty note to his adjutant: "There is a large crowd of soldiers in the grove below, engaged in the interesting game called chuck-a-luck. My chaplain is running his church on the other side of me, but chuck-a-luck has the largest crowd. I think this unfair, as the church runs only once a week but the game goes on daily. I suggest that one or the other of the parties be dispersed." Somewhat in the same vein is a short but far-ranging diary entry of a Pennsylvania soldier: "The company was paid off to-day, and went on a general drunk. Eight p.m., held prayer-meeting services, conducted by Peter Tippin."[43]

During the 1862 Seven Days campaign in front of Richmond, the Reverend Joseph Clay Stiles addressed a large contingent of soldiers near the front lines. The men were on their knees, eyes tightly closed, as Stiles offered a prayer. Without warning a Federal battery began firing into the area. "Faith and devotion were not strong enough to prevent my opening my eyes and glancing around," one soldier confessed. The other men refused to be distracted—until the shells got closer. Then the praying soldiers "felt it would be wise and well to supplement the protection of heaven by the trees and stumps of earth, if they could find them, and so they were actually groping for them with arms wide extended but eyes tight closed, and still on their knees."[44]

Some soldiers were unsympathetic with the evangelism sweeping the camps. "It seems to me," wrote a member of the 21st Alabama, "that wherever I go I can never get rid of the Psalm-'singers'—they are in full blast with a Prayer meeting a few rods off." When patience became exhausted, troops rebelled physically against the loud zeal of their compatriots. Night after night during one wintry period, gunners in the Surry Light Artillery of Virginia gathered in a sergeant's tent for prayers and hymn-singing. To every song the men shouted a fervent refrain: "Scotland's burning! Cast on water!"

Several battery members grew tired of the monotonous noise. The next evening, as the faithful soldiers extolled: "Scotland's burning! Cast on water!" down the chimney of the tent's fireplace came a large bucket of water. The water extinguished both the fire and the singing as smoke sent worshippers scurrying from the tent. "Cast on water!" was not heard again in the battery.[45]

The greatest supplement to the work of Northern chaplains was the U.S. Christian Commission. Organized in 1861 to improve the moral and mental welfare of troops in the field, the commission in 1864 alone dispensed over 569,700 Bibles, 4,815,000 hymnals and psalm books, plus 13,681,000 pages of religious literature.[46] It encouraged men to write home by distributing free paper and stamps. Dozens of its minister-representatives went into the field to provide assistance and material benefits. A Pennsylvania soldier was among those who praised their efforts:

"Close to the rear of the battle line, often amidst the crashing of shells and the smoke of battle, these devoted men carried fuel and water to keep their vessels of hot coffee full and steaming; and with hands tender as a woman's, fed the hungry, staunched the blood, and bound up the gashes . . . These priests of God, Catholic and Protestant, asked no questions of the sufferer, but simply obeyed the divine precept to feed the hungry, clothe the naked and bind up the wounds of both friend and foe."[47]

Assisting chaplains on both sides in spreading the faith were colporteurs. Employees of religious denominations or benevolent societies, their primary duty was to distribute Bibles and tracts to the soldiers. Colporteurs could regularly be seen wandering through the various camps. They were often visible in or near hospitals, where they found a "captive" and usually more eager reception for their materials.

Evangelical sects, especially Methodists and Baptists, literally flooded army camps with reading material. Three varieties of publications came from church presses. First were official church organs, which appeared regularly and contained not only inspirational stories but also letters from chaplains and colporteurs, news from home churches, and the like. Far at the head of this list was the Richmond-based *Religious Herald*. It was the largest of such publications and had the greatest influence of all the many Baptist periodicals. The first issues contained lengthy defenses of slavery as well as repeated assertions that Northern heathen had snatched the olive branch of peace from the hands of faithful Southerners. Subsequent issues urged all readers to support the war effort and to pray for Confederate success. Other, less militant journals were the *Southern Churchman, Southern Christian Advocate, South Western Baptist,* and *Southern Presbyterian.*

Periodicals specifically produced for servicemen comprised the second class and included the *Army and Navy Herald, Army and Navy Messenger, Soldiers Friend, Soldiers Magazine,* and *Soldiers Visitor.* All of these serials were basically tracts in newspaper form.

The third and by far the largest of the categories were religious tracts. Almost without exception they underscored the necessity of conversion and faith, the evil elements that always taunted soldiers, and the glory of God available to all who sought it. Hundreds of such pamphlets were delivered weekly to the armies. The most popular of all was an eight-page leaflet, *A Mother's Parting Words to Her Soldier Son*. Written by Richmond clergyman Jeremiah B. Jeter, the mother's message was direct and fast-paced, void of the heavy sentimentality that lessened the reality—and hence the value—of so many other tracts. *Parting Words* called on a son to uphold liberty, freedom, and Christian values; and it did so with such effectiveness that over 250,000 copies went into the Confederate armies.

An anonymously written pamphlet, *How Do You Bear Your Trials?* urged soldiers always to seek God's help in time of trouble. *Pitching the Tent toward Sodom* warned of the dangers inherent in gambling, while *The Gambler's Balance Sheet* pointed out statistically that he who waged money gained all evil and no good. Fighting the use of alcohol were such commentaries as *Liquor and Lincoln and Liquor*, plus *The Eventful Twelve Hours; or the Destitution and Wretchedness of a Drunkard*. Profanity came under attack with a pointed tract, *Why Do You Swear?*, and an interesting monograph, *The Silly Fish*, in which the author compared a swearer to a fish that bit an empty hook: neither derived any real satisfaction from the experience.

Colporteurs and missionaries claimed that the tracts always met eager receptions and were highly conducive to improved behavior. The writings of the soldiers themselves display mixed opinions about the pamphlets. Some officers resented the tracts because they felt that the repeated references to death, judgment, and hell unnerved the fighting man and made him unreliable in battle. One soldier became angry at being deluged "with a plethora of religious tracts while I for weeks lay prone upon an army cot." However, a member of the 17th Mississippi was confident that the troops "generally receive them thankfully & read them with profit to their morals."[48]

Religion in the Civil War reached its zenith in two great revivals that swept through the Confederate armies. "Revival" was a popular term in that era. It signified a new and deep interest in religion—"an awakening following a period of indifference to spiritual matters." In the armies, it applied more specifically to a first embrace with faith and to a renewal of spirit among the "back-sliders."

The revival movement in the armies began at a time when Confederate morale had just suffered twin blows of defeat at Sharpsburg, Maryland, and Perryville, Kentucky. In the autumn and winter of 1862–1863, an ecumenical outpouring burst forth in General Robert E. Lee's encamped army in Virginia. Lincoln began worrying that "rebel soldiers are praying with a great deal more earnestness . . . than our own troops."[49] Interlocked together were an acute awareness of sin, daily prayer meetings and church services, fervid exhortations by chaplains, visiting missionaries, soldiers and laymen, public confessions of wrong-doing, baptisms at nearby streams, lines of men seeking conversion, and even greater numbers reaffirming their faith.

A Confederate described the December 1862 revival in his division as "one great Methodist Camp Meeting—they build log fires, sing, pray and preach, and when they ask for the morners they come in hundreds some falling on the ground crying for mercy." Three months later, a private in the 13th Georgia wrote his sister: "God is reviving his believers. The Soldiers amids hardships and privations are now more zealous for the Cause of Christ, Than our Christian friends at home. It would do you good if you could hear the tap of the drum for meeting and see the Soldiers gather for the Meeting." In the Western theater, a chaplain in General Braxton Bragg's army reported forty conversions nightly over a two-week period.[50]

The campaigns of Vicksburg and Gettysburg interrupted the revival movement. Following those two crushing defeats for the Confederacy, religious awakenings far more intense began in the autumn of 1863 and spread through both major theaters of war. Southerners now perceived the punishment of God at work in their military reversals. Moreover, with the war nowhere near an end, death lurked closer to the soldiers. A regimental correspondent stated the situation clearly to a Baptist newspaper: "There have always been among us some pious men, but until that time nothing like a general revival or even seriousness. The regiment had just returned from the disastrous Pennsylvania expedition, and a few days before had the closest and most desperate encounter with the enemy that they had ever had. The minds of the men were fresh from scenes of danger and bloodshed and were forced thereby to contemplate eternity, and in many cases, to feel the necessity of preparation."[51]

Forty chapels were thereupon built along Virginia's Rapidan River in the space of a few weeks. A missionary reported joyfully: "Men may be seen an *hour before services* running to the [meeting] house, in order that they may procure seats. They come from regiments two miles off." Out in Louisiana, a Confederate surgeon joyfully announced to his wife: "The meeting in the brigade still continues. Martin baptized 23 today making a total of 134 in two months. You who have never seen it cannot imagine such scenes as are daily transpiring here. From daylight until the late hours of the night nothing is heard but hymns and prayers. May God speed on the work until not a sinner is left in the command."[52]

One of Lee's brigade chaplains described his schedule: prayers at sunrise, "inquiry meeting" at 8 A.M., preaching at 11 A.M., prayers for Confederate success at 4 P.M., and preaching again at night.[53]

Inclement weather did not deter the faithful. A group of soldiers once waited forty minutes in a driving rain to have a service. At another camp meeting, fourteen barefooted soldiers were among a large group who stood in several inches of snow in anticipation of the arrival of a missionary. Chaplain J. William Jones recalled on another occasion that he had to cut ice from a millpond in order to conduct baptism, and soldiers eagerly awaited their turn to plunge into the icy water.

Backlash by the less-than-devout was to be expected. When a group of men in a New Hampshire regiment decided to organize an antidrinking group to be called the Sons of Temperance, some of their less ardent comrades quickly combined the first letters of the three words and dubbed the crusaders "SOTS." The society disbanded shortly thereafter. In January 1864, a Confederate soldier attended a civilian church service near the camp. What he saw was hardly inspiring. "The church was filled to overflowing with soldiers—the doors, windows, and even the loft was full when the excitement commenced. They got upon the benches and every ten minutes a bench would break down and then someone would fall out of the window and I never heard such loud singing in my life. It seems that they would make me Deaf. One lady said that she had seen Jesus and a soldier said, 'she was mistaken, that it was a soldier in the loft that she saw' and a thousand other expressions too sacreligious to repeat."[54]

In spite of such incidents, the Confederate army revivals of 1862–1864 were sweeping, exciting, and dramatic. They stimulated some 15,000 conversions—almost 1,000 men in September 1863 alone. One might assume that these professions of faith would have been more permanent than in civilian life because of the uncertain and dangerous environment of war. However, subsequent court-martial findings, statements of chaplains, and similar sources make it fairly clear that the consequences of revivals were short-lived. The desire for more entertaining outlets, and the accessibility of temptation, were too keen. Hence, for every soldier forever "cleansed" by the religious experience, two or three fellow converts soon lapsed into previous ways.

Still, trust in God reached to the soul of most Union and Confederate soldiers. Typical of the expressions made in letters was that of Pennsylvania soldier Milton Ray to his sister: "I hope you may continue in earnest prayer for the preservation of my life if it is God's holy will that I should be spared. If it is his will that I should sacrifice my life for my country then the Lord Jesus will receive my spirit. Pray that I may be a faithful soldier of the cross and of my country."

In strikingly similar vein, Tennessee infantryman Jim Parrott informed his wife: "God has bin my sheal and I hope that he will be until I dy what has bin the Cauze of him being my friend [is that] I have ask him for his blessing you rote to me that you prade for mee I do believe that God has ancered your parers for he has blest me in every thing and I Request you to Continyou tu ask god far to extend his blessings to wards us as a family if we shal never sea each other a gain in this life I hope that we will meat in heaven where there is no ware."[55]

Many veterans in the Army of Northern Virginia never forgot seeing a dead Confederate on one of the Richmond battlefields. His hand rested on a Bible, which was opened to the 23rd Psalm and the words: "Thy rod and Thy staff they comfort me."[56]

· 10 ·

"In the Prison Cell I Sit"

Of dozens of songs written during the Civil War by George F. Root, none tugged more at the heartstrings than his 1863 composition, "Tramp, Tramp, Tramp." Its lyrics began:

In the prison cell I sit, thinking, Mother dear, of you,
And our bright and happy home so far away.
And the tears they fill my eyes, spite of all that I can do,
Tho' I try to cheer my comrades and be gay.

Johnny Rebs and Billy Yanks went off to war with many expectations: novel sights, new friends, camp life, combat, martial glory, perhaps "a red badge of courage" (a battle wound), and possibly a heroic death. Few recruits ever envisioned capture, or the nightmarish existence as a prisoner of war. Yet 408,000 Civil War soldiers fell into the hands of the enemy. Over 56,000 of that number died painfully and neglected while locked in the remote and makeshift compounds of North and South.[1]

It did not have to be that way; but because it was, the subject of Civil War prisons inspired more embittered accusations and sparked more violent passions than did any aspect of the 1861–1865 period. The controversy still rages today. Andersonville had a well-publicized record that remains vile even by modern standards. Yet so did a dozen other prisons, both Union and Confederate. The sordidness and suffering that took place stemmed not so much from deliberation and malice as from clumsiness and inexperience. A combination of indifference and incompetence caused prisons of the 1860s to become factories of disease and death. Men perished under conditions of filth and terror never known before and not to be equaled until World War II.

Neither side started out with the intention of abusing prisoners of war. The ill-treatment that developed was the direct result of short-sightedness and, in some instances, lack of resources. North and South went to war without a single prison on the continent capable of holding more than a handful of men. Southerners convinced themselves from the beginning that there would be no real war. Northerners were confident that the uprising down south was a local disturbance that could last no more than ninety days. Hence, after the surrender of Fort Sumter, South Carolina, Major Robert Anderson and his small Federal garrison were shown every courtesy and allowed to leave Charleston as conquered heroes.

Meanwhile, in far-off Texas, 1,500 Federals who had surrendered to state authorities were preparing to return home when they were suddenly detained because of fears that their numbers would greatly reinforce the North. Most of those U.S. Regulars would spend the next two years in crude prisons. They were the first wave of soldier-prisoners in the Civil War.

The limited military action of 1861 did not yield enough prisoners to create a problem. Barely 1,300 men were captured at First Manassas in the Eastern theater. They were sent to Richmond and locked in several tobacco factories and warehouses converted into temporary holding pens. In the West, the only significant action in those first months of the war was an engagement at Wilson's Creek, Missouri, and only 300 prisoners were taken there. Such manageable numbers were easily accommodated in tent camps or converted warehouses. The first year of the war thus passed with—at best—haphazard attention to the natural by-product of any war.

What was a minor issue in 1861 became a crisis in 1862. Battle exploded, at Forts Henry and Donelson, Shiloh, Corinth, and Perryville in the West, Roanoke Island, Williamsburg, Seven Pines, the Shenandoah Valley, the Seven Days, Cedar Mountain, Second Manassas, and Antietam Creek in the East. An original trickle of prisoners became a flood. Yet both sides seemed content to use Band-Aids for major wounds. Exchanges and paroles, informally arranged by opposing commanders, were a common practice. Men who surrendered simply gave their paroles as prisoners of war and then were shipped to a rendezvous point for formal exchange. Once exchanged, former prisoners returned to their regiments.

In actual practice, however, many of the paroled soldiers considered themselves through with the war and wanted no further part in it. They were difficult to keep in the parole camps. A Union soldier at Annapolis estimated that three-fourths of the men under his charge were stern shirkers, and that not 500 of the men either knew or cared to which units they belonged. "If the men in my camp were a sample of our army," he stated, "we would have nothing but a mob of stragglers and cowards."[2]

Pressure for some sort of release originated with families, newspapermen, and politicians; and this pressure increased as the struggle entered its second year. Both sides relented, and on July 22, 1862, Federal General John A. Dix and Confederate General D. Harvey Hill formalized an official cartel applicable to all military theaters. The system was cumbersome but fairly effective. All prisoners were to be released within ten days after capture, or as soon thereafter as practical. Enlisted troops would be exchanged man for man; officers would be swapped on a one-for-one basis according to rank or on a complex scale of values: 2 lieutenants for a captain, 6 privates for a captain, 30 enlisted men for a major general, and so forth. Surplus prisoners were to be paroled until they could be officially exchanged. Paroled soldiers were not to bear arms or perform other military duties. Any misunderstandings that might arise over the cartel would become the "subject of friendly discussions" while the exchange continued.[3]

Implementing the cartel meant an enormous amount of paperwork. Delays were both regular and exasperating. The procedure worked well for only a few months. What went wrong was simply that the whole system rested on gentlemen's agreements; and once the war passed the boundaries of gentlemanly conduct, prisoner exchange disintegrated. As examples: Southern authorities refused to swap black soldiers on a parity with whites; Northern generals complained that the exchange policy was so lenient as to induce soldiers to be captured so that they could be paroled and sent home. Each side accused the other of repeated violations, and the misunderstandings intensified to the breaking point.

The cartel collapsed in 1863; thereafter, the number of prisoners in Northern and Southern stockades zoomed upward to oftentimes uncontrollable levels and forced the creation of many new compounds. Both sides converted what they could find into military prisons: jails, training camps, warehouses, school buildings, even open fields. It was a situation that became particularly acute for the South. The largest influx of prisoners came at a time when the Confederacy's transportational and supply systems were disintegrating.

What transpired in those hastily improvised quarters was a terrible combination of neglect and suffering. Yet the two sides were equally guilty of displaying congestion plus unfitness and mismanagement in the officer personnel supervising the prison systems. From every one of the twenty major prisons of the Civil War came nauseating stories of filth, vermin, disease, poor food, abominable sanitary practices, and inadequate medical care. These in turn produced widespread sickness, mental depression, and—for thousands—slow death.

It was late in 1861 before North or South even got around to placing an official in charge of prisons. The Northern commandant was Colonel William Hoffman. He was an energetic and patriotic officer, yet at the same time a dollar-conscious administrator whose miserly qualities bode ill for Confederate prisoners. Hoffman never fully grasped the magnitude of his task. Even worse, he proved to be little more than an errand boy for the vindictive Secretary of War Edwin M. Stanton.

One of Hoffman's first assignments was to establish a new prison solely for captured southerners. He thought an island somewhere deep in the North to be the ideal site. After a long search, Hoffman selected Johnson's Island in Lake Erie and a couple of miles offshore from Sandusky, Ohio. The commissary-general of prisoners, as Hoffman was called, specified that the compound should be large enough to hold 1,000 prisoners. Early in 1862 Hoffman proudly announced that Johnson's Island was ready for occupancy. Two weeks later, Fort Donelson, Tennessee, fell to forces under Gen. U. S. Grant. That one capture resulted in the largest surrender of American troops in the nation's history to that time. Suddenly Hoffman had 12,000 Confederate prisoners to accommodate. The disorderly manner in which they were scattered throughout the North became the norm thereafter.

Hoffman's counterpart on the Southern side was Brigadier General John H. Winder. A military bureaucrat with an abrasive personality and little sympathy for captured enemy soldiers, Winder got his job because he had been the tight-fisted provost marshal of Richmond in the first months of the war. In Winder's defense, it can be said that he had few material resources for handling large numbers of Federals, and he had even less authority for implementing any kind of uniform policy for a balanced and humane treatment of prisoners. Winder responded to the problem by establishing prison camps here and there and leaving each one pretty much to fend for itself.

More than 150 military prisons sprang into existence during the Civil War. Only about 20 (10 on each side) reached major notoriety. All of the compounds can be grouped under one of five types. First were coastal fortifications, with Fort Warren in Boston harbor, Fort Delaware on Pea Patch Island in the Delaware River, and Castle Pinckney in Charleston harbor being the most well known. Next were enclosed barracks: groups of wooden buildings set up on a large plot of ground. Originally constructed as basic-training camps or as rendezvous points for recruits, this type existed only in the North. The principal prisons in this category were Camp Chase in Columbus, Ohio, Camp Douglas at Chicago, and Camp Morton in Indianapolis.

A third type of compound, found primarily in the South, were old buildings converted into prisons. Libby Prison in Richmond, Castle Thunder at Petersburg, and six tobacco warehouses at Danville, Virginia, became the most notorious among this class. Fourth were clusters of tents enclosed by a high fence. Only two major prisons were in this category: Point Lookout, Maryland, near the junction of the Potomac River and the Chesapeake Bay, and Belle Isle, located in the James River a little west of downtown Richmond. The last type of compound were barren stockades with no shelter save what the prisoners themselves were able to construct. This class existed only in the South and included Camp Sorghum, South Carolina, Salisbury, North Carolina, Camp Ford, Texas, and Camp Sumter (more familiarly known as Andersonville), Georgia.

Officers and enlisted men were always kept in separate compounds, the rationale being that as long as enlisted men had no superiors, they were a leaderless—and hence helpless—mass. For example, Johnson's Island was an officer prison, while Andersonville held only enlisted men.

After every battle, lines of disarmed enemy troops were led to the rear under guard. These captives spent several hours in some sort of holding pens while their names and units were being recorded. Provost marshals then made arrangements for the prisoners to be sent to one of the central compounds far behind the lines. Transportation was by rail, boat, or foot, depending in part on the distance involved and in part on what conveyances were available.

Civilians along the way gathered to watch the men pass. Sometimes they hurled invectives at the prisoners. George Hegeman of the 52nd

New York recalled being led with a long line of prisoners through Warrenton, Virginia. The sight of captured Yankees attracted a large crowd of "the Reb Ladies who before when our army passed through the town were all Union." Now, Hegeman snorted, they "came out in their true colors and gave us a beautiful blessing, using the choicest language."[4]

The prisoners were usually taken to "depot prisons" such as Point Lookout, Maryland, and Libby Prison, Virginia, then reassigned to another stockade for however long the incarceration was to be. Once the men arrived at their final destination, their names and units were again checked, the prisoners underwent another search, after which they entered the compound and began the ordeal of survival.

For captured soldiers, life in confinement followed a drab and demoralizing routine. The men arose at dawn, answered roll call, and received some type of breakfast. After that meal, a Massachusetts soldier confined at Libby wrote, "the men had ample time for reflection. I thought of home and the dear ones that were left behind, not knowing whether we were dead or alive."[5] Conversation, sleep, thoughts, and sporadic activity occupied the day. A second meal came in late afternoon. Roll call occurred again around 7 P.M., followed by lights out two hours later. The next day was a repetition, as was the next, and the next.

Whether at Johnson's Island in Lake Erie, Belle Isle in the James River, Camp Douglas on Chicago's outskirts, Cahaba Prison deep in Alabama pine country, or any other of the major stockades, the thoughts and complaints of captured soldiers were the same. For starters, and with few exceptions, prison commandants were universally damned. Among those praised was Colonel Charles W. Hill at Johnson's Island. A Confederate there termed Hill "a good friend to the prisoners, all of whom esteemed him very highly for his kindness of heart . . ."[6]

Colonel Richard D. Owen, in command of Camp Morton, Indiana, proved so caring and benevolent that after the war former prisoners commissioned a bust of the colonel. It still remains on display in the Indiana capitol. Federal prisoners at Danville, Virginia, described the prison commandant, Lieutenant Colonel Robert C. Smith, as "a kind, sympathetic man" who "would not voluntarily inflict any unnecessary hardships upon those under his charge." Yet as Smith helplessly watched conditions at Danville deteriorate, he took refuge in whiskey and became a victim of his own system.[7]

Inmates tended to regard most prison officials, however, as little more than sadistic monsters. The 53rd Illinois' George R. Lodge described one of Libby's prison clerks as "the little snotty pup" and a prison officer as an "Ass of a Lieut.—with a head the shape of a cocoanut."[8] Captain Henry Wirz of Andersonville emerged in prisoners' recollections as the Devil incarnate. Described as "a most savage looking man, and who was as brutal as his looks would seem to indicate," the Swiss-born Wirz was the perpetrator of a host of alleged atrocities. A Massachusetts artilleryman, for example, asserted that when he arrived at the Georgia prison, he and his fellow captives were forced to stand in line while Wirz, a huge cavalry pistol in his hand, strolled up and down in front of the men and shouted: "What'd you come down here for? First god-dam man that falls out of line I blow him to hell! I will make you wish you stay at home!"[9]

Libby Prison's Dick Turner was another jailer around whom atrocity stories swirled. An "eyewitness" testified that this officer, variously categorized as "a vulgar, coarse brute" and "the greatest scoundrel that ever went unhung," once entered a room, saw a dying prisoner lying on the floor and, for no reason (it was charged), kicked the man in the side. Confederate prisoners at Fort Delaware thought Lieutenant Abraham Wolf possessed of "all the mean, cowardly, and cruel instincts of the beast from which his name was taken." Point Lookout's Major Allen G. Brady supposedly enjoyed galloping his horse through crowds of prisoners, trampling those unable to get out of the way. Speaking of Fort Delaware's commandant and two of the guards, a Tennesseean snorted: "I Dont Think Thar is any Place in Hell Hot anuf for Thos 3 men."[10]

A few of the criticisms were more than unfounded opinion. When a Federal inspector made his first tour of the prison at Camp Chase, Ohio, he disgustingly noted that Commandant Charles W. B. Allison "is entirely without experience and utterly ignorant of his duties and he is surrounded by the same class of [officers]." The inspector added dryly: "But he is a lawyer and a son-in-law of the Lieutenant-Governor."[11]

Prison guards were more loathsome and hateful in the eyes of captives for several reasons. The anonymity of the enemy disappeared in prison. Whereas soldiers viewed their foe as opponents barely visible across a no-man's land, opposing soldiers now saw each other as individuals with appearance and personality. Further, when large groups of men, motivated by enthusiasm and patriotism, are suddenly denied the opportunity to continue fighting for those emotions because of capture, and when captors find themselves masters over men who may be their superiors in the number of ways, sharp antagonisms develop. The old axiom that no prisoner loves his jailer was certainly true in the 1860s, but so was the likelihood that few jailers sympathized with the inmates under their charge.

Troops assigned to guard captured soldiers consisted in the main of men mentally or physically unfit for duty in the field. On both sides prison sentries appeared to possess a combination of good-natured indifference mixed with heavy parts of half-witted cruelty. An Andersonville inmate wrote: "we are under the Malishia & their ages range from 10 to 75 & they are the Dambst set of men I ever had the Luck to fall in with yet." Another prisoner described the guards as "the worst looking scallawags. . . . from boys just large enough to handle a gun, to old men who . . . , ought to have been dead years ago for the good of their country." Even Andersonville's commandant admitted to the guards' "carelessness" and "inefficiency," adding that their "worthlessness" was "on the increase day by day."[9]

In countless affidavits from prisoners in every major Civil War compound, allegations were made that guards shot prisoners in cold blood without provocation—and that guards received bounties, furloughs, or promotions for their acts. Prisoners on both sides viewed the sentries with the same sentiment expressed by a Texan: "An ambitious coward loves authority where he is secure from danger and can vent his fiendish nature on his fellow man."[13]

A combination of wartime shortages and wartime psychoses accounted for much of the suffering that prisoners of war had to endure. Drab quarters and inadequate supplies existed for captured Federals because the embattled South did not possess the necessary materiel. The rations distributed to Union prisoners was often no worse than Confederate soldiers in the field were receiving. Indeed, early in the war the Confederate Congress passed legislation stipulating that "the rations furnished prisoners of war shall be the same in quantity and quality as those furnished to enlisted men in the Confederacy."[14] Unfortunately, Union officials seemed never to have been aware of the straitened condition.

Thus, when reports began filtering northward through the lines that Southern authorities were purposefully subjecting Federal prisoners to starvation, the North responded in kind. Rations in Northern prisons were reduced, sometimes by half. A Confederate officer complained directly to Colonel Hoffman about the "inhuman treatment" he had received at Camp Chase. The commissary-general dismissed the charge by declaring that the new Union treatment was "retaliation for innumerable outrages which have been committed on our people." On another occasion, Hoffman stated in an official directive: "It is not expected that anything more will be done to provide for the welfare of Rebel prisoners than is absolutely necessary."[15]

Northern propagandists buttressed this countermovement with tales of "sleek fat rebels" living the good life in Northern prison camps. The Union quartermaster general even complained publicly of prison officials treating inmates as "Southern gentlemen," and feeding them so lavishly that "they die of gout."[16]

As prison conditions in the South worsened with the course of the war, so did Northern accusations. Newspaper editors, utilizing both history and sensationalism, borrowed atrocity stories from the War of 1812 and the American Revolution in "reporting" Confederate mistreatment of prisoners. In 1864 the U.S. Sanitary Commission issued a blatantly distorted report of the state of affairs in Union and Confederate stockades. Southerners, the document charged, were practicing cruelty and deprivations as part of "a predetermined plan for destroying and disabling the soldiers of their enemy."[17] In contrast, the Sanitary Commission intoned, Confederate prisoners enjoyed mess funds so generous that the surpluses were being used to provide luxuries for the captured men. Colonel Hoffman, meanwhile, continued to make severe cuts in prisoner rations, and at the end of the war he proudly returned two million dollars to the Federal Treasury!

In truth, conditions of Southern soldiers incarcerated in a land of plenty were as inhuman as those for Union soldiers imprisoned in a land being systematically destroyed.

Food issues provoked more negative comments than any other subject; for with mealtime being the only break in the boredom of the day, thinking about food became a dominant part of life in captivity. Prison fare was qualitatively drab, monotonous, and suspect in content. The amounts rationed to the men were such as merely to keep appetites whetted. Captain John W. Lavender of the 4th Arkansas wrote of his stay at Johnson's Island: "Men in there was Just as Every place Else. Some had no get up aboute them, never tried to shift around and help themselves but sit around Draw their Rashions, Growl and talk aboute home and how good mother Could cook."

A New England officer confined at Libby swore that his rations "consisted of about twenty-two ounces of bread and thirty ounces of meat for one week. We had something else that they gave us one week; I do not know what the name of it was." Tennessee prisoner Joseph Hoover knew what his prison fare was on one occasion at Camp Douglas. Hoover swore that he ate a hunk of mule neck with the hair still attached.[18]

Randolph Shotwell of the 8th North Carolina termed the bacon distributed at Fort Delaware "rusty" and "very slimy;" the soup ("slop") was "filled with white worms a half inch long." It was a standing joke, Shotwell commented, "that the soup was too weak *to drown* the rice worms and pea bugs, which, however, came to their death by starvation."[19]

In fact, a starvation atmosphere existed inside every prison. South Carolina Sergeant James T. Wells catalogued his food issues in November 1863: "For breakfast, half-pint coffee, or, rather, slop water; for dinner; half-pint greasy water (called soup for etiquette), also a small piece of meat, perhaps three or four ounces. For bread we were allowed eight ounces per day; this you could press together in your hand and take at a mouthful. . . . The writer has known large, stout men to lay in their tents at night and cry like little babies from hunger . . . " A Virginia soldier wrote of Point Lookout: "I have heard men pray to be made sick that the appetite might be taken away."[20]

With hunger so prevalent, prisoners quickly pounced on any source of meat. A dog or cat that wandered into a prison became a feast for whoever caught it. Soldiers were equally quick in seizing rats that inhabited every prison. Let a rodent make an appearance, and minutes later it would be sizzling over a fire. Captain Lavender stated of Johnson's Island fare: "We traped for Rats and the Prisoners Eat Every one they Could get. I taken a mess of Fried Rats. They was all right to a hungry man, was liked Fried squirrels . . . "

Tennesseean Joseph Ripley was so adept at catching rats that he often treated fellow inmates to nightly banquets. "These feasts are pleasant memories to me yet," he stated years later. They "broke the monotony of prison life, and to play host to a rat dinner [which relieved] your comrades of that awful torture of gnawing hunger, gave you the consciousness of having done well."[21]

Regardless of the nature of the food received, prisoners learned to eat it immediately lest it be wrenched from their hands by starved-crazy inmates. Vicious brawls often exploded over nothing more than a morsel of food.

Drinking water inside the prisons was usually less than desirable.

The few wells furnishing Salisbury Prison in North Carolina produced so little water that they ran dry after sunrise each day. At Point Lookout, the drinking water was heavy with coppera and tasted brackish. One Southern prisoner with a gift for words described the water there as "so impregnated with some mineral as to offend every nose, and induce diarrhea in almost every alimentary canal. It colors everything black in which it is allowed to rest, and a scum rises on the top of the vessel, if it is left standing during the night, which reflects the prismatic colors as distinctly as the surface of a stagnant pool."[22]

Inadequate clothing was also a widespread source of misery. Most soldiers were wearing lightweight summer issue when captured and were unprepared for the frigid gales of winter in open and drafty stockades. One group of Confederate prisoners arrived at Rock Island Prison, Illinois, on a wintry afternoon. A cold wind was whipping across the Mississippi River compound. The new arrivals spent the next hours pounding themselves to keep warm as they as they trotted back and forth through the drafty barracks. In the days that followed, several comrades dozed off from coldness and quietly died. Topcoats were rarely in evidence, and as a rule only one man in three would possess even a scrap of a blanket. The need for clothing became so acute that the rags of dead comrades were eagerly seized by those still living.[23]

Never was there such a thing as a clean Civil War prison. Especially where buildings served as compounds, inmates made little effort to keep their quarters reasonably free of filth; and authorities did not enforce rules of cleanliness. Filth at all stockades bred epidemics of fleas, lice, and bedbugs. A wounded prisoner from the 22nd Massachusetts wrote of his first days at Libby: "I was painfully aware that ownership of my clothing would be disputed by other occupants, inch by inch. It was no uncommon thing for the men during the warm days to remove all their clothing, and so get temporary relief from their bloodthirsty tormentors. The flies were also a source of great annoyance. Not only were their bites painful, but we were obliged to be constantly on the watch to prevent their depositing eggs on our bandages, and so produce maggots." A Tennessee prisoner stated of life at Rock Island: "About one million or more Cooties Chas[ed] Each other up and down my Spine and now an then Stop to dig into [my] Small Pocks Sores."[24]

Vermin were so plentiful in prison, a Rhode Islander commented, "that the boys said they had regimental drill." A Confederate at Washington's Old Capitol Prison wrote of regular attacks by bedbugs. He sighed: "Sometimes we get together and have . . . a promiscuous slaughter, regardless of age or sex. But they must recruit from the other side, like the Yankee army, as we can notice no dimunition in the forces."[25]

George H. Putnam of the 176th New York found fleas particularly obnoxious. "The beasts crawled over the ground from body to body, and their attacks seemed to become more aggravating as the men became more emaciated. By daylight, they could be picked off and the first occupation of the morning was usually to free oneself from their immediate presence, but in the darkness there was nothing to do but suffer with patience." The 19th Massachusetts' John G. B. Adams added: "We hunted them three times each day but could not get the best of them. They are very prolific and great-grandchildren would be born in twenty-four hours after they struck us."[26]

Lack of nourishment and proper sanitation, plus limited medical facilities and short supplies of medicine, triggered extensive sickness in all prisons. The long wide trenches that served as latrines at Old Capitol were immediately adjacent to the prison itself. They were never cleaned or covered with layers of dirt. A Confederate inmate overlooked the health problem when he stated tersely: "The presence of these sinks . . . did not contribute to the beauty of the scenery or add sweetness to the tainted air."

Every factor was present to make prisoners seriously ill. Confederate Surgeon Joseph Jones made an inspection of Andersonville, and part of his report easily applied to every Civil War compound: "From the crowded conditions, filthy habits, bad diet and dejected, depressed condition of the prisoners, their system had become so disordered that the smallest abrasion of skin, from the rubbing of a shoe, or from the effects of the sun, the prick of a splinter or the scratching of a mosquito bite, in some cases took on a rapid and frightful ulceration and gangrene."[27]

Scurvy and chronic diarrhea complicated any illness or outbreak of disease. Prisoners lived in particular dread of scurvy, a "deep-sea malady" caused by lack of fresh fruits and vegetables. Without such foods, there was no way to block or control it. Soldiers could only watch for it by pushing a thumb or finger inside some soft part of the flesh and waiting to see if a discoloration followed or if the indentation vanished. The later, more dread signs of scurvy were teeth loosening and hair falling out, followed by a third stage in which the legs could no longer support the body. Scurvy was common in many Civil War prisons and epidemic in some. In mid-September, 1864, no less than 1,870 cases existed at Elmira—a compound then but three months old.[28]

Later that year, one of every nine Confederates at Fort Delaware fell victim to the disease. Fresh vegetables existed in abundance on the nearby mainland, and a prison fund was available to purchase needed items; yet Colonel Hoffman in Washington insisted that money be spent only on absolute necessities. Hence, at a time when scurvy was rampant, some $23,000 languished in the Fort Delaware "relief fund."[29]

Prison hospitals were a hellish farce. At the Camp Douglas ward, sick Confederates had to lie on cots without mattresses, sheets, or bedding. The rooms reeked from foul air. During one twenty-two-day period in 1863, 130 prisoners died in the hospital. Another 130 Southerners, unable to gain admission there, breathed their last in the barracks.[30] Yet this was mild compared to medical conditions at Andersonville.

There the hospital was a five-acre plot of ground outside the stockade. Ill prisoners were placed in sheds open on all sides and thus vulnerable to every element of weather. Patients lay on boards with no covering unless the Federal soldier himself had a piece of blanket. Hospital stewards were other prisoners known largely for ignorance, carelessness, and neglect. Wounds were cleaned merely by pouring water over them and letting everything seep into the ground on which the men lay. Such unsanitary conditions attracted millions of flies that tended to collect on men too weak to offer resistance.

Two prisons that opened simultaneously in 1864 represent the basest horrors of Civil War compounds.

By the beginning of that year, Virginia prisons were filled beyond capacity; and Union forces shortly would resume their advance through the state. Confederate authorities decided to transfer most of the captured Union enlisted men in Virginia to a new prison farther south where security would be greater and food supplies supposedly more abundant. The site selected was an open, treeless plain in south central Georgia. Officially named Camp Sumter, it became known more for the nearby settlement: Andersonville.

The twenty-six acres were never sufficient for the number of men who flowed into it. In addition, the locale was so isolated that getting building materials to it was extremely difficult. Hence, the only structures were a few shanty-like outbuildings used for headquarters, cookhouse, hospital, and morgue. The commandant reported in the prison's second month of existence that he was burying the dead without coffins because he did not have enough lumber to begin to meet the needs of the living.[31] Prisoners had to construct lean-tos out of blankets, clothing, sticks, and any other materials they could procure. Many dug depressions in the ground and placed scraps of blankets or shirts over them to make crude dugouts.

Federal prisoners began arriving at Andersonville in February 1864 while the camp was still being laid out. Prison officials were caught completely unprepared. Before even reasonable arrangements could be made, transferred prisoners swamped Andersonville's primitive facilities. From 7,500 inmates in March, the population jumped to 15,000 in May, and 29,000 in July. By August—the peak month for Andersonville—33,000 emaciated Federals were crammed into a shelterless expanse that offered each inmate about twenty-five square feet of space (roughly the space consumed in lying down).[32] At that time, only four cities in the Southern Confederacy had a higher population.

The crowded conditions at Andersonville produced massive pollution. There was no room for needed latrines. Bisecting the compound was a small stream known as Sweet Water Branch. It was simultaneously a garbage dump for the hospital and cookhouse, a latrine for thousands of prisoners, and the only source of water for the entire prison. Mosquitoes, fleas, lice, flies, and maggots were everywhere. The remoteness of Andersonville, plus critical food shortages in the South during the last year of the war, reduced rations to the point where authorities often could not provide daily bread.

Bands of criminal elements inside the stockade preyed unmercifully on their own. By far the largest and most vicious of these groups was led by William Collins of Pennsylvania and called itself the "Mosby Rangers." The band looted and murdered at will until it, not the Confederate guards, dominated life inside Andersonville. Other prisoners soon banded together out of desperation. With the permission of the commandant, they took matters into their own hands. Inmates arrested the raiders and brought them to trial before a vigilante court. Six of the culprits were hanged. Eighteen others were sentenced to "run the gauntlet" between two rows of angry prisoners. Three of them died from the severe beating they received.[33]

Andersonville quickly gained a reputation for infamy still unmatched in the Western Hemisphere. A Confederate surgeon who inspected the compound in the most crowded period was appalled by what he found. The 30,000 prisoners were jammed together "with little or no attention to hygiene, with festering masses of filth at the very doors of their rude dens and huts." More than 10,000 Federals had died in the past seven months; another 5,000 were desperately ill with diarrhea, dysentery, hospital gangrene, scurvy, and a host of other illnesses. Some 90–130 deaths were occurring daily.[34]

Federals who survived confinement at Andersonville later sought to outdo each other in describing the horrors of that stockade. "Eyewitness accounts" even appeared from men who were never there. Those who did endure Andersonville wrote of "men almost skeletons," of others "bloated with scurvy," of prisoners "clothed in rags" and living in a filth beyond comprehension, of the weak and dying "creeping upon their hands and knees" in search of help that never came. One New England prisoner gave up trying to enumerate the full extent of the misery. "The lexicographers of our language have not yet invented the words of proper strength to express condemnation of the studied inhumanities of Andersonville." And if any doubts remained as to Andersonville being one vast execution chamber, its critics charged, 13,000 deaths in less than a year formed a seemingly irrefutable indictment.[35]

In truth, while the situation at the Georgia compound would have taxed the endurance of hale and hearty men, few of the Federals sent there could in any wise be termed able-bodied. Rather than being "fresh fish" (as newly captured prisoners were dubbed by longterm inmates), most of the Union soldiers who filed through Andersonville's large wooden doors and into the crowded pen beyond had been in long confinement elsewhere and were seriously ill when they reached the prison.

Fifty percent of the prisoners were reported sick in each of Andersonville's first six months of existence. Final statistics for the prison leave little doubt but that practically every captive required some kind of medical treatment at some point. Thus, Andersonville was more a vast, badly organized, thoroughly inadequate hospital than a military prison. Medical facilities, surgeons, drugs, and sick diet were needed more than anything else. The lack of those essentials was unquestionably the principal cause of the high mortality rate at that stockade.[36]

Another post-1863 prison became the Northern counterpart to Andersonville. No compound struck a deeper chill of terror in the minds of Confederate soldiers than the enclosed-barracks stockade at Elmira, New York. For six of its twelve months, this prison led all Northern compounds in number of deaths with an average of ten per day. Elmira also had the largest sick list of any Federal prison for the last half-year of the Civil War. A Texas soldier spoke for every inmate when he declared: "If there was ever hell on earth, Elmira prison was that hell."[37]

This prison, which opened in July, 1864, could not have been in a worse location. It was a thirty-acre expanse alongside—and actually below—the Chemung River. Flooding was a constant danger. In the middle of the area was a stagnant lagoon 40 feet wide and 3–6 feet deep. This backwash was called Foster's Pond, and it received all cookhouse refuse plus thousands of gallons of human sewage daily. Foster's Pond rapidly became a veritable cesspool, its "festering mass of corruption" producing such "pestilential odors" that the mere smell of the pond caused vomiting.[38]

Thirty-five two-storied wooden barracks, each 100 by 20 feet, comprised the prison camp. The green lumber used in construction held for no more than six months, after which it began "cracking, splitting, and warping in every direction." Because none of the barracks had foundations, the floors were always cold and damp. Officials were repeatedly warned in advance to expect 10,000 prisoners. Preparations were inexplicably made for half that number. By mid-August 1864, after a mere six weeks in operation, Elmira contained 9,600 Confederates.[39] Shortsighted authorities hastily began to jam the overflow into tents that provided no protection from the severe temperatures of winter. When the supply of tents ran out, hundreds of prisoners were forced to sleep in the open.

Diarrhea and dysentery were the first illnesses that prostrated Southerners in droves. One official described the prisoners as "pale and emaciated, hollow-eyed and disspirited in every act and movement." In September, scurvy multiplied the suffering by afflicting fully 20 percent. A month later, while the post surgeon was stating with relief that "the number of deaths this week is but forty," the prison commandant warned officials in Washington that if the volume of sickness continued at the current rate, the entire prison population would be dead within a year.[40]

The winter of 1864–1865 was the coldest and most prolonged of the war. At Elmira, each barracks had one stove, which was pitifully insufficient for the 100 inhabitants in the building. Every wintry morning, a Virginia cavalryman stated, "the men crawled out of their bunks shivering and half frozen, when a scuffle, and frequently a fight, for a place by the fire occurred. God help the sick or the weak, as they were literally left out in the cold." Indeed they were. On one occasion, over

1,600 half-naked Confederates, lacking any semblance of a blanket or tent, stood ankle-deep in snow to answer morning roll call. Pneumonia became an epidemic, as did an outbreak of smallpox which began in December. By then, one of the prison guards stated, Confederates were dying "as sheep with the rot." Official figures confirm that observation: 2,980 of the 12,147 Confederates locked inside Elmira perished before the compound abandoned operations in the summer of 1865.[41]

Living conditions inside all the prisons were an abomination. Every captured soldier would have summarized his involuntary home in the same vein as an Alabamian characterized Fort Delaware: "It is useless to attempt a description of the place. A respectable hog would have turned up his nose in disgust at it."[42] That kind of environment, plus the sometimes laxity of guards and proximity to one's own lines, led to countless escape attempts. They occurred at every prison because, wrote one Federal, "freedom was more desired than salvation, more sought after than righteousness."[43] To escape from the living nightmare became the hope of every prisoner at one time or another.

The largest prison break of the Civil War happened not in some remote, sparsely populated outpost but in the very heart of the Confederate capital.

Libby Prison was the most widely known of several Richmond warehouses converted into prison compounds. Situated near the James River and only blocks from the downtown area, Libby was a large building three stories high in front and four in the rear as the land fell away toward the river. It contained as many as 1,200 Federal officers for most of the war, and the prison became notorious for draftiness and vermin.

By late 1863, the cartel had collapsed and further exchange seemed unlikely. One Federal inmate at Libby observed: "We fumed and fretted, and our restraint grew more and more irksome. At last we settled down to the conviction that we were in for the war, unless we affected escape . . . " Another officer, likewise "brooding over his confinement," was thirty-three-year-old Colonel Thomas E. Rose of the 77th Pennsylvania.[44] A heavy-set, fully bearded man with piercing eyes, Rose had been captured in September at the battle of Chickamauga. He was impatient to rejoin his command.

Rose began discussing escape possibilities with two youthful subalterns, Major Andrew G. Hamilton of the 12th Kentucky Cavalry and Captain Isaac N. Johnston of the 6th Kentucky Infantry. Soon they had an unwanted ally: the 51st Indiana's Colonel Abel D. Streight, a flamboyant officer who somehow learned of the plot in its first stages. Streight would bear watching, the others agreed.

A tunnel was to be the means of escape. Although streets bounded Libby on three sides, a forty-foot open field adjoined the east face. At the far end of the field was a high board fence enclosing a lot on which stood a storage building. If a tunnel could be dug from the prison to a point in the storage lot, the fence would serve as a screen for prisoners making their escape. Where and how to begin the tunnel were the immediate as well as the major problems. Several of the Federals made a thorough inspection of the Libby building over the course of several days and then arrived at a course of action.

The center room on the main floor was an abandoned kitchen unguarded and open to the prisoners. Colonel Rose discovered that the hearthstones in the fireplace were loose; once pulled away, they gave access to the unused basement below. "Sufficient of the masonry was removed from the fireplace to admit the passage of a man through a diagonal cut to the store room below," Colonel Harrison Hobart of the 21st Wisconsin wrote; and Lieutenant Warren H. Mead of the 6th Kentucky Cavalry added: "Crawling through that aperture, feet foremost, and dropping down ten feet, would bring a person into the dark and empty basement under the adjoining room."[45] Accumulated ashes in the fireplace were used to mask the stones removed and replaced as the men went to and from work.

Rose enlisted perhaps as many as 200 of the 1,200 prisoners in the scheme. Each swore an oath of secrecy and began toiling when possible in around-the-clock shifts. Those prisoners too weak to perform hard labor acted as sentinels to cover the absence of the diggers. The only tools that the men had were a table knife, an old chisel, a wooden box that had been serving as a spittoon, some string from a clothing shipment, and a few candles.

The digging procedure was painfully simple, Colonel Hobart stated. "But two persons could work at the same time. One would enter the hole with his tools and a small tallow candle, dragging the spittoon after him attached to a string. The other would fan air into the passage with his hat, and with another string would draw out the novel dirt cart when loaded, concealing its contents beneath the straw and rubbish of the cellar."[46]

For thirty days the excavation proceeded tediously. The tunnel was eight feet below street level, the men judged, and barely large enough for a person to travel through by groping with hands and feet. Detection by Confederates seemed imminent on several occasions, but luck held for the prisoners.

Shortly after dark on February 7, 1864, the tunnel reached what seemed to be the fifty-foot mark. Success was just a few inches away. It was then that the fame-seeking Colonel Streight stepped forward. Insisting that the tunnel was long enough, and apparently exerting seniority of rank, Streight personally crawled through the tunnel to have the honor of digging upward and breaking through the ground. When he did so, the colonel found himself not behind the storage building fence but out in the open field—and a few feet from two Confederate sentinels.

Streight, his head protruding from the hole, crouched motionless and barely breathed. One of the guards looked into the darkness and said: "I have been hearing a strange noise in the ground there."

The two Confederates listened intently for several moments. Then the second sentry replied: "Oh, it's nothing but rats," and the two walked away.[47]

Hastily, Streight made his way back through the tunnel. One of the Federal prisoners donated his shirt, and the premature hole was quickly plugged. Digging resumed, now with more urgency. On Tuesday, February 9, Rose announced to his fellow miners that the breakout would take place at 9:00 that evening. To mask the escape, other prisoners would stage a musical show guaranteed to be loud and boisterous.

Rose, followed by Hamilton, led the first contingent through the dark and cramped passage. The feet of one prisoner became a beacon for the hands of the prisoner behind him, so that a veritable chain of men snaked through the tunnel. Rose broke ground on target in the storage lot; and as escapees emerged on the streets, prisoners watching from Libby's windows became overenthusiastic and rushed to the basement to join in the exodus. Suddenly someone shouted that guards had discovered the plot and were hastening into Libby with loaded muskets. Enthusiasm gave way to momentary pandemonium as some prisoners scurried back up the floors of the prison while fortunate ones continued to file through the underground passage. The cries of alarm, unfounded though they were, greatly restricted the number who went through the tunnel. Yet all told, six colonels, six lieutenant colonels, seven majors, thirty-two captains, and fifty-eight lieutenants made their escape that night.[48]

Once on the outside, the Federals broke up by individuals or groups of twos and walked off in different directions. Colonel Hobart explained how he avoided detection: "My face being very pale and my beard long, clinging to the arm of Col. West, I assumed the part of a discrepit old man who seemed to be in exceeding ill-health and badly affected with a consumptive cough. In this manner we passed beneath the glaring gas lights, and through the crowded streets, without creating a suspicion as to our real character."[49] The men headed either for the homes of known loyalists in the area or else they struck northward or eastward in search of the Federal lines.

The breakout was not discovered until roll call the following morning. The resultant indignation was intense, an Ohio prisoner commented. "When the rebel officers counted the men they found one hundred and nine too few. They were excited and counted again. . . . In a twinkling, church bells were ringing, cavalrymen were out with horns blaring, and all hounds obtainable were yelping. The excitement was at white-heat. The cavalry and hounds started in every direction. The prison guards were all arrested, charged with bribery."[50]

Of the 109 Federals who escaped, 59 made it back to their lines, 48 were recaptured, and 2 drowned in swollen streams. Among those returned to Libby and placed in solitary confinement was Colonel Rose. Yet, one of the Federals proudly asserted, the mass escape was "the grandest thing that ever took place in Libby Prison."[51]

The vast majority of group escape attempts were unsuccessful, and what happened in a Danville, Virginia, warehouse-prison ten months after the Libby breakout was typical.

Federals in Danville were locked on the upper floors of six warehouses. Each evening a small contingent was permitted downstairs to the anteroom so as to be escorted outside to collect water and firewood. Two prisoners—Brigadier General Alfred N. Duffie, a French adventurer known mainly for oratory and pomp, and William C. Raulston, the popular colonel of the 24th New York Cavalry—concocted a plan whereby the two of them, acting as a water detail, would go to the anteroom and occupy the attention of the guards while all the other prisoners in the building massed in the darkness of the stairwell. The two sentries would be overpowered, the Federals would dash from the warehouse, capture the other guards, destroy all military installations in the town, and then head for the nearest Union forces in the Shenandoah Valley.

The plan initially worked. Raulston and Duffie grabbed the two inside guards as scores of prisoners rushed into the anteroom. However, the noise of men bounding down wooden stairs instantly aroused the suspicions of the sergeant of the guard outside. He cracked open the main door for a quick peek; at that moment, the Confederate whom Duffie was holding around the neck with both hands broke loose and began screaming: "Escape! Escape!"

Duffie later confessed: "I try to shut off ze wind, but ze more I choke, ze more he holly!"

Sounding the general alarm, the sergeant of the guard slammed and bolted the main door. Prisoners tried to batter down the entrance but the oak door was too thick. With Confederate troops rushing to the scene, Raulston yelled: "Too late! Go back!" Then a veritable traffic jam ensued as prisoners clambered to get back up the narrow stairs. Raulston was one of the last to start up; as he passed an open window, a shot rang out and the twenty-nine-year-old colonel fell against the wall from a mortal wound. This December 1864 attempt at freedom was the last such effort made at any of the Danville compounds.[52]

Thoughts of escape first faded and then disappeared as months of incarceration sapped strength and diluted determination. For most prisoners of war, the days were long, depressing, and dull. "Will no one send a little word to cheer us in our gloomy hours of activity?" a prisoner at Johnson's Island wrote in his journal. "Oh, God, how dreadful are these bitter feelings of hope deferred. . . . Thus we linger, thus we drag the slow, tedious hours of prison life."[53]

Men spent the slowly passing hours in every way possible. They read anything at hand; they played cards, checkers, chess, dice, and marbles; they whittled trinkets from bones and woods; they pitched ball or stones; they took brisk walks (when allowed) around the compound to keep muscles loose and circulation flowing.

Some men experimented with poetry. Most of the compositions were crude and somber, such as:

> Bless all, O Lord, and speed the time
> When freedom shall deliverance bring
> The fetters from the captive fall,
> The prison doors wide open spring.[54]

Conversation on every conceivable subject was a favorite pastime. The smallest tidbit of news would be retold and magnified until it reached unbelievable levels. This was especially true in the case of the most popular topic in prison: exchange. A Minnesota private at Andersonville wrote in his diary: "There is considerable excitement this morning about Paroling, but it is all gass I reckon for there never was so ignorant a lot of men to gether since the World stood that is in reguard to matters outside of the Bull Pen."[55]

Prisoners wrote letters when they could, which was seldom. Paper was scarce and outgoing mail was limited in length and severely censored. Some authorities restricted letter-writing by prisoners still further. As the commandant at Fort Delaware stated, "I found it impossible to permit them to write to everybody as they please, for the reason that four clerks in the post-office could not read 2,000 letters a day. . . . Another reason for this restriction is that they found out the names of notorious rebel sympathizers, to whom hundreds of letters were daily directed asking for assistance."[56]

Many captured soldiers found comfort in religion. On the last day of 1864, Kentucky soldier Thee Jones wrote his sister from Camp Douglas: "I pass a great portion of my time in reading the Holy Bible. I have read it through more than twice." The 28th North Carolina's William Norman stated of his routine at Johnson's Island: "Often while walking the floor of the prison, I repeat the Lord's Prayer, and I find my whole mind absorbed upon the subject of my future state of existence or my appearing before God."[57] Prisoners eagerly welcomed any minister, regardless of denomination, who came into the stockade to conduct services. Informal prayer meetings were common sights in every Civil War prison.

A large percentage of Union and Confederate prisoners simply became victims of their own existence. The lack of privacy, the harassment by prison officials who limited communications and reneged on promises of improved conditions, the claustrophobic nature of prison, critical shortages of food, clothing and shelter, an unknown future, the ever presence of death, broke the mental stability of many men. A New Yorker confined at Camp Sorghum, South Carolina, observed inmates who "sit moping for hours with a look of utter dejection, their elbow upon their knee, and their chin resting upon their hand, their eyes having a vacant, far-away look . . . "

Such catatonic behavior was not difficult to explain, a New Hampshire officer stated. "The sufferings of the body were not equal to the tortures of the mind. The uncertainty as to our prospects of release, the strange sense of isolation from the outer world, absence of news, the false rumors of intended exchange circulated throughout the camp, the hopes deferred, the longing for news from home, the many thoughts and desires that continually haunted us, the monotonous character of our daily life, the gradual but sure weakening of the body—all had a depressing effect upon the mind, and finally many became insane."[58]

Early in 1865 an exchange program resumed. Yet by then the damage had been done. Captain John G. B. Adams of the 19th Massachusetts was at Goldsboro, North Carolina, when, in mid-February of that year, some 200 released Federal prisoners arrived by train. It was, he declared, "the worst sight that the eyes of mortal [man] ever gazed upon. They had been three days on the road . . . As they were unloaded not one in fifty was able to stand. Many were left dead on the cars, the guards rolling them off as they would logs of wood; most of them were nearly naked, and their feet and hands were frozen; they had lost their reason; could not tell the State they came from, their regiment or company. We threw them what rations we had, and they would fight for them like dogs, rolling over each other in their eagerness to get the least morsel." Adams then stated: "I took a little fellow in my arms and carried him across the street; he could not have been over sixteen years old, and did not weight more than fifty pounds; he died just as I laid him down."[59]

With the coming of peace, prison doors everywhere sprang open. Emaciated soldiers were paroled and left to get home the best way they could. Yet while the suffering ended, the bitterness did not. Hysteria and exaggeration swelled to new heights. A New England cavalryman held for a time in one southern prison asserted that "for some very trifling offense of language, I have seen prisoners knocked down by the guard with iron bars and clubs, and have seen Union men stripped of their clothing and ducked in the freezing cold water, and their rations cut off for the day." Confederates were just as quick to get into the act. Southern soldiers charged that at Camp Douglas prisoners were regularly placed in solitary confinement for days on end, beaten with sticks and leather straps for such "crimes" as picking up snow to quench thirst, and "tortured with the thumb-screw until they fainted with pain."[60]

One might overlook such far-fetched allegations, but cold statistics on prison deaths could not be ignored. About 211,000 Federal soldiers had been captured in the course of the war; and of 194,000 imprisoned in the South, 30,000 had perished. Some 214,000 luckless Confederates had been sent to Northern prisons, where 26,000 had died.

The victors demanded revenge. General John H. Winder would have been the logical target, but the Confederate prison superintendent had died in February 1865 from overwork. The publicity—and propaganda—associated with Andersonville turned attention to its commandant, Captain Henry Wirz. He became an ideal "pound of flesh." A native of Switzerland, Wirz had served nine years in European armies before coming to America and establishing a medical practice in Louisiana. That background instilled in Wirz sharp characteristics of organization and discipline. He had joined the Confederate army shortly after civil war began. At the 1862 battle of Seven Pines he had received a wound that left an arm permanently useless and Wirz constantly in pain. He had then agreed to serve as a prison superintendent. His foreign accent remained pronounced and seemed to grow thicker when he became angry. Hence, this crippled foreigner, with martinet-like insistence on detail, engendered every prejudice among prisoners in his charge. Even before the war ended, Wirz had been labeled "the inhuman wretch," "the infamous Captain," and "the Andersonville savage."

In May 1865, Wirz was arrested. He was taken to Washington, brought before a military tribunal, and accused of "combining, confederating, and conspiring . . . to injure the health and destroy the lives of soldiers in the military service of the United Stated, then held and being prisoners of war, and . . . murder in violation of the laws and customs of war."[61] The trial was held that summer, with Wirz escorted daily from his cell in Old Capitol Prison to the courtroom. The proceedings were a mockery of justice: a parade of witnesses gave perjured testimony, evidence was manipulated, defense counsel was denied one motion after another. Wirz continually protested that he was merely a soldier carrying out orders in a situation of want.

Callous judges gave no heed to Wirz's statements. The court found him guilty of all charges and ordered him hanged. On the morning of November 10, 1865, calmly and with resignation, Wirz mounted the gallows and went to his death. It is, to say the least, ironic that on the site where Wirz was executed now stands the U.S. Supreme Court building.[62]

Wirz was the final casualty of Civil War prison camps. However, the charges and countercharges raged for years thereafter in veterans' meetings, in the testimony of countless, physically impaired former prisoners, and in hundreds of published "memoirs" that embellished truth on behalf of sensationalism, sales, and notoriety. The complete and true story of Civil War prisons will perhaps never be known. Perhaps it is best that the full horror remain in the dimness of America's past.

· 11 ·

Beyond the Call of Duty

The passing of winter always heralded the coming of battle. As snows melted and warm weather began drying out roads, it became time for soldiers to perform their ultimate task: fight. Johnny Rebs and Billy Yanks may have left a good deal to be desired in camp and on the march, but they more than compensated for these deficiencies by their overall performance in battle. Their heroism is a foundation of American military glory. Yet, for most of them, learning how to engage collectively in combat was slow, suspenseful, and archaic by modern-day standards.

Orders to break winter camp were the first sure signs that a new campaign was getting underway. Rumors then multiplied as to where the army was heading, what its objective was this time, when it expected to meet the enemy, comparative strengths of the two hosts, and the like. Men cleaned their weapons with a new fervor. Gear was carefully stowed away. Then the regiments began marching toward the confrontation. The advance might take days, even weeks, but all too soon the two opposing armies were facing each other at a distance ranging from a few hundred yards to a mile.

On the night before the battle, troops usually received orders to prepare or secure three days' rations in the event the conflict became protracted. The soldiers always obeyed that directive—but many men ate the rations as soon as they were in hand. Soldiers liked to go into battle with a full stomach; in addition, they preferred carrying as little on their person as was necessary. Later in the evening came a final regimental preparation: the dispensing of ammunition. The usual allotment was sixty rounds per man. Then a night of waiting began. Some troops might nap fitfully; others prayed fervently for deliverance; if campfires were permitted, a few men penned hasty notes to loved ones. Most soldiers, however, simply stared through the darkness while a flood of thoughts tumbled through their minds.

Around 3 A.M., with dawn but a couple of hours away, an insistent rattle of drums sounding "The Long Roll" signaled the call to arms. Troops promptly formed into lines. Officers made a last, quick inspection of the ranks. It was customary at that point for a commanding officer to give the men a final morale-building talk. The contents of those addresses varied widely.

Typical of a positive declaration was that of Confederate General A. Sidney Johnston on the eve of Shiloh: "The eyes and hopes of eight millions of people rest upon you. You are expected to show yourselves worthy of your race and lineage; worthy of the women of the South, whose noble devotion in this war has never been exceeded at any time. With such incentives to brave deeds and with the trust that God is with us, your general will lead you confidently to the combat, assured of success."[1]

These prebattle "pep-talks" could be brief. A major in command of the 13th New Hampshire had prepared a long and moving address to give his troops before they entered combat for the first time. Yet seeing their determined looks, and caught in the fury of the action already beginning, the major shouted to the aligned ranks: "Thirteenth New Hampshire! You love your country, you are brave men, and you came out here to fight for her! Now go in! Forward!"[2]

Just before battle resumed on the second day at Chancellorsville, Colonel Robert Riley of the 75th Ohio gathered his troops around him and made a similarly short but far more pointed speech. "Some of you will not see another sunrise," he stated. "If there is a man in the ranks who is not ready to die for his country, let him come to me and I will give him a pass to go to the rear, for I want no half-hearted, unwilling soldiers or cowards in the ranks."[3] No one accepted the offer. Among the fatalities in the combat which followed was Colonel Riley.

One of the most negative of these supposedly inspirational messages came from the colonel of a Midwestern regiment. In the attack about to begin, he shouted, "the secessionists have ten thousand men and forty rifled cannon. They are strongly fortified. They have more men and more cannon than we have. They will cut us to pieces. Marching to attack such an enemy, so entrenched and so armed, is marching to a butcher shop rather than to a battle. There is bloody work ahead. Many of you boys will go out who will never come back again." After the battle, dissatisfaction over the colonel was so widespread that he resigned from service.[4]

Every now and then, these prebattle speeches had unintended humor. At Murfreesboro, Tennessee, late in 1862, Colonel Granville Moody called his 74th Ohio together for its send-off. Moody was a minister. The men expected a religious exhortation, and they were getting it. Moody had just reached his climactic point. "Now, boys," he roared, "fight for your country and your God and . . . " At that moment, a volley of Confederate bullets whistled through the staging area. Moody, instead of giving the expected benediction, bellowed: "Aim low!" For weeks thereafter, whenever Moody passed through the camp, his "mischievous rascals" in the 74th Ohio would chortle: "Aim low! Aim low!"[5]

All speeches completed—one way or the other, the units moved forward, peeling left and right through woods and across fields as they took assigned positions in line of battle. Then came another period of waiting, and for many troops, the minutes now became hours in length. Veterans were easily distinguishable from recruits. The old-timers became quieter and displayed less concern, even to the point of napping while everything was quiet. For the uninitiated, fear came, and it came in many ways. Extreme dryness of throat and mouth, shortness of breath, a churning in the stomach, clammy perspiration— all were common reactions. Tension would course through the ranks, and sometimes even a quick cough would cause men nearby to jump.

For other soldiers, fear manifest itself in an unusual sharpness of memory, whereby childhood events and scenes long forgotten suddenly appeared in sharp focus. Moments away from battle, some men became strangely observant of nature. Over and over in their writings the men of blue and gray told how, just before the explosion of combat, they remembered the birds singing, spring flowers in bloom, a warm scent in the air.

The type of fear most prevalent among untested soldiers was not of being wounded (many men coveted "a red badge of courage" provided it was not too serious), or even of being killed. What they dreaded above all was "showing the white feather"—displaying cowardice. The majority of troops feared its presence as much as the enemy. Many remembered the biblical admonition: "If thou faint in the day of adversity, thy faith is small." Just as important, no conscientious soldier wanted his conduct in battle to bring humiliation to family and friends back home.

As David Beem of the 14th Indiana confided to his wife in May 1861: "If I was to turn back now, many would say I was a coward. I would rather be shot at once than to have such a stigma rest on me." An Alabama soldier expressed the same sentiments to his wife. "I want to come home as bad as any body can . . . but I shant run away . . . I don't want it throwed up to my children after I am dead and gone that I was a deserter . . . I don't want to do anything if I no it will leave a stain on my posterity hereafter."[6]

Along with uncertainties of courage were guilt feelings about past sins. Most soldiers of that day regarded God, final judgment, and eternal hell as very real things. Men might enjoy earthly pleasures when they were available; but with battle imminent, hundreds of soldiers sought to get their lives in order through intense reading of the Bible, fervent prayers, and whispered supplications. Time and again, men would swear loudly that they would never drink, gamble, curse, or whore again if the Almighty would just get them through this particular engagement.

Some soldiers got into the habit of writing their names and units on little pieces of paper and pinning them to their shirts or overcoats, so that burial details could make easy identification. And there was always one soldier who would walk up and down the assembled ranks, shaking hands with one and all as he observed: "Well, goodbye, boys, this means death."[7]

In the final seconds before the attack, the column generally became completely quiet as each man wrestled with his emotions and prepared for the ordeal at hand. A Connecticut artilleryman described that time in poetic and philosophical terms. The soldier "feels a certain sinking of the heart, as though the lead of the enemy has already lodged there. His soul becomes a theater where the two star actors, HOPE and FEAR, supported by Imagination, Apprehension, Patriotism, Courage, Doubt, Resolution, Ambition, and a host of supernumeraries, rehearse the coming battles. Fierce and doubtful is the fight, even on that mimic stage . . . "[8]

Often one man would get so overcome from anxiety as to break the silence momentarily. Such an "intruder" was James F. Wilcox of the 33rd Illinois. He was waiting for the signal to charge the enemy works at Vicksburg when he could no longer bear the strain. "Oh how my heart palpitated!" he admitted. "It seemed to thump the ground (I lay on my face) as hard as the enemy's bullets. The sweat from off my face run in a stream from the tip ends of my whiskers. . . . Twice I exclaimed aloud . . . *'My God, why dont they order us to charge!'* "[9]

Eventually the order to advance would come.

Fighting in the Civil War was an elemental and intimate thing. One side would usually line up to attack across an expanse of ground against the fortified position of the other side. The soldier making the assault was to keep his place in the tight formation, touching the elbow of the man on either side of him, and maintaining a distance of 1–2 feet from the soldier in his front. File closers were to keep the lines as intact as possible. The officers were inside the ranks or just behind them.

The enemy's bristling guns and gleaming bayonets could almost always be seen because only a few hundred yards separated the two armies. It looked so easy and so obvious; yet open-field assaults by then—because of improved weaponry and the size of armies—were murderous. Even some of the commanders of that day realized the odds against the attacking force. Federal General John M. Schofield put it succinctly: "To mass troops against the fire of a covered line is simply to devote them to destruction. The greater the mass, the greater the loss— that is all."[10] Nevertheless, such tactics persisted to war's end.

"This was my first experience at being shot at," a member of the 6th Mississippi wrote, "and I was as scared as the next man." Yet, a Tennessee soldier commented, "as the movement goes on you get into the thick of the fight, this [fear] goes out and you become, for the most part, indifferent to time and danger." Private Edwin Weller of the 107th New York shared the same reactions. In reply to his sweetheart's query of what it felt like going into battle, Weller stated: "When we first Started from our position as a reserve to the Woods near where the Rebels were, I thought of Home, friends, and most everything else, but as Soon as we Entered the Woods where the Shells and Balls were flying thick and fast I lost all fear and thought of Home and friends, and a Reckless don't care disposition Seemed to take possession of me. . . . I have heard other Soldiers Say the Same."[11]

Eagerness for action sometimes caused troops in the rear to dash through the ranks toward the front of the line, thereby breaking down all order. Moreover, the habit of men double-timing into battle—often at an incredible 165 steps per minute—did little to protect the soldiers but much to wear them out before they entered the center of action.

Joseph A. Higginbotham summarized the 19th Virginia's charge at First Manassas by writing: "We started in double quick from our entrenchments and went until we were near broke down. I never came so near giving out in my entire life." An officer in the 59th Georgia explained that unit's failure at Gettysburg by stating in his official report: "We were repulsed the first charge, because the men were so completely exhausted when they made it, having double-quicked a distance of some 400 yards, under a severe shelling and a scorching sun."[12]

In contrast to Currier & Ives paintings and other orderly depictions of the Civil War, the actual fighting was just not that visual or that clean at all. An attack was not an uninterrupted, steady advance across a field with fixed bayonets. The assaulting soldiers would rush forward a few yards, fire a volley, reload, and dash a few more yards before firing again, and then make a final run toward the enemy works. Lying down to load took time; besides, out in the open a man was an inviting target whether he was prone or standing erect. No matter how precise or meticulous an assault, or how organized or prepared a defense, the whole situation seemed to disintegrate once the battle began.

Thick, acrid smoke settled over the area; and in the bitter taste of gunpowder, the crash of musketry, the explosion of cannon fire, the shouts and screams of men fighting and dying, a soldier saw only what was directly in front of him. A New Jersey infantryman described the noise of one engagement as "the terrible power and grandour of a mighty church organ, played by twice ten thousand brave soldiers, and the keys they were striking were men." Intelligence ceased to function. "I did not think of the bullets what was whizing around me," a Wisconsin private stated, "about all I thought of was just what I was doing my self but I thought about home."[13]

Combat and confusion became one and the same. At First Manassas, a captain heroically led his 100-man company into the smoke-filled action. When the gunfire ended, he turned to thank his brave soldiers—and saw that what he was leading were three of his own men, two other foot soldiers, a lost artillerist, three dismounted cavalrymen, a surgeon, a quartermaster's clerk, and the chaplain of another regiment.[14]

A Maine private described one typical action: "The air was filled with a medley of sounds, shouts, cheers, commands, oaths, the sharp report of rifles, the hissing shot, dull heavy thuds of clubbed muskets, the swish of swords and sabers, groans and prayers. . . . Many of our men could not afford the time necessary to load their guns . . . but they clubbed their muskets and fought. Occasionally, when sorely pressed, they would drop their guns and clinch the enemy in single combat, until Federal or Confederate would roll upon the ground in the death struggle." Tennessee soldier Robert Gates was just as vivid in his recollections. He once described a Federal charge as "with a rush, like ocean waves driven by a hurricane, trampling their own dead and wounded, sweeping on as if by an irresistible impulse, to dash and break and reel and die against the Confederate works, and stagger back like drunken men, broken and routed."[15]

The 19th Massachusetts was in the thick of the fighting at Gettysburg. One of its members stated of the melee: "Foot to foot, body to body and man to man they struggled, pushed, and strived and killed. Each had rather die than yield. The mass of wounded and heaps of dead entangled the feet of the contestants, and, underneath the trampling mass, wounded men who could no longer stand, struggled, fought, shouted and killed—hatless, coatless, drowned in sweat, black with powder, red with blood, stifling in the horrid heat, parched with smoke and blind with dust, with fiendish yells and strange oaths they blindly plied the work of slaughter."[16]

Gruesome deaths became commonplace. After a battle in Mississippi, a Georgia soldier wrote his wife: "Maj. John C. Lamb was Killed instantly by a round Ball. . . . his head was half shot off, his brains all flew about 4 feet & mostly fell in a pile. his cap was not found & his skul flew in every directsion. our men were turablely Shocked but all acted the part of a Soldier."[17]

Baptism into battle certainly strengthened powers of concentration, as many Civil War troops affirmed. William A. Fletcher and other members of the 8th Texas Cavalry had a particular dread as they entered combat for the first time. "I with a number of others," Fletcher explained, "were sufferers from camp diarrhea, and up to that time we had found no cure—so, entering the battle, I had quite a great fear that something disgraceful might happen and it was somewhat uppermost in my mind; but to my surprise the excitement or something else had effected a cure."[18]

Anger also did much to overcome the initial fear of soldiers. After two years in the field, a Texas officer stated of his conduct in an 1863 battle: "See how they do fall, like leaves in the fall of the year . . . Oh this is fun to lie here and shoot them down and we not get hurt." Having close friends slain could cause a man's adrenalin to erase uncertainty. At Gaines's Mill, the 83rd Pennsylvania's Oliver Norton saw two messmates fall in action. "I acted like a madman," he confessed, "a kind of desperation seized me. . . . I snatched a gun from the hands of a man who was shot through the head, as he staggered and fell. . . . Then I jumped over dead men with as little feeling as I would over a log. The feeling that was uppermost in my mind was a desire to kill as many rebels as I could."[19]

The total disorder of a battle made it inevitable that soldiers forgot to do basic things. On more than one occasion, troops in the second or third line became so excited that they fired wildly into their own front rank. A notable instance of this occurred at Antietam Creek, when the 59th New York "did as much harm to their friends as to their enemies" by sending several volleys into the ranks of the 15th Massachusetts.[20]

A common failure in those battles was the improper loading and firing of muskets. Men caught up in the action would go through the motions of preparing their weapons for firing and then forget the final step of pulling the trigger. Of 27,500 muskets collected on the field after the battle of Gettysburg, over 12,000 of them contained two charges, 6,000 contained anywhere from three to ten powder-loads and balls, while one musket had twenty-three complete rounds of ammunition. Had any of those muskets been fired, the results would have been fatal to the man who pulled the trigger.

In the blazing hell of every Civil War battle occurred instances when men would "show the white feather." Soldiers usually referred to cowards as men suffering from "cannon fever" or "chicken heart disease." Such loss of heart could take the form of a subtle expression. A company of the 22nd Massachusetts was once pinned down by heavy Confederate musketry. The Yankees could not move. Finally one soldier (who either was a schoolteacher or a civic official before the war) cried aloud: "I move that we be taken out of here by some responsible officer!"[21]

Other soldiers without the necessary stamina called attention to themselves by unique actions. During the Fredericksburg campaign, Confederates began an artillery bombardment of the area where the 84th New York was posted. One of the New Yorkers failed to show "any trunk a tall," a compatriot snorted. "he grubed his nose all away by laying down when the sheling was going on for he nearly plowed the hole field up with his nose."[22]

Cowardice on many occasions was collective as well as contagious. Sergeant Edward Eggleston of a Mississippi battery wrote after the 1864 debacle at Nashville: "The infantry ran like cowards and the miserable wretches who were to have supported us refused to fight and ran like a herd of stampeded cattle." At Chickamauga, what remained of the 17th Georgia suddenly broke from the field under severe artillery fire. General Henry Benning saw the men bolting to the rear. "Hold on there!" the colorful brigadier shouted at them. "Damn you! If you are going back to Georgia, wait and I will go with you!"[23]

More often, however, individual shirkers would break from ranks and flee from the action. Soldiers despised such cowards and took delight in lampooning their lack of courage. One of the standard jokes on both sides was about the slacker who boasted that when the battle was at its most intense, he could be found where the bullets were thickest— far to the rear, hiding under an ammunition wagon. Yet there were many instances when truth reinforced this anecdote.

For example, Austin Stearns of the 13th Massachusetts never forgot one soldier racing toward the rear and shouting: "Give 'em hell, boys, we got 'em started!" A member of the 14th Wisconsin, writing after Shiloh, informed his parents: "The story about Lawtons being so brave was all a hoax. As soon as the battle commenced he was making for the river about as fast as his legs would carry him. When asked where he was going he replied 'that he was going down to the river to draw rations, so that the boys could have something to eat as soon as they were done fighting.' Very thoughtful, wasn't he."[24]

A few soldiers freely admitted taking leave of the action. Writing of one of the battles fought at Petersburg, a Michigan infantryman told how his brigade got flanked and was being cut to pieces. He then added seriously: "Of course it would not be gallant to say that anybody run, but if there was any tall walking done during the war, we did it crossing that field."[25]

For every man lacking in fortitude, the record is clear that 100 or more rose to heights of heroism in the Civil War. When a Federal shell tore off both hands of a Kentucky soldier, the man stared numbly at his two bleeding stumps and mumbled only: "My Lord, that stops my fighting."[26] Official reports of unit commanders North and South referred time and again to the gallantry of citizen-soldiers. When charging against concentrated musketry, they were known to lean forward as if they were advancing into the face of a hailstorm. Calling for volunteers to perform perilous tasks would bring a shout of responses. Repeatedly men jumped atop parapets to yell defiances at the enemy; they denounced and even struck officers who played the coward; they begged for the privilege of carrying the colors; they took command without being told when all the officers were disabled; many refused to leave the field although seriously wounded.

In his official report of Second Manassas, Major James D. Waddell of Georgia stated that he "carried into the fight over 100 men who were barefoot, many of whom left bloody footprints among the thorns and briars through which they rushed, with Spartan courage and really jubilant impetuosity, upon the serried ranks of the foe." During another battle in Virginia, a Louisiana battery commander was directing the fire of his guns when a Federal shell tore off his left arm at the shoulder. The officer grabbed the reins of his horse with his right hand, swung the animal around in an attempt to hide his injury, and shouted: "Keep it up, boys! I'll be back in a moment!" He started riding down the hill and pitched forward dead.[27]

The post of colorbearer was of great danger on any battlefield. Since the regimental flag was the most visible badge of pride, the man who carried it had to be in front as a defiant and inspirational beacon. The flagbearers knew that they were the first targets of the enemy, but pride and patriotism at their chosen post caused them to display extraordinary valor—and sacrifice.

At Kennesaw Mountain, Georgia, Confederate John Hagan witnessed the heroism of one Union colorbearer. The Southerners, he wrote, "poord volley after volly until the yanks was forced back. [Then] one of there coller guards reached our works & planted his collars & 40 Ball was Shot through him." Colorbearer J. M. Rice of the 8th Tennessee was leading the regiment into action at Murfreesboro when he fell with a bullet wound. Rice crawled forward on his knees, with the flag still held aloft, until a second bullet killed him. A Virginia soldier wrote of the fighting at Cedar Mountain: "Our colorbearer knocked down a Yankee with his flag staff—and was shot to death at once. One of the color guard took the flag, and he also was killed. Another . . . bayoneted a Yankee, then was immediately riddled with bullets—three going through him. Four colorbearers were killed with the colors in their hands."[28]

No regiment suffered a greater loss of flagbearers at one time than did the 2nd Iowa at Fort Donelson. Every member of the color guard except one was killed in the assault. Two had already fallen dead, the regimental historian wrote, when Corporal Harry Doolittle picked up the colors. He "receives four wounds instantaneously and the flag is stretched upon the ground; it is raised by Corporal Page, who is shot dead; Corporal Churcher then takes the colors and has his arm broken [and subsequently died] and is succeeded by Corporal Twombly, who is knocked down by a spent ball but jumps up and carries the colors to the close of the engagement."[29]

Uncommon valor was a common virtue in most battles of that war. Thousands of soldiers demonstrated that they loved something more than life itself. When the 19th Massachusetts' Henry Jackson How fell mortally wounded at Frayser's Farm, he murmured: "Let me die here on the field; 'tis more glorious to die on the field of battle.' "[30]

Following a bloody encounter at Tupelo, Mississippi, Iowa soldier Joseph Sweney went to one of the field hospitals to care for his wounded brother. Next to his brother, Sweney beheld "a man whose abdomen was largely torn away by a shell." Shortly after Sweney arrived, the man asked amid intense pain: "How has the fight gone?"

"We have whipped them," Sweney replied proudly. "We have driven them off the field, we have won the day!"

"Good," the wounded soldier mumbled. "I can die contented."

A few minutes later, he was dead.[31]

For the living, the end of a battle brought numb exhaustion. Rest, food, and water during the hours of fighting had been practically nonexistent. The anxiety over one's self, the heavy expenditure of nervous energy, the exuberance of success or the despair of defeat, took such a profound toll that by midafternoon many soldiers were barely able to stand, much less to load and fire a gun; and the weariness would linger for days after the engagement.

So would the shock and sadness at comrades lost in battle. That realization first struck hard when an officer formed his company and called the roll. As last names were shouted, from the ranks would come such responses as: "John was killed before we fired a shot" . . . "I saw Frank throw up his arms and fall just after we fired the first volley" . . . "Jim was shot through the head" . . . "Charley was killed while we were charging across the plain this side of the brick house." Theodore Upson of the 100th Indiana confessed in his diary after writing the wife of a fellow soldier killed in action: "But when it come to telling about the way he died and how we buried him I could hardly write. I had to get away of by my self, and I am affraid she will have hard work to read it for I could not help blotting the paper some."[32]

The knowledge that one or more close friends were suddenly gone produced gloom inside the ranks, and the nearby sight of the arena where men had sacrificed everything only intensified the heavy-heartedness. "None can realize the horrors of war, save those actually engaged," a member of the 6th Georgia told the homefolk a couple of days after an engagement. "The dead lying all around, your foes unburied to the last, horses & wagons & troops passing heedlessly along . . . The stiffened bodies lie, grasping in death the arms they bravely bore, with glazed eyes, and features blackened by rapid decay. Here sits one against a tree in a motionless stare. Another has his head leaning against a stump, his hands over his head. They have paid the last penalty. They have fought their last battle. The air is putrid with decaying bodies of men & horses. My God, My God, what a scourge is war."[33]

A necessary task after every battle was the burial of the dead; and with summer's heat working rapidly on hundreds of corpses, the gruesome and nauseous job was done with haste rather than reverence. "We commenced gathering the dead for burial," a soldier in the 130th Pennsylvania wrote two days after Antietam Creek. "The bodies were . . . so greatly swollen that the clothing could hardly contain them, and they were of a livid blue-black color. One way for gathering them was for six men to take three rails, and placing one or two dead men on them by putting one rail under the shoulders, one under the hips and one under the knees, and so carry them to the place of burial. They were there placed side by side in long rows, and a trench dug to a sufficient depth to cover them well, and long enough so they might be laid side by side."[34]

Neatness was rarely in evidence when burying the enemy's dead, as James Phillips of the 92nd Illinois told his wife after the battle of Perryville. "The rebles went off and left their men lying just as they fell, and our men pressed the citisans to bury them. They dug shallow holes as the ground was verry hard and stony and throwed them in and throwed a few leaves and a little dirt over them and the first rain that come washed it all off and the hogs have rooted them out and are eating them up."[35]

Even in the presence of death, another Illinois soldier commented, "the average soldier will jest and have his little joke at the expense of the dead." His regiment was passing through the Shiloh battlefield a month after the fighting. Half-buried soldiers were visible everywhere. A dead hand stuck up from one grave, and in it one of the marching soldiers placed a hardtack biscuit. From the ranks came the shout that "that fellow was not going off hungry if he could help it!"[36]

The revulsion and weariness and grief tended to become less with each battle. "I can look at a dead man or help a wounded man from the field and think no more of it than I would of eating my dinner," Private Henry Schafer wrote home. "I am ashamed to say it but I have seen so much of it that in one sens of the word I have become hardened and it does not affect me but little to walk over the field of strife and behold its horrors."[37]

As those farm boys, students, clerks, merchants, and immigrants moved from one bloodstained field to another, seeking peace somewhere down a long and treacherous road, those who continued to survive displayed an increased resoluteness such as voiced by the 14th Iowa's Peter Wilson. To his father late in January 1863, Wilson declared: "I see no reason to dread the future. . . . I trust that the Almighty hand that has kept me in health thus far will keep me still in safety although much danger may be before me. If it is God's will that I find my grave in the South I hope to be ready. Let it come when it may, I am determined to do my duty and come home honorably or never."[38]

John Moseley also had that resolve. Moseley was one of the youngest members of the 3rd Alabama, with his manhood still before him. On July 3, 1863, he took part in an assault against the Union lines at Gettysburg. The next morning he penned this note home:

Battlefield, Gettysburg Penn. July 4, 1863
Dear Mother

I am here a prisoner of war & mortally wounded. I can live but a few hours more at farthest—I was shot fifty yards [from] the enemy's lines. They have been exceedingly kind to me.

I have no doubts as to the final results of this battle and I hope I may live long enough to hear the shouts of victory yet, before I die.

I am very weak. Do not mourn my loss. I had hoped to have been spared, but a righteous God has ordered it otherwise and I feel prepared to trust my case in his hands.

Farewell to you all. Pray that God may receive my soul.

Your unfortunate son John

The youthful Alabamian was buried in an unmarked grave on the outskirts of Gettysburg, a town totally unfamiliar to him until he came there to die.[39]

Appomattox brought the war to a close. For the victor and for the vanquished, the feelings were deep. A New Yorker wrote on that Palm Sunday: "For some time the Cheers and Actions of the men are strongly contrasted with their appearance a few short hours before. Men who could hardly keep up in the line now shout and run around almost crazy with joy." Across the way, "strong men wept like children." A North Carolina soldier asked his general if the reports of Lee's surrender were true. The officer then replied: "It is, I am sorry to say, too true."

At that, the veteran burst into tears and cried out: "Blow, Gabriel, blow! I do not want to live another day!"[40]

Many survivors of that conflict went home feeling only an abhorrence for the cruelty and killing they had witnessed. Mississippian George Gibbs began his private memoirs with the assertion: "War is not the fine adventure it is often represented to be by novelists and historians, but a dirty, bloody mess, unworthy of people who claim to be civilized." Illinois surgeon John L. Hostetter felt the same way. "There is no God in war. It is merciless, cruel, vindictive, unchristian, savage, relentless. It is all that devils could wish for." Sergeant Boyd of the 15th Iowa agreed to a point. "War is hell broke loose and benumbs all the tender feelings of men and makes of them brutes. I do not want to see any more such scenes and yet I would not have missed this for any consideration."[41]

For many Confederates, anticipated joy at going home changed abruptly to heartache. Josia Reams returned to McNairy County, Tennessee, in the spring of 1865 to find his family decimated. "My father and stepmother . . . [had] died. My only brother was killed . . . and a half brother on the Union side . . . died. So our home was broken up and I was penniless."[42]

There is a wide consensus that the Civil War is the central theme of American history. Whether that is true, the war was surely the central theme in the lives of Northern and Southern men who fought in it. A Wisconsin soldier stated in one of his last wartime letters: "What an experience the last few years have been! I would not take any amount of money & have the events which have transpired in that length of time blotted out from my memory."[43]

With the passing years, the men of blue and gray aged gracefully. Time healed most wounds and obliterated scars of body and mind. "Some good to the world must come from such sacrifice," a North Carolinian wrote near the end of his life. When John Mason, a former Tennessee artillerist, was asked in the 1920s about his war experiences, the old veteran responded humbly: "I fired a cannon. I hope I never kill[ed] any one."[44]

They are all gone now. Today, in cemeteries all across this broad land, Johnny Rebs and Billy Yanks sleep the last sleep. Thousands of those men who loved America each in his own way lie beneath orderly rows of gleaming white headstones. A Regular Army officer of that day might snort that at last those damned volunteers were in a straight formation, and a callous person might conclude that one cross looks no different from another. And yet, beneath those stones is the simple reminder—and the lasting realization—that when the great challenges come, this nation's common people can and will show that they value some ideals more than they value their lives.

As America matured into one, indivisible nation—a country that Lincoln proclaimed "the last great hope of earth," the last survivors of the great Civil War came to possess a common pride and a common legacy. Men of North and South alike surely felt like the Indiana farm boy-turned-solder who wrote that "from those who have lived to return comes no words of regrets. They are content their duty is done, and well done. What matters the loss of all these years! What matters the trials, the sickness, the wounds! What we went out to do is done. The war is ended, and the Union is saved!"[45]

Notes

Preface
1. Amos M. Judson, *History of the Eighty-third Regiment Pennsylvania Volunteers* (Dayton, OH, 1986), 2–3.
2. George Alphonso Gibbs reminiscences, in possession of George Fugate, Lexington, KY.

Chapter 1—Rallying 'round the Flag
1. William Howard Russell, *My Diary North and South* (Boston, 1863), 92; U.S. War Department. (comp.), *War of the Rebellion: A Compilation of the Official Records of the Union and Confederate Armies* (Washington, 1880–1902), Ser. IV, Vol. I, 380 (cited hereafter as *Official Records*; unless otherwise stated, all references will be to Ser. I).
2. Allan Nevins, *The War for the Union* (New York, 1959–1971), I, 88; *OR*, Ser. III, Vol. I, 101.
3. John A. Sloan, *Reminiscences of the Guilford Grays, Co. B, 27th N.C. Regiment* (Washington, 1883), 18; Bob Womack, *Call Forth the Mighty Men* (Bessemer, AL, 1987), 19; Military Order of the Loyal Legion (MOLLUS) Iowa Commandery, *War Sketches and Incidents*, I (1893), 159.
4. *Herald of the South*, Dec. 31, 1859; Howard C. Perkins (ed.), *Northern Editorials on Secession* (New York, 1942), II, 731; James M. McPherson, *Ordeal by Fire* (New York, 1982), 149–50; Fred Arthur Bailey, *Class and Tennessee's Confederate Generation* (Chapel Hill, 1987), 78; Frederick S. Daniel, *The Richmond Examiner during the War* (New York, 1868), 13.
5. Cyrus F. Boyd, *The Civil War Diary of Cyrus F. Boyd, Fifteenth Iowa Infantry, 1861–1863* (Iowa City, IA, 1953), 7; Henry E. Schafer to wife, Mar. 1, 1863, in possession of William A. Schaeffer III, Houston, TX; James I. Robertson, Jr., *Tenting Tonight: The Soldier's Life* (Alexandria, VA, 1984), 24.
6. William A. Smith, *The Anson Guards: Company C, Fourteenth Regiment North Carolina Volunteers, 1861–1865* (Charlotte, 1914), 18; William E. Paxton, " 'Dear Rebecca:' The Civil War Letters of William Edwards Paxton," *Louisiana History* XX (1979), 183; Henry E. Schafer to wife, Mar. 1, 1863, Schaeffer Papers.
7. Iowa Commandery—MOLLUS, *War Sketches and Incidents*, I (1893), 167.
8. John L. Parker, *Henry Wilson's Regiment: History of the Twenty-second Massachusetts Infantry* . . . (Boston, 1887), 39.
9. Thaddeus C. C. Brown et al., *Behind the Guns: The History of Battery I, 2nd Regiment, Illinois Light Artillery* (Carbondale, IL, 1965), 6; Henry C. Bear, *The Civil War Letters of Henry C. Bear: A Soldier in the 116th Illinois Volunteer Infantry* (Harrogate, TN, 1961), 8; Ira M. B. Gillaspie, *From Michigan to Murfreesboro: The Diary of Ira Gillaspie of the Eleventh Michigan Infantry* (Mount Pleasant, MI, 1965), 7.
10. Francis A. Lord, *They Fought for the Union* (Harrisburg, PA, 1960), 10–11.
11. William Clark Corson, *My Dear Jennie* (Richmond, VA, 1982), 93–94.
12. John W. Hagan, *Confederate Letters of John W. Hagan* (Athens, GA, 1954), 28.
13. Joseph T. Glatthaar, *The March to the Sea and Beyond* (New York, 1985), 40.
14. Robertson, *Tenting Tonight*, 24.
15. Robert U. Johnson and C. C. Buel (eds.), *Battles and Leaders of the Civil War* (New York, 1884–1887), I, 87.
16. Andrew E. Ford, *The Story of the Fifteenth Regiment, Massachusetts Volunteer*

Infantry, in the Civil War, 1861–1864 (Clinton, 1898), 26; Frank T. Robinson, *History of the Fifth Regiment, M. V. M.* (Boston, 1879), 9.

17. A Tennessee soldier felt that most of these emotional orations were long and loud. Moreover, "what was wanting in quality was made up in quantity. On some occasions we remember well to have heard men try to make war speeches who never before or since lifted their voices in strains of eloquent patriotism to stir the souls of their countrymen." [J. G. Carrigan] *The Cheat Mountain Campaign* (Nashville, 1885), 18.

18. Robertson, *Tenting Tonight*, 21–22.

19. Albert B. Moore, *Conscription and Conflict in the Confederacy* (New York, 1924), 71n.

20. Walter A. Clark (ed.), *Histories of the Several Regiments and Battalions from North Carolina in the Great War, 1861–'65* (Raleigh, 1901), I, 221.

21. John D. Billings, *Hardtack and Coffee; or, The Unwritten Story of Army Life* (Boston, 1887), 200. For a reaction of a single man, see Marcus B. Toney, *The Privations of a Private* (Nashville, 1907), 15.

22. J. P. Cannon, *Inside of Rebeldom: The Daily Life of a Private in the Confederate Army* (Washington, 1900), 20.

23. David E. Johnston, *The Story of a Confederate Boy in the Civil War* (Portland, OR, 1914), 41–42. A similar scene is described in Joseph R. C. Ward, *History of the One Hundred and Sixth Regiment, Pennsylvania Volunteers, 2d Brigade, 2d Division, 2d Corps, 1861–1865* (Philadelphia, 1906), 4–5.

24. Gibbs reminiscences; Robert A. Moore, *A Life for the Confederacy* (Jackson, TN, 1959), 28. See also Parker, *22nd Massachusetts*, 32.

25. Francis H. Buffum, *A Memorial of the Great Rebellion: Being a History of the Fourteenth Regiment, New Hampshire Volunteers* (Boston, 1882), 13; Alfred Bellard, *Gone for the Soldier: The Civil War Memoirs of Private Alfred Bellard* (Boston, 1975), 4.

26. R. L. T. Beale, *History of the Ninth Virginia Cavalry in the War between the States* (Richmond, 1899), 9.

27. John S. Robson, *How a One-legged Rebel Lives* (Durham, NC, 1898), 9–10.

28. Ansel D. Dickerson, *A Raw Recruit's Experiences* (Providence, 1888), 12–13.

29. George H. Allen, *Forty-six Months with the Fourth R.I. Volunteers in the War of 1861 to 1865* (Providence, 1887), 15–16.

30. Charles W. Cowtan, *Services of the Tenth New York Volunteers (National Zouaves) in the War of the Rebellion* (New York, 1882), 50–51.

31. Val C. Giles, *Rags and Hope: The Recollections of Val C. Giles, Four Years with Hood's Brigade, Fourth Texas Infantry* (New York, 1961), 23.

32. George N. Carpenter, *History of the Eighth Regiment, Vermont Volunteers, 1861–1865* (Boston, 1886), 30.

33. *History of the Thirty-fifth Regiment, Massachusetts Volunteers, 1862–1865* (Boston, 1884), 5; William P. Hopkins, *The Seventh Regiment, Rhode Island Volunteers, in the Civil War, 1862–1865* (Providence, 1903), 2. Similar misfits in uniform are itemized in Henry F. W. Little, *The Seventh Regiment, New Hampshire Volunteers, in the War of the Rebellion* (Concord, 1896), 17.

34. William A. Spicer, *History of the Ninth and Tenth Regiments, Rhode Island Volunteers, and the Tenth Rhode Island Battery, in the Union Army in 1862* (Providence, 1892), 141.

35. Nelson Stauffer, *Civil War Diary* (Northridge, CA, 1976), entry of Mar. 25, 1862.

36. George K. Collins, *Memoirs of the 149th Regt. NY Vol. Inft . . .* (Syracuse, 1891), 159; John L. Smith, *History of the Corn Exchange Regiment, 118th Pennsylvania Volunteers* (Philadelphia, 1888), 11.

37. Theodore F. Upson, *With Sherman to the Sea* (Bloomington, IN, 1958), 25.

38. J. T. Pool, *Under Canvass; or, Recollections of the Fall and Summer Campaign of the 14th Regiment, Indiana Volunteers* (Terre Haute, 1862), 7.

39. Richmond *Enquirer*, Oct. 15, 1861.

40. William F. Wagner, *Letters of William F. Wagner, Confederate Soldier* (Wendell, NC, 1983), 15.

Chapter 2—Mixing the Ingredients

1. Sylvanus Cadwallader, *Three Years with Grant* (New York, 1955), 175.

2. James I. Robertson, Jr. (ed.), "An Indiana Soldier in Love and War," *Indiana Magazine of History* LIX (1963), 255.

3. John Smith Kendall (ed.), "Recollections of a Confederate Officer," *Louisiana Historical Quarterly* XXIX (1946), 1208.

4. James A. Connolly, *Three Years in the Army of the Cumberland* (Bloomington, IN, 1959), 333; William M. Dame, *From the Rapidan to Richmond and the Spotsylvania Campaign* (Baltimore, 1920), 103. However, it should be noted, Union Gen. William T. Sherman considered Confederate horsemen "the best cavalry in the world." William T. Sherman, *Memoirs of General W. T. Sherman* (New York, 1875), I, 336.

5. Leo M. Kaiser, "Letters from the Front," *Journal of the Illinois State Historical Society* LVI (1963), 156. In April 1864 Pvt. James Hall of the 44th Mississippi wrote home: "Col. Sawyer says that every cavalry man ought to have a board tied on his back and the word 'thief' written on it so that honest men could know him when they came about and hid their horses." Charles T. Jones, Jr., "Five Confederates: The Sons of Bolling Hall in the Civil War," *Alabama Historical Quarterly* XXIV (1962), 194.

6. Connolly, *Three Years in the Army of the Cumberland*, 185.

7. Clark, *N.C. Regiments*, III, 376.

8. Upson, *With Sherman to the Sea*, 138.

9. Theodore F. Vaill, *History of the Second Connecticut Volunteer Heavy Artillery* (Winsted, CT, 1868), 43.

10. Thomas L. Livermore, *Numbers and Losses in the Civil War in America, 1861–65* (Boston, 1901), 68.

11. John William De Forest, *A Volunteer's Adventures* (New Haven, 1946), 35–36.

12. Asa W. Bartlett, *History of the Twelfth Regiment, New Hampshire Volunteers, in the War of the Rebellion* (Concord, 1897), 85–86.

13. Charles E. Davis, *Three Years in the Army* (Boston, 1894), 258.

14. Lurton D. Ingersoll, *Iowa and the Rebellion* (Philadelphia, 1867), 501, 513.

15. Herbert Adams, "Enemy of Rebels and Rum Lovers," *Civil War Times Illustrated* XXV (Mar., 1986), 47–48.

16. Collins, *149th New York*, 56–57; Kaiser, "Letters from the Front," 151.

17. Benjamin F. Cook, *History of the Twelfth Massachusetts Volunteers (Webster Regiment)* (Boston, 1882), 21–22, 142; Parker, *Henry Wilson's Regiment*, 48, 100, 163.

18. Robert Tilney, *My Life in the Army* (Philadelphia, 1912), 153.

19. Glatthaar, *March to the Sea*, 28.

20. George Fowle, *Letters to Eliza from a Union Soldier, 1862–1865* (Chicago, 1963), 131.

21. *OR*, X, Pt. 1, 589.

22. Dame, *From the Rapidan to Richmond*, 2–3; Weymouth T. Jordan (comp.), *North Carolina Troops, 1861–1865: A Roster* (Raleigh, 1966–), V, 180.

23. *Roster and Record of Iowa Soldiers in the War of the Rebellion* (Des Moines, 1908–1911), V, 788.

24. Theodore Lyman, *Meade's Headquarters, 1863–1865* (Boston, 1922), 327.

25. Robertson, *Tenting Tonight*, 28.

26. Susan L. Blackford (comp.), *Letters from Lee's Army* (New York, 1947), 48–49.

27. Adin B. Underwood, *The Three Years' Service of the Thirty-third Mass. Infantry Regiment, 1862–1865* (Boston, 1881), 11.

28. Davis, *Three Years in the Army*, 48.

29. William Corby, *Memoirs of Chaplain Life* (Notre Dame, IN, 1894), 357.

30. Peter Welsh, *Irish Green and Union Blue: The Civil War Letters of Peter Welsh* (New York, 1986), 27; Upson, *With Sherman to the Sea*, 67.

31. Troops in the 8th Michigan thought the 79th New York to be "a set of foreigners and sots," while the Highlanders looked on the heterogeneous Michiganders as "a lot of undrilled bushwhackers tinged with verdancy." Ralph Ely, *With the Wandering Regiment: The Diary of Captain Ralph Ely of the Eighth Michigan Infantry* (Mount Pleasant, MI, 1965), 21.

32. John M. Gould, *History of the First—Tenth—Twenty-ninth Maine Regiment* (Portland, 1871), 41.

33. Lyman, *Meade's Headquarters*, 208.

34. Worthington C. Ford (ed.), *A Cycle of Adams Letters, 1861–1865* (Boston, 1920), I, 23.

35. James H. Langhorne to sister, Nov. 4, 1861, Langhorne Letters, in possession of James I. Robertson, Jr.

36. *Official Records*, Ser. IV, Vol. III, 1009–10.

37. Nevins, *War for the Union*, II, 516.

38. Ford, *Adams Letters*, I, 171; Thaddeus H. Capron, "War Diary of Thaddeus H. Capron, 1861–1865," *Journal of the Illinois State Historical Society* XII (1919), 358.

39. *Official Records*, XIV, 377.

40. James I. Robertson, Jr., "Negro Soldiers in the Civil War," *Civil War Times Illustrated* VII (Oct., 1968), 22; William H. Crouse to "Jack," Feb. 20, 1863, letter in possession of William J. Downer, Pitman, NJ.

41. Isaac J. Wistar, *Autobiography of Isaac Jones Wistar, 1827–1905* (Philadelphia, 1937), 446; Ford, *Adams Papers*, II, 195, 216–17.

42. Boyd, *Civil War Diary*, 118; Johnson and Buel, *Battles and Leaders*, IV, 418.

43. *Official Records*, XXIV, Pt. 2, 448, 467.

44. John A. Kress, *Memoirs of Brigadier General John Alexander Kress* (n.p., 1925), 32; Benjamin F. Butler, *Private and Official Correspondence of Gen. Benjamin F. Butler, during the Period of the Civil War* (Norwood, MA, 1917), V, 192. General George H. Thomas rode over the battlefield of Nashville and observed "the bodies of colored men side by side with the foremost on the very works of the enemy." He turned to his staff and said: "Gentlemen, the question is settled; negroes will fight." Thomas J. Morgan, *Reminiscences of Service with Colored Troops in the Army of the Cumberland, 1863–65* (Providence, 1885), 48.

45. *Official Records*, Ser. II, Vol. V, 940–41.

46. Ibid., Vol. VI, 163.

47. James K. Newton, *A Wisconsin Boy in Dixie: The Selected Letters of James K. Newton* (Madison, WI, 1961), 28.

48. Dudley Taylor Cornish, *The Sable Arm: Negro Troops in the Union Army, 1861–1865* (New York, 1956), 288.

49. Military Historical Society of Massachusetts, *Civil and Mexican Wars, 1846, 1861* (Boston, 1913), 313.

50. Henry Lee Swint (ed.), *Dear Ones at Home: Letters from Contraband Camps* (Nashville, 1966), 123.

51. *Under the Maltese Cross; Antietam to Appomattox: The Loyal Uprising in Western Pennsylvania, 1861–1865* (Pittsburgh, 1910), 50.

52. Bear, *Civil War Letters*, 9.

53. Samuel Merrill, "Letters from a Civil War Officer," *Mississippi Valley Historical Review* XIV (1928), 510.

54. David R. Garrett, *The Civil War Letters of David R. Garrett, Detailing the Adventures of the 6th Texas Cavalry, 1861–1865* (Marshall, TX, 1963), 53; Jesse W. Reid,

History of the Fourth Regiment S.C. Volunteers, from the Commcement of the War until Lee's Surrender (Greenville, SC, 1892), 76.

55. Davis, *Three Years in the Army*, 265; Glatthaar, *March to the Sea*, 42; S. Millett Thompson, *Thirteenth Regiment of New Hampshire Volunteer Infantry in the War of the Rebellion, 1861–1865* (Boston, 1888), 217. A New Hampshire officer estimated that only one of every ten conscripts and substitutes made a good soldier. Lyman Jackman, *History of the Sixth New Hampshire Regiment in the War for the Union* (Concord, 1891), 11.

56. McPherson, *Ordeal by Fire*, 410; Judson, *83rd Pennsylvania*, 152–53; Austin C. Stearns, *Three Years with Company K* (Cranbury, NJ, 1976), 215–16. See also Bartlett, *12th New Hampshire*, 153; Vaill, *2nd Connecticut Heavy Artillery*, 45.

57. Charles T. Loehr, *War History of the Old First Virginia Infantry Regiment* (Richmond, 1884), 53; J. W. Eggleston to mother, Dec. 31, 1863, letter in possession of James I. Robertson, Jr.

58. Thomas L. Livermore, *Days and Events, 1860–1866* (Boston, 1920).

59. Lincoln, *34th Massachusetts*, 152; Glatthaar, *March to the Sea*, 36.

60. Henry Orendorff, *We Are Sherman's Men: The Civil War Letters of Henry Orendorff* (Macomb, IL, 1986), 56.

Chapter 3—Novelties of Camp Life

1. Peter Wilson, "Peter Wilson in the Civil War," *Iowa Journal of History and Politics*, XL (1942), 157; Charles W. Wills, *Army Life of an Illinois Soldier* (Washington, 1906), 14; William H. Morgan to sister, Aug. 26, 1861, letter in possession of Melvin M. Scott, Falls Church, VA; Edwin Weller, *A Civil War Courtship: The Letters of Edwin Weller from Antietam to Atlanta* (Garden City, NY, 1980), 27.

2. Thompson, *13th New Hampshire*, 35.

3. Davis, *Three Years in the Army*, 7.

4. Gould, *1st-10th-29th Maine*, 21; Spicer, *9th and 10th Rhode Island*, 84–85.

5. Boyd, *Civil War Diary*, 23.

6. Robson, *How a One-legged Rebel Lives*, 10.

7. John Day Smith, *The History of the Nineteenth Regiment of Maine Volunteer Infantry, 1862–1865* (Minneapolis, 1909), 3; Spicer, *9th and 10th Rhode Island*, 172.

8. Henry E. Handerson, *Yankee in Gray: The Civil War Memoirs of Henry E. Handerson* (Cleveland, 1962), 9.

9. Spicer, *9th and 10th Rhode Island*, 102–3. Of sleeping "spoon fashion" in a tent, another New England soldier commented: "Long practice has got us pretty well drilled in this respect, and all that is necessary is to sing out 'About face!' and immediately all the sleepers turn over on the other side, together, without disturbing the blankets or bed." Allen, *4th Rhode Island*, 32.

10. Abner Dunham, "Civil War Letters of Abner Dunham, 12th Iowa Infantry," *Iowa Journal of History* LIII (1955), 307–8; Alexander Hunter, *Johnny Reb and Billy Yank* (New York, 1905), 239; Billings, *Hardtack and Coffee*, 47.

11. *History of the Twelfth Regiment, Rhode Island Volunteers, in the Civil War, 1862–1863* (Providence, 1904), 135–36.

12. Weller, *A Civil War Courtship*, 24; Billings, *Hardtack and Coffee*, 52; Albert H. DeRosier, Jr. (ed.), *Through the South with a Union Soldier* (Johnson City, TN, 1969), 102.

13. Davis, *Three Years in the Army*, 69–70.

14. Hunter, *Johnny Reb and Billy Yank* 160; James M. Phillips, *Civil War Diary & Letters of James Martin Phillips, Company G. 92nd Illinois Volunteers* (St. Louis, 1982), 136. See also Ernest L. Waitt, *History of the Nineteenth Regiment, Massachusetts Volunteer Infantry, 1861–1865* (Salem, 1906), 110.

15. Thomas L. Livermore, *Days and Events, 1860–1866* (Boston, 1920), 34; R. F. Aden (ed.), "In Memoriam, Seventh Tennessee Cavalry, C. S. A.," *West Tennessee Historical Society Papers* XVII (1963), 110; John H. Worsham, *One of Jackson's Foot Cavalry* (Jackson, TN, 1964), 91.

16. George Crooke, *The Twenty-first Regiment of Iowa Volunteer Infantry* (Milwaukee, 1891), 22.

17. William S. Lincoln, *Life with the Thirty-fourth Mass. Infantry in the War of the Rebellion* (Worcester, 1879), 45.

18. Jackman, *6th New Hampshire*, 3–4.

19. Collins, *149th New York*, 32; W. G. Bean, *The Liberty Hall Volunteers: Stonewall's College Boys* (Charlottesville, VA, 1964), 31; Thompson, *13th New Hampshire*, 19.

20. Ibid.; Elbridge J. Copp, *Reminiscences of the War of the Rebellion, 1861–1865* (Nashua, NH, 1911), 22.

21. Oliver W. Norton, *Army Letters, 1861–1865* (Chicago, 1903), 28.

22. Smith, *118th Pennsylvania*, 12.

23. George C. Eggleston, *A Rebel's Recollections* (New York, 1875), 20; Thompson, *13th New Hampshire*, 3.

24. Buffum, *14th New Hampshire*, 45.

25. Thompson, *13th New Hampshire*, 99.

26. Gillaspie, *From Michigan to Murfreesboro*, 13; Vaill, *2nd Connecticut Heavy Artillery*, 22, 28.

27. Hunter, *Johnny Reb and Billy Yank*, 79.

28. Frank Wilkeson, *Recollections of a Private Soldier in the Army of the Potomac* (New York, 1886), 22.

29. Hunter, *Johnny Reb and Billy Yank*, 79.

30. Thomas Head, *Campaigns and Battles of the Sixteenth Regiment, Tennessee Volunteers* (Nashville, 1885), 197; John K. Bettersworth (ed.), *Mississippi in the Confederacy* (Baton Rouge, 1961), I, 178.

31. W. W. Lenoir Civil War Diary, July 27, 1862, Lenoir Family Papers, University of North Carolina; Giles, *Rags and Hope*, 68; Charles E. Cort, *"Dear Friends:" The Civil War Letters and Diary of Charles Edwin Cort* (n.p., 1962), 11.

32. W. J. McMurray, *History of the Twentieth Tennessee Regiment Volunteer Infantry, C. S. A.* (Nashville, 1904), 187; William M. Wood, *Reminiscences of Big I* (Jackson, TN, 1956), 8.

33. Bean, *Liberty Hall Volunteers*, 28.

34. Charles T. Quintard, *Doctor Quintard, Chaplain C. S. A. and Second Bishop of Tennessee; Being His Story of the War (1861–1865)* (Sewanee, TN, 1905), 20.

35. Robertson, *Tenting Tonight*, 53.

36. Thomas J. Pierce, *Letters Home* (Burlington, IA, 1957), 28.

37. Lincoln, *34th Massachusetts*, 200.

38. Smith, *118th Pennsylvania*, 13; Gould, *1st-10th-29th Maine*, 53.

39. Ephraim A. Wilson, *Memoirs of the War* (Cleveland, 1893), 32.

40. Gould, *1st-10th-29th Maine*, 296.

41. Giles, *Rags and Hope*, 48.

42. *History of the Fifth Massachusetts Battery* (Boston, 1902), 139–42.

43. *Official Records*, Ser. III, Vol. I, 561.

44. Cannon, *Inside of Rebeldom*, 22–23; John B. Landis, "Personal Experiences in the War of the Rebellion, 1862–1863" (typescript in possession of James I. Robertson, Jr.), 4–5; John B. Lindsley, *The Military Annals of Tennessee: Confederate* (Nashville, 1886), 207–8.

45. Sloan, *Guilford Grays*, 5; Buffum, *14th New Hampshire*, 54.

46. Cyril B. Upsham, "Arms and Equipment for the Iowa Troops in the Civil War," *Iowa Journal of History and Politics* XVI (1918), 18.

47. William Camm, "Diary of Colonel William Camm, 1861 to 1865," *Journal of the Illinois State Historical Society* XVII (1926), 802, 813; John O. Casler, *Four Years in the Stonewall Brigade* (Dayton, OH, 1971), 54; Ulysses S. Grant, *Personal Memoirs of U. S. Grant* (New York, 1885), I, 95.

48. Albert W. Mann (comp.), *History of the Forty-fifth Regiment, Massachusetts Volunteer Militia* (Boston, 1908), 39.

49. Grenville W. Dodge, "Gen. James A. Williamson," *Annals of Iowa* VI (1903), 164.

50. Grady McWhiney, *Southerners and Other Americans* (New York, 1973), 107.

51. Hopkins, *7th Rhode Island*, 16.

52. L. W. Day, *Story of the One Hundred and First Ohio Infantry* (Cleveland, 1894), 39.

53. Buffum, *14th New Hampshire*, 70; George H. Otis, *The Second Wisconsin Infantry* (Dayton, OH, 1984), 35–36.

54. Howard Thomas, *Boys in Blue from the Adirondack Foothills* (Prospect, NY, 1960), 17; *History of the 121st Pennsylvania Volunteers* (Philadelphia, 1893), 15.

55. William W. H. Davis, *History of the 104th Pennsylvania Regiment, from August 22nd, 1861, to September 30th, 1864* (Philadelphia, 1866), 161; Reid, *4th South Carolina*, 15.

56. Gibbs reminiscences; Fred A. Shannon, *The Organization and Administration of the Union Army, 1861–1865* (Cleveland, 1928), I, 139.

57. Vaill, *2nd Connecticut Heavy Artillery*, 65–66.

58. Thompson, *13th New Hampshire*, 221.

59. Sheldon B. Thorpe, *The History of the Fifteenth Connecticut Volunteers in the War for the Defense of the Union, 1861–1865* (New Haven, 1893), 13.

60. Chattahoochee Valley Historical Society (comp.), *War Was the Place. A Centennial Collection of Confederate Soldier Letters* (Chambers County, AL, 1961), 18.

61. Davis, *Three Years in the Army*, 4.

62. Moore, *A Life for the Confederacy*, 104; Thompson, *13th New Hampshire*, 4.

63. *History of the Thirty-sixth Regiment, Massachusetts Volunteers, 1862–1865* (Boston, 1884), 6; William B. Stevens, *History of the Fiftieth Regiment of Infantry, Massachusetts Volunteer Militia, in the Late War of the Rebellion* (Boston, 1907), 97.

64. Welsh, *Irish Green and Union Blue*, 38.

Chapter 4—The Novelties Wear Off

1. William C. Davis (ed.), *Shadows of the Storm* (Garden City, NY, 1981), 124.

2. Oliver Wendell Holmes, Jr., *Touched with Fire: Civil War Letters and Diary of Oliver Wendell Holmes, Jr., 1861–1864* (Cambridge, MA, 1947), 142

3. William Child, *A History of the Fifth Regiment, New Hampshire Volunteers, in the American Civil War, 1861–1865* (Bristol, NH, 1893), 99.

4. Bruce Catton, *A Stillness at Appomattox* (Garden City, NY, 1953), 201.

5. Norton, *Army Letters*, 59; Ernest L. Waitt, *History of the Nineteenth Regiment Massachusetts Volunteer Infantry, 1861–1865* (Salem, 1906), 281.

6. Davis, *Three Years in the Army*, 37; Tilney, *My Life in the Army*, 52; Hunter, *Johnny Reb and Billy Yank*, 238–39.

7. Waitt, *19th Massachusetts*, 217.

8. Parker, *Henry Wilson's Regiment*, 185. See also the reminiscences of George C. Parker, in *Civil War Times Illustrated* XVI (Apr., 1977), 14.

9. Lewis Bissell, *The Civil War Letters of Lewis Bissell* (Washington, 1981), 293; Wilson, *Memoirs of the War*, 49.

10. Waitt, *19th Massachusetts*, 218.

11. Bissell, *Civil War Letters*, 248; Marcus B. Toney, *The Privations of a Private* (Nashville, 1905), 40; Bellard, *Gone for a Soldier*, 79. For a particularly gruesome account of taking water from nearby gullies, see *History of the 35th Massachusetts*, 139.

12. A. J. Bennett, *The Story of the First Massachusetts Light Battery* (Boston, 1886), 62; Allen, *4th Rhode Island*, 32–33.

13. Thomas, *Boys in Blue*, 209; John W. Lavender, *The War Memoirs of Captain John W. Lavender, C.S.A.* (Pine Bluff, AR, 1956), 34.

14. DeRosier, *Through the South*, 108.

15. George A. Bowen, "George A. Bowen Memoirs," Salem County (NJ) Historical Society, 3–4; Justus M. Silliman, *A New Canaan Private in the Civil War: Letters of Justus M. Silliman, 17th Connecticut Volunteers* (New Canaan, CT, 1984), 16; Spicer, *9th & 10th Rhode Island*, 203.

16. Cort, *"Dear Friends,"* 18; Bean, *Liberty Hall Volunteers*, 77.

17. Joseph P. Blessington, *The Campaigns of Walker's Texas Division* (New York, 1875), 63.

18. Eggleston, *A Rebel's Recollections*, 208–9; Bailey, *Confederate Generation*, 82. A similar statement about the Union commissariat is in Bennett, *1st Massachusetts Light Battery*, 42.

19. E. H. C. Cavins to his father, July 18, 1862, Cavins Collection, Indiana Historical Society.

20. George W. Adams, *Doctors in Blue: The Medical History of the Union Army in the Civil War* (New York, 1952), 16; Edgar Jackson (ed.), *Three Rebels Write Home* (Franklin, VA, 1955), 16.

21. *Under the Maltese Cross*, 84–85.

22. Joseph K. Newell, *"Ours:" Annals of 10th Regiment, Massachusetts Volunteers, in the Rebellion* (Springfield, 1875), 90. See also Edwin B. Houghton, *The Campaigns of the Seventeenth Maine* (Portland, 1866), 18; *Civil War Times Illustrated* XIV (Oct., 1875), 11.

23. Bellard, *Gone for a Soldier*, 120. See also *History of the 35th Massachusetts*, 94.

24. Lincoln, *34th Massachusetts*, 319; Lenoir diary, Jan. 2, 1863; Bellard, *Gone for a Soldier*, 188.

25. Fowle, *Letters to Eliza*, 132.

26. Bean, *Liberty Hall Volunteers*, 53; Chattachoochee Society, *War Was the Place*, 87; Robert Patrick, *Reluctant Rebel: The Secret Diary of Robert Patrick, 1861–1865* (Baton Rouge, 1959), 138.

27. Thompson, *13th New Hampshire*, 439; Bellard, *Gone for a Soldier*, 119–20.

28. Adams, *Doctors in Blue*, 208; Spicer, *9th and 10th Rhode Island*, 141.

29. Bean, *Liberty Hall Volunteers*, 15.

30. Casler, *Stonewall Brigade*, 221; Hunter, *Johnny Reb and Billy Yank*, 440; John W. Green, *Johnny Green of the Orphan Brigade: The Journal of a Confederate Soldier* (Lexington, 1956), 136.

31. Robert W. Glover (ed.), *"Tyler to Sharpsburg:" The Letters of Robert H. and William H. Gaston* (Waco, 1960), 12.

32. See Philip F. Brown, *Reminiscences of the War of 1861–1865* (Roanoke, VA, 1912), 29; Carlton McCarthy, *Detailed Minutae of Soldier Life in the Army of Northern Virginia. 1861–1865* (Richmond, 1882), 59.

33. Luther S. Dickey, *History of the Eighty-fifth Regiment, Pennsylvania Volunteer Infantry, 1861–1865* (New York, 1915), 10; Stearns, *Company K*, 22; DeRosier, *Through the South*, 32–33; Weller, *A Civil War Courtship*, 97.

34. Royal W. Figg, *Where Men Only Dare to Go! or, The Story of a Boy Company (C.S.A.)* (Richmond, 1885), 20; Otis, *2nd Wisconsin*, 136; Stephen G. Cook, *The "Dutchess County Regiment" (150th Regiment of New York State Volunteer Infantry) in the Civil War* (Danbury, CT, 1907), 103.

35. Thompson, *13th New Hampshire*, 494; Adams, *Doctors in Blue*, 208; Kaiser, "Letters from the Front," 158. See also Charles W. Cowtan, *Services of the Tenth New York Volunteers (National Zouaves) in the War of the Rebellion* (New York, 1882), 152.

36. Waitt, *19th Massachusetts*, 18.

37. Welsh, *Irish Green and Union Blue*, 56.

38. Day, *101st Ohio*, 77–78.

39. Crooke, *21st Iowa*, 21.

40. Davis, *Three Years in the Army*, 13; Boyd, *Civil War Diary*, 53. See also Bellard, *Gone for a Soldier*, 119.

41. David Brett, *"My Dear Wife:" The Civil War Letters of David Brett, 9th Massachusetts Battery, Union Cannoneer* (Little Rock, AR, 1964), 9; Moore, *A Life for the Confederacy*, 56; Bartlett, *12th New Hampshire*, 140–41.

42. Bellard, *Gone for a Soldier*, 119.

43. Schafer diary; Dame, *From the Rapidan to Richmond*, 26.

44. Cort, *"Dear Friends,"* 162; H. H. Cunningham, *Doctors in Gray: The Confederate Medical Service* (Baton Rouge, 1958), 176. Six weeks after Gettysburg a North Carolina soldier wrote from camp: "I don't think that this war will last long without the[y] give us more to eat for I have [heard] some say the[y] wood runaway that I thought never would runaway but we can't stand everything & not get half enuf to eat . . . " Samuel R. Flynt to brother, Aug. 16, 1863, Flynt Letters, in possession of Vicki Heilig, Germantown, MD.

45. C. C. Briant, *History of the Sixth Regiment, Indiana Volunteer Infantry* (Indianapolis, 1891), 254–55.

46. John Obreiter, *History of the Seventy-seventh Pennsylvania Volunteers* (Harrisburg, 1905), 137; Thomas J. Ford, *With the Rand and File: Incidents and Anecdotes during the War of the Rebellion* (Milwaukee, 1895), 25–26; Hunter, *Johnny Reb and Billy Yank* 267. In a similar vein, see also Stearns, *Company K*, 277.

47. Samuel R. Watkins, *"Co. Aytch," Maury Grays, First Tennessee Regiment* (Nashville, 1882), 121–22.

48. W. S. Dunlop, *Lee's Sharpshooters; or, the Forefront of Battle* (Little Rock, 1899), 55.

49. Davis, *Three Years in the Army*, 160.

50. Joseph R. C. Ward, *History of the One Hundred and Sixth Regiment, Pennsylvania Volunteers, 2d Brigade, 2d Division, 2d Corps, 1861–1865* (Philadelphia, 1906), 101; Bear, *Civil War Letters*, 19; Oliver C. Hamilton to father, May 17, 1863, Eli Spinks Hamilton Papers, University of North Carolina.

51. Parker, *Henry Wilson's Regiment*, 203. For other instances of raids on sutlers' wagons, see ibid., 73; Thorpe, *15th Connecticut*, 49–50; Smith, *19th Maine*, 56; Benjamin W. Crowninshield, *A History of the First Regiment of Massachusetts Cavalry Volunteers* (Boston, 1891), 159; Hopkins, *7th Rhode Island*, 22.

52. *Under the Maltese Cross*, 88; Penrose G. Mark, *Red: White: and Blue Badge, Pennsylvania Veteran Volunteers: A History of the 93rd Regiment . . .* (Harrisburg, 1911), 352; Theodore Gerrish, *Army Life: A Private's Reminiscences of the Civil War* (Portland, ME, 1882), 99.

53. Schafer diary, Nov. 30, 1862; Smith *19th Maine*, 18; Casler, *Stonewall Brigade*, 78. Contrary to the widely maintained belief that Lee's army refrained from pillaging during the 1863 campaign into Pennsylvania, more than one Confederate soldier later confessed to "some depredations on private property." See Moore, *A Life for the Confederacy*, 152.

54. Connolly, *Army of the Cumberland*, 311.

55. Benjamin Borton, *On the Parallels; or, Chapters of Inner History: A Story of the Rappahannock* (Woodstown, NJ, 1903), 39–40.

56. Hunter, *Johnny Reb and Billy Yank*, 44.

57. Figg, *"Where Men Only Dare to Go,"* 64.

58. Thompson, *13th New Hampshire*, 103; James Greenalch, "Letters of James Greenalch," *Michigan History* XL (1960), 206.

59. Terry L. Jones, *Lee's Tigers: The Louisiana Infantry in the Army of Northern Virginia* (Baton Rouge, 1987), 140.

60. Thompson, *13th New Hampshire*, 95–96; Dame, *From the Rapidan to Richmond*, 18–19.

61. For various accounts of the construction and appearance of winter quarters, see Vaill, *2nd Connecticut Heavy Artillery*, 137; William Batts, "A Foot Soldier's Account: Letters of William Batts, 1861–1862," *Georgia Historical Quarterly* L (1966), 91; Stearns, *Company K*, 247–48; Newell, *10th Massachusetts*, 248; D. Augustus Dickert, *History of Kershaw's Brigade* (Newberry, SC, 1899), 83–84.

62. See William M. Owen, *In Camp and Battle with the Washington Artillery* (Boston, 1885), 68–69; Billings, *Hardtack and Coffee*, 57; Thompson, *13th New Hampshire*, 106–7.

63. Tilney, *My Life in the Army*, 51; Robertson, "Indiana Soldier," 253; Womack, *Call Forth the Mighty Men*, 351–52.

64. Davis, *Three Years in the Army*, 85; Parker, *Henry Wilson's Regiment*, 219; Stephen A. Repass to Mrs. Peter Shirey, Feb. 16, 1862, letter in possession of Mary McCauley, Salem, VA.

65. Glatthaar, *March to the Sea*, 109.

66. Bellard, *Gone for a Soldier*, 147; Samuel R. Flynt to brother, Aug. 15, 1863, Flynt Letters; Connolly, *Army of the Cumberland*, 120–21; Reid, *4th South Carolina*, 74; Bailey, *Confederate Generation*, 84. The war was barely eighteen months old when a North Carolinia soldier wrote of the Army of Northern Virginia: "One-fifth of Lee's army was barefooted, one-half in rags and the whole of them half famished. The marvel of it is that any of us were able." Smith, *The Anson Guards*, 161. Similar comments will be found in Wood, *Reminiscences of Big I*, 87, and Benjamin H. Freeman, *The Confederate Letters of Benjamin H. Freeman* (Hicksville, NY, 1974), 44.

67. *History of the 35th Massachusetts*, 200; Giles, *Rags and Hope*, 138.

68. Glatthaar, *March to the Sea*, 114–15.

69. George E. Parks, "One Story of the 109th Illinois Volunteer Infantry Regiment," *Journal of the Illinois State Historical Society* LVI (1963), 286; Davis, *Three Years in the Army*, 15.

70. Hopkins, *7th Rhode Island*, 66.

71. Wilson, *Memoirs of the War*, 58.

72. Smith, *19th Maine*, 55.

73. *Official Records*, LII, Pt. 2, 252; Crowninshield, *1st Massachusetts Cavalry*, 109.

74. McHenry Howard, *Recollections of a Maryland Confederate Soldier and Staff Officer under Johnston, Jackson and Lee* (Dayton, OH, 1975), 254n.

75. Abner R. Small, *The Sixteenth Maine Regiment in the War of the Rebellion, 1861–1865* (Portland, 1886), 159.

76. George P. Prowell, *History of the Eighty-seventh Regiment, Pennsylvania Volunteers* (York, PA, 1903), 117.

Chapter 5—Fun, Frolics, and Firewater
1. Adam S. Rader to Simon Rader, May 7, 1862, letter in the possession of James I. Robertson, Jr.; William A. Schafer to wife, Jan. 18, 1863, Schaeffer Papers.

2. Chattahoochee Society, *War Was the Place*, 20. A similar expression of contentment is in Nancy Niblack Baxter, *Gallant Fourteenth* (Traverse City, IN, 1980), 36.

3. Glatthaar, *March to the Sea*, 93; John T. Smith to family, Feb. 1, 1863, letter in possession of Melvin M. Scott, Falls Church, VA; Boyd, *Civil War Diary*, 24. See also Robertson, *Tenting Tonight*, 56.

4. Day, *101st Ohio*, 19; Henry E. Schafer to wife, Apr. 9, 1865, Schaeffer Papers.

5. Asbury L. Kerwood, *Annals of the Fifty-seventh Regiment Indiana Volunteers* (Dayton, OH, 1868), 188–89; *Religious Herald*, May 8, 1862; Charles Ross, "Diary of Charles Ross," *Vermont History* XXX (1962), 135.

6. Kaiser, "Letters from the Front," 157; Davis, *104th Pennsylvania*, 15.

7. Otis, *2nd Wisconsin*, 135.

8. Arthur J. L. Fremantle, *Three Months in the Confederate States* (London, 1863), 71; [Thomas E. Caffey] *Battle-fields of the South, by an English Combatant* (London, 1863), II, 101; Moore, *A Life for the Confederacy*, 66.

9. Bruce Catton, *Mr. Lincoln's Army* (Garden City, NY, 1951), 19.

10. Wood, *Reminiscences of Big I*, 115.

11. Weller, *A Civil War Courtship*, 14; Smith, *The Anson Guards*. 163.

12. Tilney, *My Life in the Army*, 53.

13. Leander W. Cogswell, *A History of the Eleventh New Hampshire Regiment, Volunteer Infantry, in the Rebellion War, 1861-1865* (Concord, 1891), 64. For similar incidents, see Thorpe, *15th Connecticut*, 41; Toney, *Privations of a Private*, 73.

14. Thompson, *13th New Hampshire*, 104.

14. Ibid., 447.

16. Henry Hotze, *Three Months in the Confederate Army* (University, AL, 1952), 22.

17. For example, see Thompson, *13th New Hampshire*, 106, 235.

18. *History of the 35th Massachusetts*, 155.

19. Norton, *Army Letters*, 327–28.

20. Gould, *1st-10th-29th Maine*, 245; Davis, *104th Pennsylvania*, 14–15.

21. Moore, *A Life for the Confederacy*, 82.

22. James Smart Warnell Diary, May 25, 1862, copy in possession of Edward H. Hahn, Pittsburgh, PA.

23. Figg, "Where Men Only Dare to Go," 100–1; Martin A. Haynes, *A History of the Second Regiment, New Hampshire Volunteer Infantry, in the War of the Rebellion* (Lakeport, 1896), 212.

24. E. H. C. Cavins to wife, Sept. 25, 1861, Cavins Collection.

25. Dame, *From the Rapidan to Richmond*, 23.

26. Figg, "Where Men Only Dare to Go," 95.

27. James A. Emmerton, *A Record of the Twenty-third Regiment Mass. Vol. Infantry in the War of the Rebellion, 1861-1865* (Boston, 1886), 161; Smith, *118th Pennsylvania*, 378.

28. Jay Monaghan, "Civil War Slang and Humor," *Civil War History* III (1957), 125–33.

29. Wilson, *Memoirs of the War*, 171; Chattachoochee Society, *War Was the Place*, 20.

30. Worsham, *One of Jackson's Foot Cavalry*, xxi–xxii; Crooke, *21st Iowa*, 17.

31. Davis, *Three Years in the Army*, 29.

32. Ward, *106th Pennsylvania*, 13; Kaiser, "Letters from the Front," 152.

33. Thompson, *13th New Hampshire*, 2.

34. Ibid., 542; Figg, "Where Men Only Dare to Go," 98.

35. Johnston, *The Story of a Confederate Boy*, 103.

36. For example, see *Under the Maltese Cross*, 220; Boyd, *Civil War Diary*, 57; Gould, *1st-10th-29th Maine*, 46–47.

37. Orendorff, *We Are Sherman's Men*, 30.

38. Wilson, "Peter Wilson in the Civil War," 402–3.
39. Bettersworth, *Mississippi in the Confederacy*, I, 346; Glatthaar, *March to the Sea*, 96.
40. Wilbur F. Hinman, *The Story of the Sherman Brigade* (Alliance, OH, 1897), 225–26.
41. Thompson, *13th New Hampshire*, 25.
42. Hunter, *Johnny Reb and Billy Yank*, 75.
43. Toney, *Privations of a Private*, 56; Giles, *Rags and Hope*, 157.
44. Newton, *A Wisconsin Boy in Dixie*, 77; Stephen F. Blanding, *In the Defences of Washington* (Providence, 1889), 9. See also Bettersworth, *Mississippi in the Confederacy*, I, 187.
45. Thompson, *13th New Hampshire*, 254.
46. General Order Book, 37th N.C. Troops, 1862–1863, Duke University.
47. Davis, *Three Years in the Army*, 307; John T. Smith to family, Feb. 1, 1863, Smith Letter.
48. For example, see Green, *Orphan Brigade*, 122.
49. Judson, *83rd Pennsylvania*, 164.
50. James P. Douglas, *Douglas's Texas Battery, CSA* (Tyler, TX, 1966), 53; Edwin E. Bryant, *History of the Third Regiment of Wisconsin Veteran Volunteer Infantry, 1861–1865* (Madison, 1891), 285–86.
51. Tilney, *My Life in the Army*, 55.
52. Newell, *10th Massachusetts*, 159; Hunter, *Johnny Reb and Billy Yank*, 244.
53. Clark, *N.C. Regiments*, I, 753. See also Douglas, *Douglas's Texas Battery*, 146.
54. Welsh, *Irish Green and Union Blue*, 17.
55. Davis, *104th Pennsylvania*, 38; McClellan order quoted in Bell I Wiley, *The Life of Billy Yank* (Indianapolis, 1952), 252.
56. John H. Morgan to sister, Aug. 9, 1861, letter in possession of Melvin M. Scott, Falls Church, VA; Davis, *Three Years in the Army*, 299. A soldier in the 25th Georgia wrote his wife in November, 1861: "I thought I had quit liquor but I find it is absolutely necessary to life & therefore drink mean whiskey that is worth about 40 cts a gallon at home that cost me $5 a gallon here." Theodorick W. Montfort, *Rebel Lawyer: Letters of Theodorick W. Montfort, 1861–1862* (Athens, GA, 1965), 30–31.
57. Patrick, *Reluctant Rebel*, 115; Gillaspie, *From Michigan to Murfreesboro*, 22.
58. Reid, *4th South Carolina*, 11.
59. Gould, *1st-10th-29th Maine*, 51; Spicer, *9th & 10th Rhode Island*, 233.
60. Newell, *10th Massachusetts*, 52.
61. William D. F. Landon, "Fourteenth Indiana Regiment: Letters to the Vincennes Western Sun," *Indiana Magazine of History* XXXIV (1938), 87; Crowninshield, *1st Massachusetts Cavalry*, 298–99.
62. Davis, *Three Years in the Army*, 300.
63. Bear, *Civil War Letters*, 7.
64. Elbridge Hadley, "A Young Soldier's Career," *Annals of Iowa* XIII (1922), 337.
65. Livermore, *Days and Events*, 183; Allen, *4th Rhode Island*, 126.
66. Perry Mayo, *The Civil War Letters of Perry Mayo* (East Lansing, 1967), 194–95; Cort, *"Dear Friends,"* 36; Livermore, *Days and Events*, 297.
67. Onley Andrus, *Civil War Letters of Sgt. Onley Andrus* (Urbana, IL, 1947), 72. For a similar Christmas celebration in the 7th Tennessee, see Womack, *Call Forth the Mighty Men*, 139.
68. Hudson Hyatt (ed.), "Captain Hyatt: Being the Letters Written during the War Years 1863–1864 to His Wife Mary," *Ohio State Archaeological and Historical Quarterly* LIII (1944), 169.
69. Hunter, *Johnny Reb and Billy Yank*, 98.
70. Bellard, *Gone for a Soldier*, 33. See also Lincoln, *34th Massachusetts*, 126.

71. DeRosier, *Through the South*, 92; Boyd, *Civil War Diary*, 93.
72. James M. Nichols, *Perry's Saints; or the Fighting Parson's Regiment in the War of the Rebellion* (Boston, 1886), 113.
73. DeRosier, *Through the South*, 45.
74. *History of the 35th Massachusetts*, 220.
75. Wilson, *Memoirs of the War*, 167–68; Reid, *4th South Carolina*, 44; Glatthaar, *March to the Sea*, 99.
76. Wilson, "Peter Wilson in the Civil War," 403.

Chapter 6—Heartstrings vs. Playthings
1. Douglas, *Douglas's Texas Battery*, 44; John W. Cotton, *Yours till Death: Civil War Letters of John W. Cotton* (University, AL, 1951), 14.
2. Alfred L. Hough, *Soldier in the West: The Civil War Letters of Alfred Lacey Hough* (Philadelphia, 1957), 157; Samuel L. Sawyer to mother, Sept. 29, 1863, Charles H. Sawyer Letters, University of Tennessee; DeRosier, *Through the South*, 56.
3. Figg, *"Where Men Only Dare to Go,"* 112.
4. Bailey, *Confederate Generation*, 81; Gillaspie, *From Michigan to Murfreesboro*, 16; Cunningham, *Doctors in Gray*, 4–5.
5. Joel Angle to Mary Ann Angle, undated letter, collection in possession of James I. Robertson, Jr.
6. Cotton, *Yours till Death*, 32.
7. Giles, *Rags and Hopes*, 61; Boyd, *Civil War Diary*, 125.
8. Ira S. Dodd, *The Song of the Rappahannock: Sketches of the Civil War* (New York, 1898), 206; Carrie Esther Spencer (ed.), *A Civil War Marriage in Virginia: Reminiscences and Letters* (Boyce, VA, 1956), 123.
9. Crooke, *21st Iowa*, 19.
10. Corson, *My Dear Jennie*, 26; Connolly, *Army of the Cumberland*, 274; Glatthaar, *March to the Sea*, 89. A regimental historian wrote of late summer, 1861: "Home letters were the only relief for the homesickness by which some of the men were still bitterly afflicted." Ford, *15th Massachusetts*, 62.
11. Bear, *Civil War Letters*, 7.
12. Joel Angle to Mary Ann Angle, Nov. 24, 1862, Angle Letters; Harrison A. Loflin to mother, Sept. 7, 1862, in possession of James I. Robertson, Jr.
13. Cotton, *Yours till Death*, 36.
14. Dunham, "Civil War Letters," 331; Leo W. and John I. Faller, *Dear Folks at Home: The Civil War Letters of Leo W. and John I. Faller* (Carlisle, PA, 1963), 18; Mayo, *Civil War Letters*, 191.
15. Fowle, *Letters to Eliza*, 65; C. G. Hamilton to father, Dec. 29, 1862, Eli Spinks Hamilton Letters, University of North Carolina; Edna J. S. Hunter, *One Flag, One Country and Thirteen Greenbacks a Month* (San Diego, 1980), 97.
16. Glatthaar, *March to the Sea*, 88.
17. Wiley, *Life of Billy Yank*, 187.
18. Spencer, *Civil War Marriage*, 134; Orendorff, *We Are Sherman's Men*, 12; Bean, *Liberty Hall Volunteers*, 172.
19. Kaiser, "Letters from the Front," 159.
20. Phillips, *Civil War Diary & Letters*, 142.
21. Hunter, *One Flag, One Country*, 96–97; Cotton, *Yours till Death*, 23.
22. Ibid., 9.
23. Ira S. Jeffers, "Letters from Ira S. Jeffers, 137 New York Inf., Co. F" (typescript copy in possession of James I. Robertson, Jr.), 7.
24. Chattahoochee Society, *War Was the Place*, 57.
25. Ford, *15th Massachusetts*, 62; Wagner, *Letters*, 44.

26. Worsham, *One of Jackson's Foot Cavalry*, 98.
27. J. Whit Johnson to cousin, July 2, 1862, in possession of Melvin M. Scott, Falls Church, VA; Glatthaar, *March to the Sea*, 90; Phillips, *Civil War Diary & Letters*, 138.
28. Spencer, *Civil War Marriage*, 120.
29. Cotton, *Yours till Death*, 6; Newton, *A Wisconsin Boy in Dixie*, 56, 59.
30. John H. Morgan to sister, Aug. 9, 1861, Morgan letters.
31. Phillips, *Civil War Diary & Letters*, 110; Douglas, *Douglas's Texas Battery*, 80; Charles S. Brown to family, Jan. 15, 1865, Charles S. Brown Papers, Duke University.
32. Thompson, *13th New Hampshire*, 21; William H. Sutherland to "My Dear Sir," July 27, 1862, in possession of Mrs. D. K. Brown, Vinton, VA.
33. Womack, *Call Forth the Mighty Men*, 264.
34. William J. Rogers, "William J. Rogers' Memorandum Book" *West Tennessee Historical Society Papers* IX (1955), 83.
35. George Baylor, *Bull Run to Bull Run* (Richmond, 1900), 290.
36. Roscoe B. G. Cowper to William H. Cross, Mar. 31, 1864, copy in the possession of James I. Robertson, Jr.
37. Upson, *With Sherman to the Sea*, 19; Henry E. Sterkx, *Partners in Rebellion: Alabama Women in the Civil War* (Cranbury, NJ, 1970), 73.
38. William H. Morgan to sister, Aug. 26, 1861, Morgan Letters.
39. Andrew Crockett to "Henry P." May 22, 1862, letter in possession of Mary C. Fugate, Danville, VA.
40. Hunter, *One Flag, One Country*, 68; Lord, *They Fought for the Union*, 215.
41. William R. Hartspence, *History of the Fifty-first Indiana Veteran Volunteer Infantry* (Cincinnati, 1894), 49.
42. Hunter, *One Flag, One Country*, 68; Glatthaar, *March to the Sea*, 68; *History of the 12th Rhode Island*, 153.
43. Kaiser, "Letters from the Front," 162.
44. Leander and Lydia Catherine Starks, *Throb of Drums in Tennessee, 1862–1865* (Philadelphia, 1973), 268.
45. E. H. C. Cavins to wife, Sept. 22, 1863, Cavins Collection; Douglas, *Douglas's Texas Battery*, 31. See also John Q. Anderson, *A Texas Surgeon in the C.S.A.* (Tuscaloosa, AL, 1957), 33.
46. John Jay Good and Susan Anna Good, *Cannon Smoke: The Letters of Captain John J. Good, Good-Douglas Texas Battery, CSA* (Hillsboro, TX, 1971), 12; Ruffin Barnes, "The Confederate Letters of Ruffin Barnes of Wilson County," *North CArolina Historical Review* XXXI (1964), 99.
47. Robert Hugh Martin, *A Boy of Old Shenandoah* (Parsons, WV, 1977), 55. See also Spencer, *Civil War Marriage*, 148.
48. Robert Selph Henry, *The Story of the Confederacy* (Indianapolis, 1931), 301.
49. Corson, *My Dear Jennie*, 15.
50. Charles N. Cook, "Letters of Privates Cook and Ball," *Indiana Magazine of History* XXVII (1931), 250, 260–61.
51. Peter Dekle, "Peter Dekle's Letters," *Civil War History* IV (Dec. 1958), 16.
52. E. H. C. Cavins to wife, Jan. 18, 1863, Cavins Collection.
53. Ibid., Dec. 21, 1862.
54. W. G. Bean, *Stonewall's Man: Sandie Pendleton* (Chapel Hill, 1952), 163, 173, 191, 229, 231.
55. Cotton, *Yours till Death*, 104; Jones, *Louisiana Tigers*, 191.
56. Chattachoochee Society, *War Was the Place.* 86–87.
57. E. H. C. Cavins to wife, Jan. 1, 1862, Cavins Collection.
58. Worsham, *One of Jackson's Foot Cavalry*, xx.
59. Newton, *A Wisconsin Boy in Dixie*, 113; Regis de Trobriand, *Four Years with the Army of the Potomac* (Boston, 1889), 604–5; Corby, *Memoirs of Chaplain Life*, 246–48.

60. Greenalch, "Letters," 230.

61. Boyd, *Civil War Diary*, 57.

62. Robertson, *Tenting Tonight*, 60; Margaret Leech, *Reveille in Washington, 1860–1865* (New York, 1941), 262–64.

63. David E. Beem to wife, Apr. 8, 1863, David E. Beem Papers, Indiana Historical Society.

64. E. H. C. Cavins to wife, Aug. 17, 1863, Cavins Collection.

65. Richmond *Daily Dispatch*, May 6, 1862.

66. Seth J. Temple, "Camp McClellan during the Civil War," *Annals of Iowa* XXI (1937), 44.

67. Bernt Olmanson, *Letters of Bernt Olmanson: A Union Soldier in the Civil War, 1861–1865* (n.p., n.d.), 13.

68. Phillips, *Civil War Diary & Letters*, 102–3.

69. Reid, *4th South Carolina*, 15.

70. Bear, *Civil War Letters*, 6.

71. Richmond *Enquirer*, Oct. 31, 1864.

72. E. H. C. Cavins to wife, Sept. 16, 1863, Cavins Collection.

73. *Medical Affairs*, II (1961), 17, 20.

74. Mayo, *Civil War Letters*, 170.

75. Greenalch, "Letters," 223; Phillips, *Civil War Diary & Letters*, 103, 107.

76. Elnathan L. and Jane Keeler, *Portrait of Elnathan Keeler, a Union Soldier* (New York, 1977), 21.

77. Howell, *Going to Meet the Yankees*, 169–70.

Chapter 7—Problems of Discipline

1. Edith Armstrong Talbot, *Samuel Chapman Armstrong: A Biographical Study* (New York, 1904), 68–69.

2. *History of the 127th Regiment, Pennsylvania Volunteers* (Lebanon, PA, 1902), 146–47.

3. Douglas S. Freeman, *Lee's Lieutenants: A Study in Command* (New York, 1942–1944), I, 13.

4. *Official Records*, XLVII, Pt. 2, 1276–77.

5. MOLLUS—Iowa, *War Sketches and Incidents*, I (1893), 163.

6. Howell, *Going to Meet the Yankees*, 39.

7. Bruce Catton, *America Goes to War* (Middletown, CT, 1958), 53.

8. John Gerber, "Mark Twain's 'Private Campaign,' " *Civil War History* I (1955), 55; Smith, *The Anson Guards*, 25–26.

9. Giles, *Rags and Hope*, 73.

10. James S. Beavers to Isham S. Upchurch, July 2, 1861, Isham Sims Upchurch Papers, Duke University; Davis, *Shadows of the Storm*, 125.

11. Smith, *The Anson Guards*, 11.

12. Jeffers, "Letters," 9; Leander Stillwell, *The Story of a Common Soldier of Army Life in the Civil War, 1861–1865* (Erie, KS, 1920), 12.

13. Davis, *Three Years in the Army*, 261.

14. *The Diary of an Unknown Soldier, September 5, 1862, to December 7, 1862, Found on a Battlefield* (Van Buren, AR, 1959), 38; Stearns, *Three Years with Company K*, 12.

15. Cotton, *Yours till Death*, 73; Kaiser, "Letters from the Front," 154.

16. Boyd, *Civil War Diary*, 28–29.

17. Ibid., 110.

18. Glatthaar, *March to the Sea*, 22.

19. Wilson, "Peter Wilson in the Civil War," 301; Boyd, *Civil War Diary*, 44.

20. Samuel A. Craig, "Captain Samuel A. Craig's Memoirs of Civil War and Reconstruction," *Western Pennsylvania Historical Magazine* XIII (1930), 229.

21. Evan R. Jones, *Four Years in the Army of the Potomac* (London, 1881), 45.

22. W. W. Scott (ed.), *Two Confederate Items* (Richmond, 1927), 14.

23. Collins, *149th New York*, 95.

24. *Official Records*, XVI, Pt. 1, 1062.

25. Jones, *Louisiana Tigers*, 45; George N. Bliss, "Chaos Still Reigns in This Camp— Letters of Lieutenant George N. Bliss, 1st New England Cavalry, March-September, 1862," *Rhode Island History* XXXVI (1977), 18–19.

26. Moore, *A Life for the Confederacy*, 48; Connolly, *Army of the Cumberland*, 252.

27. Cyrus C. Carpenter, "A Commissary in the Union Army: Letters of C. C. Carpenter," *Journal of Iowa History* LIII (1955), 65; Underwood, *33rd Massachusetts*, 15; James T. Ayers, *The Diary of James T. Ayers, Civil War Recruiter* (Springfield, IL, 1947), 34; Newton, *A Wisconsin Boy in Dixie*, 72.

28. Collins, *149th New York*, 38; Robert H. Strong, *A Yankee Private's Civil War* (Chicago, 1961), 83–84.

29. See Henry F. W. Little, *The Seventh Regiment New Hampshire Volunteers in the War of the Rebellion* (Concord, 1896), 88.

30. Cotton, *Yours till Death*, 58; Jackman, *6th New Hampshire*, 27.

31. Casler, *Stonewall Brigade*, 102.

32. James G. Hudson, "A Story of Company D, 4th Alabama Infantry Regiment, C.S.A.," *Alabama Historical Quarterly*, XXIII (1961), 156–57.

33. Child, *5th New Hampshire*, 89, 208, 213, 314. For other praise of good officers, see Thomas, *Boys in Blue*, 62–63; Carpenter, *8th Vermont*, 154.

34. George B. McClellan, *McClellan's Own Story* (New York, 1887), 86, 99–100. See also William Todd, *The Seventy-ninth Highlanders, New York Volunteers, in the War of the Rebellion, 1861–1865* (Albany, 1886), 56–58; Mayo, *Civil War Letters*, 179.

35. Greenalch, "Letters," 192–93.

36. Boyd, *Civil War Diary*, 18; Davis, *Three Years in the Army*, 11.

37. Hagan, *Confederate Letters*, 17.

38. Catton, *Mr. Lincoln's Army*, 181.

39. Bartlett, *12th New Hampshire*, 156; Thompson, *13th New Hampshire*, 152. For examples of similar punishments, see Henry E. Schafer diary, Oct. 23, 1862, Schaeffer Papers; Ford *15th Massachusetts*, 244–45; Gould, *1st-10th-29th Maine*, 102; Quintard, *Doctor Quintard*, 13.

40. Thorpe, *15th Connecticut*, 40.

41. Bellard, *Gone for a Soldier*, 27–28.

42. Joseph Gould, *The Story of the Forty-eighth: A Record of the Campaigns of the Forty-eighth Regiment Pennsylvania Veteran Volunteer Infantry during the Four Eventful Years of Its Service in the War for the Preservation of the Union* (Philadelphia, 1908), 177–78.

43. Catton, *A Stillness at Appomattox*, 136.

44. *Official Records*, XXXII, Pt. 2, 654.

45. Bartlett, *12th New Hampshire*, 57; *Official Records*, XXV, Pt. 2, 73; Henry Robinson Berkeley, *Four Years in the Confederate Artillery* (Chapel Hill, 1961), 65.

46. Waitt, *19th Massachusetts*, 274; Ward, *106th Pennsylvania*, 72; Luther Rice Mills, "Letters of Luther Rice Mills—A Confederate Soldier," *North Carolina Historical Review* IV (1927), 307.

47. Lindsley, *Military Annals*, 487.

48. Ella Lonn, *Desertion during the Civil War* (New York, 1928), 12–13.

49. John G. B. Adams, *Reminiscences of the Nineteenth Massachusetts Regiment* (Boston, 1899), 94.

50. H. Clay Trumbull, *War Memories of an Army Chaplain* (New York, 1906), 181–

83; Herbert W. Beecher, *History of the First Light Battery, Connecticut Volunteers, 1861–1865* (New York, 1901), II, 535; Massachusetts Adjt. Gen. (comp.), *Massachusetts Soldiers, Sailors, and Marines in the Civil War* (Norwood, MA, 1931), II, 808; Alfred S. Roe, *The Twenty-fourth Regiment, Massachusetts Volunteers, 1861–1865* (Worcester, 1907), 424–32.

51. Little, *7th New Hampshire*, 343–45. For an account of an unbelievably mishandled execution of two deserters, see Thomas F. Galwey, *The Valiant Hours* (Harrisburg, PA, 1961), 143–45.

52. Carpenter, *8th Vermont*, 129.

53. Thomas, *Boys in Blue*, 221.

54. George Drake, *The Mail Goes Through; or, The Civil War Letters of George Drake, 1846–1918* (San Angelo, TX, 1964), 86.

55. Ford, *15th Massachusetts*, 56.

56. Nelson V. Hutchinson, *History of the Seventh Massachusetts Volunteer Infantry in the War of the Rebellion of the Southern States against Constitutional Authority, 1861–1865* (Taunton, MA, 1890), 123; Crooke, *21st Iowa*, 101.

57. Giles, *Rags and Hope*, 157.

58. John B. Gordon, *Reminiscences of the Civil War* (New York, 1903), 110–12.

59. *History of the 36th Massachusetts*, 29–30.

60. Charles H. Banes, *History of the Philadelphia Brigade* (Philadelphia, 1876), 247.

61. DeRosier, *Through the South*, 141; Gilbert A. Hays, *Under the Red Patch: Story of the Sixty-third Regiment, Pennsylvania Volunteers, 1861–1864* (Pittsburgh, 1908), 270–71.

62. Wilson, *Memoirs of the War*, 236–37. See also James L. Bowen, *History of the Thirty-seventh Regiment, Mass. Volunteers, in the Civil War of 1861–1865* (Holyoke, MA, 1884), 402.

63. Lyman, *Meade's Headquarters*, 181.

64. Charles A. Cuffel, *History of Durrell's Battery in the Civil War* (Philadelphia, 1904), 229.

65. See Charles E. Belknap, "Christmas Day near Savannah in Wartime," *Michigan History* VI (1922), 591–96.

66. Figg, *"Where Men Only Dare to Go,"* 142.

67. Womack, *Call Forth the Mighty Men*, 369.

68. Henry E. Schafer to wife, July 16, 1863, and Schafer diary, July, 1863, Schaeffer Papers.

69. Hunter, *Johnny Reb and Billy Yank*, 431.

Chapter 8—The Grimmest Reaper

1. *Official Records*, X, Pt. 1, 771; Kate Cumming, *Kate, The Diary of a Confederate Nurse* (Baton Rouge, 1959), 14.

2. George H. Atkin to parents, Sept. 22, 1862, in possession of Arthur Donald Gill, Glen Rock, NJ.

3. *Official Records*, XXVII, Pt. 1, 28; Cornelia Hancock, *South of Gettysburg: Letters of Cornelia Hancock, 1863–1868* (New York, 1956), 7.

4. Gillaspie, *From Michigan to Murfreesboro*, 16; Cunningham, *Doctors in Gray*, 4–5; Bailey, *Confederate Generation*, 81.

5. John H. Morgan to sister, Aug. 9, 1861, Morgan Letters; *Medical Affairs*, II (1961), 7; U.S. Army Surgeon General, *Medical and Surgical History of the War of the Rebellion* (Washington, 1870–1888), III, 1.

6. Ohio Commandery, MOLLUS, *Sketches of War History*, II (1888), 90.

7. Adams, *Doctors in Blue*, 12–13; Bellard, *Gone for a Soldier*, 5.

8. Buffum, *14th New Hampshire*, 15.

9. Cunningham, *Doctors in Gray*, 164; *Official Records*, V, 82.

10. Boyd, *Civil War Diary*, 108.

11. Parker, *Henry Wilson's Regiment*, 204; Catton, *Mr. Lincoln's Army*, 189–90.

12. Gould, *1st-10th-29th Maine*, 30; William H. Morgan, *Personal Reminiscences of the War of 1861-5* (Lynchburg, VA, 1911), 86; Iowa Commandery, MOLLUS, *War Sketches and Incidents*, I (1893), 107–8.

13. L. J. Wilson, *The Confederate Soldier* (Fayetteville, AR, 1902), 19–20.

14. Green, *Orphan Brigade*, 12; Corson, *My Dear Jennie* 50; Iowa Commandery, MOLLUS, *War Sketches and Incidents*, I (1893), 107–8.

15. Gillaspie, *From Michigan to Murfreesboro*, 12; Cunningham, *Doctors in Gray*, 196.

16. Newell, *10th Massachusetts*, 61–62; Hopkins, *7th Rhode Island*, 162.

17. Anderson, *Texas Surgeon*, 61; Cunningham, *Doctors in Gray*, 194; Green, *Orphan Brigade*, 45; Emmerton, *23rd Massachusetts*, 79–84.

18. Thorpe, *15th Connecticut*, 24.

19. Thomas Kirwan, *Memorial History of the Seventeenth Regiment, Massachusetts Volunteer Infantry . . .* (Salem, 1911), 122–23.

20. Samuel H. M. Byers, *Iowa in War Times* (Des Moines, 1888), 560.

21. Cunningham, *Doctors in Gray*, 185; Wagner, *Letters*, 17.

22. Maine Commandery, MOLLUS, *War Papers*, I (1898), 141; Bailey, *Confederate Generation*, 89.

23. Stewart Brooks, *Civil War Medicine* (Springfield, IL, 1966), 117.

24. Cort, *"Dear Friends,"* 39; Charles S. Wainwright, *A Diary of Battle* (New York, 1962), 33–34.

25. Child, *5th New Hampshire*, 40.

26. Brooks, *Civil War Medicine*, 108.

27. Joseph Merrill diary, Mar. 5, 1863, in possession of Charles M. Neinas, Boulder, CO.

28. Boyd, *Civil War Diary*, 124; Newell, *10th Massachusetts*, 84.

29. Cunningham, *Doctors in Gray*, 169; William T. Poague, *Gunner with Stonewall* (Jackson, TN, 1957), 137–38.

30. Cotton, *Yours till Death*, 58; Wilson, *Memoirs of the War*, 276.

31. Hunter, *Johnny Reb and Billy Yank*, 279–80.

32. Hutchinson, *7th Massachusetts*, 43; Phillips, *Civil War Diary & Letters*, 155; Bean, *Liberty Hall Volunteers*, 155.

33. Brown, *2nd Illinois Light Artillery*, 8; George O. Bailey to brother, from camp near Glasgow, KY, undated letter in possession of John C. Melkerson, Thomasville, GA; Hutchinson, *7th Massachusetts*, 42–43.

34. Boyd, *Civil War Diary*, 15; Womack, *Call Forth the Mighty Men*, 496.

35. Thompson, *13th New Hampshire*, 103.

36. Brooks, *Civil War Medicine*, 6.

37. Benjamin F. Pearson, "Benjamin F. Pearson's Civil War Dairy," *Annals of Iowa* XV (1926), 520.

38. Jones, *Louisiana Tigers*, 26.

39. Davis, *Three Years in the Army*, 94; Brooks, *Civil War Medicine*, 63.

40. See Tilney, *My Life in the Army*, 51; Hutchinson, *7th Massachusetts*, 89; Newell, *10th Massachusetts*, 75; Smith, *The Anson Guards*, 36.

41. Patrick, *Reluctant Rebel*, 88; Cunningham, *Doctors in Gray*, 214n.; Bear, *Civil War Letters*, 17; Bailey, *Confederate Generation*, 89.

42. Enos B. Vail, *Reminiscences of a Boy in the Civil War* (Brooklyn, 1915), 29.

43. Adams, *Doctors in Blue*, 54–55; Phoebe Y. Pember, *A Southern Woman's Story* (Jackson, TN, 1959), 124. See also Cuningham, *Doctors in Gray*, 259.

44. Hays, *Under the Red Patch*, 70–71.

45. Beers quoted in Cunningham, *Doctors in Gray*, 262–63; Hutchinson, *7th Massachusetts*, 235–36.

46. Adams, *Doctors in Blue*, 80.

47. *Civil War Times Illustrated* XVII (June 1978), 16–17.

48. Edwin S. Barrett, *What I Saw at Bull Run* (Boston, 1886), 26.

49. Ohio Commandery, MOLLUS, *Sketches of War History*, II (1888), 92–93.

50. Glatthaar, *March to the Sea*, 173; Hunter, *Johnny Reb and Billy Yank*, 550.

51. Bellard, *Gone for the Soldier*, 146. See also Hunter, *Johnny Reb and Billy Yank*, 345–46.

52. Richard Slade to sister, June 28, 1864, Dallas (TX) Historical Society.

53. Parker, *Henry Wilson's Regiment*, 137.

54. Womack, *Call Forth the Mighty Men*, 132.

55. Cowtan, *10th New York*, 272.

56. George T. Stevens, *Three Years in the Sixth Corps* (New York, 1870), 343–45.

57. Ohio Commandery, MOLLUS, *Sketches of War History*, II (1888), 86–87; Horace H. Cunningham, *Field Medical Services at the Battle of Manassas (Bull Run)* (Athens, GA, 1968), 18; Adams, *Doctors in Blue*, 26.

58. Womack, *Call Forth the Mighty Men*, 408.

59. Allen, *4th Rhode Island*, 134.

60. Hunter, *Johnny Reb and Billy Yank*, 348.

61. Daniel Aaron, *The Unwritten Civil War* (New York, 1973), 60–68; Walter Lowenfels (ed.), *Walt Whitman's Civil War* (New York, 1961), 92, 181–82, 293.

62. For the most part, the material on Chimborazo is from Joseph P. Cullen, "Chimborazo Hospital," *Civil War Times Illustrated* XIX (Jan. 1981), 36–42.

63. Nicholas A. Davis, *Chaplain Davis and Hood's Texas Brigade* (San Antonio, 1962), 103–4.

64. Pember, *A Southern Woman's Story*, 45, 146.

65. Anna Morris Holstein, *Three Years in Field Hospitals of the Army of the Potomac* (Philadelphia, 1867), 55; Marjorie Barstow Greenbie, *Lincoln's Daughters of Mercy* (New York, 1944), 173; Berkeley, *Confederate Artillery*, 19.

Chapter 9—Gathering at the River

1. Kaiser, "Letters from the Front," 152; David Lathrop, *The History of the Fifty-ninth Regiment, Illinois Volunteers* (Indianapolis, 1865), 126.

2. John Shepard, Jr., "Religion in the Army of Northern Virginia," *North Carolina Historical Review* XXV (1948), 341.

3. Timothy L. Smith, *Revivalism and Social Reform* (New York, 1957), 17.

4. Fannie A. Beers, *Memories: A Record of Personal Experience and Adventure during Four Years of War* (Philadelphia, 1889), 38.

5. Sidney J. Romero, *Religion in the Rebel Ranks* (New York, 1983), 129; Edwin H. Fay, *This Infernal War: The Confederate Letters of Edwin H. Fay* (Austin, TX, 1958), 34.

6. William H. Brown, "Soldier of the 92nd Illinois: Letters of William H. Brown to His Fiancee, Emma Jane Fraley," *Bulletin of the New York Public Library* II (1969), 124; *Southern Presbyterian*, July 6, 1861.

7. Collins, *149th New York*, 34.

8. Womack, *Call Forth the Mighty Men*, 362.

9. Romero, *Religion in the Rebel Ranks*, 101.

10. [Figg], *"Where Men Only Dare to Go,"* 69–70, 209; James A. Graham, *The James A. Graham Papers* (Chapel Hill, 1928), 185.

11. Womack, *Call Forth the Mighty Men*, 409–10; Hinman, *Sherman Brigade*, 357.

12. Charles T. Quintard to George C. Harris, Nov. 5, 1861, Tennessee State Library.

13. Soldiers and Sailors Historical Society of Rhode Island, *Personal Narratives of Events in the War of the Rebellion* (Providence, 1878–1915), II (1891–1893), 17; *Religious Herald*, July 17, 1862; William H. Newlin et al., *A History of the Seventy-third Regiment of Illinois Infantry Volunteers* (Springfield, 1890), 680.

14. Lord, *They Fought for the Union*, 253–54.

15. John Paris to W. H. Wills, Apr. 9, 1863, Wills Papers, Southern Historical Collection, University of North Carolina; W. W. Bennett, *A Narrative of the Great Revival Which Prevailed in the Southern Armies during the Late Civil War between the States and the Federal Union* (Philadelphia, 1877), 276–77; *Central Presbyterian*, Sept. 24, 1863.

16. Edwin C. Bennett, *Musket and Sword* (Boston, 1900), 179.

17. Romero, *Religion in the Rebel Ranks*, 39–40; Bennett, *Musket and Sword*, 183.

18. Warnell diary, July 16 and Aug. 31, 1862.

19. *Diary of an Unknown Soldier*, 37; Sale diary, June 19, 1864; Robertson, *Tenting Tonight*, 147.

20. Catton, *Mr. Lincoln's Army*, 180; Catton, *A Stillness at Appomattox*, 215.

21. Charles M. Clark, *History of the Thirty-ninth Illinois Volunteer Veteran Infantry* (Chicago, 1889), 208.

22. Romero, *Religion in the Rebel Ranks*, 17–18.

23. Paul J. Engel (ed.), "A Letter from the Front," *New York History* XXXIV (1953), 206.

24. Alexander D. Betts, *Experience of a Confederate Chaplain, 1861–1864* [n.p., n.d.], 17.

25. John F. Moors, *History of the Fifty-second Regiment, Massachusetts Volunteers* (Boston, 1893), 45.

26. Ford, *15th Massachusetts*, 62; Richard Eddy, *History of the Sixtieth Regiment, New York State Volunteers* (Philadelphia, 1864), 89.

27. Ford, *15th Massachusetts*, 51; Quintard, *Doctor Quintard*, 64; Moors, *52nd Massachusetts*, 71.

28. Wilson, *The Confederate Soldier*, 130.

29. John Beatty, *The Citizen-Soldier; or, Memoirs of a Volunteer* (Cincinnati, 1879), 43; *Confederate Veteran* XXX (1922), 391.

30. J. William Jones, *Christ in the Camp; or, Religion in Lee's Army* (Richmond, 1887), 537; *Religious Herald*, May 1, 1862.

31. B. W. McDonnold, *History of the Cumberland Presbyterian Church* (Nashville, 1888), 637; *Official Records*, XXV, Pt. 1, 873.

32. Edwin Porter Thompson, *History of the Orphan Brigade* (Louisville, 1898), 274; Richard F. Fuller, *Chaplain Fuller* (Boston, 1863), 299, 302–3.

33. McDonnold, *Cumberland Presbyterian Church*, 427, 430.

34. Edward N. Botts, "Civil War Letters of E. N. Botts from New Bern and Plymouth," *North Carolina Historical Review* XXXVI (1959), 214–15; Jones, *Christ in the Camp*, 365; Cort, *"Dear Friends,"* 79.

35. Silliman, *A New Canaan Private*, 78; Gould, *1st-10th-29th Maine*, 180.

36. James I. Robertson, Jr., and Richard M. McMurry (eds.), *Rank and File: Civil War Essays in Honor of Bell Irvin Wiley* (San Rafael, CA. 1976), 119–20.

37. Quintard, *Doctor Quintard*, 72–73; Hopkins, *7th Rhode Island*, 38.

38. *Religious Herald*, Feb. 27, 1862.

39. Romero, *Religion in the Rebel Ranks*, 76.

40. Thompson, *13th New Hampshire*, 112; Jones, *Army of the Potomac*, 190.

41. John H. Kiracofe to wife, Aug. 26, 1861, John H. Kiracofe Papers, Duke University.

42. James Hamilton to brother, Apr. 1, 1862, Ruffin-Roulhac-Hamilton Papers, Southern Historical Collection, University of North Carolina.

43. Curtis, *24th Michigan*, 138; *Under the Maltese Cross*, 220.
44. Robert Stiles, *Four Years under Marse Robert* (New York, 1903), 114.
45. James M. Williams, *From That Terrible Field: Civil War Letters of James M. Williams, Twenty-first Alabama Infantry Volunteers* (University, AL, 1981), 13; Benjamin W. Jones, *Under the Stars and Bars: A History of the Surry Light Artillery* (Richmond, 1909), 81–82.
46. Lord, *They Fought for the Union*, 132.
47. *Under the Maltese Cross*, 337–38.
48. Hutchinson, *7th Massachusetts*, 146; Moore, *A Life for the Confederacy*, 164.
49. Roy P. Basler (ed.), *The Collected Works of Abraham Lincoln* (New Brunswick, NJ, 1953–1955), V, 420.
50. Romero, *Religion in the Rebel Ranks*, 116; Chattachoochee Society, *War Was the Place*, 85; Bennett, *Narrative of the Great Revival*, 313.
51. Quoted in Drew Gilpin Faust, "Christian Soldiers: The Meaning of Revivalism in the Confederate Army," *Journal of Southern History* LIII (1987), 72.
52. *Religious Herald*, Feb. 11, 1864; Anderson, *Texas Surgeon*, 83; Jones, *Christ in the Camp*, 224, 248–49.
53. Ibid., 504.
54. Thompson, *13th New Hampshire*, 214; Romero, *Religion in the Rebel Ranks*, 89–90.
55. J. Milton Ray to Elizabeth Ray, May 5, 1863, John Milton Ray Papers, Soldiers and Sailors Memorial Hill, Pittsburgh, PA; Womack, *Call Forth the Mighty Men*, 416–17.
56. *The Grayjackets And How They Lived, Fought and Died for Dixie* (Richmond, 1867), 268.

Chapter 10—"In the Prison Cell I Sit"
1. James Ford Rhodes, *History of the United States from the Compromise of 1850* (New York, 1893–1906), V, 507–8. For different, propagandized statements, see *Official Records*, Ser. II, Vol. VIII, 946–48.
2. Ibid., Vol. V, 194.
3. The cartel is published in full in ibid., IV, 266–67.
4. Robertson, *Tenting Tonight*, 113.
5. Ford, *15th Massachusetts*, 110.
6. Dunlop, *Lee's Sharpshooters*, 327.
7. Hattie Lou Winslow and Joseph R. H. Moore, *Camp Morton, 1861–1865* (Indianapolis, 1940), 262; James I. Robertson, Jr., "Houses of Horror: Danville's Civil War Prisons," *Virginia Magazine of History and Biography* LXIX (1961), 339–40.
8. George R. Lodge, "In the Bastile of the Rebels," *Journal of the Illinois State Historical Society* LVI (1963), 324.
9. Henry A. Willis, *Fitchburg in the War of the Rebellion* (Fitchburg, MA, 1866), 193; Alfred S. Roe and Charles Nutt, *History of the First Regiment of Heavy Artillery, Massachusetts Volunteers* (Worcester, 1917), 256.
10. Military Historical Society of Massachusetts, *Civil War and Miscellaneous Papers* (Boston, 1918), 181; William P. Derby, *Bearing Arms in the Twenty-seventh Massachusetts Regiment of Volunteer Infantry during the Civil War, 1861–1865* (Boston, 1883), 410; Hyland C. Kirk, *Heavy Guns and Light: A History of the 4th New York Heavy Artillery* (New York, 1890), 403–4; Bailey, *Confederate Generation*, 97.
11. J. Ogden Murray, *The Immortal Six Hundred* (Winchester, VA, 1905), 58; *Southern Historical Society Papers* XXIII (1895), 162 [cited hereafter as *SHSP*]; *Official Records*, Ser. II, IV, 197.
12. Ovid Futch, "Prison Life at Andersonville," *Civil War History* VIII (1962), 129–30; *Official Records*, Ser. II, VII, 708.

13. See *SHSP*, I (1876), 235; John K. Burlingame (comp.), *History of the Fifth Regiment of Rhode Island Heavy Artillery, during Three Years and a Half of Service in North Carolina* (Providence, 1892), 225; Louis N. Beaudry, *Historic Records of the Fifth New York Cavalry, First Ira Harris Guard* (Albany, 1868), 267; James E. Paton, "Civil War Journal of James E. Paton," *Register of the Kentucky Historical Society* LVI (1963), 228.

14. William B. Hesseltine, *Civil War Prisons: A Study in War Psychology* (Columbus, OH, 1930), 55.

15. *Official Records*, Ser. II, Vol. V, 468, 477, 487.

16. Ibid., VI, 893–94.

17. William B. Hesseltine, "The Propaganda Literature of Confederate Prisons," *Journal of Southern History* I (1935), 58; U.S. Sanitary Commission, *Narrative of Privations and Sufferings of United States Officers and Soldiers While Prisoners of War in the Hands of Rebel Authorities* (Philadelphia, 1864), passim.

18. Lavender, *War Memoirs*, 132; MOLLUS—Mass., *Civil War Papers*, I (1900), 111; Bailey, *Confederate Generation*, 96.

19. Randolph A. Shotwell, *Papers of Randolph Abbot Shotwell* (Raleigh, 1931), II, 140.

20. *SHSP*, VII (1879), 327–28; XVIII (1890), 432.

21. Lavender, *War Memoirs*, 132; Bailey, *Confederate Generation*, 96–97.

22. *SHSP*, XVIII (1890), 116; Anthony M. Keiley, *In Vinculis; or, The Prisoner of War* (Petersburg, VA, 1866), 66–67.

23. Bailey, *Confederate Generation*, 95–96; Robertson, "Houses of Horror," 341; John W. Urban, *My Experiences mid Shot and Shell and in Rebel Den* (Lancaster, PA, 1882), 599; Louis A. Brown, *The Salisbury Prison: A Case Study of Confederate Military Prisons, 1861–1865* (Wendell, NC, 1980), 114.

24. Parker, *Henry Wilson's Regiment*, 144; Bailey, *Confederate Generation*, 97.

25. Frederic Denison, *Sabres and Spurs: The First Regiment, Rhode Island Cavalry, in the Civil War, 1861–1865* (Central Falls, RI, 1876), 196; James J. Williamson, *Prison Life in the Old Capitol and Reminiscences of the Civil War* (West Orange, NJ, 1911), 68.

26. George H. Putman, *A Prisoner of War in Virginia, 1864–5* (New York, 1912), 40–41; Adams, *19th Massachusetts*, 124.

27. Williamson, *Old Capitol*, 55; John McElroy, *Andersonville: A Story of Rebel Military Prisons* (Toledo, OH, 1879), 310.

28. MOLLUS—Maine, *War Papers*, I (1898), 168; James E. Robertson, Jr., "The Scourge of Elmira," *Civil War History* VIII (1962), 192.

29. Nancy Travis Dean, "Confederate Prisoners of War at Fort Delaware," *Delaware History* XIII (1968), 8.

30. Richard F. Hemmerlein, *Prisons and Prisoners of the Civil War* (Boston, 1934), 61–62.

31. *Official Records*, Ser. II, VII, 40; Ovid L. Futch, *History of Andersonville Prison* (Gainesville, FL, 1968), 32–36.

32. Francis T. Miller (ed.), *The Photographic History of the Civil War* (New York, 1911), VII, 76; Hemmerlein, *Prisons and Prisoners*, 36–37.

33. See Futch, *Andersonville*, 63–74.

34. *Official Records*, Ser. II, VII, 1092–93.

35. *History of the 35th Massachusetts*, 334–35; Willis, *Fitchburg in the War of the Rebellion*, 194; William C. Walker, *History of the Eighteenth Regiment, Conn. Volunteers, in the War for the Union* (Norwich, CT, 1885), 376; J. Waldo Denny, *Wearing the Blue in the Twenty-fifth Mass. Volunteer Infantry* (Worcester, 1879), 366.

36. Hemmerlein, *Prisons and Prisoners*, 63–64; Hesseltine, *Civil War Prisons*, 152; Futch, *Andersonville*, 97.

37. *SHSP*, IX (1891), 48; *Official Records*, Ser. II, VIII, 997–1003; Robertson, "Scourge of Elmira," 184, 200.

38. Berry Benson, *Berry Benson's Civil War Book* (Athens, GA, 1962), 127; *Official Records*, Ser. II, VII, 603–4.

39. Hemmerlein, *Prisons and Prisoners*, 43–44; *Official Records*, Ser. II, VII, 1135; Robertson, "Scourge of Elmira," 185.

40. Ibid., 187; *SHSP*, XXXVI (1908), 230; *Official Records*, Ser. II, VII, 997, 1092.

41. John N. Opie, *A Rebel Cavalryman with Lee, Stuart, and Jackson* (Chicago, 1899), 318; Robertson, "Scourge of Elmira," 191; Wilkeson, *Recollections of a Private Soldier*, 225.

42. Edmund D. Patterson, *Yankee Rebel: The Civil War Journal of Edmund DeWitt Patterson* (Chapel Hill, 1966), 120.

43. Abner R. Small, *The Road to Richmond* (Berkeley, CA, 1939), 175.

44. MOLLUS—Ohio, *Sketches of War History* IV (1896), 340; Frederick A. Bartleson, *Letters from Libby Prison* (New York, 1956), 37.

45. MOLLUS—Wisconsin, *War Papers*, I (1891), 399–400; MOLLUS—Minnesota, *Glimpses of the Nation's Struggle*, III (1893), 211.

46. MOLLUS—Wisconsin, *War Papers*, I (1891), 400; MOLLUS—Ohio, *Sketches of War History*, II (1888), 362. For a description of how Federal prisoners tunneled from a Savannah, GA, compound, see MOLLUS—Massachusetts, *Civil War Papers*, I (1900), 113.

47. George N. Bliss, *Prison Life of Lieut. James M. Fales* (Providence, 1882), 20–22; MOLLUS—Wisconsin, *War Papers*, I (1891), 400.

48. Bliss, *Fales*, 24; MOLLUS—Ohio, *Sketches of War History*, IV (1896), 341–42; Bartleson, *Letters from Libby Prison*, 35.

49. MOLLUS—Wisconsin, *War Papers*, I (1891), 408.

50. Day, *101st Ohio*, 334–35.

51. MOLLUS—Wisconsin, *War Papers*, I (1891), 408.

53. Clark, *N.C. Regiments*, IV, 677.

54. Bartleson, *Letters from Libby Prison*, 43.

55. Futch, "Prison Life," 123.

56. *Official Records*, Ser. II, VI, 809–10.

57. Thee Jones to sister, Dec. 31, 1864, University of Kentucky; William M. Norman, *A Portion of My Life* (Winston-Salem, NC, 1959), 205.

58. Alonzo Cooper, *In and Out of Rebel Prisons* (Oswego, NY, 1888), 267; Cogswell, *11th New Hampshire*, 531.

59. Adams, *19th Massachusetts*, 177–78.

60. Denison, *Sabres and Spurs*, 317; *SHSP*, I (1876), 238, 240–41.

61. Miller, *Photographic History*, VII, 180.

62. Darrett B. Rutman, "The War Crimes and Trial of Henry Wirz," *Civil War History* VI (1960), 117–23.

Chapter 11—Beyond the Call of Duty

1. *Official Records*, X, Pt. 2, 389.

2. Thompson, *13th New Hampshire*, 57. Bee also Borton, *On the Parallels*, 65.

3. Augustus C. Hamlin, *The Battle of Chancellorsville* (Bangor, ME, 1896), 62.

4. Beatty, *The Citizen-Soldier*, 25–26.

5. William D. Bickham, *Rosecrans' Campaign with the Fourteenth Army Corps, or the Army of the Cumberland* (Cincinnati, 1863), 362.

6. Baxter, *Gallant Fourteenth*, 41; Cotton, *Yours till Death*, 65.

7. Mark, *93rd Pennsylvania*, 321.

8. Vaill, *2nd Conn. Heavy Artillery*, 49–50.

9. James F. Wilcox, "With Grant at Vicksburg, from the Civil War Diary of Capt. James F. Wilcox," *Journal of the Illinois State Historical Society* XXX (1938), 479–80.

10. John M. Schofield, _Forty-six Years in the Army_ (New York, 1897), 146.

11. Howell, _Going to Meet the Yanks_, 84; John Johnston, "The Civil War Reminiscences of John Johnston, 1861–1865," _Tennessee Historical Quarterly_ XIV (1955), 51; Weller, _A Civil War Courtship_, 19–20.

12. _Official Records_, X, Pt. 1, 465; XXVII, Pt. 2, 403; Joseph A. Higginbotham diary, July 21, 1861, University of Virginia.

13. William P. Haines, _History of the Men of Co. F, with Description of the Marches and Battles of the 12th New Jersey Vols._ (Mickleton, NJ, 1897), 57; Glatthaar, _March to the Sea_, 164.

14. T. C. DeLeon, _Four Years in Rebel Capitals_ (Mobile, 1890), 131.

15. Gerrish, _Army Life_, 177; Lindsey, _Military Annals_, 219.

16. Waitt, _19th Massachusetts_, 242.

17. Hagan, _Confederate Letters_, 23.

18. William A. Fletcher, _Rebel Private Front and Rear_ (Austin, TX, 1908), 20.

19. Samuel T. Foster, _One of Cleburne's Command: The Civil War Reminiscences and Diary of Capt. Samuel T. Foster, Granbury's Texas Brigade, CSA_ (Austin, TX, 1980), 62; Norton, _Army Letters_, 106–9.

20. Ford, _15th Massachusetts_, 195–96.

21. Parker, _Henry Wilson's Regiment_, 228.

22. George H. Atkin to mother, Dec. 25, 1862, Atkin Letters.

23. Edmund T. Eggleston, "Excerpts from the Civil War Diary of E. T. Eggleston," _Tennessee Historical Quarterly_ XVII (1958), 356; Giles, _Rags and Hope_, 204.

24. Stearns, _Company K_, 87; Newton, _A Wisconsin Boy in Dixie_, 19–20.

25. Daniel G. Crotty, _Four Years Campaigning in the Army of the Potomac_ (Grand Rapids, MI, 1874), 160.

26. Green, _Orphan Brigade_, 26.

27. _Official Records_, XII, Pt. 2, 593; Stiles, _Four Years under Marse Robert_, 197.

28. Hagan, _Confederate Letters_, 45; Womack, _Call Forth the Mighty Men_, 208; Worsham, _Jackson's Foot Cavalry_, 65.

29. John T. Bell, _Tramps and Triumphs of the Second Iowa Infantry_ (Des Moines, 1961), 10.

30. Waitt, _19th Massachusetts_, 97.

31. Joseph H. Sweney, "Nursed a Wounded Brother," _Annals of Iowa_ XXXI (1951), 192.

32. Smith, _19th Maine_, 73; Upson, _With Sherman to the Sea_, 143.

33. William F. Plane, "Letters of William Fisher Plane, C.S.A., to His Wife," _Collections of the Georgia Historical Society_ XLVIII (1964), 223. See also Reid, _4th South Carolina_, 25–26.

34. Landis, "Personal Reminiscences," 24–25.

35. Phillips, _Civil War Diary & Letters_, 109. A similar description of the same battlefield is in DeRosier, _Through the South_, 34.

36. Wilson, _Memoirs of the War_, 112–13. See also Samuel Toombs, _New Jersey Troops in the Gettysburg Campaign_ (Orange, 1888), 92–93.

37. Henry E. Schafer to wife, June 23, 1864, Schaeffer Papers.

38. Wilson, "Peter Wilson in the Civil War," 344–45.

39. C. F. Moseley to William W. Moseley, Nov. 10, 1863, Xerox copy in the possession of James I. Robertson, Jr.

40. Alexander G. Rose, _The Civil War Diaries of Alexander Grant Rose (1838–1920)_ (Baltimore, 1974), 72; Bailey, _Confederate Generation_, 105; Clark, _N.C. Regiments_, I, 275.

41. Gibbs reminiscences; Edward W. Payne, _History of the Thirty-fourth Regiment of Illinois Volunteers Infantry_ (Clinton, IA, 1903), 173; Boyd, _Civil War Diary_, 42.

42. Bailey, _Confederate Generation_, 114.

43. Newton, *A Wisconsin Boy in Dixie*, 160.
44. Clark, N.C. Regiments, II, 423; Bailey, *Confederate Generation*, 86.
45. Upson, *With Sherman to the Sea*, 181.

Works Cited

MANUSCRIPTS

Angle, Joel, Letters. In possession of James I. Robertson, Jr., Blacksburg, VA.

Atkin, George H., Letters. In possession of Arthur Donald Gill, Glen Rock, NJ.

Bailey, George, Letter. In possession of John C. Melkerson, Thomasville, GA.

Beem, David J., Papers. Indiana Historical Society.

Bowen, George A., Memoirs. Salem County, NJ, HIstorical Society.

Brown, Charles S., Papers. Duke University.

Cavins, E. H. C., Letters. Cavins Collection, Indiana Historical Society.

Cowper, Roscoe B. G., Letter. In possession of James I. Robertson, Jr.

Crockett, Andrew, Letter. In possession of Mary C. Fugate, Danville, VA.

Crouse, William H., Letter. In possession of William J. Downer, Pitman, NJ.

Eggleston, J. W., Letter. In possession of James I. Robertson, Jr.

Flynt, Samuel R., Letters. In possession of Vicki Heilig, Germantown, MD.

General Order Book, 37th N.C. Troops, 1862–1863. Duke University.

Gibbs, George Alphonso, Reminiscences. In possession of George Fugate, Lexington, KY.

Hamilton, Eli Spinks, Letters. University of North Carolina.

Higginbotham, Joseph A., Diary. University of Virginia.

Jeffers, Ira S., "Letters from Ira S. Jeffers, 137 New York Inf., Co. F." Typescript copy in possession of James I. Robertson, Jr., Blacksburg, VA

Johnson, J. Whit, Letter. In possession of Melvin M. Scott, Falls Church, VA.

Jones. Thee, Letter. University of Kentucky.

Kiracofe, John H., Papers. Duke University.

Landis, John B., "Personal Experiences in the War of the Rebellion, 1862–1863." Typescript copy in possession of James I. Robertson, Jr.

Langhorne, James H., Letters. In possession of James I. Robertson, Jr.

Lenoir, W. W., Civil War Diary. Lenoir Family Papers, University of North Carolina.

Works Cited

Loflin, Harrison A., Letter. In possession of James I. Robertson, Jr.
Merrill, Joseph, Diary. In possession of Charles M. Neinas, Boulder, CO.
Morgan, William H., Letters. In possession of Melvin M. Scott.
Moseley, C. F., Letter. Copy in possession of James I. Robertson, Jr.
Quintard, Charles T., Letter. Tennessee State Library.
Rader, Adam S., Letter. In possession of James I. Robertson, Jr.
Ray, John Wilton, Papers. Soldiers and Sailors Memorial Hall, Pittsburgh, PA.
Repass, Stephen A., Letter. In possession of Mary McCauley, Salem, VA.
Ruffin-Roulhac-Hamilton Papers. University of North Carolina.
Sale, John F., Diary. Virginia State Library.
Sawyer, Samuel L., Letters. University of Tennessee.
Schafer Papers. In possession of William A. Schaeffer III, Houston, TX.
Slade, Richard, Letter. Dallas (TX) Historical Society.
Smith, John T., Letter. In possession of Mrs. D. K. Brown, Vinton, VA.
Upchurch, Isham Sims, Papers. Duke University.
Warnell, James Smart, Diary. Copy in possession of Edward H. Hahn, Pittsburgh, PA.
Willis Papers. University of North Carolina.

SOLDIERS' LETTERS AND REMINISCENCES

Anderson, John Q., *A Texas Surgeon in the C.S.A.* Tuscaloosa, AL: Confederate Publishing Co., 1957.
Ayers, James T., *The Civil War Diary of James T. Ayers, Civil War Recruiter.* Springfield: The State of Illinois, 1947.
Barnes, Ruffin, "The Confederate Letters of Ruffin Barnes of Wilson County," *North Carolina Historical Review* XXXI (1964).
Barrett, Edwin S., *What I Saw at Bull Run.* Boston: Beacon Press, 1886.
Bartleson, Frederick A., *Letters from Libby Prison.* New York: Greenwich Book Publishers, 1956.
Batts, William, "A Foot Soldier's Account: Letters of William Batts, 1861–1862," *Georgia Historical Quarterly* L (1966).
Baylor, George, *Bull Run to Bull Run; or, Four Years in the Army of Northern Virginia.* Richmond: B. F. Johnson Publishing Co., 1900.
Bear, Henry C., *The Civil War Letters of Henry C. Bear: A Soldier in the 116th Illinois Volunteer Infantry.* Harrogate, TN: Lincoln Memorial University Press, 1961.
Beatty, John, *The Citizen-Soldier; or, Memoirs of a Volunteer.* Cincinnati: Wilstach, Baldwin & Co., 1879.
Bellard, Alfred, *Gone for a Soldier: The Civil War Memoirs of Private Alfred Bellard.* Boston: Little, Brown and Co., 1975.

Bennett, Edwin C., *Musket and Sword; or, The Camp, March, and Firing Line in the Army of the Potomac.* Boston: Coburn Publishing Co., 1900.

Benson, Berry, *Berry Benson's Civil War Book.* Athens: University of Georgia Press, 1962.

Berkeley, Henry Robinson, *Four Years in the Confederate Artillery.* Chapel Hill: University of North Carolina Press, 1961.

Betts, Alexander D., *Experiences of a Confederate Chaplain.* n.p.,n.d.

Billings, John D., *Hardtack and Coffee; or, The Unwritten Story of Army Life.* Boston: G. M. Smith & Co., 1887.

Bissell, Lewis, *The Civil War Letters of Lewis Bissell.* Washington: Field School Educational Foundation Press, 1981.

Blackford, Susan (comp.), *Letters from Lee's Army.* New York: Charles Scribner's Sons, 1947.

Bliss, George N., "Chaos Still Reigns in This Camp—Letters of Lieutenant George N. Bliss, 1st New England Cavalry, March–September, 1862," *Rhode Island History* XXXVI (1977).

————, *Prison Life of Lieut. James M. Fales.* Providence, RI: N. Bangs Williams & Co., 1882.

Borton, Benjamin, *On the Parallels; or, Chapters of Inner History: A Story of the Rappahannock.* Woodstown, NJ: Monitor-Register Press, 1903.

Botts, Edward N., "Civil War Letters of E. N. Botts from New Bern and Plymouth," *North Carolina Historical Review* XXXVI (1959).

Boyd, Cyrus F., *The Civil War Diary of Cyrus F. Boyd, Fifteenth Iowa Infantry, 1861–1863.* Iowa City: State Historical Society of Iowa, 1953.

Brett, David, *"My Dear Wife:" The Civil War Letters of David Brett, 9th Massachusetts Battery, Union Cannoneer.* Little Rock: Pioneer Press, 1964.

Brown, Philip F., *Reminiscences of the War of 1861–1865.* Roanoke, VA: Union Printing Co., 1912.

Brown, William H., "Soldier of the 92nd Illinois: Letters of William H. Brown to His Fiancee, Emma Jane Fraley," *Bulletin of the New York Public Library* II (1969).

Butler, Benjamin F., *Private and Official Correspondence of Gen. Benjamin F. Butler, during the Period of the Civil War.* 5 vols. Norwood, MA: The Plimpton Press, 1917.

[Caffey, Thomas L.] *Battle-fields of the South, by an English Combatant.* 2 vols. London: Smith, Elder and Co., 1863.

Camm, William "Diary of Colonel William Camm, 1861 to 1865," *Journal of the Illinois State Historical Society* XVII (1926).

Cannon, J. P., *Inside of Rebeldom: The Daily Life of a Private in the Confederate Army.* Washington: National Tribune, 1900.

Capron, Thaddeus H., "War Diary of Thaddeus H. Capron, 1861–1865," *Journal of the Illinois State Historical Society* XII (1919).

Carpenter, Cyrus C., "A Commissary in the Union Army: Letters of C. C.

Works Cited

Carpenter," *Journal of Iowa History* LIII (1955).

[Carrigan, J. G.] *The Cheat Mountain Campaign*. Nashville: Albert B. Tavel Co., 1885.

Casler, John O., *Four Years in the Stonewall Brigade*. Dayton, OH: Morningside Bookshop, 1971.

Chattahoochee Valley Historical Society (comp.), *War Was the Place: A Centennial Collection of Confederate Soldier Letters*. Chambers County, AL: The Society, 1961.

Connolly, James A., *Three Years in the Army of the Cumberland*. Bloomington: Indiana University Press, 1959.

Cook, Charles N., "Letters of Privates Cook and Ball," *Indiana Magazine of History* XXVII (1931).

Cooper, Alonzo, *In and Out of Rebel Prisons*. Oswego, NY: R. J. Oliphant, 1888.

Copp, Elbridge J., *Reminiscences of the War of the Rebellion, 1861–1865*. Nashua, NH: Telegraph Publishing Co., 1911.

Corby, William, *Memoirs of Chaplain Life*. Notre Dame, IN: "Scholastic" Press, 1894.

Corson, William Clark, *My Dear Jennie*. Richmond: Dietz Press, 1982.

Cort, Charles E., *"Dear Friends:" The Civil War Letters and Diary of Charles Edwin Cort*. n.p., 1962.

Cotton, John W., *Yours till Death: Civil War Letters of John W. Cotton*. University: University of Alabama Press, 1951.

Craig, Samuel A., "Captain Samuel A. Craig's Memoirs of Civil War and Reconstruction," *Western Pennsylvania Historical Magazine* XIII (1930).

Crotty, Daniel G., *Four Years Campaigning in the Army of the Potomac*. Grand Rapids, MI: Dygert Bros. & Co., 1874.

Dame, William M., *From the Rapidan to Richmond and the Spotsylvania Campaign*. Baltimore: Green-Lucas Co., 1920.

Davis, Nicholas A., *Chaplain Davis and Hood's Texas Brigade*. San Antonio: Principia Press of Trinity University, 1962.

De Forest, John William, *A Volunteer's Adventures: A Union Captain's Record of the Civil War*. New Haven: Yale University Press, 1946.

Dekle, Peter, "Peter Dekle's Letters," *Civil War History* IV (1958).

DeRosier, Arthur H., Jr. (ed.), *Through the South with a Union Soldier*. Johnson City: East Tennessee State University, 1969.

Diary of an Unknown Soldier, September 5, 1862, to December 7, 1862, Found on a Battlefield. Van Buren, AK: Press-Argus Printing Co., 1959.

Dickerson, Ansel D., *A Raw Recruit's War Experiences*. Providence: The Press Co., 1888.

Dodd, Ira A., *The Song of the Rappahannock: Sketches of the Civil War*. New York: Dodd, Mead and Co., 1898.

Drake, George, *The Mail Goes Through; or, The Civil War Letters of George

Drake, 1846–1918. San Angelo, TX: Anchor Publishing Co., 1964.

Dunham, Abner, "Civil War Letters of Abner Dunham, 12th Iowa Infantry," *Iowa Journal of History* LIII (1955).

Dunlop, W. S., *Lee's Sharpshooters; or, The Forefront of Battle.* Little Rock: Tunnah & Pittard, 1899.

Eggleston, George C., *A Rebel's Recollections.* New York: Hurd and Houghton, 1875.

Ely, Ralph, *With the Wandering Regiment: The Diary of Captain Ralph Ely of the Eighth Michigan Infantry.* Mount Pleasant: Central Michigan University Press, 1965.

Engel, Paul J. (ed.), "A Letter from the Front," *New York History* XXXIV (1953).

Faller, Leo W., and John I. Faller, *Dear Folks at Home: The Civil War Letters of Leo W. and John I. Faller.* Carlisle, PA: Cumberland County Historical Society, 1963.

Fay, Edwin H., *This Infernal War: The Confederate Letters of Edwin H. Fay.* Austin: University of Texas Press, 1958.

Ford, Worthington C. (ed.), *A Cycle of Adams Letters.* 2 vols. Boston: Houghton Mifflin Co., 1920.

Foster, Samuel T., *One of Cleburne's Command: The Civil War Reminiscences and Diary of Capt. Samuel T. Foster, Granbury's Texas Brigade, CSA.* Austin: University of Texas Press, 1980.

Fowle, George, *Letters to Eliza from a Union Soldier, 1861–1865.* Chicago: Follett Publishing Co., 1963.

Freeman, Benjamin H., *The Confederate Letters of Benjamin H. Freeman.* Hicksville, NY: Exposition Press, 1974.

Fuller, Richard F., *Chaplain Fuller: Being a Life Sketch of a New England Clergyman and Army Chaplain.* Boston: Walker, Wise and Co., 1863.

Galwey, Thomas F., *The Valiant Hours: Narrative of "Captain Brevet," An Irish-American in the Army of the Potomac.* Harrisburg, PA: Stackpole, 1961.

Garrett, David R., *The Civil War Letters of David R. Garrett, Detailing the Adventures of the 6th Texas Cavalry, 1861–1865.* Marshall, TX: Port Caddo Press, 1963.

Gerrish, Theodore, *Army Life: A Private's Reminiscences of the Civil War.* Portland, ME: Hoyt, Fogg & Donham, 1882.

Giles, Val C., *Rags and Hope: The Recollections of Val C. Giles, Four Years with Hood's Brigade, Fourth Texas Infantry.* New York: Coward-McCann, 1951.

Gillaspie, Ira M. B., *From Michigan to Murfreesboro: The Diary of Ira Gillaspie of the Eleventh Michigan Infantry.* Mount Pleasant: Central Michigan University Press, 1965.

Glover, Robert W. (ed.), *"Tyler to Sharpsburg:" The Letters of Robert H. and William H. Gaston.* Waco: W. M. Morrison, 1960.

Works Cited

Good, John Jay, and Susan Ann Good, *Cannon Smoke: The Letters of Captain John J. Good, Good-Douglas Texas Battery, CSA*. Hillsboro, TX: Hill Junior College Press, 1971.

Gordon, John B., *Reminiscences of the Civil War*. New York: Charles Scribner's Sons, 1903.

Graham, James A., *The James A. Graham Papers*. Chapel Hill: University of North Carolina Press, 1928.

Grant, Ulysses S., *Personal Memoirs of U. S. Grant*. 2 vols. New York: Charles L. Webster & Co., 1885.

Grayjackets, The: and How They Lived, Fought and Died for Dixie. Richmond: Jones Brothers & Co., 1867.

Green, John W., *Johnny Green of the Orphan Brigade: The Journal of a Confederate Soldier*. Lexington: University of Kentucky Press, 1956.

Greenalch, James, "Letters of James Greenalch," *Michigan History* XL (1960).

Hadley, Elbridge, "A Young Soldier's Career," *Annals of Iowa* XIII (1922).

Hadley, John V., "An Indiana Soldier in Love and War," *Indiana Magazine of History* LIX (1963).

Hagan, John W., *Confederate Letters of John W. Hagan*. Athens: University of Georgia Press, 1954.

Handerson, Henry E., *Yankee in Gray: The Civil War Memoirs of Henry E. Handerson*. Cleveland: Press of Western Reserve University, 1962.

Head, Thomas A., *Campaigns and Battles of the Sixteenth Regiment Tennessee Volunteers*. Nashville: Cumberland Presbyterian Publishing House, 1885.

Holmes, Oliver W., Jr., *Touched with Fire: Civil War Letters and Diary of Oliver Wendell Holmes, Jr., 1861–1864*. Cambridge: Harvard University Press, 1947.

Hotze, Henry, *Three Months in the Confederate Army*, University: University of Alabama Press, 1952.

Hough, Alfred L.: *Soldier in the West: The Civil War Letters of Alfred Lacy Hough*. Philadelphia: University of Pennsylvania Press, 1957.

Howard, McHenry, *Recollections of a Maryland Confederate Staff Officer under Johnston, Jackson and Lee*. Dayton, OH: Morningside Bookshop, 1975.

Hunter, Alexander, *Johnny Reb and Billy Yank*. New York: Neale Publishing Co., 1905.

Hunter, Edna J. S., *One Flag, One Country and Thirteen Greenbacks a Month*. San Diego: Hunter Publications, 1980.

Hyatt, Hudson (ed.), "Captain Hyatt: Being the Letters Written during the War Years 1863–1864 to His Wife Mary," *Ohio State Archaeological and Historical Quarterly* LIII (1944).

Jackson, Edgar (ed.), *Three Rebels Write Home*. Franklin, VA: News Publishing Co., 1955.

Johnston, David E., *The Story of a Confederate Boy in the Civil War*. Portland, OR: Glass & Prudhomme, 1914.

Johnston, John, "The Civil War Reminiscences of John Johnston, 1861–1865," *Tennessee Historical Quarterly* XIV (1955).

Jones, Charles T., Jr., "Five Confederates: The Sons of Bolling Hall in the Civil War," *Alabama Historical Quarterly* XXIV (1962).

Jones, Evan R., *Four Years in the Army of the Potomac*. London: Tynbe Publishing Co., 1881.

Kaiser, Leo M., "Letters from the Front," *Journal of the Illinois State Historical Society* LVI (1963).

Keiley, Anthony M., *In Vinculis; The Prisoner of War*. Petersburg, VA: "Daily Index" Office, 1866.

Kendall, John Smith (ed.), "Recollections of a Confederate Officer," *Louisiana Historical Quarterly* XXIX (1946).

Kress, John A., *Memoirs of John Alexander Kress*. n.p., 1925.

Lavender, John W., *The War Memoirs of Captain John W. Lavender*. Pine Bluff, AR: W. M. Hackett and D. R. Perdue, 1956.

Livermore, Thomas L., *Days and Events, 1860–1866*. Boston: Houghton Mifflin Co., 1920.

Lodge, George R., "In the Bastile of the Rebels," *Journal of the Illinois State Historical Society* LVI (1963).

Lyman, Theodore, *Meade's Headquarters, 1863–1865*. Boston: Atlantic Monthly Press, 1922.

McCarthy, Carlton, *Detailed Minutae of Soldier Life in the Army of Northern Virginia, 1861–1865*. Richmond: C. McCarthy and Co., 1882.

McClellan, George B., *McClellan's Own Story*. New York: C. L. Webster & Co., 1887.

McElroy, John, *Andersonville: A Story of Rebel Military Prisons*. Toledo: D. R. Locke, 1879.

Martin, Robert Hugh, *A Boy of Old Shenandoah*. Parsons, WV: McClain Printing Co., 1977.

Mayo, Perry, *The Civil War Letters of Perry Mayo*. East Lansing: Michigan State University, 1967.

Merrill, Samuel, "Letters from a Civil War Officer," *Mississippi Valley Historical Review* XIV (1928).

Military Order of the Loyal Legion of the United States—Iowa Commandery, *War Sketches and Incidents*. Vol. I. Des Moines: P. C. Kenyon, 1893.

———, Maine Commandery, *War Papers*. 2 vols. Portland: Lafavor-Tower Co., 1898–1902.

———, Massachusetts Commandery, *Civil War Papers*. 2 vols. Boston: The Commandery, 1900.

———, Minnesota Commandery, *Glimpses of the Nation's Struggle*. 6 vols. St. Paul: The Commandery, 1887–1909.

———, Ohio Commandery, *Sketches of War History, 1861–1865*. 6 vols. Cincinnati: R. Clarke & Co., 1888–1908.

Works Cited

———— , Wisconsin Commandery, *War Papers*. 3 vols. Milwaukee: Burdick, Armitage & Allen, 1891–1903.

Mills, Luther Rice, "Letters of Luther Rice Mills—A Confederate Soldier," *North Carolina Historical Review* IV (1927).

Montfort, Theodorick W., *Rebel Lawyer: Letters of Theodorick W. Montfort, 1861–1862*. Athens: University of Georgia Press, 1965.

Moore, Robert, *A Life for the Confederacy*. Jackson, TN: McCowat-Mercer Press, 1959.

Morgan, Thomas J., *Reminiscences of Service with Colored Troops in the Army of the Cumberland, 1863–65*. Providence: The Society, 1885.

Morgan, William H., *Personal Reminiscences of the War of 1861–65*. Lynchburg, VA: J. P. Bell Co., 1911.

Murray, J. Ogden, *The Immortal Six Hundred: A Story of Cruelty to Confederate Prisoners of War*. Winchester, VA: Eddy Press Corp., 1905.

Newton, James K., *A Wisconsin Boy in Dixie: The Selected Letters of James K. Newton*. Madison: University of Wisconsin Press, 1961.

Norman, William M., *A Portion of My Life*. Winston-Salem, NC: J. F. Blair, 1959.

Norton, Oliver, W., *Army Letters, 1861–1865*. Chicago: O. L. Deming, 1903.

Olmanson, Bernt, *Letters of Bernt Olmanson: A Union Soldier in the Civil War, 1861–1865*. n.p., n.d.

Opie, John N., *A Rebel Cavalryman with Lee, Stuart, and Jackson*. Chicago: W. B. Conkey Co., 1899.

Orendorff, Henry, *We Are Sherman's Men: The Civil War Letters of Henry Orendorff*. Macomb: Western Illinois University, 1986.

Parks, George E., "One Story of the 109th Illinois Volunteer Infantry," *Journal of the Illinois State Historical Society* LVI (1963).

Paton, James E., "Civil War Journal of James E. Paton," *Register of the Kentucky Historical Society* LVI (1963).

Patrick, Robert D., *Reluctant Rebel: The Secret Diary of Robert Patrick, 1861–1865*. Baton Rouge: Louisiana State University Press, 1959.

Patterson, Edmund D., *Yankee Rebel: The Civil War Journal of Edmund DeWitt Patterson*. Chapel Hill: University of North Carolina Press, 1966.

Paxton, William E., " 'Dear Rebecca:' The Civil War Letters of WIlliam Edwards Paxton," *Louisiana History* XX (1979).

Pearson, Benjamin F., "Benjamin F. Pearson's Civil War Diary," *Annals of Iowa* XV (1926).

Phillips, James M., *Civil War Diary & Letters of James Martin Phillips, Company G, 92nd Illinois Volunteers*. St. Louis: Genealogical Research & Productions, 1982.

Pierce, Thomas J., *Letters Home*. Burlington, IA: Ellen B. Korbitz, 1957.

Plane, William F., "Letters of William Fisher Plane, C.S.A., to His Wife," *Collections of the Georgia Historical Society* XLVIII (1964).

Poague, William T., *Gunner with Stonewall: Reminiscences of William*

Thomas Poague. Jackson, TN: McCowat-Mercer Press, 1957.

Pool, J. T., *Under Canvass; or, Recollections of the Fall and Summer Campaign of the 14th Regiment, Indiana Volunteers*. Terre Haute: O. Bartlett, 1862.

Putnam, George H., *A Prisoner of War in Virginia, 1864–5*. New York: G. P. Putnam's Sons, 1912.

Quintard, Charles T., *Doctor Quintard, Chaplain C.S.A. and Second Bishop of Tennessee: Being His Story of the War (1861–1865)*. Sewanee, TN: The University Press, 1905.

Rhode Island Soldiers and Sailors Historical Society, *Personal Narratives of Events in the War of the Rebellion*. 10 vols. Providence: The Society, 1878–1915.

Robson, John S., *How a One-legged Rebel Lives*. Durham, NC: Educator Co., 1898.

Rogers, William J., "William J. Rogers' Memorandum Book," *West Tennessee Historical Society Papers* IX (1955).

Rose, Alexander G., *The Civil War Diaries of Alexander Grant Rose (1838–1920)*. Baltimore: A. G. Rose III, 1974.

Ross, Charles, "Diary of Charles Ross," *Vermont History* XXX (1962).

Schofield, John M., *Forty-six Years in the Army*. New York: Century Co., 1897.

Sherman, William T., *Memoirs of W. T. Sherman*. 2 vols. New York: Charles L. Webster and Co., 1886.

Shotwell, Randolph A., *Papers of Randolph A. Shotwell*, 2 vols. Raleigh: North Carolina Historical Commission, 1929–1931.

Silliman, Justus M., *A New Canaan Private in the Civil War: Letters of Justus M. Silliman, 17th Connecticut Volunteers*. New Canaan: New Canaan Historical Society, 1984.

Small, Abner R., *The Road to Richmond*. Berkeley: University of California Press, 1939.

Spencer, Carrie Esther (ed.), *A Civil War Marriage in Virginia: Reminiscences and Letters*. Boyce, VA: Carr Publishing Co., 1956.

Stauffer, Nelson, *Civil War Diary*. Northridge: California State University, 1976.

Stearns, Austin C., *Three Years with Company K*. Cranbury, NJ: Fairleigh Dickinson University Press, 1976.

Stevens, George T., *Three Years in the Sixth Corps*. New York: D. Van Nostrand, 1870.

Stiles, Robert, *Four Years under Marse Robert*. New York: Neale Publishing Co., 1903.

Stillwell, Leander, *The Story of the Common Soldier of Army Life in the Civil War, 1861–1865*. Erie, PA: Franklin Hudson Publishing Co., 1920.

Strong, Robert Hale, *A Yankee Private's Civil War*. Chicago: Henry Regnery Co., 1961.

Works Cited

Sweney, Joseph H., "Nursed a Wounded Brother," *Annals of Iowa* XXXI (1952).

Swint, Henry Lee (comp.), *Dear Ones at Home: Letters from Contraband Camps.* Nashville: Vanderbilt University Press, 1966.

Tilney, Robert, *My Life in the Army: Three Years and a Half with the Fifth Army Corps, Army of the Potomac, 1862–1865.* Philadelphia: Ferris & Leach, 1912.

Toney, Marcus B., *The Privations of a Private.* Nashville: M. E. Church, South, 1907.

Trobriand, Regis de. *Four Years with the Army of the Potomac.* Boston: Ticknor and Co., 1889.

Trumbull, Henry Clay, *War Memories of an Army Chaplain*, New York: C. Scribner's Sons, 1906.

Upson, Theodore, *With Sherman to the Sea.* Bloomington: Indiana University Press, 1958.

Urban, John W., *My Experience mid Shot and Shell and in Rebel Den.* Lancaster, PA: The Author, 1882.

Vail, Enos B., *Reminiscences of a Boy in the Civil War.* Brooklyn: The Author, 1915.

Wagner, William F., *Letters of William F. Wagner, Confederate Soldier.* Wendell, NC: Broadfoot's Bookmark, 1983.

Wainwright, Charles S., *A Diary of Battle.* New York: Harcourt, Brace & World, 1962.

Weller, Edwin, *A Civil War Courtship: The Letters of Edwin Weller from Antietam to Atlanta.* Garden City, NY: Doubleday & Company, 1980.

Welsh, Peter, *Irish Green and Union Blue: The Civil War Letters of Peter Welsh.* New York: Fordham University Press, 1986.

Wilcox, James F., "With Grant at Vicksburg, from the Civil War Diary of Capt. James F. Wilcox," *Journal of the Illinois State Historical Society* XXX (1938).

Wilkeson, Frank, *Recollections of a Private Soldier in the Army of the Potomac.* New York: G. P. Putnam's Sons, 1886.

Williams, James M., *From That Terrible Field: Civil War Letters of James M. Williams, Twenty-first Alabama Infantry Volunteers.* University: University of Alabama Press, 1981.

Williamson, James J., *Prison Life in the Old Capitol and Reminiscences of the Civil War.* West Orange, NJ: The Author, 1911.

Wills, Charles W., *Army Life of an Illinois Soldier*, Washington: Globe Printing Co., 1904.

Wilson, Ephraim A., *Memoirs of the War.* Cleveland: W. M. Bayne Printing Co., 1893.

Wilson, Legrand J., *The Confederate Soldier.* Fayetteville, AR: M'Roy Printing Co., 1902.

Wilson, Peter, "Peter Wilson in the Civil War," *Iowa Journal of History and*

Politics XL (1942).

Wistar, Isaac J., *Autobiography of Isaac Jones Wistar, 1827–1905*. Philadelphia: Wistar Institute of Anatomy and Biology, 1937.

Wood, William W., *Reminiscences of Big I*. Jackson, TN: McCowat-Mercer Press, 1956.

Worsham, John W., *One of Jackson's Foot Cavalry*. Jackson, TN: McCowat-Mercer Press, 1964.

UNIT HISTORIES

Adams, John G. B., *Reminiscences of the Nineteenth Massachusetts Regiment*. Boston: Wright & Potter Printing Co., 1899.

Aden, R. F. (ed.), "In Memoriam, Seventh Tennessee Cavalry, C.S.A.," *West Tennessee Historical Society Papers* XVII (1963).

Allen, George H., *Forty-six Months with the Fourth R. I. Volunteers in the War of 1861 to 1865*. Providence: J. A. & R. A. Reid, 1887.

Banes, Charles H., *History of the Philadelphia Brigade*. Philadelphia: J. B. Lippincott & Co., 1876.

Bartlett, Asa W., *History of the Twelfth Regiment, New Hampshire Volunteers, in the War of the Rebellion*. Concord: I. C. Evans, 1897.

Baxter, Nancy Niblack, *Gallant Fourteenth*. Traverse City, IN: Study Center Press, 1980.

Beale, R. L. T., *History of the Ninth Virginia Cavalry in the War between the States*. Richmond: B. F. Johnson Publishing Co., 1899.

Bean, W. G., *The Liberty Hall Volunteers: Stonewall's College Boys*. Charlottesville: University Press of Virginia, 1964.

Beaudry, Louis N., *Historic Records of the Fifth New York Cavalry, First Ira Harris Guard*. Albany: J. Munsell, 1868.

Beecher, Herbert W., *History of the First Light Battery, Connecticut Volunteers, 1861–1865*. New York A. T. De La Nare Ptgt. and Pub. Co., 1901.

Bell, John T., *Tramps and Triumphs of the Second Iowa Infantry*. Des Moines: Kieffer Associates, 1961.

Bennett, A. J., *The Story of the First Massachusetts Light Battery*. Boston: Deland and Barta, 1886.

Blessington, Joseph P., *The Campaigns of Walker's Texas Division*. New York: J. P. Blessington, 1875.

Bowen, James L., *History of the Thirty-seventh Regiment, Mass. Volunteers, in the Civil War of 1861–1865*. Holyoke, MA: C. W. Bryan & Co., 1884.

Briant, C. C., *History of the Sixth Regiment, Indiana Volunteer Infantry*. Indianapolis: William B. Burford, 1891.

Brown, Thaddeus C. C., et al., *Behind the Guns: The History of Battery I, 2nd Regiment, Illinois Light Artillery*. Carbondale: Southern Illinois University Press, 1965.

Bryant, Edwin E., *History of the Third Regiment of Wisconsin Veteran Volun-*

Works Cited

teer Infantry, 1861–1865. Madison: Veteran Association of the Regiment, 1891.

Buffum, Francis H., *A Memorial of the Great Rebellion: Being a History of the Fourteenth Regiment, New Hampshire Volunteers.* Boston: Rand, Avery, & Co., 1882.

Burlingame, John K. (comp.), *History of the Fifth Regiment of Rhode Island Heavy Artillery, during Three Years and a Half of Service in North Carolina.* Providence: Snow & Farnham, 1892.

Carpenter, George N., *History of the Eighth Regiment, Vermont Volunteers.* Boston: Press of Deland & Barta, 1886.

Child, William, *A History of the Fifth Regiment, New Hampshire Volunteers, in the American Civil War, 1861–1865.* Bristol, NH: R. W. Musgrove, 1893.

Clark, Charles M., *The History of the Thirty-ninth Regiment, Illinois Volunteer Veteran Infantry (Yates Phalanx), in the War of the Rebellion.* Chicago: Veteran Assn., 1889.

Clark, Walter (ed.), *Histories of the Several Regiments and Battalions from North Carolina, in the Great War 1861–'65.* 5 vols. Raleigh: E. M. Uzzell, 1901.

Cogswell, Leander, *A History of the Eleventh New Hampshire Regiment, Volunteer Infantry, in the the Rebellion War, 1861–1865.* Concord: Republican Press Assn., 1891.

Collins, George K., *Memoirs of the 149th Regt., N.Y. Vol. Inft., 3d Brig., 2d Div., 12th and 20th A.C.* Syracuse, NY: The Author, 1891.

Cook, Benhamin F., *History of the Twelfth Massachusetts Volunteers (Webster Regiment).* Boston: Twelfth (Webster) Regiment Assn., 1882.

Cook, Stephen G., *The "Dutchess County Regiment" (150th Regiment of New York State Volunteer Infantry) in the Civil War.* Danbury, CT: Danbury Medical Printing Co., 1907.

Cowtan, Charles W., *Services in the Tenth New York Volunteers (National Zouaves) in the War of the Rebellion.* New York: C. H. Ludwig, 1882.

Crooke, George, *The Twenty-first Regiment of Iowa Volunteer Infantry.* Milwaukee: King, Fowle & Co., 1891.

Crowninshield, Benjamin W., *A History of the First Regiment of Massachusetts Cavalry Volunteers.* Boston: Houghton, Mifflin and Co., 1891.

Cuffel, Charles A., *History of Durell's Battery in the Civil War.* Philadelphia: Craig, Finley & Co., 1903.

Davis, Charles E., *Three Years in the Army: The Story of the Thirteenth Massachusetts Volunteers from July 16, 1861, to August 1, 1864.* Boston: Estes and Lauriat, 1894.

Davis, William W. H., *History of the 104th Pennsylvania Regiment, from August 22nd, 1861, to September 30th 1864.* Philadelphia: J. B. Rogers, 1866.

Day, L. W., *Story of the One Hundred and First Ohio Infantry.* Cleveland: W. M. Bayne Printing Co., 1894.

Denison, Frederic, *Sabres and Spurs: The First Regiment Rhode Island Cav-*

alry in the Civil War, 1861–1865. Central Falls, RI: The First Rhode Island Cavalry Veteran Assn., 1876.

Denny, J. Waldo, *Wearing the Blue in the Twenty-fifth Mass. Volunteer Infantry.* Worcester, MA: Putnam & Davis, 1879.

Derby, William P., *Bearing Arms in the Twenty-seventh Massachusetts Regiment of Volunteer Infantry during the Civil War, 1861–1865.* Boston: Wright & Potter Printing Co., 1883.

Dickert, D. Augustus, *History of Kershaw's Brigade.* Newberry, SC: E. H. Aull Co., 1899.

Dickey, Luther S., *History of the Eighty-fifth Regiment, Pennsylvania Volunteer Infantry, 1861–1865.* New York: J. C. & W. E. Powers, 1915.

Douglas, James P., *Douglas's Texas Battery, CSA.* Tyler, TX: Smith County Historical Society, 1966.

Eddy, Richard, *History of the Sixtieth Regiment New York State Volunteers.* Philadelphia: The Author, 1864.

Emmerton, James A., *A Record of the Twenty-third Regiment Mass. Vol. Infantry in the War of the Rebellion, 1861–1865.* Boston: W. Ware & Co., 1886.

Figg, Royal W., *"Where Men Only Dare to Go:" The Story of a Boy Company (C.S.A.).* Richmond: Whittet & Shepperson, 1885.

Ford, Andrew E., *The Story of the Fifteenth Regiment, Massachusetts Volunteer Infantry, in the Civil War, 1861–1864.* Clinton, MA: Press of W. J. Coulter, 1898.

Gould, John M., *History of the First—Tenth—Twenty-ninth Maine Regiment.* Portland: S. Berry, 1871.

Gould, Joseph, *The Story of the Forty-eighth: A Record of the Campaigns of the Forty-eighth Regiment Pennsylvania Veteran Volunteer Infantry during the Four Eventful Years of Its Service in the War for the Preservation of the Union.* Philadelphia: Alfred M. Slocum Co., 1908.

Haines, William P., *History of the Men of Co. F, with Description of the Marches and Battles of the 12th New Jersey Vols.* Mickleton, NJ: C. S. Magrath, 1897.

Hartspence, William R., *History of the Fifty-first Indiana Veteran Volunteer Infantry.* Cincinnati: Robert Clarke Co., 1894.

Haynes, Martin A., *A History of the Second Regiment, New Hampshire Volunteer Infantry, in the War of the Rebellion.* Lakeport, NH: The Author, 1896.

Hays, Gilbert A., *Under the Red Patch: Story of the Sixty-third Regiment, Pennsylvania Volunteers, 1861–1864.* Pittsburgh: Sixty-third Pennsylvania Regimental Assn. 1908.

Hinman, Wilbur F., *The Story of the Sherman Brigade.* Alliance OH: The Author, 1897.

History of the Fifth Massachusetts Battery. Boston: L. E. Cowles, 1902.

Works Cited

History of the 121st Pennsylvania Volunteers. Philadelphia: Burk & McFetridge Co., 1893.

History of the 127th Regiment, Pennsylvania Volunteers. Lebanon, PA: Report Publishing Co., 1902.

History of the Thirty-fifth Regiment, Massachusetts Volunteers, 1862–1865. Boston: Rockwell and Churchill, 1884.

History of the Thirty-sixth Regiment, Massachusetts Volunteers, 1862–1865. Boston: Mills, Knight & Co., 1884.

History of the Twelfth Regiment, Rhode Island Volunteers, in the Civil War, 1862–1863. Providence: Snow & Farnham, 1904.

Hopkins, William P., *The Seventh Regiment, Rhode Island Volunteers, in the Civil War, 1862–1865.* Providence: The Providence Press, 1903.

Houghton, Edwin B., *The Campaigns of the Seventeenth Maine.* Portland: Short & Loring, 1866.

Howell, H. Grady, *Going to Meet the Yankees: A History of the "Bloody Sixth" Mississippi Infantry, C.S.A.* Jackson, MS: Chickasaw Bayou Press, 1981.

Hudson, James C., "A Story of Company D, 4th Alabama Infantry Regiment, C.S.A." *Alabama Historical Quarterly* XXIII (1961).

Hutchinson, Nelson V., *History of the Seventh Massachusetts Volunteer Infantry in the War of the Rebellion of the Southern States against Constitutional Authority, 1861–1865.* Taunton, MA: The Regimental Assn., 1890.

Jackman, Lyman, *History of the Sixth New Hampshire Regiment in the War for the Union.* Concord: Republican Press Assn., 1891.

Jones, Benjamin W., *Under the Stars and Bars: A History of the Surry Light Artillery.* Richmond: E. Waddey Co., 1909.

Judson, Amos J., *History of the Eighty-third Regiment, Pennsylvania Volunteers.* Dayton, OH: Morningside, 1986.

Kerwood, Asbury L., *Annals of the Fifty-seventh Regiment Indiana Volunteers.* Dayton, OH: W. J. Shuey, 1868.

Kirk, Hyland C., *Heavy Guns and Light: A History of the 4th New York Heavy Artillery.* New York: C. T. Dillingham, 1890.

Kirwan, Thomas, *Memorial History of the Seventeenth Regiment, Massachusetts Volunteer Infantry (Old and New Organizations) in the Civil War from 1861–1865.* Salem, MA: Salem Press Co., 1911.

Landon, William D. F., "Fourteenth Indiana Regiment: Letters to the Vincennes Western Sun," *Indiana Magazine of History* XXXIV (1938).

Lathrop, David, *The History of the Fifty-ninth Regiment Illinois Volunteers.* Indianapolis: Hall & Hutchinson, 1865.

Lincoln, William S., *LIfe with the Thirty-fourth Mass. Infantry in the War of the Rebellion.* Worcester, MA: Noyes, Snow & Co., 1879.

Lindsley, John B. (ed), *The Military Annals of Tennessee: Confederate.* Nashville: J. M. Lindsley & Co., 1886.

Little, John F. W., *The Seventh Regiment, New Hampshire Volunteers, in the*

War of the Rebellion. Concord: Ira C. Evans, 1896.

Loehr, Charles T., *War History of the Old First Virginia Infantry Regiment, Army of Northern Virginia*. Richmond: W. E. Jones, 1884.

McMurray, W. J., *History of the Twentieth Tennessee Regiment Volunteer Infantry, C.S.A.* Nashville: The Publication Committee, 1904.

Mann, Albert W. (comp.), *History of the Forty-fifth Regiment, Massachusetts Volunteer Militia*. Boston: Wallace Spooner, 1908.

Mark, Penrose G., *Red: White: and Blue Badge, Pennsylvania Veteran Volunteers: A History of the 93rd Regiment . . . Harrisburg: Aughinbaugh Press, 1911.*

Moors, John F., *History of the Fifty-second Regiment, Massachusetts Volunteers*. Boston: G. H. Ellis, 1893.

Newell, Joseph K., *"Ours:" Annals of 10th Regiment, Massachusetts Volunteers, in the Rebellion*. Springfield: C. A. Nichols & Co., 1875.

Newlin, William H., et al., *A History of the Seventy-third Regiment of Illinois Infantry Volunteers*. Springfield: Regimental Reunion Assn., 1890.

Nichols, James M., *Perry's Saints; or, The Fighting Parson's Regiment in the War of the Rebellion*. Boston: D. Lathor and Co., 1886.

Obreiter, John, *History of the Seventy-seventh Pennsylvania Volunteers*. Harrisburg: Harrisburg Publishing Co., 1905.

Otis, George H., *The Second Wisconsin Infantry*. Dayton, OH: Morningside, 1984.

Parker, John L., *Henry Wilson's Regiment: History of the Twenty-second Massachusetts Infantry, the Second Company Sharpshooters, and the Third Light Battery, in the War of the Rebellion*. Boston: Regimental Assn., 1887.

Payne, Edwin W., *History of the Thirty-fourth Regiment of Illinois Volunteer Infantry*. Clinton, IA: Allen Printing Co., 1903.

Prowell, George R., *History of the Eighty-seventh Regiment, Pennsylvania Volunteers*. York, PA: Press of the York Daily, 1903.

Reid, Jesse W., *History of the Fourth Regiment S.C. Volunteers, from the Commencement of the War until Lee's Surrender*. Greenville, SC: Shannon & Co., 1892.

Robinson, Frank T., *History of the Fifth Regiment, M. V. M.* Boston: W. F. Brown, 1879.

Roe, Alfred S., and Nutt, Charles, *History of the First Regiment of Heavy Artillery, Massachusetts Volunteers*. Worcester: Regimental Assn., 1917.

————— , *The Twenty-fourth Regiment, Massachusetts Volunteers, 1861–1865*. Worcester: Twenty-fourth Veteran Assn., 1907.

Sloan, John A., *Reminiscences of the Guilford Grays, Co. B, 27th N.C. Regiment*. Washington: R. O. Polkinhorn, 1883.

Small, Abner R., *The Sixteenth Maine Regiment in the War of the Rebellion, 1861–1865*. Portland: Regimental Assn., 1886.

Smith, John Day, *The History of the Nineteenth Regiment of Maine Volunteer Infantry, 1862–1865*. Minneapolis: The Great Western Printing Co., 1909.

Works Cited

Smith, John L., *History of the Corn Exchange Regiment, 118th Pennsylvania Volunteers, from Their First Engagement at Antietam to Appomattox.* Philadelphia: J. L. Smith, 1888.

Smith, William A., *The Anson Guards: Company C, Fourteenth Regiment North Carolina Volunteers, 1861–1865.* Charlotte: Stone Publishing Co., 1914.

Spicer, William A., *History of the Ninth and Tenth Regiments, Rhode Island Volunteers, and Tenth Rhode Island Battery, in the Union Army in 1862.* Providence: Snow & Farnham, 1892.

Stevens, William B., *History of the Fiftieth Regiment of Infantry, Massachusetts Volunteer Militia, in the Late War of the Rebellion.* Boston: Griffith-Stillings Press, 1907.

Thompson, Edwin Porter, *History of the Orphan Brigade.* Louisville: L. N. Thompson, 1898.

Thompson, S. Millett, *Thirteenth Regiment of New Hampshire Volunteer Infantry in the War of the Rebellion, 1861–1865.* Boston: Houghton Mifflin Co., 1888.

Thorpe, Sheldon B., *The History of the Fifteenth Connecticut Volunteers in the War for the Defense of the Union, 1861–1865.* New Haven: Price, Lee & Adkins Co., 1893.

Todd, William, *The Seventy-ninth Highlanders, New York Volunteers, in the War of the Rebellion, 1861–1865.* Albany: Brandow, Barton & Co., 1886.

Under the Maltese Cross: Antietam to Appomattox: The Loyal Uprising in Western Pennsylvania, 1861–1865. Pittsburgh: The 155th Regimental Assn., 1910.

Underwood, Adin B., *The Three Years' Service of the Thirty-third Mass. Infantry Regiment, 1862–1865.* Boston: A. Williams & Co., 1881.

Vaill, Theodore F., *History of the Second Connecticut Volunteer Heavy Artillery.* Winsted: Winsted Printing Co., 1868.

Waitt, Ernest L., *History of the Nineteenth Regiment, Massachusetts Volunteer Infantry, 1861–1865.* Salem: Salem Press Co., 1906.

Walker, William C., *History of the Eighteenth Regiment Conn. Volunteers in the War for the Union.* Norwich: The Committee, 1885.

Ward, Joseph R. C., *History of the One Hundred and Sixth Regiment, Pennsylvania Volunteers, 2d Brigade, 2d Division, 2d Corps, 1861–1865.* Philadelphia: F. McManus, Jr., & Co., 1906.

Watkins, Samuel R., *"Co. Aytch," Maury Grays, First Tennessee Regiment.* Nashville: Cumberland Presbyterian Publishing House, 1882.

OTHER PRIMARY SOURCES

Beers, Fannie A., *Memories: A Record of Personal Experience and Adventure during Four Years of War.* Philadelphia: J. B. Lippincott Co., 1888.

Bennett, William W., *A Narrative of the Great Revival Which Prevailed in the*

Southern Armies during the Late Civil War between the States of the Federal Union. Philadelphia: Claxton, Remsen & Heffelfinger, 1877.

Bickham, William D., *Rosecrans' Campaign with the Fourteenth Army Corps, or the Army of the Cumberland.* Cincinnati: Moore, Wilstach, Keys & Co., 1863.

Byers, Samuel H. M., *Iowa in War Times.* Des Moines: W. D. Condit & Co., 1888.

Cadwallader, Sylvanus, *Three Years with Grant.* New York: Alfred A. Knopf, 1955.

Cumming, Kate, *Kate, The Diary of a Confederate Nurse.* Baton Rouge: Louisiana State University Press, 1959.

Daniel, Frederick S., *The Richmond Examiner during the War.* New York: Printed for the author, 1868.

DeLeon, T. C., *Four Years in Rebel Capitals.* Mobile: Gospel Printing Co., 1890.

Ford, Thomas J., *With the Rank and Rile: Incidents and Anecdotes during the War of the Rebellion.* Milwaukee: Evening Wisconsin Co., 1895.

Fremantle, Arthur J. L., *Three Months in the Confederate States.* London: William Blackwood and Sons, 1863.

Hancock, Cornelia, *South after Gettysburg: Letters of Cornelia Hancock from the Army of the Potomac, 1863-1865.* New York: Thomas Y. Crowell Co., 1956.

Holstein, Anna Morris, *Three Years in Field Hospitals of the Army of the Potomac.* Philadelphia: J. B. Lippincott & Co., 1867.

Johnson, Robert U., and Buel, C. C. (eds.), *Battles and Leaders of the Civil War.* 4 vols. New York: The Century Co., 1885-1887.

Jones, J. William, *Christ in the Camp: or, Religion in Lee's Army.* Richmond: B. F. Johnson & Co., 1887.

Jordan, Weymouth T. (comp.), *North Carolina Troops, 1861-1865: A Roster.* Raleigh: North Carolina Division of Archives and History, 1966-).

Keeler, Elnathan L., and Jane Keeler, *Portrait of Elnathan Keeler, A Union Soldier.* New York: Goldlief Reproductions, 1977.

Lincoln, Abraham, *The Collected Works of Abraham Lincoln.* 9 vols. New Brunswick, NJ: Rutgers University Press, 1953-1955.

Lowenfels, Walter (ed.), *Walt Whitman's Civil War.* New York: Alfred A. Knopf, 1961.

Massachusetts Adjt. Gen. (comp.), *Massachusetts Soldiers, Sailors, and Marines in the Civil War.* 9 vols. Norwood, MA: Norwood Press, 1931-1937.

Military Historical Society of Massachusetts, *Civil and Mexican Wars, 1846, 1861.* Boston: The Society, 1913.

——————, *Civil War and Miscellaneous Papers.* Boston: The Society, 1918.

Pember, Phoebe Yates, *A Southern Woman's Story: Life in Confederate Richmond.* Jackson, TN: McCowat-Mercer Press, 1959.

Works Cited

Perkins, Howard C. (ed.), *Northern Editorials on Secession*. New York: D. Appleton-Century Co., 1942.

Roster and Record of Iowa Soldiers in the War of the Rebellion. 6 vols. Des Moines: Published by the General Assembly, 1908–1911.

Russell, William Howard, *My Diary North and South*. New York: O. S. Felt, 1863.

Toombs, Samuel, *New Jersey Troops in the Gettysburg Campaign*. Orange, NJ: Evening Mail Publishing House, 1888.

U.S. Sanitary Commission, *Narrative of Privations and Sufferings of United States Officers and Soldiers While Prisoners of War in the Hands of Rebel Authorities*. Philadelphia: King and Baird, 1864.

U.S. Surgeon-General's Office (comp.), *The Medical and Surgical History of the War of the Rebellion (1861–65)*. 6 vols. Washington: Government Printing Office, 1870–1888.

U.S. War Dept., (comp.), *War of the Rebellion: A Compilation of the Official Records of the Union and Confederate Armies*. 128 vols. Washington: Government Printing Office, 1880–1901.

Willis, Henry A., *Fitchburg in the War of the Rebellion*. Fitchburg, MA: S. Shepley, 1866.

PERIODICALS

Central Presbyterian, 1863.

Confederate Veteran. 40 vols. Nashville: S. A. Cunningham, 1893–1932.

Herald of the South, 1859.

Religious Herald, 1862, 1864.

Richmond *Daily Dispatch*, 1862.

Richmond *Enquirer*, 1864.

Southern Historical Society Papers. 52 vols. Richmond: Southern Historical Society, 1876–1952.

Southern Presbyterian, 1861.

SECONDARY SOURCES

Aaron, Daniel, *The Unwritten Civil War: American Writers and the Civil War*. New York: Alfred A. Knopf, 1973.

Adams, George W., *Doctors in Blue: The Medical History of the Union Army in the Civil War*. New York: H. Schuman, 1952.

Adams, Herbert, "Enemy of Rebels and Rum Lovers," *Civil War Times Illustrated* XXV (Mar., 1986).

Bailey, Fred Arthur, *Class and Tennessee's Confederate Generation*. Chapel Hill: University of North Carolina Press, 1987.

Bettersworth, John K. (ed.), *Mississippi in the Confederacy*. 2 vols. Baton Rouge: Louisiana State University Press, 1961.

Brooks, Steward, *Civil War Medicine.* Springfield, IL: Charles C. Thomas, 1966.

Brown, Louis A., *The Salisbury Prison: A Case Study of Confederate Military Prisons, 1861–1865.* Wendell, NC: Broadfoot's Bookmark, 1980.

Catton, Bruce, *America Goes to War.* Middletown, CT: Wesleyan University Press, 1958.

————, *Mr. Lincoln's Army.* Garden City, NY: Doubleday, 1951.

————, *A Stillness at Appomattox.* Garden City, NY: Doubleday, 1953.

Cornish, Dudley Taylor, *The Sable Arm: Negro Troops in the Union Army, 1861–1865.* New York: Longman, Green, 1956.

Cullen, Joseph P., "Chimborzao Hospital," *Civil War Times Illustrated* XIX (Jan., 1981).

Cunningham, H. H., *Doctors in Gray: The Confederate Medical Service.* Baton Rouge: Louisiana State University Press, 1958.

————, *Field Medical Services at the Battle of Manassas (Bull Run).* Athens: University of Georgia Press, 1968.

Davis, William C. (ed.), *Shadows of the Storm.* Garden City, NY: Doubleday, 1981.

Dean, Nancy Travis, "Confederate Prisoners of War at Fort Delaware," *Delaware History* XIII (1968).

Dodge, Grenville M., "Gen. James A. Williamson," *Annals of Iowa* VI (1903).

Faust, Drew Gilpin, "Christian Soldiers: The Meaning of Revivalism in the Confederate Army," *Journal of Southern History* LIII (1987).

Freeman, Douglas S., *Lee's Lieutenants: A Study in Command.* 3 vols. New York: Charles Scribner's Sons, 1942–1944.

Futch, Ovid L., *History of Andersonville Prison.* Gainesville: University of Florida Press, 1968.

————, "Prison Life at Andersonville," *Civil War History* VIII (1962).

Gerber, John, "Mark Twain's 'Private Campaign,'" *Civil War History* I (1955).

Glatthaar, Joseph T., *The March to the Sea and Beyond.* New York: New York University Press, 1985.

Greenbie, Marjorie L., *Lincoln's Daughters of Mercy.* New York: G. P. Putnam's Sons, 1944.

Hamlin, Augustus C., *The Battle of Chancellorsville.* Bangor, ME: The Author, 1896.

Hemmerlein, Richard F., *Prisons and Prisoners of the Civil War.* Boston: Christopher Publishing House, 1934.

Henry, Robert Selph, *The Story of the Confederacy,* Indianapolis: Bobbs-Merrill Co., 1931.

Hesseltine, William B., *Civil War Prisons: A Study in War Psychology.* Columbus: Ohio State University Press, 1930.

Works Cited

———, "The Propaganda Literature of Confederate Prisons," *Journal of Southern History* I (1935).

Ingersoll, Lurton D., *Iowa and the Rebellion*. Philadelphia: J. B. Lippincott and Co., 1867.

Jones, Terry L., *Lee's Tigers: The Louisiana Infantry in the Army of Northern Virginia*. Baton Rouge: Louisiana State University Press, 1987.

Leech, Margaret, *Reveille in Washington, 1860–1865*. New York: Harper & Brothers, 1941.

Livermore, Thomas L., *Numbers and Losses in the Civil War in America, 1861–65*. Boston: Houghton, Mifflin and Co., 1901.

Lonn, Ella, *Desertion during the Civil War*. New York: Century Co., 1928.

Lord, Francis A., *They Fought for the Union*. Harrisburg, PA: Stackpole Co., 1960.

McDonnold, B. W., *History of the Cumberland Presbyterian Church*. Nashville: Board of Publications of the Cumberland Presbyterian Church, 1888.

McPherson, James M., *Ordeal by Fire: The Civil War and Reconstruction*. New York: Alfred A. Knopf, 1982.

McWhiney, Grady, *Southerners and Other Americans*. New York: Basic Books, 1973.

Miller, Francis T. (ed.), *The Photographic History of the Civil War*. 10 vols. New York: Review of Reviews Co., 1911.

Monaghan, Jay, "Civil War Slang and Humor," *Civil War History* III (1957).

Moore, Albert B., *Conscription and Conflict in the Confederacy*. New York: Macmillan Co., 1924.

Nevins, Allan, *The War for the Union*. 4 vols. New York: Scribner, 1959–1971.

Rhodes, James Ford, *History of the United States from the Compromise of 1850*. 9 vols. New York: Macmillan Co., 1893–1906.

Robertson, James I., Jr., "Houses of Horror: Danville's Civil War Prisons," *Virginia Magazine of History and Biography* LXIX (1961).

———, "Negro Soldiers in the Civil War," *Civil War Times Illustrated* VII (Oct., 1968).

———, and McMurry, Richard (eds.), *Rank and File: Civil War Essays in Honor of Bell Irvin Wiley*. San Rafael, CA: Presidio Press, 1976.

———, "The Scourge of Elmira," *Civil War History* VIII (1962).

———, *Tenting Tonight: The Soldier's Life*. Alexandria, VA: Time-Life Books, 1984.

Romero, Sidney J., *Religion in the Rebel Ranks*. New York: University Press of America, 1983.

Rutman, Darrett B., "The War Crimes and Trial of Henry Wirz," *Civil War History* VI (1960).

Scott, W. W. (ed.), *Two Confederate Items*. Richmond: Virginia State Library, 1927.

Shannon, Fred A., *The Organization and Administration of the Union Army,*

1861–1865. 2 vols. Cleveland: Arthur H. Clark Co., 1928.

Shepard, John, Jr., "Religion in the Army of Northern Virginia," *North Carolina HIstorical Review* XXV (1948).

Smith, Timothy L., *Revivalism and Social Reform*. New York: Abingdon Press, 1957.

Starks, Leander and Lydia Catherine, *Throb of Drums in Tennessee, 1862–1865*. Philadelphia: Dorrance, 1973.

Sterkx, Henry E., *Partners in Rebellion: Alabama Women in the Civil War*. Cranbury, NJ: Fairleigh Dickinson University Press, 1970.

Talbot, Edith Armstrong, *Samuel Chapman Armstrong: A Biographical Study*. New York: Doubleday, Page & Co., 1904.

Temple, Seth J., "Camp McClellan during the Civil War," *Annals of Iowa* XXI (1937).

Thomas, Howard, *Boys in Blue from the Adirondack Foothills*. Prospect, NY: Prospect Books, 1960.

Upsham, Cyril B., "Arms and Equipment for the Iowa Troops in the Civil War," *Iowa Journal of History and Politics* XVI (1918).

Winslow, Hattie Lou, and Moore, Joseph P. H., *Camp Morton, 1861–1865*. Indianapolis: Indiana Historical Society, 1940.

Womack, Bob, *Call Forth the Mighty Men*. Bessmer, AL: Colonial Press, 1987.

Index

Index

Index

Index